SOLDIERS AND SCHOLARS

Modern War Studies

Theodore A. Wilson
General Editor

Raymond A. Callahan
J. Garry Clifford
Jacob W. Kipp
Jay Luvaas
Series Editors

SOLDIERS AND SCHOLARS

The U.S. Army and the Uses
of Military History, 1865–1920

Carol Reardon

University Press of Kansas

To my mother and father

Published by the University Press of Kansas (Lawrence, Kansas
66045), which was organized by the Kansas Board of Regents and is
operated and funded by Emporia State University, Fort Hays State
University, Kansas State University, Pittsburg State University,
the University of Kansas, and Wichita State University

Library of Congress Cataloging-in-Publication Data
Reardon, Carol.
    Soldiers and scholars : the U.S. Army and the uses of military
history, 1865-1920 / Carol Reardon.
        p.   cm. — (Modern war studies)
    Includes bibliographical references.
    ISBN 0-7006-0466-9 (alk. paper)
    1. United States—History, Military—Historiography. 2. Military
art and science—United States—History. 3. United States. Army—
History. I. Title. II. Series.
    E181.R29   1990
    973'.072—dc20   90-50111
                                                                          CIP

British Library Cataloguing in Publication Data is available.

Printed in the United States of America
10 9 8 7 6 5 4 3 2 1

The paper used in this publication meets the minimum requirements of the
American National Standard for Permanence of Paper for Printed
Library Materials Z39.48-1984.

CONTENTS

ACKNOWLEDGMENTS

I take this opportunity to express my thanks to those who supplied aid and comfort along the way to this work's completion. Just as the officers of the Old Army learned that the success of a mission often rested on the commander's ability to bring together reliable intelligence, so too have I discovered that an author requires great quantities of the same kind of help.

Several years ago, on one of many tours of the Antietam battlefield with the Allegheny College battalion of the Army of the Cussawago, Jay Luvaas inspired me to study military history with a sharper and more critical eye than I had in my days as a mere Civil War buff. I thank him for helping me to "see the light" and for encouraging this one-time biologist to take up the historian's craft. I owe him much, not only for long years of friendship and several enduring nicknames, but also for his unflagging attention to my ideas and to the completion of this volume.

Three members of the History Department of the University of Kentucky have also left their marks on this manuscript. Profs. Charles P. Roland, George C. Herring, and Robert Seager II all must bear some of the responsibility for urging me to attempt this intellectually challenging project. They have been good friends and advisers, and I trust they will approve of the product. A special thanks to Professor Herring for his wise counsel as this raw typescript became a published book.

A number of individuals at various institutions made my work easier. At the United States Army Military History Institute, Carlisle Barracks, Pennsylvania, Richard J. Sommers and especially David Keough opened up to me the world of the Army War College curricular archives and did not allow me to overlook any manuscript collection that showed even a hint of usefulness. I thank Alan C. Aimone of the United States Military Academy Library for his hospitality during my research trip to West Point. At the U.S. Army Center of Military History in Washington, D.C., Hannah Zeidlik helped uncover several important files on the early history of the army's history office that had gone astray a number of years before. Kirby Van Mater of the Theosophical Society Library of Pasadena, California, provided valuable information on noted soldier-scholar Arthur L. Conger. My very special thanks go to Dr. Timothy K. Nenninger of the Old Army and Navy

Branch of the National Archives for sharing with me his knowledge of the Leavenworth schools, for guiding me through the voluminous records of those institutions, and for his thoughtful reading of the entire manuscript.

The good people of the University Press of Kansas have earned my thanks for their skillful and professional handling of my manuscript. Despite a tight publication schedule, the entire process from typescript to printed page went wonderfully smoothly.

Finally, from the very start of this project, my parents stood behind me all the way. They unfailingly and absolutely believed in the value of my work. I am delighted to dedicate this volume to them.

Carol Reardon
Athens, Georgia
January 1990

1

INTRODUCTION

In 1971 the Department of the Army established an Ad Hoc Committee on the Army Need for the Study of Military History. Since World War II, according to the directive that authorized the committee's formation, the U.S. Army had "moved away from its traditional reliance upon the experience of history."[1] After more than twenty-five years of the Cold War and the quagmire of Vietnam, the army was searching for ways to restore its sense of mission and reinforce the spirit of professionalism and pride in honorable service to the nation. Among the committee's solutions was the introduction of a "progressive coordinated history program" into officer education.[2]

The proposed remedy revealed just how far the army had strayed from its intellectual roots. The committee's proposal, far from being novel, followed a path already marked by an earlier generation of American soldiers. In the fifty years between the Civil War and World War I, the Old Army had also looked to a "progressive coordinated history program" to kindle a vital spirit of professionalism among its officers and to elevate the study of the art of war to an intellectual level consistent with other learned professions in American society. The Old Army's experience with military history in officer education before World War I offers many relevant insights to the soldiers of the post-Vietnam generation. That they did not look back, or even know to look back, to the tribulations of their predecessors gives even more poignancy to one general's lament to the ad hoc committee: "The U.S. Army is notorious for failing to apply lessons learned."[3]

During the Progressive Era, members of the officer corps of the Old Army shared many of the same concerns that fueled the professionalization of other occupational groups. Like a chemist or a social worker or a member of any emerging specialized field of knowledge at that time, the army officer demanded that others recognize his authority in matters dealing with his unique service: national defense.

These changes began slowly in the army, first emerging at a time when signs reading "No Dogs or Soldiers Allowed" still hung in mute testimony to the military man's status in a nation at peace. Accorded little respect or attention by the civilian world and seemingly isolated from the rest of American society by their service in frontier garrisons and seacoast defenses, the soldiers of the Old Army appeared condemned to find their own way into the new century; for the first half of the twentieth century, few observers of the American military establishment would have doubted that the seeds of the Old Army's reform agitation were sown solely from within. Indeed, as late as the 1950s, no less an authority on military affairs than Samuel P. Huntington claimed that it was the introspection of hundreds of American soldiers in dozens of far-flung posts that inspired "the standard of professional excellence essential to national success in the struggles of the twentieth century."[4]

But the image of the Old Army's isolation was largely illusory. Its officers could not be entirely immune to the social and intellectual trends reshaping the civilian society in which they had been raised. Indeed, the strength of the American soldier's bond with the society that produced him was not lost on nineteenth-century army officers.[5] Nonetheless, modern scholars have been slow to seek out and examine potential "areas of harmony between the trends in society and developments in the military establishment."[6]

In the true spirit of the "new military history" of the post-World War II years, however, scholars have amassed much convincing evidence to support the idea that the forces of modernization and reform in the Old Army and in civilian society in the Progressive Era shared many elements. Russell F. Weigley's examination of the creation of the General Staff as an example of the Progressive Era's organizational revolution and James L. Abrahamson's analysis of the various political, social, and military imperatives that combined to forge a modern military establishment as the United States entered the twentieth century show just how profitable this search for common ground can be.[7]

The process of professionalization is an especially provocative "area of harmony" that demonstrates the similarity of the challenges facing both army officers and members of emerging civilian occupational specialties. According to the standards of the late nineteenth century, for any such calling to be recognized as a learned profession, initial membership and future advancement required mastery of a body of theoretical knowledge unique to its service.[8] Whether a man chose to be a scientist, an educator, or an army officer, his competence would be measured as much by his ability to understand the principles that defined his field of expertise as by his technical skill in applying them.

In civilian circles, the new standards for professional identity could be met in a number of ways. In American universities, graduate programs in dozens of different fields validated with advanced degrees competence in many professions. Hundreds of new specialized journals made available to members of the emerging professions all the most recent developments in their fields. Practitioners in many of these new specialties formed professional associations or societies to protect their own interests from outside challenges and to establish and maintain the standards required of members for the privilege of identifying with that special "closed society."[9]

The officer corps of the Old Army, like its civilian counterparts, used all these measures to establish its claim to professional status. In the years between the Civil War and World War I, a number of specialized military journals found loyal readerships among infantry, cavalry, artillery, and engineer officers. Semi-official professional organizations such as the Military Service Institution, inaugurated formally in 1879, offered forums for discussion and promotion of the special concerns that affected every officer's career. Soldiers debated the merits of all kinds of organizational and practical reforms to promote the efficiency and readiness of the army, just as corporate leaders discussed ways to streamline the production line and increase output.

Still, at the center of the officer corps' new spirit of professionalism lay a commitment to infuse into all its members a thorough grounding in the art and science of war that would clearly qualify them as unassailable experts in military affairs. The key to achieving this ambitious goal lay in the Old Army's new postgraduate officer education system, designed to guarantee its future leaders career-long opportunities for studying the art of war.[10] Understanding the need for a theoretical core to underpin the essentially practical coursework in tactics, strategy, logistics, and other elements of the soldier's art, the most perceptive of the Old Army's educators turned to what they considered to be the heart of any advanced instruction in their profession: the systematic study of military history.

The study of past wars served the professionalization of the Old Army in a number of important ways. Most commonly, battles and campaigns provided a wealth of examples to illustrate the proper and improper applications of acknowledged principles of war. In "military science," as this kind of instruction was frequently called, military history served as the soldier's laboratory. He could use historical examples to test the validity of accepted axioms under a wide variety of conditions, or he could buttress a theoretical discussion of any principle of war with demonstrations of its practical applications in the field. This was the kind of education from which the most junior lieutenant and the most senior general could benefit. In its simplest form, history-as-illustration was undeniably an effective teaching tool in army schools. In its more sophisticated form, the "applicatory method" developed at the Leavenworth schools, a student's understanding of each principle of war emerged only after an examination of a great variety of its applications, many drawn directly from the pages of history.[11] In these ways, a sound foundation in the military affairs of the past contributed greatly to the professional education of the American commanders of the future.

In addition to teaching practical lessons, the study of military history helped to inculcate the officer corps with the concept of "safe leadership," the command philosophy that guided the Old Army on the eve of World War I.[12] Even the most perceptive army leader could not guess all the ways in which recent advances in weaponry, communications, and other military technology would complicate the art of high command. At the same time, students of the military art increasingly recognized that certain intangibles of war, such as weather, fatigue, or morale, could determine the outcome of a campaign or battle but found that these elements had no formal place in the traditional maxims of warfare. It was clear that modern war had become so complex that an army commander could no longer be expected to lead his troops solely by personal example. He had to rely to an unprecedented degree on the abilities of his staff officers, his subordinates, and his subordinates' staffs to gather intelligence about these and many more factors, and then he had to depend on them to make decisions that might well decide the outcome of a battle. The concept of safe leadership stressed the teamwork and cooperation between commanders and staffs at all levels of command required to achieve victory on the modern battlefield.

Army educators believed a thorough grounding in military history would expose American officers to that vast array of tangibles and intangibles that could contribute to victory or defeat in battle. The history of the Civil War, for example, offered dozens of examples of successful and unsuccessful frontal assaults. If commanders and their chief staff officers learned in the classroom during a period of peace why each attack succeeded or failed, they would be more apt to reach a proper decision if they faced a similar situation in time of war. This developed their confidence in their ability to make sound decisions under pressure. A historical awareness among commanders at all operational levels, combined with extensive work in the practical routine of staff work, reduced the likelihood of gross misjudgment in battle. This was the essence of safe leadership.

The least recognized, and least understood, role of military history in the professionalization of the Old Army is its utility as an intellectual discipline in its own right. Embracing the rigorous standards of the new "scientific history" taught in the graduate seminars of American universities, a small number of army instructors attempted to train the "military minds" and "military eyes" of their students. They used historical rides to Civil War battlefields, staff exercises on the march between sites, and, in the classroom, the "source method" of document evaluation and analysis to train officers in the thought processes of a commander on the battlefield. An officer who received information from a variety of sources in the heat of battle must be able to discern the true from the false, the reliable from the unreliable; this was merely the historical method applied to military leadership.

The army's use of the source method deserves special notice. True, any intensive study of a past campaign would offer practical lessons in the kinds of fine detail that had affected the outcome. But by applying the source method to campaign studies, officers who had reconstructed historical events from a voluminous documentary record were far more likely to discern whether the information on which they based their command decisions was incomplete or contradictory. Such men were more apt to consider the full range of options open to them, and the infusion of this flexibility into the decision-making process prevented soldiers from overt reliance on a single textbook solution. A smart soldier, not just an obedient one, was critical to the success of safe leadership. The Old Army's experiment with the source method of studying history at the Staff College at Fort Leavenworth was so effective, it drew the admiration of the American Historical Association (AHA).[13]

The postgraduate school system was only the most obvious avenue open to soldiers who wished to improve their intellectual proficiency in their profession. But not all officers were lucky enough to receive assignment to even one of the advanced schools. Still others found their brief tours at the schools insufficient to satisfy their desire to know more about the art of war. Naturally, then, military intellectualism found other ways to express itself.

In increasing numbers form the 1880s on, army officers contributed to an explosion of specialized literature on the art of war. This new professional writing appeared in several forms. A number of professional journals, issued monthly or quarterly, offered officers in each of the combat arms the news of the latest developments in their own arms. Others, especially the *Journal of the Military Service Institution of the United States* (*JMSIUS*), tried to provide officers of all branches a "broad *service* (not simply corps) platform" to address issues "essential to healthy military progress."[14] Military history served the journal's contributors well. Whether it was history-as-illustration, history-as-application, or even history-as-inspiration or history-as-advocate, the events of past wars offered military writers—and thus military readers—many of the same advantages it provided to army educators.

Officers also promoted their own professional education by writing many of the textbooks used in the army schools. This literature broke new ground in several ways. It was the first attempt by American military men to speak with authority on the theory of war. They realized that they could not continue to bow to the pronouncements of European military theorists to guide their thinking about the art of war in North America. A whole new body of theoretical literature on the art of war, based on the experiences of American soldiers fighting in North America, replaced European military texts no longer considered relevant to officers of the Old Army. That so many soldiers "took pen in hand" was in itself proof positive of the flourishing spirit of professionalism sweeping through their ranks.

If the army's turn to military history in the pre–World War I years was so successful, however, why did later generations of officers fail to follow the paths blazed by their predecessors? Why did the army, as the ad hoc committee had been told, "turn away from its traditional reliance upon the lessons of history?" The army's inability to maintain a long-term commitment to military history in the education of its officers can also be traced to the Progressive Era.

At the dawn of the twentieth century, the officer corps of the Old Army was not the only claimant to intellectual authority over the study of the wars of the past. Among the other occupational specialties organizing and demanding recognition of its professional status at this time was the American historical community.[15] No evaluation of the origins of history's place in the foundation of the professional education of the American military officer is complete without considering the tensions that developed between—and then separated—soldiers and scholars, each group presuming to speak with authority on the military past of the United States.

The American Historical Association spoke for the scholarly community. Much as their counterparts in uniform resented civilian dilettantes who claimed to be experts on modern warfare, university-trained historians in the first decade of the twentieth century were determined to wrest control of the AHA from the antiquarians, genealogists, and state librarians—all "dabblers" with no scholarly credentials to validate them as historians—who had made up the bulk of organization's membership since its founding in 1884. The methodology of scientific history provided the unique body of theory that defined their professional identity, just as the principles of war defined the soldier's sphere of expertise.[16]

To the AHA, the Old Army's flagrant disregard for the scholarly standards of scientific history could not be tolerated. Part of the army's use of military history, instruction in the source method of historical research, fully met these standards, but this one bright spot did not compensate for the many other ways in which the spirit of scientific history was abused in officer education. Certainly history-as-illustration and the applicatory method did not live up to the standards of modern historical scholarship, but to the credit of army instructors, they freely admitted that they were not teaching "history." They taught tactics, strategy, and other military specialties, and they had not confused history the instructional tool with history the intellectual discipline. This was not an explanation the historical community could accept at a time when its own status among the professions was still insecure.

Civilian scholars, entering the lists considerably after military history had found a niche in the professional culture of the Old Army, saw only an interloper on their rightful territory. Few in the historical community were sufficiently knowledgeable about the army's use of history to realize that each profession viewed military history from a different perspective. At the annual meeting of the AHA in 1912, Prof. Albert Bushnell Hart explained the complexity of the problem: "Military history includes two terms, the subject and the method, and military science and discussion of military events and principles."[17] Most soldiers would have recognized the second half of Hart's definition as the kind of military history they usually studied; indeed, except for the source-method courses, this was the case. Academic historians, on the other hand, recognized only the methodology—the first half of Hart's description—as the proper province of their professional authority. Where military history was concerned, then, Hart had described a "history gap" between soldiers and scholars.

More than philosophical differences split the soldiers from the scholars, however. Institutional priorities inadvertently deepened the tensions between the two groups, which, it would seem, actually shared a common interest in desiring an objective, accurate record of the American military past. Scholars resented their inability to gain open access to records that The Adjutant General's Office controlled and demanded the War Department allow historians to take over or at least accept their advice concerning the army's documentary editing projects. Efforts by the AHA to set up cooperative or collaborative programs with the War Department to write American military history together invariably required greater concessions from the soldiers than from the scholars. The army for its part, saw only that any of these demands would have required the changing of long-standing policies or the surrender of control over traditional responsibilities never before challenged by outsiders. The army's resistance to changes of this magnitude, combined with the requirements of professional identity in both camps, effectively closed important channels of intellectual interchange that might have promoted a healthy interest in military history in the army and in the historical community. Instead, the study of military history thrived in neither after World War I.

This first experiment with the use of military history in the professional education of the officer corps of the Old Army would leave behind a mixed legacy. On the one hand, military history served well in a number of different ways in army classrooms. As an instructional tool, it lived up to its billing as "the laboratory of the military profession" in its ability to provide object lessons in any aspect of military science. Military history also comprised a body of common experiences that American soldiers could dissect, analyze, and use as the basis for learning how to "speak the same language" in discussing sophisticated questions of contemporary military strategy. It unquestionably improved the intellectual quality of professional education in the Old Army.

On the other hand, the study of military history could not live up to every claim its advocates made for it. Even after a generation of officers had been educated to their profession in the army's advanced schools, many nagging questions remained. Officers could not reach consensus on exactly why a soldier should study military history. They also could not agree on how soldiers should study military history to obtain the greatest benefits. Nor could they decide on what level or levels of a soldier's career instruction in military history would serve him best. And though they could make a strong case for military history's usefulness for any professional soldier, they could not shake entirely the arguments of the doubters and naysayers who would not be swayed from their belief that "only war teaches war." There would always be those who believed the study of military history only prepared a soldier to fight a war that had already been fought.

Most important, perhaps, when the validity of the army's methods of studying military history came under the scrutiny of the historical community, the army chose to redefine the limits of its intellectual authority. For all intents and purposes, the army took a backward step and restricted its perception of military history to the second half of Professor Hart's definition—to traditional military science. This last alone explains some of the discontinuities in the U.S. Army's institutional commitment to military history: Without an understanding of historical method or the historical context of other elements of scientific history, it was too easy for soldiers in the wake of a major event such as World War I to consider the distant past irrelevant to the immediate doctrinal and command problems they had just uncovered. For all its promise in officer training, there were also limits to military history's usefulness. The Old Army considered all these questions and more, and it even took important first steps toward implementing some of the tentative decisions it had reached about the benefits of military history in officer education. The officers of that earlier generation have much to say to students of Progressive Era reform and offer a striking look at the professionalization process when two groups fight over common ground. They also have much to suggest to advocates and critics of the study of military history in the post-Vietnam U.S. Army. It is time for a fresh look at the "lessons learned" close to a century ago.

2

MILITARY HISTORY:
"THE FOUNDATION OF OUR ART,
THE BASIS OF OUR PROFESSION"

"It is the *Science* of War in the broadest sense, not simply the *Art* of War, that we are to study," Maj. Gen. John M. Schofield admonished an audience of American army officers in 1877. A responsible soldier, the general advised, must study and reflect upon the art of war during times of peace. He must take every opportunity to learn from his own "observation, experience, and the careful study of the experiences of others who have gone before us" the fine points of military leadership.[1] Schofield's counsel hints at one especially important force that helped to transform the scattered frontier garrisons and seacoast defenses of the post–Civil War years into the modernized U.S. Army of World War I: the professionalization of the officer corps.

Like much of the United States at the turn of the century, the Old Army felt the effects of widespread agitation for reform. In factories, in scientific laboratories, in corporate headquarters, in university classrooms, and in countless other parts of a rapidly growing and modernizing society, the winds of change inspired new goals: efficiency in operations, proficiency in personnel. The U.S. Army heeded the call. Large-scale organizational changes, such as the creation of the General Staff and the Military Information Bureau, centralized and streamlined important elements of army administration. The drive for a more efficient military establishment behind these major institutional changes reached even into the smallest details of soldier life; so small a matter as the proper pace for infantrymen on the march — measured in steps per minute — was not too insignificant for military men to discuss in depth. The army, like many parts of civilian society, underwent its own "search for order" during the Progressive Era.[2]

But organizational efficiency was not enough. "The mass is never better than the elements which compose it," Capt. William E. Birkhimer correctly asserted.[3] General Schofield reminded his subordinates that "the duties of a military officer are becoming, year by year, more complex and more difficult to perform."[4] Perceptive officers in increasing numbers realized that the art of war had not "escaped the regulating force of modern industrial specialization. Starting as an instinct and the natural business of the entire body

9

of adult males, it has steadily shrunk in its scope until it has become, with the advance of civilization, a distinct profession and a special science."[5] Proficiency in the art of war now required special training.

In Progressive America, to lay claim to the status of a "profession" was no small matter. New areas of intellectual investigation emerged annually, and as part of the drive for efficiency, older fields of study tended to splinter into their component specialties. These trends created a whole new class of educated men—and some women—who demanded society's validation of their specific fields of expertise. They asked to be accorded what they felt was their rightful place among the traditional "learned professions" such as medicine and law. Indeed, as individuals, officers sought the same goal as civilian professionals: in the parlance of the time, the status of "learned gentlemen."[6]

Not every group claiming professional status was deemed worthy of the title. In Progressive America, a true profession had to satisfy certain informally accepted criteria. Possession of a unique service, society's recognition of its members' authority in that field, and the establishment of standards for admission to and advancement in that specialty all served as yardsticks for acceptance into the American professional class. But, more important than all these requirements, a profession was set above and apart from mere occupations or skills by the possession of an intellectual component. Mastery of a body of theoretical knowledge unique to his special service, acquired only through intensive study, separated the true professional from the dilettante. The emergence of great numbers of graduate programs and the establishment of "professional schools" in the American university system revealed the centrality of the intellectual component to the many new professions.[7]

These developments were not lost on the officer corps. "Much as science has progressed of late years, the art of war has kept even pace. The former specialties of military science, technical as well as practical, are now complete sciences in themselves and the special art of generalship, which must utilize all the others to best advantage, has been pushed so far that no longer will the artillerist or cavalryman or infantryman necessarily make a good general. . . . To be a good general now requires not only talent, but special training," wrote one captain.[8] Officers of the Old Army knew it was time to erase "a popular notion that he who was of good stature, well-proportioned figure and handsomely uniformed, possessed all the requisites of a good officer."[9]

They fully admitted that there was still a place for the traditional qualities of a good soldier. A good officer must meet certain physical standards. He must also cultivate his "moral nature" by developing the "honesty of thought and action, an uprightness of conduct, and the highest regard for truthfulness" consistent with the honor of a gentleman.[10] Growing numbers of them, however, also admitted that

> the high (and ever-essential) attributes of physical and moral courage, coolness, power of quick and correct thought and action, patriotism and zeal, no longer suffice to make the perfect military leader, but must be supplemented by careful training in the many branches of human knowledge which are not used in every feature of the profession of arms. The army officer of the present day should differ as much from his predecessor of fifty years ago as a locomotive differs from a stage-coach, or a magazine rifle from a flint-lock musket.[11]

The professionalization of the officer corps of the Old Army required some immediate changes in the traditions of military service. "We separate for service" had been the motto of one West Point class, but it applied equally well to the entire U.S. Army of the post–Civil War years. Except in time of war, an officer seldom enjoyed an opportunity to appreciate the workings of his profession outside his own branch of the service.[12] Unless he learned something of the management of all the arms and auxiliary services, however, "he cannot reasonably hope for success either in high command or in directing the duties of the general staff," one soldier complained.[13] The Old Army needed new ways to bring together the scattered officer corps under a single professional identity as specialists in the art of war.

In the classrooms of its new system of schools for the advanced education of its officers, in the meeting halls of a growing number of military societies and associations, and in the pages of the new professional journals and textbooks that soldiers wrote for other soldiers, the Old Army found ways to forge this common bond. Constant attention to the developments in the art of war preserved "the apprehension of war, without which there is no efficiency. For being in time of peace its only raison d'etre, this apprehension is to an Army the basis of self-respect; and professional self-respect – the surface of which constitutes professional pride – is the mother-earth of professional zeal, of which efficiency is the fruit."[14]

To secure that professional identity in the eyes of civilian society, however, the Old Army still had to prove its mastery over an esoteric body of theoretical knowledge unique to its service. The so-called principles of war – such accepted axioms as security, celerity, surprise, unity of command, and the superiority of the offensive – provided the framework for this body of theory. These concepts were only words unless an officer knew how to apply each one to the rapidly changing face of modern warfare. Schofield's plea to study the past to prepare for the future suggested one way to accomplish this goal.

And indeed, as the new century dawned, the Old Army had made an important discovery: Military history "is the foundation of our art, the basis of our profession."[15]

The study of military history was not a strikingly new idea to officers of the Old Army. For a generation before the Civil War, Dennis Hart Mahan, the influential instructor of military engineering at West Point and a committed advocate of professionalism, had taught his cadets that "it is in military history that we are to look for the source of all military science."[16] But Mahan's one-semester course in military art was often his students' only classroom exposure to the campaigns of the great captains of history. Moreover, once a cadet graduated, he had to design his own reading program of military biographies and battle studies if he was sufficiently motivated to improve his understanding of his profession.[17] If he chose not to further his studies, it was not likely to reflect poorly on him; before the Civil War, few officers devoted much time to any kind of systematic self-instruction.

In the years immediately after Appomattox, the old standards continued largely unchanged. By the 1880s, however, increasing numbers of ambitious young officers refused to give in to the intellectually stultifying "island community" mentality that tended to squelch a soldier's desire to broaden his knowledge of his art beyond what he needed to perform his everyday duties.[18] Even army officers serving at frontier outposts in Arizona Territory felt the winds of change sweeping through mainstream America. Temporary assignments to ordnance boards, staff duties, or court-martial service brought many of them close enough to the great urban centers to observe firsthand the efforts of reformers to improve efficiency and competence in government and industry. Still others assigned as professors of military science and tactics at land-grant colleges and universities all across the United States witnessed for themselves the growing impact of formal education on the advancement of professional knowledge in many different fields.[19] It did not take long for the Young Turks in the officer corps to conclude that they too needed a more comprehensive system of formal education.

To be sure, there was an element of self-interest in the push for a system of advanced officer education. In an army in which promotion was slow, and middle-aged Civil War veterans created a bottleneck at the higher ranks, ambitious junior officers looked into all kinds of reforms that might open the door to quicker advancement. One especially attractive plan called for replacing the traditional system of promotion based on seniority with a new set of standards that required objective evidence of an officer's capacity to perform the duties of the next higher rank. Outstanding performances in the classroom might provide just that kind of evidence and perhaps permit qualified subalterns to rise through the ranks more quickly.

Balancing personal career goals with a commitment to improve their institution—and the realization that they had to deal with a rigid bureaucracy highly resistant to change—was a difficult business at best.[20] Nonetheless, reformist officers, like their counterparts in other emerging professions, placed their hope for the future advancement of the military art in what one of its detractors called "education mania."[21]

The push for advanced education was largely a grass-roots movement that relied heavily on the efforts of individual officers committed to the improvement of professional culture in the Old Army. Even at small frontier posts, groups of officers could be found meeting informally to discuss military topics or work out practical problems in minor tactics. "The life of a line officer is what the post commander makes of it," Lt. John Bigelow decided. "He is fortunate if he comes to a post commander who is active and energetic, zealous and able." Unfortunately, "two neighboring posts may be as different from each other as the armies of two neighboring nations."[22]

Lt. Matthew Forney Steele's experiences corroborated Bigelow's comments. At his first duty station, he was met by two drunken lieutenants who introduced him to their equally inebriated captain. But later, at Fort Yates, he met "officers interested in professional study beyond the little so-called 'Tactics'" and saw "military text books other than the elementary books we had at West Point." Steele's commander, Capt. Hugh Brown, was "a student of the soldier's profession and a fine example for younger officers." Brown's penchant for *kriegsspiel*, or war gaming, "made us youngsters study all we could find in minor tactics and troop leading."[23]

Although these post discussion groups clearly indicated that the army contained a number of soldiers who wanted to "take this profession seriously enough to master it,"[24] the army took no immediate step to introduce the practice to all its garrisons. Instead, the first formal attempt to upgrade the intellectual quality of military instruction for the army's future leaders took place at an institution already more than fifty years old. A new era in military professionalism began when Col. Emory Upton arrived at the Artillery School at Fortress Monroe in 1877 to redesign its curriculum.

Established in 1824, the Artillery School still leaned heavily on its pre-Civil War curriculum based on practical exercises with small caliber, muzzle-loading, smoothbore cannons. Technological advances such as the casting of bores of much larger calibers, the introduction of rifling to cannon barrels, and the adoption of breech-loading guns were still such new developments in the late 1870s that "were the most skillful officer of the Mexican War to rise from his grave he would be an infant in the use of modern artillery."[25]

Upton decided to revise the curriculum from top to bottom. He emphasized two subjects: first, as before, the practical uses of modern guns on the battlefield; second, the theory of "kindred subjects," with relevant applications to the employment of artillery, including cavalry and infantry tactics, and "engineering, law, and military history." He required students to investigate for themselves and report to the class how artillery had been used in different battles of the Civil War. In his lectures and discussions, he himself borrowed frequently from the mistakes and victories of the past to underscore important concepts in the use of artillery alone and with other arms.[26] No longer could artillery officers, at least, entirely "separate for service" from their colleagues in other arms. The education offered at the Artillery School now gave a battery commander "the opportunity fully to understand and appreciate . . . . [How] futile his labors would be without the efficient cooperation of the others."[27]

The rapid improvement of instruction at the Artillery School encouraged Gen. William T. Sherman to attempt to give officers from other arms the same kinds of opportunities for advanced education. Too many young officers, he feared, considered their professional training complete when they received their commissions. West Point graduates especially seemed "too apt to regard their education as complete when they leave the Academy, whereas, like workmen, they have simply acquired the rudiments and a knowledge of their tools."[28]

In 1881, at Sherman's urging, the Infantry and Cavalry School was established at Fort Leavenworth, Kansas. Using the curriculum of the Artillery School as his model, Sherman expected the new institution to provide both practical training and a sound theoretical education in the art of war. The school's earliest years did not live up to Sherman's goals. Too many of the students were young lieutenants newly commissioned directly from civilian life and totally lacking in even the basics of military science, or they were undesirables dumped on the institution by commanding officers anxious to rid themselves of troublesome subordinates. All the school could do for these men was provide basic instruction in military and nonmilitary subjects; for a while, the curriculum even included reading aloud and penmanship. During the 1880s, the Infantry and Cavalry School was known derisively as "the kindergarten," and few ambitious officers chose to attend.[29]

By the 1890s, however, the school rediscovered its original mission. Indeed, the Infantry and Cavalry School became the backbone of the Old Army's education system. Each year, from the 1890s until the school closed at the outset of World War I, dozens of officers—including such exceptional subalterns as 1st Lt. George C. Marshall—became "Leavenworth men." As army reformers had hoped, graduation from this school and others like it came to be viewed as important professional credentials, worthy of special consideration during selections for choice assignments or early promotion. By the turn of the century, both faculty and students could find their names listed prominently in the annual *Army Register*.[30] By 1904, when the school reopened after the Spanish-American War with an even more advanced curriculum, faculty and administrators believed they had "set a pace that will make the diploma well worth having."[31]

Even as the Infantry and Cavalry School returned to its original purpose, it became increasingly clear that the army's education system was developing rather haphazardly. From the time an officer first qualified for his commission—either by graduating from West Point or by passing a competitive examination for a direct appointment from civilian life—until he gained sufficient seniority to attend the Artillery or the Leavenworth school, seven to ten years might have passed with no formal direction in the study of professional subjects.

To fill this void, General Schofield in 1891 ordered each garrison manned by troops of the line to establish an officers' lyceum. Schofield essentially had done little more than create a formal organizational niche for the discussion groups that had flourished in their unofficial capacity for several decades. But that was no small contribution. Under this new system, each post commander was now required to set aside time for his subordinates' professional education. He also had to design "a carefully considered scheme of theoretical instruction . . . with special reference to the requirements of examinations for promotion" to the ranks of first lieutenant and captain.[32] Officers not only completed a reading program in professional subjects, they also prepared essays for the further information and critiques of their colleagues. Suitable subjects included military law, field engineering, signaling, minor tactics, administration, drill regulations, and military topography. Outstanding work in the lyceum, as many military reformers had hoped, became a major consideration not only for promotion but for coveted assignments to more advanced schools.

Finally, as the most senior of the Old Army's professional schools, the Army War College was established at Washington in 1901. Secretary of War Elihu Root believed the new school to be absolutely essential both to national defense and to the encouragement of military professionalism among the army's high command:

Only an institution, perpetual but always changing in its individual elements, in which by conference and discussion, a consensus of matured opinion can be reached, can perpetuate the results of individual effort, secure continuity of military policy, and command for its authorized con-

clusive expressions of military judgment upon military questions the
respect and effectiveness to which that judgment is entitled.[33]

The first administrative board of the Army War College adopted an educational philosophy stated succinctly by Gen. Tasker H. Bliss: Officers must
"learn things by doing things." Before World War I, its students would prepare war plans, solve hundreds of map problems and exercises that forced
them to consider the employment of large bodies of troops, design still more
problems for instructional use at all levels of the army school system, and
attempt an "official history" of the Civil War that would reflect the doctrinal
views of the General Staff.[34] The varied experience educated a small cadre
of American soldiers—mostly majors and colonels—in the practical and
theoretical skills required either for high command or for the responsibilities
of staff work at division, corps, or army level.

The army's commitment to advanced officer education beyond West Point
did not end with these few schools. By 1917, thirty-four other schools had
opened for the instruction of officers from the Signal Corps, Medical Corps,
and other military specialties. Successful completion of the curriculum of
these schools, too, was noted next to each graduate's name in the official
Army Register. The advocates of progressive career-long education had made
great strides in creating an institutional framework that would help develop
the all-important intellectual component of their professional culture. But
their success had not come easily; indeed, the very subject of professional
education had generated much heated debate in the officers corps, the War
Department, Congress, and among interested civilian observers. More than
one soldier saw the wisdom of Gen. Ulysses S. Grant's complaint that the
only time the army had any peace was when it was at war.[35]

The study of military history became a lightning rod for critics' attacks
upon the army's new concern with its officers' intellectual development.
Even if many soldiers agreed that it was "the foundation of our art, the basis
of our profession," it did not find its way easily into the curricula of the new
schools. Military history had secured its place much more readily in the U.S.
Navy, where the commitment of Adm. Stephen Luce and Capt. Alfred
Thayer Mahan to the study of the past guaranteed that students at the Naval War College would learn the "science of their profession—the Science
of War"—with a strong awareness of the conduct of naval affairs across the
ages.[36] The Old Army, however, produced no influential intellectual god-
father of equal stature who could step forward and define the place of military history in the education of its officers. In the absence of such a spokesman, advocates of military history touted the ability of the study of the past

to contribute to the development of professional culture in a wide variety of ways. And at times, théy created more cacophony than consensus.

Military history's supporters fell into three not entirely exclusive categories. One group looked to the study of military history chiefly as a way to promote the intellectual component of the officer corps' professional identity; it would provide the foundation on which to build a soldier's understanding of the theories and maxims of modern war. A second group viewed it primarily as a practical instructional tool, especially useful for introducing officers to unusual command problems and for teaching them how to solve such situations responsibly. A third group, probably history's most effective advocates, made a strong case for the discipline's ability not only to serve the army's need for theory but to fulfill its practical needs as well. All three groups agreed that military history deserved a place in officer education, but beyond that they could not concur on precisely why a soldier should study it or what specific benefits he could expect to reap from that study.

Officers who expected the study of history to provide the intellectual framework for the military profession had only to compare a soldier's education with that of already acknowledged professions in the civilian world. An unnamed graduate of the Infantry and Cavalry School drew a direct comparison between the importance of military history to soldiers and the significance of laboratory experiments to professional chemists:

The chemist studying his science, has constant recourse to the experiment in the laboratory. . . . Assume now that, for some reason, it should be impossible to conduct experiments in chemistry, in a given century, except for two periods of two years each. . . . Would the science of chemistry perish? Not at all! It might progress in the intervals just as military science does in peace periods. But a new phase of science would appear; the history of the experiments would become the field of study. . . . This is precisely the status of the study of the profession of arms. During times of peace no experiments are possible. . . . [In combat] an officer must deduce from his knowledge of past events how troops have behaved and also the influence of each of the innumerable factors governing their behavior.[37]

Usually, the staunchest advocates of history as the intellectual foundation of the military profession drew upon a comparison that portended the direst of consequences if their pleas were ignored. The theoretical education of any army officer, they asserted, was as important to the preservation of national life as a medical student's training was to saving human life. "When it is a question, not of the life of one man, but of hundreds, not the well being of a community, but of a nation, how much greater is the necessity for legal protection against ignorant practice, no matter how patriotic or well meaning the individual?" asked Maj. William Murray Black. Since "the immense swiftness and concentration and the implacable onset of modern warfare . . . leaves no time for the painful acquirement in the field" of the military art, an officer who devoted himself to the study of past wars would be more likely to win battles and less likely to condemn a soldier under his command to a fate as "a mere bullet-stopper or typhoid victim."[38]

Graduates of the army's more advanced schools could not fathom why members of learned professions would not accept them into the "society of gentlemen." Capt. Campbell A. King, an infantryman who graduated from the Infantry and Cavalry School and became an instructor in its tactics department, understood the giant intellectual leap the army had taken by introducing theoretical instruction into officer education. With the zeal of a convert, King railed against the lack of respect extended to army officers as compared with that accorded members of other professions:

> In civil life men undergo for every profession a special training and preparation before they can successfully practice it. Those dealing indirectly with life and death such as medicine, pharmacy, surgery, are protected by law from practice by men not specially trained for their profession whatever may be their mental attainments in other directions. But war, that which deals most directly with life and death, whose agencies are the most destructive that human ingenuity can prevent, is hedged about with no safeguard.

King had also come to understand the importance of military history to the ability of an officer to master his art: "The conduct of the armies of today is both a profession and a colossal business in one. . . . A knowledge of the result which will follow certain combinations, and practice in the preparation of combinations is as essential to the profession of arms as a like knowledge and practice is essential to the profession of medicine."[39]

The advocates of military history as an intellectual discipline were not obsessed solely by a desire to elevate the army officer to the special social status claimed by the learned professions. If the study of past wars promoted a soldier's mastery of military theory, it was enough that the army had gained an officer who could think critically. A soldier who had given long years of thought and study to the military campaigns of the great captains and could translate what he had learned into action on the battlefield would vindicate the supporters of these views and undermine critics of spending time in the study of military history.

Additionally, if an officer cultivated his "military mind," he probably also enhanced his "military character," the moral component also essential to a professional soldier. To the civilian middle class of the Progressive Era, character "stood for power, permanence, and fortitude," virtues that were equally important to a professional soldier.[40] The ideal military character, which Lt. Hugh Kelly defined as "truth, honor, loyalty, courage, duty and self-sacrifice," was best inspired by the example of the great soldiers of history.[41] Unquestionably, the cause of military professionalism could only benefit as soldiers of strong military character naturally sought out like-minded colleagues and served as role models for others.

Gradually, at least among reform-minded soldiers, a new image of the model army officer of the future emerged. He would be equally comfortable in the field or in the classroom. He must "begin to wield the pen as well as the bayonet and sabre."[42] Older officers must write textbooks, submit articles based on their experiences to the new professional journals, and use the classroom to disseminate what they had learned in the field to their younger colleagues. More and more, it became apparent that the rapidly changing face of warfare now required army officers to accept "the absolute necessity of studying and reading in the art of war—and for their constant reading at that."[43]

Although military history's strongest supporters did not need to be convinced further that the professional education of the officer corps would best be advanced by studying the wars of the past, the more perceptive among them also looked for ways to overcome the equally strong reservations of some of their colleagues. Other subjects considered by some to be unimportant to the soldier's art, especially foreign languages and law, already had inspired heated debate. To secure history's place in professional education, therefore, some of its proponents deftly turned the discipline's intellectual nature into a practical plus for any officer. Their fundamental argument was straightforward. The more an officer knew about the capabilities of modern weapons, and the different ways various formations, tactics, and strategies might be employed in war, the more likely he would be prepared to face his ultimate practicum: combat. The study of military history "lays in supplies of which there must be the right and prompt use on occasion."[44]

There were many other practical advantages to studying history as well. An officer who took time to understand how campaigns throughout history were won or lost was apt to develop greater confidence in his ability to make decisions on the battlefield. An officer with a sound military mind, General Schofield repeatedly warned, had to be able to do far more than copy uncritically the tactics of some successful Civil War hero. That only invited disaster. An intelligent soldier "must intently study the history of military contests and endeavor therefrom to learn the facts . . . [and] ascertain what influence each of the ascertained conditions exercised in producing the known result."[45] Military history, viewed this way, offered a treasure trove of practical examples in leadership an officer could draw upon if faced with a similar situation on the battlefield.

Shrewd proponents of the study of military history also knew how to make it appeal directly to the practical concerns of ambitious younger officers. Captains and lieutenants should take time to study their art to better their own career opportunities. Among the officers most in demand — and most likely to be promoted — during a national emergency were those who had developed in peacetime the intellectual and analytical skills needed in war. The mind-numbing routine of garrison duty had killed too many young officers' interest in military studies. But as the army moved from a promotion system based solely on seniority toward one based on merit, junior officers were urged to consider time spent in serious study a practical investment toward quicker advancement. A few hours well spent in the deep study of professional subjects each day promised greater long-term benefits than did frittering away their time tiring "appetite and muscle in the capture or search for trout, turkey, and antelope."

Moreover, if a young officer failed to keep up with military developments, he ran the risk of damaging his future usefulness to the nation. "The science of war widens with all the rest [of the professions] and the preparations and conditions of success here as elsewhere become more and more complex," one instructor warned. A junior officer should approach his professional studies with an active, inquisitive mind. Quality of study — not quantity — mattered most, he assured them: "A few campaigns well studied and carefully reflected on, will do more to develop a capacity for hard thinking than would a whole course of lectures on a score of battles."[46]

History's most ardent supporters ignored no viable argument that might convince a skeptical officer to sharpen his military mind. A favorite tactic was to point out the ability of battles and campaigns, even from the distant past, to provide a sense of vicarious experience with untold numbers of unusual or unfamiliar elements that might affect the outcome of a fight. Lt. Albert Bjornstad advised studying both major victories and decisive defeats to discover "the vagaries of the human mind under conditions of stress, danger, and excitement." If a soldier understands the factors that contributed to the results of a past campaign and he finds himself in a similar situation, his historical insights are likely to check "whatever tendency there may be to depart from true principles." The study of history "marks the line between the possible and impossible, the good and the bad; not always distinctly, it is true, but with a fair accuracy not otherwise obtainable."[47]

The army's most effective and forceful proponents of military history ably combined—and acknowledged—both the intellectual and the practical benefits of studying the campaigns of the past. Never in the life of the United States was the need for a trained standing army so pressing as it was during the quarter-century before World War I. Advances in military technology and the rapidity with which a major power's industrial capacity could be turned to the large-scale production of armaments led many soldiers to believe future wars would be brief and decisive. There would be no time to teach an officer the soldier's art on the battlefields of such conflicts. Moreover, it was necessary to educate all officers, not just those slated for high command. All these "modern changes . . . bring into far greater prominence than ever before the functions of commander, which officers of all grades must exercise. Blind obedience, courage, and even discipline, however great, can no longer be relied upon to gain victories. Every captain and lieutenant should be, in no small degree, a real general."[48] If for no other reason, therefore, the study of military history deserved a special place in any comprehensive system of officer education.

More immediately pressing, the modernization of warfare inspired the Old Army to articulate a new philosophy of military command, a concept officers generally referred to as "safe leadership." The usefulness of military history in spreading the spirit of safe leadership throughout the officer corps provided all the evidence needed of its ability to contribute to both the intellectual and practical elements of professional culture.

Even in the few years since the Civil War, the profession of arms had been so drastically transformed by the effects of modernization and industrialization that the responsibilities of military command demanded redefinition. The longer ranges of modern weapons and the introduction of the telegraph (and later, the field telephone and "the wireless") had greatly increased the size of the battlefield. A commander could no longer direct all parts of a battle through personal exertion. As commanders found themselves farther and farther behind the front lines, they discovered that for victory "under modern conditions, the cooperation of many elements must be secured."[49]

Analogies made the point for officers who did not grasp the complexities of command in modern warfare. One particularly apt illustration during this time of rapid industrial growth compared safe leadership to an intricate mechanical apparatus that, like any finely tuned mechanism, works most effectively only if all the cogs meshed perfectly. In this model of high com-

mand, the "natural" leader, the individualist, or the unpredictable and spec-
tacularly lucky "military genius" were just so much sand to foul the cogs.[50]
Officers must become the kind of cogs that fit with the others. Other com-
parisons worked well, too. The Army War College Class of 1912 heard a
high-ranking officer compare safe leadership to the teamwork on a successful
football team. Everyone had to stay on the same page of the playbook to
ensure a victory.[51]

Army educators, especially, thought the best way to infuse the spirit of
safe leadership into the officer corps was through the study of military history. Soldiers could learn much from dissecting the command decisions
made by previous generations of generals and analyzing how those decisions
contributed to victory or defeat. In the classroom, for instance, officers
could unravel Robert E. Lee's complex tactical and strategic challenges from
the Gettysburg campaign, isolate and identify the factors most important
to a successful solution of each problem, suggest a course of action consistent with the principles of war, and evaluate the soundness of Lee's own decisions. This kind of intense study reproduced the conditions of a real campaign without "the sense of responsibility, the excitement and the physical
strain."[52] Long series of case studies based on historical examples, each stressing both the principles of war and their applications in specific situations,
helped an officer to understand "what to expect from every other and what
to do himself."[53] An officer who cultivated "the proper habit of thought and
action" and who could "render decisions quickly and accurately" was a soldier endowed with the spirit of safe leadership.[54]

Mastery of the concept of safe leadership required an understanding of
much that was not essentially military in nature. Late in his career, Col.
Arthur L. Wagner, one of the army's first and most influential proponents
of the new command philosophy, explained how military history might
teach a professional soldier a wide array of subtle but important lessons. The
study of past campaigns can inspire an appreciation of the "perplexities and
embarrassments" that generals face at all times; it dispels the notion that
successful commanders are endowed with "supernatural prescience"; it teaches
that the "ablest of generalship is merely human wisdom applied to human
knowledge"; it reminds soldiers that human wisdom is not infallible; and it
underscores the costliness of misinformation, inefficiency, indolence, treach-
ery, loss of orders, or undue delays.[55]

Additionally, Wagner and most other military educators urged soldiers to
study battles from both the perspective of the victor and that of the van-
quished. Both had lessons to teach. During the 1890s, in his first years on
the faculty of the Infantry and Cavalry School, Capt. Eben Swift, Wagner's
colleague and kindred spirit and a firm believer that "the secrets of the art

of war are to be found in the pages of history,"[56] refined an instructional technique to expose his students to large numbers of historical and imaginary military situations, drawn directly from or based loosely on the great victories and massive defeats of the past. Each case study demonstrated not merely a principle of war but also an application or misapplication of that axiom. A student of Swift's "applicatory system" could not fail to gain confidence in his own ability to make command decisions based soundly on an appropriate principle of war. Swift made him flex his "military mind." Thus he was more likely to be a "safe leader."[57]

Still, despite such carefully reasoned and effectively articulated arguments for officer education and the attractiveness of the concept of safe leadership in modern war, not all American soldiers viewed these changes as good for the service. Indeed, the officer corps was divided against itself on many questions concerning military professionalism. An unsympathetic traditionalist element in the Old Army made especially clear its resentment of the most obvious manifestation of the professionalization process: the intellectualization of the officer corps. This group's criticism of the army's postgraduate school system in general, and the education of officers in the theory of the art of high command in particular, inevitably placed the study of military history under its close scrutiny.

The most hostile military conservatives, including many senior officers who had been commissioned directly from civilian life or owed their positions to their long-ago Civil War heroics, held stubbornly to their conviction that the battlefield was the only teacher of the art of war. As products of the citizen-soldier tradition whose own careers seemed to prove that schooling for soldiers was unnecessary, they saw little need for—and may even have feared—new regulations that stipulated classroom proficiency as one requirement for promotion. Indeed, many of them believed these changes might be dangerous if carried too far.

Military anti-intellectualism took many forms. Some senior officers, especially those nearing retirement and disenchanted by all the changes occurring around them, viewed professional education as just another army fad. Col. George S. Anderson, a bitter critic of the lyceum system he was supposed to direct on his post, complained in 1898 that after the flurry of interest in military signaling—a "disease of the day, now dead and buried"—and the quick demise of the "map making bacillus" that followed, the army should have realized that "we are all too old to have wisdom crammed down our throats like food down the necks of Strasburg geese." He lamented the army's fall into the "epidemic of wisdom" that plagued his last years in the service of his country. With tongue planted firmly in cheek, he reviewed the many innovations introduced into and then discarded from officer education during the previous decade and complained caustically that if theology were not added to the curriculum in the next eighteen months, "I fear that I shall be able to miss it."[58]

Other critics of the army's intellectual pursuits borrowed freely from charges leveled at similar trends in civilian circles. As historian Richard Hofstadter has argued, the American public during the Progressive Era demanded leaders in the Theodore Roosevelt mold, the "kind of men who could join the sphere of ideas and moral scruples with the virile qualities of action and assertion."[59] Too much book learning, the critics argued, could actually work against the betterment of the service by creating an effeminate officer corps.

Traditionalists agreed with progressives that a sound military character was important to every officer, but they also believed the necessary qualities required only the development of innate characteristics; a man could not be "educated" to be a soldier. Physical and moral courage, attention to duty, boldness, perception, and justice could not be taught to a man who was not born with them. Moreover, too close attention to book learning might even destroy such hearty virtues.

Old soldiers were furious that a man who had been "a bookworm at home and knows it all by dint of hard study" received a lieutenant's commission more often than "the stronger and better man" who was rejected because as an "undeveloped soldier or scholar [he] can't tell us who fought at the battle of Bladensburg or matters of equal import."[60] The sentiment against excessive book learning remained so strong that—in jest, one hopes—Col. Charles B. Hall pleaded with the entering class of the School of the Line in 1906 "not to be stampeded by the many reports that have gone out from here as to the physical wrecks caused by overstudy."[61]

Still other traditionalists simply held on tenaciously to an outdated and romantic notion that a warrior was born, not made.[62] Classroom study could not teach a man how to command in war if he had not been born with the intangibles that make a good leader. Capt. James Chester, a frequent and vocal critic of professional education, asserted that mastery of the military art consisted simply of an ability to diagnose a situation and the spirit of command. Neither quality, he believed, could be taught. The "immutable scientific deductions" that passed for military theory could be upset by "any greasy mechanic" in one day. "Success in the next succeeding war will depend on the ability to grasp the meaning of the new conditions and not familiarity with the old," he concluded, and this could not be taught in school.[63]

Chester's gripes struck responsive chords in many officers of the Old Army. In many cases, their career decisions had been shaped by a long-standing admiration of the battlefield heroics of the great chieftains of the United

States. When Grant, Sherman, and Sheridan visited West Point during the 1880s, Cadet George Duncan spoke for many when he recalled that "to see these great soldiers was an inspiration to all of us."[64] Even young officers commissioned directly from civilian life looked to these role models as the ideal of what it meant to be a soldier. Few seemed to recall that the three generals' glories on the field of battle followed the best military education the army could offer to that generation of American officers.

Grant, Sherman, and Sheridan were the products of a time just a few years earlier when personal leadership on the battlefield was still expected of a commanding general. Now, as the army moved toward the philosophy of safe leadership, many officers of all grades regretted the passing of the active heroic warrior and the elevation of the intellectual decision maker and the efficient staff officer to prominent places in the army's command structure.

Some admitted that they felt uncomfortable with the feeling of becoming little more than a nameless, interchangeable cog in the modern military machine. They just did not feel like soldiers. Lt. John P. Wisser compared this feeling to the musings of an old Persian parable about a drop of water that fell into the sea: "Alas what an inconsiderable creature am I in this prodigious ocean of water! I am reduced to a kind of nothing, and am less than the least of the works of God!"[65]

Wisser's Persian parable was a dramatic response to the rapidity of change in the army, but it is also evidence that even young officers with strong sympathies for certain progressive changes could not always accept the entire reform agenda. Wisser represented a second type of military anti-intellectualism unlike that of Chester and other hardline traditionalists. Wisser was a firm believer in professional education; he was a graduate of Upton's Artillery School and had even served briefly in 1888 as a member of the faculty of the Naval War College.[66]

Despite this background, Wisser did not fit comfortably into the mold of most other army education reformers. In his frequent contributions to professional military journals, Wisser insisted that the army should limit the course work in the postgraduate schools to practical and technical instruction only. "Instead of devoting all the time now given to the Art of War, to the study of campaigns, and military history, the course should strike much lower" to teach the "every-day duties of a subaltern officer in the field; instead of teaching the construction of a military bridge by laborious drawings in the section room, would it not be better to actually construct bridges," he wondered.[67] As an artilleryman, he knew, for instance, that any gunner could benefit from learning as much as he could about ballistics, range finding, metallurgy, and other useful ordnance topics. But to expend time, effort, and money to teach each artillery officer anything more than the fundamentals of military theory was wasteful; only the army's highest ranking soldiers would ever have the opportunity to use what they had learned in the classroom, and few artillerymen ever reached those heights.

Wisser was not alone among army progressives who criticized the content of the curriculum of the army schools. Another skeptic, Lt. E. H. Plummer, noted that if military history was really critical to an officer's education, then the Civil War commanders, especially those who remained in the army after 1865, would have written textbooks for the classroom. When they did not do so, Plummer concluded that they must have been convinced that knowledge of past campaigns was not a key to successful command in future wars. After all, he added, military science was not really a science at all. It was more like forecasting the weather; just like the "fickle" fortunes of war, "scientific prediction of the weather twenty-four hours hence" can only be based on "'probabilities.'"[68]

Other like-minded contemporaries agreed. "There is history and there is history," another junior officer explained. "There is much that is interesting and valuable to a scholar and the man who reads for general culture, that is of little use to the practical soldier; and there is much else that is as dry as the multiplication tables, yet has direct bearing upon the questions of the day."[69] As late as 1914, when Chief of Staff Leonard Wood ordered soldiers familiar with the army school system to evaluate the curriculum, Col. C. G. Morton summarized his comments with, "all military education must be severely practical, eliminate books as far as possible except for purposes of reference."[70]

Despite the grousing of the traditionalists, the school system, professional organizations such as the Military Service Institution, new journals, and other evidences of military intellectualism thrived in the decades before the United States entered the Great War. However, if the Old Army's advocates of theoretical education had convinced many of their fellow officers of the importance of reading, studying, and writing about the art of war as matters of professional responsibility, they had met only one part of the challenge facing them. To clinch their place among the learned professions, army officers still needed to convince mainstream America of their intellectual authority over military affairs.

Most distressing to reform-minded officers, but an unavoidable consequence of military service in a republic, the U.S. Army could not control its own destiny. As Wagner noted, "It is clear that our military future will not be shaped by theories based on military principles alone. The military policy of the United States will be strongly affected by the popular predilection for economical expenditures in time of peace; by a jealousy of large standing armies; by reliance upon volunteers in time of war; and by a more or less active influence of popular opinion in the direction of armies in the field."[71] The officer corps, then, did not enjoy the autonomy it needed to remold its institution to comply with all professional standards. Although remaining nearly unanimous in their support for civilian control over the army, advocates of military professionalism chafed at the War Department's constant need to cultivate the good favor of a frequently indifferent and parsimonious Congress and executive.

Unable to exert complete control over its affairs, the Old Army could not always fend off incursions by Congress or other recognized professional groups designed to strip it of its traditional authority over some of its nonmilitary responsibilities. As the organized professions in the civilian world set standards of practice for their certified members, an officer in the Medical Corps or the Corps of Engineers, for instance, suddenly found that any measure of his professional proficiency could no longer be judged solely on his ability to carry out his assigned duties as a commissioned officer in the U.S. Army.[72] He must also live up to the standards of an essentially civilian profession over which the military establishment exerted no authority at all.

The Old Army could afford to surrender some of its responsibilities to civilian competitors without harming irreparably the cause of military professionalism. Indeed, the army could benefit from allowing many of its officers to affiliate with and adhere to the standards of appropriate professional organizations in civilian society. It could ill afford, however, to surrender its authority over the study of the art of war, the theoretical foundation that defined the U.S. Army's specific and unique mission.

During the last part of the nineteenth century, the army's claim to authority over military history seemed secure. In fact the intensive study of military history evoked little interest outside the army before 1900. Consistent with the nationalistic school of historical writing that flourished before the turn of the century, most civilian authors either steered clear of military events entirely or glossed over them superficially as just another thread in the fabric of American history. A perceptive few who cared to delve more deeply into military subjects actively sought out and often deferred to the professional opinions of army officers.

John Codman Ropes, perhaps the best-known nineteenth-century civilian student of American military history, was among those who accepted the soldier as master in the art of war. He had even written apologetically in the preface to his much heralded *The Army under Pope* that "it may be considered presumptuous in a civilian to attempt a history of a campaign."[73] Ropes's deference set the tone of the relations between soldiers and scholars

during the nineteenth century. This kind of collaboration could prove fruitful. When Ropes began a study of the Waterloo campaign in the late 1880s,
he wrote often to then Capt. Tasker H. Bliss, who answered the scholar's
questions in long, handwritten letters, often complete with diagrams to illustrate complex tactical maneuvers and attack formations.[74] When Ropes
rushed one of the first copies of his newly published book to Bliss, the officer admitted that he turned first to the "account of the incidents of the battle which had been the subject of conversation and correspondence between us." Bliss approved of what he saw. "In this age of books when so
many are and have been written upon every important incident of war—and
more on the Waterloo campaign than on any other—you have conferred the
greatest possible boon upon the military student. . . . I think he can con-
fidently accept your conclusions and let the dust accumulate upon the other
volumes."[75]

Even as Ropes published his Waterloo monograph, the era of good relations between soldiers and scholars was drawing to a close. Just as the officer
corps in the Old Army took great pains to establish its professional identity,
the historical community in American universities underwent the same
kind of pressure to assert its claim to membership among the learned professions. In the late nineteenth century, historians, too, were seeking to define
the limits of their specific sphere of authority.[76]

Like the officer corps, this new generation of scholarly historians needed
a theoretical framework on which to base its claim to professional status.
Until they embraced the methodology of German scientific history,[77] American scholars struggled to carve out a place for the study of the past among
the more traditional intellectual disciplines. "History is the youngest of the
studies to claim a place in higher education, and as a disciplinary study it
is still regarded by many as on trial—on probation," wrote Prof. George E.
Howard of the University of Nebraska in 1885. Its critics still claimed that
history "is not a science, and therefore not entitled to a large space in the
academic course."[78] Until this new breed of historians secured its right to set
the intellectual standards for historical scholarship, the army's authority in
military history remained unchallenged.

Informed army officers were not unaware of the stirrings of professionalism
in the historical community. But they did seem to misunderstand what
these developments might mean to their own efforts. At first they welcomed
the discipline of scientific history; its inclusion in the army curriculum only
improved the intellectual content of officer education. Rather than examine
deeply the scholars' new methodology, however, army instructors and writers seemed content to limit their interpretation of the term "scientific" to
mean "accurate" or "true."[79] The army's profuse praise of the merits of scien-

tific history was misleading; the methodology of the scholars found its way into officer education only in the form of a single source-method research course taught at the Staff College at Fort Leavenworth in the decade before World War I.[80]

The progressive impulse that spurred the Old Army toward the professionalization of its officer corps had also inspired the historical community. Had it played a less important role in the professional identity of either group, military history might have provided common ground for a fruitful collaboration. Unfortunately, it found itself caught between the two, claimed by both and fated to promote conflict. The army felt completely entitled to assert its authority in this case because, after all, it was *military* history. The scholars merely shifted the emphasis: It was military *history*.

The nineteenth century had seen armed conflict undergo a transition from limited wars for territorial gains to all-out ideological war. The army in this clash with historians showed that it could still fight both kinds. Neither side would be completely satisfied with only partial victory, but in the end, partial victories are all either side could claim. Although the Old Army did not surrender its grip on the kind of military history that best served its needs—the sort Professor Hart had termed "military science"—it did make small "territorial" concessions to the historical community in matters such as access to War Department documents. Despite these minor victories, historians had to accept that they could not erode overnight the strength of traditional War Department practices; they could not, for instance, wrest control of the army's documentary editing projects from the clerks at The Adjutant General's Office and impose their scholarly standards where they were not welcome.[81]

If a winner must be named, however, the Old Army should claim the crown of victory. It had not permitted the unconditional surrender of the intellectual foundation of its art to civilian interlopers. The struggle to exert intellectual authority over military history was at the same time a fight for the survival of a carefully crafted professional identity. The army had won. It had taken minor territorial losses but had not given in on any decisive front. Even the public press sensed what had happened. In 1914 liberal editors were complaining about the effectiveness of "our military propagandists" who were attempting to "influence the writing of American history so that it will be treated from the military point of view; and the American Historical Association has fallen into line by offering a prize for military essays."[82] Historians could take pride in the inroads they had made, but at this point—to borrow a Jominian concept—they had failed to capture "decisive points" from the army.

The likelihood of bringing together the two sides at this stage of their professionalization was small. The great irony, of course, is that both sides were fighting a war that really was unnecessary. In fact, neither side realized that they were fighting two essentially different wars. Here was the root of Professor Hart's "history gap." The army demanded authority over its perception of the nature of military history—the narratives of battles and military science that composed one half of Hart's definition of the discipline. The historical community, on the other hand, based its claim on its expertise in the scholarly methodology of scientific history, the other half of Hart's definition. Still, as long as each group remained rigid in its defense of its professional identity and what it perceived to be its intellectual foundation, attempts at collaboration or even cooperation were doomed to fail.

The two sides would try to find common ground. With the entry of the United States into World War I, the War Department and the historical community, especially the American Historical Association, attempted an interesting experiment to combine the talents of soldiers and scholars to compile the official history of American involvement in the Great War.[83] The project failed to live up to expectations, however, and the growing hesitancy of civilian historians to deal with the War Department in any capacity helped to turn Hart's history gap from a difference in intellectual perspective into a bona fide institutional split.

When General Schofield urged his junior officers to study the past to prepare for the future, he may not have known just how sound his advice was. He may not have realized that the discovery of a common heritage with the great captains of the American military past and the acceptance of a shared obligation to defend the United States would unite the officer corps and obliterate the "island community" mentality that had plagued the frontier army. In 1877 he saw only the first hints of the spirit of safe leadership that would create a new kind of military commander in the American army, one who could think as well as fight. Schofield could not have known then— although he certainly knew when he became commanding general in the 1890s—that past battles and campaigns offered examples of applied principles of war that would effectively inculcate the officer corps with a vibrant spirit of professionalism at the dawn of the new century.

Schofield would have been among the first to admit that the Old Army embraced the study of military history on its own terms and for its own ends. That it did not always meet the scholarly standards of scientific history was by and large irrelevant to the army's educators and to the officers who studied under them. It was sufficient that examples drawn from past wars had proved themselves unmatchable for teaching the theory of the art of war and for imparting important practical lessons in command. When the army required the intellectual rigor of scientific history to teach critical analysis and evaluation of military information, its educators were not hesitant to use that either. Forgotten in the shuffle is the contribution of military history to the officer corps' overarching goal: the development of an essential intellectual component to underpin the spirit of professionalism that would deliver the leaders of the Old Army into the company of other learned gentlemen in American society.

PART 1
MILITARY HISTORY
AND OFFICER EDUCATION

The rapid advance of military science during the nineteenth century increased the responsibilities of army officers far beyond the small-unit tactical evolutions they had learned at West Point or on garrison duty. Such prominent military progressives as Secretary of War Elihu Root recognized that by 1901 only two-thirds of the American officer corps had enjoyed even the smallest opportunity to study the art of war systematically. In order to gain a proper understanding of the theory of warfare, the complex problems of transportation, supply, hygiene, and civil-military relations, "the soldier, above all others, should be familiar with the history and imbued with the spirit of our institutions," Root asserted. A "thorough and broad education for military officers" was essential.[1]

The teaching of military history in the army's major postgraduate schools addressed both halves of Professor Hart's description of a history gap. In army classrooms, faculty members used the events of military history to teach both the theory and the practice of war. The goal of advanced instruction in the art of war was to promote the army's philosophy of responsible command, or safe leadership. Most often, instructors used the applicatory method to design classroom or open-air exercises that were based on hypothetical or historical situations and taught both the important theoretical principles of military leadership and the practical application of those axioms under different conditions.

The applicatory method without doubt helped to create a historical awareness in army officers at the postgraduate schools. Although military history provided the examples, "under the idea that all the military problems which the masters have encountered can be reduced to situations, we attempt to repeat those situations so frequently . . . that when a similar situation arises, the best solution may at once be apparent as much from habit as from historical example," explained Army War College president Gen. W. W. Wotherspoon.[2] This utilitarian approach to history was undoubtedly an important element of military education. Since it was also the most obvious use of the discipline, it is easy to underestimate the intellectual content of military history as practiced in the U.S. Army before World War I.

But the applicatory method was not the only way army instructors used history to promote the spirit of safe leadership. In some parts of the army schools' curriculum, instruction in military history closely complied with the tenets of historical scholarship. Civil War battlefield tours forced an officer to sharpen his military mind and to exercise his military eye for terrain by evaluating the command decisions of an earlier generation of soldiers on the very ground where the events unfolded. Few officers faced with the evidence of terrain, time, and distance failed to appreciate the folly of breaking important rules of war and violating the principles of safe leadership.

In its most refined form, especially as practiced at the Leavenworth schools and at the Army War College, historical research held an important place in the curriculum. Like the other applications of history, the source method promoted safe leadership. A historian who deals with a wide variety of evidence, an observer of Capt. Arther L. Conger's research seminar recalled, is much like a soldier on the battlefield.[3] A commander in the field also accumulated much information that he had to scrutinize, analyze, and interpret to prepare orders to his troops. A soldier who learned to use historical methods in the classroom to evaluate the command decisions of the great captains would be more confident in his own ability to untangle the complex factors he might encounter in military decision making.

Military history found many useful applications in officer education. That soldiers often abused history cannot be denied. That they often used it correctly and with telling effect should not be ignored.

3

MILITARY HISTORY AND
THE SCHOOL OF "SAFE LEADERSHIP"

"The causes of the triumphs and disasters of the past form a class of study which will best lead us to an appreciation of the meaning of Strategy," Maj. Eben Swift announced to his students at the Infantry and Cavalry School in September 1904.[1] The introduction of the study of military history into the U.S. Army's pre–World War I postgraduate schools contributed to the professionalization of the American officer corps in two ways. First, illustrations from past campaigns lay at the heart of the schools' new stress on teaching applications of the principles of war, the core of any course in military theory. Second, and equally important, an intensive and systematic study of military history by all officers helped to cultivate the "uniformity of thought and uniformity of procedure" necessary to another prime professional and very practical goal: safe leadership.[2]

Military history found its greatest opportunity to contribute to both military professionalism and practical leadership in the army's advanced officer training schools. From the revitalization of the Artillery School at Fortress Monroe in the late 1870s, to the founding of the Infantry and Cavalry School in 1881, the formal institutionalization of the lyceum system in 1891, and the establishment of the Army War College and other advanced service schools before 1914, the Old Army revealed the depths of its new commitment to professional education for its officers.

Taking their cues from the highly regarded Prussian system of officer training, army educators refined, borrowed, or modified a number of effective teaching techniques that relied heavily on historical example. Map problems, map maneuvers or *kriegsspiel*, terrain exercises, and staff rides – all complementing faculty lectures – could draw upon a seemingly unending variety of situations from the pages of history to provide case studies for analysis and evaluation in peacetime classrooms. As Capt. Arthur L. Conger often noted: "Military history is the laboratory of the military profession."[3]

Official interest in the systematic study of past campaigns took root only after Appomattox and after the decisive Prussian victories of 1866 and 1870–71. Many army reformers and some Civil War veterans recognized the importance of imparting the lessons of these recent conflicts to future generations of officers. Despite the technological advances that added new twists to warfare in the late nineteenth century, many soldiers still believed their profession was guided by certain immutable principles.[4] In the absence of firsthand experience with combat, a study of past campaigns offered the best way to impress the lessons of war upon new officers and, as General Schofield argued, to "reduce the 'chances' of war to a minimum."[5]

As with many such reforms, however, the army's turn toward a systematic study of history began and was sustained by the interest and persistence of capable and dedicated individuals far from the seat of power in Washington. The credit for making military history an important element in the education of the officer corps of the Old Army belongs to a group of unheralded junior officers who nurtured the discipline in far-flung garrisons, where it flourished with little encouragement from the War Department.

Col. Emory Upton, a strong believer in military professionalism, deserves a high place in the ranks of the U.S. Army's most influential reformers in the postwar years, and his contributions to military education belong near the top of his list of accomplishments.[6] A graduate of the U.S. Military Academy in the Class of May 1861, Upton had enjoyed an almost unparalleled range of wartime experiences in command of a battery of U.S. Regular Artillery, an infantry regiment of New York volunteers, and a division of cavalry. By 1874 he had drawn upon his practical wartime experiences to rewrite the army's drill manuals for the cavalry, infantry, and artillery. A rare American soldier who recognized that success in combat requires commanders who understand the missions, capabilities, and limitations of each arm, Upton believed the responsibilities of national defense were best left to a professional army led by officers well educated in the theory and practice of the art of war.

Impressed by Upton's work, Gen. William T. Sherman chose him to lead a War Department delegation on an inspection tour of important military establishments around the world. Upton's official report, *The Armies of Asia and Europe*, provided a comprehensive agenda for reformers in the late nineteenth century, just as his better known *Military Policy of the United States* became the bible for Secretary of War Elihu Root and the generation of military progressives in the immediate pre–World War I years. Among his first and most important conclusions, Upton believed the army in peacetime must serve as a school to "prepare officers and men for efficient service in time of war." Especially enamored of the curriculum of the Prussian Kriegsakademie, which emphasized the study of military history in the training of candidates for the General Staff, Upton encouraged the War Department as early as 1878 to consider creating a similar "war academy" in the United States to "educate officers in the art of war."[7]

To Upton's satisfaction, he found a chance to leave his own mark on officer education in the Old Army as "superintendent of studies in mathematics, engineering, military art and science, law and military administration, applied tactics, infantry and grand tactics; also of practice in the same" at the reorganized Artillery School.[8] Citing Upton's work and that of other ambitious young soldiers as evidence that the army did indeed contain "officers who study and keep in the foreground of military knowledge," General Sherman successfully pushed for the establishment of the Infantry and Cavalry School at Fort Leavenworth and used Upton's curriculum as the model for the new school.[9]

After unspectacular beginnings, new regulations rescued the army's "kindergarten" and placed it back on track to teach officers the theory – and not just the practice – of the art of war. To guarantee the success of the fledgling Leavenworth school, another Upton was needed, a strong personality committed to fashioning a professional curriculum that could withstand the tide of military conservatism. Fortunately, not one but two progressive soldiers stepped forward to develop a course of study that would set the professional standards for officer education in the Old Army.

Capt. Arthur Lockwood Wagner, once described as "a kindly, friendly old man who looked like a farmer dressed up in uniform,"[10] was among the first to attempt to create a strong theoretical and practical curriculum at the Infantry and Cavalry School. Officers who criticized military education angered the mild-mannered captain. "There are officers who pose as practical soldiers, and affect to despise all theory," he wrote. "These . . . are generally ignorant and obstinate men who know as little of the practice as they do of the theory of war. . . . [H]ow can we be sure that they will not 'some day find themselves compromised on service from want of knowledge, not from want of talent'?"[11]

Early in his career, Wagner showed signs of his later preeminence in army educational affairs. A graduate of the U.S. Military Academy in 1875, he frequently neglected the formal curriculum to spend his time reading military history and editing two literary magazines. After six years on active duty with the Sixth Infantry, he served a short stint as a professor of military science and tactics at the University of Louisiana. In 1886 he was named an assistant instructor in the Department of Military Art at the Infantry and Cavalry School.

Wagner took to his new assignment with relish. A careful observer of European trends in officer education, he visited the great military schools on the Continent and freely adapted foreign instructional techniques to the needs of his own department. And Wagner's intellectual abilities equaled his zeal for teaching other soldiers the lessons of the past. Gen. George C. Marshall recalled Wagner as "the first of our military men to write anything readable on tactics."[12] He was one of the few American army officers whose ideas

European military men respected. The editors of the *Army and Navy Gazette* of London commented after the publication of Wagner's study of the Battle of Königgrätz: "If the American Army of today contains a large proportion of officers as zealous and well informed in their profession as Wagner, in charge of troops as steady and resolute as those who fought in the last years of the Great Civil War, the United States may depend with confidence on her Army in any struggle that may await the Republic."[13] From 1886 until his death, except for active service in the Spanish-American War, Wagner devoted his efforts to officer training so completely that he was dubbed the "American Pioneer in the Cause of Military Education."[14]

Wagner received this title from Capt. Eben Swift, an officer who shared his commitment to officer education and to the study of military history in this education. Swift, a West Point graduate of the Class of 1876, joined the faculty of the Department of Military Art at the Infantry and Cavalry School in 1893. Except for brief tours of duty with troops during the Spanish-American War, in the Philippines, and along the Texas border with Mexico, he spent most of his professional career at either the Leavenworth schools or the Army War College.[15]

On the surface, Wagner and Swift had little in common beyond their commitment to military education. Wagner, who was regarded by his colleagues as a military intellectual (not in an entirely complimentary way), had difficulty bridging the perceived gap between theoretical and practical soldiering; Swift was more successful at bridging this gap. A frail man of uncertain health, Wagner died in 1905 of what may have been tuberculosis.[16] By comparison, Swift, at the age of sixty-three, appeared prominently in a satirical newspaper cartoon during the military mobilization of 1917 generating a huge cloud of dust while "leading a hike" and leaving his much younger subordinates collapsing in his wake.[17]

Of Swift and Wagner, historian Timothy K. Nenninger has correctly observed: "Their work laid the basis for Leavenworth methods, course content, doctrine and overall objectives until World War I. Wagner and Swift were catalysts in breaking down the garrison mentality."[18] The "Leavenworth methods" extended to officer education at the pre–World War I Army War College and other advanced schools, making the impact of these two men a pervasive one indeed.

For many soldiers of this era, theory and practice seemed little connected. Wagner and Swift, by contrast, argued that theory and practice were merely two sides of the same coin. They made perhaps their greatest contributions when they bridged this gap. Under Swift's sure hand, especially, the applicatory method of instruction dispelled the old fallacy that "war alone teaches war." He argued that "principles are best learned by their application rather than by the abstract study of the principles themselves. Its full success depends upon the number of examples considered and upon the variety and manner in which principles are applied. It thus takes longer than other methods of study, but its results are more lasting."[19]

Map problems became the backbone of the course of instruction in military art at both the Leavenworth schools and the Army War College. These exercises provided the variety that Swift considered critical to a sound foundation in the theory of war and allowed the students to *learn one thing at a time*," a luxury a soldier would not enjoy during wartime.[20]

In its simplest form, a map exercise allowed a student to learn about a military problem by working it out on a map. "It is natural that the map should call for our first attention because we would ordinarily see it before we have a chance to examine the ground which it represents," Swift often told his students.[21] An officer who becomes familiar with the use of maps learns firsthand the uncertainty and ambiguities that emerge in the opening stages of a military campaign, Swift argued. Peacetime training with maps and without all the diversions of active campaigning developed both sound judgment and prompt decision making, two essential ingredients of safe leadership.

Like most of the examples found in the textbooks used in the earliest years of the postgraduate schools, many of the first map exercises were drawn from European military history. Otto F. Griepenkerl's *Studies in Applied Tactics* yielded a multitude of map problems for army instructors.[22] Many of his problems illustrated military situations from the Franco-Prussian War of 1870–71, and more than one American officer who fought in the area around Metz and Sedan during World War I made practical use of the lessons offered by those specific map exercises.[23] Gen. George C. Marshall, for one, took great pleasure in telling about his colleague Gen. Preston Brown, who was posted near Metz in 1918 and exacted his revenge on Griepenkerl by turning his division artillery on the Hôpital Wald, a woods that had caused him much grief during the map problems.[24] Wagner, Swift, and other army instructors also borrowed freely from map problems prepared by other Prussian officers, most notably the Litzman series, which increased in difficulty as it familiarized students with "the contents and applications of our various regulations."[25]

Griepenkerl's and Litzman's problems never lost their usefulness, but after 1900 they did begin to slip in popularity among army educators. The Prussian problems focused on small-unit actions, and the faculty at the army postgraduate schools wanted to focus their efforts on command problems at the division, corps, and army levels. More important, despite their familiarity with European military history and the curricula of foreign schools, neither Wagner nor Swift, nor the faculty who followed after them, bowed slavishly to Continental military doctrine. Indeed, in his written work, and no doubt in his lectures, Wagner was among the first to demand that the education of officers in the U.S. Army be "Americanized."

By the 1890s Wagner and other American officers began to prepare their own map exercises based on campaigns of the U.S. Army or on nonhistorical scenarios that used the terrain of North America. Officers at the Leavenworth schools, for instance, frequently solved tactical problems on specially prepared maps of eastern Kansas, where their garrison was located.[26] Later, students at the Army War College found themselves responsible not only for solving map problems as part of their own education but also for making up additional exercises for use throughout the army school system.

Army War College students took this task seriously. New problems generated much in-class discussion as the officers tried to meet the faculty's challenge: "It is desired to make these problems as perfect as possible, as they will be objects of keen criticism."[27] Not all instructors were so high minded. Capt. Malin Craig, while on assignment to the faculty of the Army War College, gleefully wrote a friend: "I am preparing problems . . . for my people. Won't it jolt those old boys to digest what I hand out?"[28] Increasingly, these new map problems became far more complex than those initially borrowed from the Prussians. Many considered the movements of large units and frequently called upon American military history to provide appropriate models. After 1910, additional problems addressed particularly thorny questions that Army War College students had first raised during the creation of war plans they were also responsible for preparing.[29]

A student's answer to a map problem often comprised two elements, usually submitted in writing for faculty evaluation and critique by the class. Students in the Army War College Class of 1907, for instance, were required to offer an "estimate of the situation" and a "solution." Both parts were designed to instill in students what their instructors called the importance of "a uniformity of arrangement" in army paperwork.[30] A properly completed "estimate of the situation" included, in this sequence, the military objective of the exercise, the situation and strength of enemy troops, the situation and strength of friendly forces, an evaluation of the courses of action open to the enemy, a similar consideration of the friendly forces' options, and a "decision." A proper "solution" required the preparation of orders to be issued by the commander of the friendly forces.[31] Of the two, the solution generated the greater discussion. Debate between students and faculty to reach a "proper" solution frequently grew intense and heated. After each hard-won point, students simply refused to accept the faculty's official stand that the solution was "not to be considered as correct in the sense that any variation from it is *prima facie* erroneous."[32]

Although each problem required students to understand and properly apply the principles that governed the art of war, the greatest value of these exercises frequently came from the practical experience of writing "proper" orders. In 1894 Swift first discussed the impact of imprecise or unwieldy orders on military affairs. His study of the changes in warfare since the campaigns of Napoleon had convinced him that modern war required that a commander rely more and more frequently upon distant subordinates to carry out his will.[33] Safe leadership demanded that an officer write orders that created no doubt or confusion in the minds of the recipients. The Confederate defeat at Gettysburg, the confusing concentration of the southern army before Shiloh, and the inaction of important segments of the Union army at First Bull Run all resulted from poorly written orders.

Swift believed each officer in the army must write orders according to an accepted system. He developed the five-paragraph order, which required the following information: information on the enemy and the general situation of friendly troops, the objective of the movement, the disposition of the troops, the necessary orders for supply trains and auxiliary troops, and the location where the commander would be found.[34] Every officer who attended the army postgraduate schools learned from sheer repetition the accepted form for written orders. A systematic approach to this important practice was essential to promoting safe leadership.

The use in map exercises of historical situations from the American military past also required soldiers to think about the principles of war that lay behind their decisions. Events from American battles became commonplace in map problems because instructors were convinced that it was "easier to apply modern methods to an actual than to a hypothetical situation. The study of history removes the mystery that surrounds great events and leads to confidence in the superiority of our modern methods."[35]

In keeping with this new philosophy, students in the Army War College Class of 1908 wrote orders to march and concentrate phantom troops for an attack on enemy forces near Shiloh Church, an exercise reminiscent of Gen. Albert S. Johnston's chief tactical problem of April 1862.[36] Others prepared orders to move troops from south and west of the Potomac River, through the District of Columbia, to positions north and west of Washington, a situation much like that in July 1864 when Union forces hurriedly marched to Fort Stevens to repulse the advance of Gen. Jubal Early's Confederates.[37] The use of such historical situations gave students both the opportunity to learn how a genuine military problem was solved and a chance to sharpen their skills in evaluating command decisions.

Equally important for the students, not all the map exercises involved operational situations. The Army War College Class of 1909 faced a complex problem based on the Antietam campaign that required the officers to decide which elements of an infantry division should be connected by wire; they then wrote orders from a divisional commander to the chief of his signal battalion, as well as the orders of the signal officer to his company commanders.[38] Subsequent classes determined the proper location for aid stations and field hospitals using a Gettysburg scenario. Increasing numbers of problems used the Antietam campaign as the basis for sophisticated logistical questions.[39]

Occasionally, students attempted a running series of map problems, each one based on the solution of the one before, replicating the unfolding of a military campaign along the lines of Lee's invasion of Pennsylvania.[40] An officer who during an academic year completed a full set of forty or more map exercises, whether individual or serial problems, became accustomed to writing all kinds of orders in a wide variety of constantly changing situations. Moreover, the theoretical bases for the officer's decisions were hammered home by linking the key military principles to their application in actual historical cases.

After students grew more comfortable with the use of maps in the application of military principles, the faculty of the army schools introduced them to more sophisticated methods that also drew upon historical examples to teach the art of war. Map maneuvers, known throughout the army as *kriegsspiel* (war games), built upon the basic skills that students learned in the map exercises by simulating continuous, unfolding campaign conditions. In map maneuvers, unlike map exercises, students no longer solved only one problem at a time. As in a genuine combat situation, they now had to take into account the factors of time and distance and the impact of terrain on the movement and deployment of troops and in the selection of offensive and defensive positions for units of various sizes.

American soldiers borrowed the concept of map maneuvers from the Prussians, who had used them successfully in officer education since the end of the Napoleonic wars. Swift always regretted that such a valuable educational tool had been so badly misnamed. He agreed with the assessment of a Prussian chief of staff who had remarked, "It is not a game; it is training for war."[41]

Army educators such as Swift claimed that map maneuvers offer five chief benefits for professional soldiers. First, they supplement a soldier's map-reading experience after the completion of map exercises. Second, map maneuvers present a whole military situation, not a limited portion. Third, they offer still more practice in issuing, interpreting, and executing orders. Fourth, especially if a historical situation serves as the basis for the problem, map maneuvers illustrate applications of the principles of strategy and tactics. Finally, they help officers to develop their ability to make quick and accurate decisions, compressing into a few hours what had occurred over several days in history. Although Swift doubted the correctness of proponents of the educational technique who "expected to teach the whole science of war by it,"[42] he did believe it intensified each officer's professional training.

American officers first discovered the Prussian version of *kreigsspiel* immediately after the Civil War, but they were quick to Americanize the war game. After a brief flirtation with a British map maneuver, U.S. Army officers designed three different Americanized editions of the Prussian *kriegsspiel* for potential use in the classrooms of the new postgraduate schools. Lt. C. A. L. Totten produced an elaborate game he called "Strategos," after the Greek word for "general." Capt. Charles Raymond of the Corps of Engineers published a pamphlet evaluating traditional Prussian war games and making suggestions for their use in the United States. Best known and by far the most popular, however, was *The American Kriegsspiel: A Game for the Practice of the Art of War*, developed by still another army engineer, Capt. William Roscoe Livermore.[43]

All the different map maneuvers had certain similarities. The "game board" was a topographical map, often illustrating a battlefield from history. Students executed "troop movements" by shifting wooden or metal blocks into the desired position or by using celluloid overlays to update the location of troops on the game board.[44] The speed and distance of a march or the rapidity of the deployment of troops depended upon terrain features and the type of forces involved in the movement. In simulated combat situations, when the troops fired upon each other, losses were assessed from formalized tables that took into account the weapons in use, the terrain, the experience of the troops, and other important factors. The students were responsible for deciding where, when, and how to move the forces and—at least in Army War College classrooms—for writing up the appropriate orders.[45] An umpire, usually an instructor, decided the acceptability of the ordered troop movement and the casualties resulting from exchanges of fire.

The creators of these American games agreed on the need for scrupulous accuracy. As Captain Raymond advised his readers: "The tables must be formed after the careful and scientific discussion of all the data furnished by the history of recent wars. The rules must conform as closely as possible to actual experience."[46] Games that relied heavily upon the use of the formal computations often were labeled rigid *kriegsspiel* in the United States.[47]

War games became part of the Infantry and Cavalry School's curriculum in the early 1890s, and they were retained in the curricula of the School of the Line and the Staff College that succeeded the Infantry and Cavalry School after the Spanish-American War. Additionally, they were included in the course work for students at the Army War College from the beginning of classroom instruction there. Under Swift's guidance, the instructors at these schools made changes in the games to reflect the growing tendency to examine the intangibles of war. Swift, for instance, did not like the formal tables that dictated the number of casualties resulting from an exchange of fire. He preferred the method adopted by Prussian general Julius von Verdy du Vernois, who discarded the formal tables and computations and sometimes just rolled dice to determine whether losses would be greater or less than the assigned number, a measure that added an important feeling of realism and unpredictability.[48] Swift was a firm believer in this method of instruction, usually called free *kriegsspiel* in the United States, and one of his subordinates on the Leavenworth faculty, Capt. Farrand Sayre, created for use in U.S. Army classrooms an Americanized version of Verdy du Vernois's war game.[49]

Army educators also made a distinction between two other kinds of war games. "Two-handed" *kriegsspiel* involved two teams whose moves and countermoves were approved or disallowed by a neutral umpire. This method most closely duplicated operations in the field.[50] Swift, who could not shake his severe reservations about the utility of war games that followed rigid rules and tables and ignored intangible factors, was among the minority of American soldiers drawn to "single-handed" *kriegsspiel*, in which the umpire himself was the student's opponent. The umpire could lead the student in predetermined directions, "brush aside the trivialities which always hamper the exercise," and teach principles of his own choosing.[51]

Like the map exercises at the army schools, map maneuvers often were drawn from the pages of American history. The prohibitively high cost of suitable topographical maps restricted most pre–World War I map maneuvers to Civil War campaigns for which appropriate maps were already available. At the Army War College, most students worked through map maneuvers that barely disguised the events of the 1862 Maryland campaign or the march to and fighting around Gettysburg in 1863. Although students at the Leavenworth schools started out using topographical maps of the post and surrounding area, they too used the Civil War maneuver problems more and more often in the years before World War I.[52]

In army classrooms, two-handed free *kriegsspiel* was the rule. In a typical map maneuver based on the Gettysburg campaign, the members of the Army War College Class of 1909 were divided into a Blue army and a Red army, roughly corresponding to the Union and Confederate armies. The Blue forces received orders to march from Maryland north into Pennsylvania, keeping Gettysburg on the army's left flank, and to prepare to attack the Red force somewhere between Gettysburg and Carlisle. After the Blue leaders issued the orders that deployed their troops along the roads into

Pennsylvania, they left the map room, and the Red leaders came in to make their first move. Told that their army was concentrated around Chambersburg, the Red forces received orders from the umpire to send a detachment to clear Gettysburg, a move that would threaten the flank of the Blue force marching into Pennsylvania. After the Red force had deployed toward Gettysburg, its leaders surrendered the map room to the Blue leaders, who then had to decide what to do about the threat to their flank.[53] The umpire could use his discretion to allow each side to maneuver its troops within the time and space limitations accepted for each arm.

One major purpose of these exercises was to encourage soldiers to think about a "theory of the art of war suited to our own terrain, based upon our own experience and limited by our own resources."[54] As the Pennsylvania map maneuver continued, after several Blue moves to secure its left flank at Gettysburg, the students received a sealed envelope containing a "special situation." In effect, the umpire changed the game a little each time he added a new complication. In this case, the Blue leaders discovered a Red cavalry force at Willoughby Run on the very outskirts of Gettysburg and had to write appropriate orders to deploy to meet it. When the Red leaders reentered the map room, they received their own special situation, including orders to attack the Union advance guard at Gettysburg. The Red leaders, like the Blue leaders, had to react to an unforeseen development and write orders to prepare to attack.[55] At this point, the students faced the same kinds of decisions that Union cavalry leader John Buford and Confederate general A. P. Hill made on June 30–July 1, 1863.

Not all soldiers liked war gaming, especially when taught on the highest levels of army education. Some of the army's most progressive educators, such as former president of the Army War College Board Tasker H. Bliss, believed students should "*learn things* by *doing things.*[56] Bliss noted, "The schools already exist where officers should be and are taught how to draw from the lessons of experience." He believed the General Staff "should omit the formal study of the theory of the subjects that are or can be sufficiently taught in the service schools, such as history."[57]

Still other officers detested war gaming because it signaled further success of the forces of intellectualization in the U.S. Army, a move some conservative soldiers considered unnecessary and even dangerous. Capt. James Chester, a notorious critic of the army's trend toward professional schooling, believed, "while a man may be educated into a kriegsspieler, he cannot be educated into a commander of men any more than he can into a poet, or an artist, or a Christian."[58] Ultimately, the utility of *kriegsspiel* was not lost on Bliss; Chester, however, represented that considerable clique of officers who resisted change at all costs, especially when it clashed with their ideas of personal leadership.

The third major portion of the applicatory method of officer instruction did take to heart Bliss's injunction to learn by doing. In assignments variously known as tactical rides, war rides, staff rides, or terrain exercises, students replaced the classroom map with real ground. Although their troops were still imaginary, the students learned through tactical rides not to become victims of "the map habit."[59]

These open-air exercises provided officers with three important practical lessons. First, they learned that even the best maps suffered from limitations that might prevent a commander from obtaining an accurate picture of the terrain. Second, terrain rides helped to convince students that a spirit of safe leadership must be instilled in all officers, especially in cases where a commander behind the lines gives only general directions to a subordinate who must then work out the details of an attack or defense on the actual ground. Third, the rides promoted each officer's ability to grasp the military features of the landscape "just by looking at it," either to ferret out an enemy or to select a sound offensive or defensive position.[60]

Like most instructional techniques adopted by the army postgraduate schools, tactical rides served both practical and theoretical ends. Incorporated into the Leavenworth curriculum in 1893, the rides taught Infantry and Cavalry School students many practical lessons about selecting offensive and defensive positions and campsites. They also learned how to resolve tactical problems complicated by difficult terrain, such as crossing rivers, assaulting a woodland, and attacking defensive positions on high ground.[61] The topography around the Fort Leavenworth post served as their laboratory.

Students who attended the Army War College after 1906 discovered the more theoretical aspects of the tactical rides. The course of American military history again suggested many terrain problems. The students applied the principles of war on their tactical rides in much the same way as they carried out their map maneuvers. The Army War College Class of 1908, for example, received the following problem: "Washington is the capital city of the 'Blue' forces. The city is threatened by the 'Red' force." Students of American military history readily recognized the model for this assignment—Jubal Early's advance on Washington in July 1864. The Blue commanders were given only four battalions of infantry and one battery of artillery, with no hope for reinforcement, to defend the approaches to Washington from Rock Creek to Piney Branch. The students assigned to the Blue force then had to work out six problems on the ground: the location of trench lines; other means of defense, perhaps obstacles of some sort; the troop positions in the line; the communications network; the preparation of an accurate, freehand map of troop dispositions; and the security measures to prevent surprise during construction of the trenches and at night.[62]

The Red force had equally tough field problems. When it arrived at Silver Spring with three infantry regiments and two artillery batteries, it received orders to encamp for the night and prepare to attack the next morning. The Red officers' assignments included locating and assigning campsites; locating and assigning outposts; ordering a reconnaissance of the Blue position; reporting on the pluses and minuses of each approach to the Blue position; and ordering the attack on the Blue position.[63] The solutions from both the Blue and the Red forces required appropriate orders and hand-drawn field maps.

The scope of the tactical rides changed to meet the lesson plans of the instructors. Frequently, they were restricted to the action of a single arm. But in keeping with the safe leadership ideal, Army War College students at least gained practice in "the tactics of combined operations" and in the disposition of large military units.[64] Five of the tactical rides for the Army War College Class of 1911, for instance, were renamed field fortification problems and required students to prepare mock defensive positions to place as many as two divisions of troops into different segments of the Civil War–era Washington defenses.[65] Other times, the tactical ride would be renamed a staff ride, to introduce students to "the practice of leading large bodies of troops of all arms, and the preparations of commanders and staff officers for . . . the issue of orders for the march, camp, outpost, and supply." These exercises were also based on Civil War campaigns in the Washington area.[66]

Swift decided to take advantage of nearby Antietam battlefield as well, to introduce the members of the Army War College Class of 1907 to staff problems that required considerably more maneuvering than those restricted to the old fortification lines around the District of Columbia. He again divided the class into the Red army, barely disguised as Lee's Army of Northern Virginia, and the Blue army, a thinly veiled Army of the Potomac.[67] He provided each "army" with an evaluation of the situation that duplicated the conditions of early morning on September 17, 1862, a day fated to become the bloodiest of the Civil War.

Relying only on their knowledge of the principles of war and their observations of the terrain, each officer received an assignment to write acceptable orders to carry out Red or Blue army maneuvers on the battlefield. One officer, for instance, wrote the orders to launch the Blue army's initial attack, which duplicated the advance of Gen. Joseph Hooker's I Corps on that fateful day; others wrote the appropriate orders to place Red or Blue artillery, set up a defensive position, arrange for hospitals and dressing stations, establish communications between components of a division, and give attack orders for units from brigade to corps size. To make the challenge even more difficult, the students assigned to explain the historical events of the 1862 battle and how the principles of war had been applied back then did so only after the practical work was completed. In this way, the Antietam trip served both the theoretical and the practical requirements that Swift demanded from a tactical or terrain ride.

Through the use of the applicatory method, military history became the intellectual backbone for much of the army's practical professional education. Although educators were not constrained to use examples from American military history in preparing map exercises, map maneuvers, and tactical rides, they found no better way to expose their students to such a spectrum of possible experiences, far more than they or their students were likely to encounter during their careers. Even these vicarious experiences increased the likelihood that a safe leader would be produced. As Army War College administrators noted nearly every year in their welcoming lecture to each new class, "The self-reliance of officers is built up by the formation of independent decisions upon historical events."[68]

By the outbreak of World War I, the army schools were meeting their primary goals. Capt. Stuart Heintzelman, a military history instructor at the Staff College, described the twofold aim of officer education: Soldiers must learn "a common doctrine as to the salient principles involved in the use of the arm or arms concerned," and they must be instilled with the "initiative and will to apply these principles."[69] A study of military history provided the inspiration and the know-how to enable an officer to do his best on both counts.

Nonetheless, methods that used historical examples to illustrate the applications and misapplications of axioms of war subscribed to only one half of Professor Hart's definition of military history.[70] In their tendency to demonstrate a priori principles with specially culled examples, instructors of the applicatory method at the Leavenworth schools violated the spirit and the letter of scientific history.

Still, the army's first generation of instructors at the postgraduate schools did share some standards with academic historians. Swift, Wagner, and their colleagues were committed to finding the truth about past military events, as the tenets of the new spirit of scientific history demanded. They did not attempt to mislead their students by disguising poor military decisions of American soldiers in the name of patriotism or institutional pride, because that would not serve the cause of safe leadership. Moreover, they did not purport to teach history courses. Their adaptation of military history to courses with more professionally acceptable titles such as "Tactics," "Strategy" or "The Art of War" was only a tool to aid students in achieving a higher degree of professional proficiency. Military history was not intended in these cases to stand apart as an intellectual discipline.

True, in its first applications of military history to officer education, the Old Army left itself open to the criticism of professional historians who saw only the abuse of the past for predetermined practical purposes. The great irony, of course, is that many of the army's most progressive instructors viewed the use of historical examples from precisely the opposite pole. They were drawn to history because it provided theoretical underpinnings to advanced officer education. These very different views of the nature of history created as wide a gulf as Hart's own history gap. The study of military history in officer education must be viewed from several perspectives: its contribution to intellectual advancement in the officer corps, its practical lessons in safe leadership, and its usefulness in the army's drive for professional recognition and acceptance.

Army educators did recognize the difference between the use of examples from the past and the study of military history as an intellectual discipline. Instructors in the postgraduate officer education system experimented successfully with other instructional methods more in tune with the standards of historical scholarship in academic circles. The historical ride that was introduced into the curriculum of both the Leavenworth schools and the Army War College combined the practical aspects of the terrain ride with the unparalleled glimpse into the past that follows from an evaluation of command decisions made on the very site of an important battle. The Staff College at Fort Leavenworth adopted a course in historical methodology that fully conformed to the strict standards of the historical profession.

But the applicatory methods that infused history into officer training were too useful to the promotion of safe leadership to be discarded, even if they offended the historian's commitment to objectivity. They remained an important part of officer training to World War I and well beyond. The army's adoption of applicatory methods was also a sound halfway step between theory and practice that sufficiently disguised genuinely innovative ideas from conservative soldiers who might wish to block radical change. The successes of Wagner and Swift, especially, reflect their appreciation of the army's need for theoretical training without making it appear too drastic a change. "Military men of all others are the most averse to change and the slowest to accept new ideas," Swift perceptively averred.[71] Wagner, Swift, and growing numbers of their colleagues had indeed convinced the army to accept Napoleon's dictum: "Study attentively the campaigns of the great masters." They simply recognized that the army was determined to do it on its own terms.

4

CIVIL WAR BATTLEFIELDS:
OPEN-AIR CLASSROOMS
FOR MILITARY HISTORY

Before the Spanish-American War, *kriegsspiel*, map exercises, and terrain rides were the standard elements of the army's professional education in small- and large-unit tactics. Between "the splendid little war" and the "war to end all wars," the army discovered yet another instructional method that offered still more opportunities to learn practical lessons in safe leadership. Easily the most popular part of advanced officer training during this period, the annual trip to Civil War battlefields came to be known first as the "historical ride," and later, in its more polished version, as the "staff ride."

From their introduction at the Staff College in 1906 until they were suspended in 1915, visits to American battlefields presented students with perspectives on the art of war they were unlikely to learn from traditional instructional methods. Personal examinations of battle sites allowed each officer to exercise his military mind by evaluating the command decisions of Civil War generals on the spot where those choices were made. Furthermore, to analyze a campaign well, a student had to sharpen his military eye for terrain features as well as understand the relation between geography and decision making on the battlefield. When instructors combined the historical ride with exercises in staff work to fill the hours of travel from one battlefield to the next, many officers agreed with Col. Robert Lee Bullard that the trips were "delightful beyond all my hopes and profitable beyond my expectation."[1]

The combination of practice and theory on these battlefield tours also helped to soften lingering doubts about the overall quality of officer education. Firsthand examination of battle sites provided a vicarious experience that partially satisfied the conviction of conservative officers that only combat was the true school of the soldier. The practical lessons in staff work also mollified the considerable number of officers who continued to believe "as an army we are given too much to theorizing," a flaw that might produce officers who were too likely to fail if faced with the "practical emergencies of thought."[2] In addition, although many participants did not realize it at the time, the rides delivered several intangible rewards that they appreciated only much later on active service in Europe in World War I.

50

Like most instructional methods used in the American army's postgraduate schools, the battlefield tour was the product of European military practices and intellectual trends. Since 1806, when Prussian general G. J. D. von Scharnhorst introduced the "staff journey" into his army's officer training after its defeat by Napoleon, field studies had complemented the classroom work required of candidates for commissions, promotions, or appointments to the General Staff. This exercise developed into a sham fight without troops to test each officer's ability to handle staff work in the field, and succeeding generations of educators took advantage of nearby battlefields of the Franco-Prussian and Austro-Prussian wars to combine the Germans' strong commitment to history with practical staff exercises.[3]

The British army, too, adopted the practice for their officer education system. By the 1880s, students at the Staff College at Camberley regularly visited the battlefields of the Napoleonic wars and the scenes of Prussia's great victories in 1866 and 1870-71. Early in the twentieth century, some prescient British officers even began to focus their studies on old battlefields along the Franco-German border, an area they felt sure would be critical in any future Continental war.[4]

The strongly nationalistic spirit that emerged in much German historical work after the 1850s also helped indirectly to pave the way for American officers to visit Civil War battlefields. The Prussian school of historiography, typified by the works of Heinrich von Treitschke and Heinrich von Sybel, stressed the glories of national union and became the dominant strain of historical thought in Bismarck's Germany. After 1890, other scholars, most notably Friedrich Meinecke, defined an even narrower German school of historical writing in which the history of the nation's political affairs—including the army's role in them—reigned supreme in Wilhelmian Germany.[5]

The military section of the German General Staff drew upon this patriotic spirit primarily to impress upon its officer corps the importance of battlefield success in preserving the recent unification of the German states and the army's responsibility for the new nation's defense. The Germans' emphasis on the importance of understanding the past to prepare for national security in the future[6] struck a responsive chord among Americans. The divisiveness of the Civil War years was still a fresh memory. Tours of Civil War battlefields could serve American soldiers in much the same way as the sites of Prussian victories served their European counterparts.

The emergence of scientific history in German universities also helped to justify the addition of Civil War battlefield tours to American officer education. The application of a strict methodology, stressing primary sources and a commitment to objectivity, forced officers to evaluate critically the American campaigns they dissected, a far greater boon to professional military education than studies inspired by a spirit of nationalism alone.

Although it is not clear whether they realized it, American officers justified their interest in visiting battlefields by using many of the innovative
ideas of German scholar Hans Delbrück. Adopting a macrohistorical philosophy that transcended the limitations of nationalistic history, Delbrück
embraced critical methodology and attention to practical details for the
study of military affairs. Although he fell well outside the narrow nationalistic German historiographical mainstream, Delbrück still ranked safely
among the practitioners of scientific history.[7]

A member of the history faculty of the University of Berlin, Delbrück offered an important intellectual rationale for studying battle sites. He named
his methodology *Sachkritic*, and it comprised three primary techniques:
determining the accuracy of "the smallest facts" of battles by examining
terrain; reconstructing tactics based on the limitations of weapons, equipment, formations, and human frailty; and analyzing reliable reports from
similar fights.[8]

Delbrück's use of *Sachkritic* outraged classicists and ancient historians. He
concluded, for instance, that most accounts of ancient battles such as Mara-
thon were as accurate as "wash-room prattle and adjutants' gossip."[9] He dismissed the account written by Herodotus — and all subsequent narratives
based upon it — as almost totally unreliable because the movements of the
Athenian phalanx described by the Greek chronicler were physically impossible. After observing similar maneuvers by disciplined Prussian troops, burdened no heavier than the civilian-soldiers of the Greek phalanx, Delbrück
decided that the Athenian force, which included many older men, would
have been too exhausted to fight the numerically superior and well-trained
Persians.[10]

Delbrück was not about to be deterred by his critics. Indeed, he had already discovered one of the most useful aspects of his research method early
in his career when he had decided to take a walking tour of the battlefield
at Waterloo before he started writing about that fight. By his own admission,
he found the tour more enlightening than many of the printed sources
because he could see the terrain, understand the distances troops had to
march, and get a feel for the amount of time maneuvers might take.[11]

The various intellectual currents and military education methods in Europe, and especially in Germany, were not lost on Capt. Arthur L. Wagner.
During a visit to Europe in the late 1880s, when he observed officer training
at leading Prussian military schools, he also toured the battlefields of Königgrätz, Prague, Austerlitz, Wagram, Mars-la-Tour, Gravelotte, and Waterloo.[12]

Although the precise source of his inspiration remains unclear, when he
returned from his trip, Wagner had been converted to the practice of battlefield visits. He assured his readers that they could trust the authority of

his widely praised study of the 1866 Prussian victory: "I have . . . personally visited the scene of the operations described, and especially in regard to the topography of the battlefield of Königgrätz, I am able to speak from my own observation."[13]

In 1894, when he became head of the tactics department at the Infantry and Cavalry School, Wagner saw his chance to extend to the American officer corps the benefits of firsthand examination of battle sites. He first set forth his plan to the directors of his own institution at Fort Leavenworth.[14] The captain seemed to realize that convincing his superiors would not be easy. Initially at least, Wagner mentioned plans for only a limited application of the new technique. He suggested that the top ten students in each Leavenworth class be detailed to take part in a tour of the battlefields of the Civil War. He hoped that the attractiveness of the assignment would encourage officers to do their best work in the classroom.

From the start, however, Wagner held expectations for these trips beyond rewarding students for proficient study. To allay fears that battlefield visits were little more than sightseeing tours, Wagner planned for each participant to prepare a professional monograph on one of the sites he visited. The captain hoped that, after visiting either Gettysburg and Antietam or Chattanooga and Chickamauga, each officer could complete a study of one of the campaigns during the following ten months.

Wagner intended to review the completed manuscripts in the hope of reprinting the best for use as army textbooks. Since these monographic studies would have to be written during the year after their authors had graduated from the Leavenworth school, Wagner tried to assure conservative senior officers that this literary work "would not necessitate" their junior officers' "being excused from ordinary duty." The captain planned to start slowly but ultimately bring substantial rewards to the entire officer corps.

Wagner's arguments revealed his deep conviction that battlefield trips were especially useful in reinforcing practically the lessons taught only theoretically in the classroom:

> The benefit to be derived by the students from battlefield trips will be so great that the entire class would be included were it not for the matter of expense alone. The best maps, in the hands of our men most accustomed to mapreading, cannot give so clear an idea of the nature of the terrain as that which can be gained by examining the ground itself. . . . [It is] a fitting capstone to class room instruction.[15]

Wagner's arguments won the support of the army's commanding general, Civil War hero John M. Schofield, who endorsed the captain's request and recommended its approval to the secretary of war. Noting that the appearance of Civil War battlefields had undoubtedly changed since the 1860s, because of timber growth or the cutting of new roads, Schofield believed Wagner's idea held special merit—the grounds would not look precisely the way veterans of the fight might have described them to the students. The addition of unexpected terrain changes could "make the study of the battlefields more profitable if done with intelligence than if it were less difficult," the general wrote.[16]

Despite Schofield's enthusiastic approval, Assistant Secretary of War Joseph Doe was not impressed. He demanded a cost estimate for a typical trip.[17] Doe closed the matter arbitrarily when he decided that Wagner's estimate of $137.51 for each officer assigned to visit Gettysburg and Antietam or $111.48 to tour Chattanooga and Chickamauga was too high a price during a time of fiscal retrenchment in the War Department.[18] Appeal was useless, and Wagner's grand design failed.

Disappointed by the rejection of his plan, Wagner waited for a more propitious time to try again. In 1903, when the Leavenworth schools reopened after the Spanish-American War, Wagner returned as assistant commandant. Determined to bring the new General Service and Staff College's curriculum into line with War Department directives to improve officer education, he suggested a two-year course of instruction that included Civil War battlefield visits as an integral part of the second year's advanced study of strategy. "The class should be divided into sections of not more than 15 officers each, and sent east to make a practical study of the battlefields of the Great War; for instance, Gettysburg, Antietam, Chickamauga, and Vicksburg."[19] Wagner knew his chances for success had improved. A precedent for such trips had been established in 1902 when first classmen from West Point began visiting Gettysburg as part of their course work in the art of war.[20] Wagner unfortunately did not live to see War Department approval of funding for his cherished plan.

In 1906 Wagner's successor, Maj. Eben Swift, succeeded where his friend had failed. He won approval for a special detail of honor graduates from the advanced Staff College course to visit the Civil War battlefields at the end of the school year.[21] When Swift was reassigned to the Army War College the following year, he introduced the practice there as well.[22] From 1906 until 1915 when the army discontinued the trips, selected officers from the Staff College at Fort Leavenworth and entire classes from the Army War College looked forward with anticipation to the annual historical ride.

Swift himself established the pattern that most of the battlefield trips followed. Since so much Civil War literature focused on the Virginia theater, he initially decided that military students would reap greater benefits from a

study of Gen. William T. Sherman's less scrutinized campaign from Chattanooga to Atlanta in 1864. In fact, Swift believed the Georgia campaign was especially useful because it conformed more closely "to those we might expect
under modern conditions." In Georgia, the armies had faced each other in constant contact for four months. The operations had covered many kinds of challenging terrain, but accurate maps were readily accessible to the students.

Most important in Swift's mind, Sherman's experiences provided excellent
lessons in safe leadership. Problems resulting from campaigns conducted on
several roads of approach, the withdrawal of a large army, the selection of
defensive positions, the accomplishment of wide turning movements, the
conduct of operations far away from bases of supply, the defense of lines of
communication, the rapid construction of defensive works, and the routine
of day-to-day, continuous staff operations could all be studied from Sherman's march from Chattanooga to Atlanta.[23]

Swift made it clear that dissecting Civil War campaigns was only one, and
not necessarily the most important, part of the historical ride. Always a practical soldier as well as a scholar, he felt strongly that a visit to a battlefield
"was not of transcendent importance unless applied to conditions which may
occur in the experience of the officer himself."[24] To make sure that battlefield
rides would not degenerate into merely a pleasant diversion from classroom
work, Swift laid down additional responsibilities for each student officer.

Under Swift's guidance, each participant was assigned in advance a specific phase of the campaign under consideration. When the class arrived at a
key point on the battlefield, the designated student then recounted the
historical events that occurred on the site. Swift also expected each officer
to suggest how Civil War decision making might be altered by modern military technology.[25] These responsibilities became standard on all pre–World
War I historical rides.

Several participants have left lively and often insightful records of their
battlefield visits. Capt. Matthew Forney Steele, an assistant instructor of tactics at the Leavenworth schools, wrote almost nightly to his wife to reveal
in an impressionistic way the highlights of several historical rides he helped
to lead. Col. Robert Lee Bullard of the Army War College Class of 1912,
a skeptic who needed to be convinced of the usefulness of the historical ride,
faithfully kept a diary that reveals the day-to-day routine from the student's
viewpoint. Lt. Col. Hunter Liggett, Capt. George Van Horne Moseley, and
other officers recalled their Civil War battlefield trips in their professional
memoirs. From these officers' substantial recollections, copies of students'
notes for their on-site discussions, and the fragmentary sentiments of other
participants, the special contributions of the battlefield tours to officer education emerge clearly.

Participants seemed to agree that personal examination of battle sites challenged them far more than map exercises in the classroom. Steele's observations were typical. He was so impressed by the ruggedness of Lookout Mountain and Missionary Ridge on his first visit to Chattanooga that he braved a trip up their slopes on a "fearful looking inclined railway" and remained obsessed with terrain features throughout his trip to Atlanta.[26] Buzzard's Roost and Rocky Face Ridge struck him as especially notable obstacles to Sherman's advance, and his admiration for the Union general rose as he recognized the intensity of Sherman's geographical problems alone.[27]

Near Resaca, Georgia, Steele came to appreciate the protection offered by "hasty entrenchments," the contemporary term for the surviving earthworks that line so many Civil War battlefields today.[28] After visiting Big Shanty where the locomotive The General was hijacked by Union soldiers, Pine Mountain where Confederate lieutenant general Leonidas Polk died, and Kennesaw Mountain where Sherman learned the folly of frontal attack on an entrenched position, Steele recalled as his only bad memory the time spent at evening colloquiums in "the hot air tent" when the officers discussed the lessons of the day.[29]

In 1908 Steele's students from Fort Leavenworth faced a far more challenging trip when they visited the battlefields of the eastern theater to complement their in-class study of the 1862 Peninsular campaign. An uneventful train ride to Virginia was lightened considerably by the uncharacteristic antics of 1st Lt. George C. Marshall, who leaped out of his railcar in Augusta, Kentucky, "to kiss all the good looking girls in town."[30] When the class began its work in the Shenandoah Valley, the student officers rediscovered Marshall's seriousness.

Instead of stressing the history of Jackson's 1862 campaign or the South's use of the valley as an invasion route into the North, Marshall designed complex staff problems to fill the several days of horseback riding required to travel down the valley to Winchester and then on to Antietam. In each problem, the students took on the responsibilities of staff officers as if they were really part of an invasion force.[31] Following the Prussian practice on staff rides, assignments changed daily to allow each student to serve as an army, corps, or division commander, as the chief of staff or supply officer to a senior commander, or in a special role as signal officer, medical officer, or cavalry commander. To solve the daily problems, each student applied lessons already learned in the classroom to make decisions and wrote up in correct form the necessary orders to move, encamp, and supply his men.

Staff problems such as those worked through by the Staff College Class of 1908 increased in sophistication on subsequent trips and sometimes overshadowed the historical aspects of the tour. To add an air of authenticity, corps commanders were forbidden to write their orders until they received appropriate communications from the army commander. Division commanders could move only after being instructed by the corps commander. Swift especially liked to encourage his assistant instructors to use these exercises because they promoted safe leadership and broke officers of the "map habit." As Swift argued, "The troops are still imaginary, but the map is replaced by real ground."[32]

Such practical experience with staff work in the field gave each officer a deep appreciation of command problems in active campaigning. The staff problems were both complex and unpredictable. Two exercises assigned to the Army War College Class of 1910 illustrate the sophistication of the officers' daily assignments. Capt. Frank Cocheu designed a continuous five-day staff problem based on the Confederate invasion of Pennsylvania in 1863. At their camp at Winchester, the class split into six groups to represent one army and five division staffs, each consisting of a commanding officer, a chief of staff, an assistant chief of staff, and a supply officer.

The problems often stressed the importance of teamwork so essential to safe leadership. The army staff chose encampment sites around Winchester, decided each division's line of march north for the next day, and delivered appropriate orders to each division staff. Only then could each division commander and his staff write up proper marching and encampment orders, based on directives from "army headquarters," for each of his mythical component units. As the theoretical invasion force moved into northern territory away from Virginia, reconnaissance and supply problems became paramount.

Cocheu was a harsh taskmaster. His critique of his class's performance revealed the wide variety of shortcomings the staff rides were designed to expose. He chastised the army staff for giving vaguely worded orders to "reconnoiter the enemy's position," which triggered a "disjointed effort" from the division commanders who interpreted the orders differently. The army high command had also maintained wide intervals between divisions, an unwise move in hostile territory. Division commanders had been too hasty in sending their ammunition trains to the rear at the first sign of trouble, making resupply both risky and uncertain if emergencies arose. Staffs at all levels marched their imaginary infantry too far too fast and rendered them unreliable if fighting broke out unexpectedly. When Cocheu, on the last day of the exercise, "surprised and routed" the invasion force, the staffs bungled the assembly of the retreating troops. Indeed, Cocheu's only praise concerned the handling of cavalry in reconnaissance missions.[33]

Capt. Fox Conner took up where Cocheu ended, and, for sheer complexity, his staff problem surpassed any exercise assigned to the Army War College class of 1910. The captain outlined an imaginary situation in which a "Southern Field Army" at Sharpsburg, Maryland, was ordered to march on Chambersburg, Pennsylvania, a scenario adapted from Lee's 1863 invasion plan. This army included three infantry divisions, one cavalry division, and one "auxiliary division" of infantry, heavy artillery, a pontoon battalion, an ammunition train, a supply train, and an aeronautical wireless battalion. Conner named Lt. Col. (later Gen.) Hunter Liggett to be army chief of staff and assigned him two assistant chiefs of staff—one was another future general, Malin Craig—and a chief supply officer. Each division staff included one chief of staff, one assistant chief of staff, and a supply officer. Told only that an enemy force was located near York, Pennsylvania, the army staff delivered marching orders to the divisions who passed them on to their imaginary components.

Conner frequently changed the situation to force the staffs to respond to rapidly developing emergencies like those they might face in active campaigning. He "moved" the enemy force from York to Gettysburg, which threatened the southern field army's security and forced the staffs to change their point of concentration in mid-march. To confuse his students further, he then interjected a strong enemy cavalry force between the southern field army and Gettysburg, which required each staff to make dispositions for combat.

When the class finally reached Gettysburg for its battlefield tour, Conner first took time to criticize its staff work. He especially chastised the officers for refusing to abide by the rules to use actual times when orders were written and received; they had destroyed the impact of the lesson on the influence of the passage of time in campaign planning. Disregarding these small details, Conner emphasized, destroyed the spirit of safe leadership.

Conner reserved the remainder of his criticism for those responsible for designing the problem. He decided that the problem was too easy because there were no real challenges in the supply effort. Next time, Conner suggested, declare certain areas of Maryland and Pennsylvania to have been stripped of useful material before the armies arrived. "Only in this way will it be possible to simulate conditions which would actually exist in campaigning a large force," he concluded. By comparison, the historical aspects of the ride were a welcome relief from the stress of the staff problems.[34]

The battlefields that especially appealed to the students were those that the federal government had seen fit to preserve as memorials to the soldiers of the Civil War. Ironically, though the War Department had been slow to approve funding for battlefield rides, it was well aware of the potential use of the sites in officer education. In the mid-1890s, when Congress debated the establishment of national military parks, the secretary of war convinced the House Committee on Military Affairs that the preservation of "the

principle battlefields of the Republic" would produce both "imperishable monuments to the patriotism of the past" and classrooms to teach "full and complete object lessons of great battles and extended tactical and strategic movements" to officers of the Regular Army and National Guard.[35] Curiously,
neither Congress nor the War Department had asked instructors in any of
the army schools for suggestions to carry out this mission.

The growing number of regimental monuments and governmental mark-
ers at Chattanooga, Chickamauga, Antietam, and Gettysburg were a boon
to military students. Steele was especially pleased because "now one can ride
over the field with no previous knowledge of the battle and by reading the
inscriptions cut upon metal tablets, can follow the operations from beginning to end." At the end of Bloody Lane at Antietam, Steele's entire class
mounted a government-funded stone observation tower to get a bird's-eye
view of the field. Benefiting from the unusual perspective, the class reached
immediate consensus: "My God what a poor general McClellan was."[36]

Steele was equally impressed with the government's preservation efforts
at Chattanooga and Chickamauga. In a poignant commentary on the army's
problems at the turn of the century, Steele reported to his wife, "Our people
are certainly generous to the memory of their dead soldiers, however little
they may appreciate the living ones."[37]

Gettysburg seemed to make the greatest impression on the student officers. Preservation efforts by private organizations had begun as early as 1864,
and a battlefield commission appointed by the War Department took care
to maintain the Peach Orchard, the Wheatfield, the entrenchments on
Culp's Hill, the copse of trees on Cemetery Ridge, and other key sites as
they stood in 1863. "This is certainly a great place to visit," Steele commented, "and I consider it a great privilege to be here."[38] Bullard, too, believed his tour of Gettysburg was "delightful, instructive, [and] a very great
privilege."[39]

The complicated staff exercises, evaluations of command decisions, and
examination of battlefield terrain that formed the core of the historical rides
rarely allowed much time for such open sentimentality as that expressed by
Steele and Bullard. Maj. Arthur L. Conger feared that trips to government-
maintained battlefields might do more harm than good. Too many of these
sites "resemble a cemetery in appearance," he argued. When "friends of the
fallen" erected monuments, they hoped only to "set up a memorial to perpetuate some gallant deed." Too often, he believed, the statues were incorrectly
located and misled rather than helped to enlighten students of a battle.[40]

Another fault of well-marked battlefields became apparent because students tended to direct their attention only to those events or sites set off
by monuments. When British officers visited Gettysburg in 1915 and asked

to be taken to the spot where Robert E. Lee first viewed the battlefield, their guide looked at them in amazement. In all the years he had led American officers around the field, not one had asked to visit the unmarked site. The British officers were appalled. After all, one argued, "it is the only way in which you can understand General Lee's actions."[41]

Army instructors hoped, however, that trips to Civil War battlefields would stimulate questions in the minds of their students, not foreclose them. They encouraged trip participants to question, criticize, and be leery of traditional explanations if their on-site examinations led them to another conclusion. Many officers were wary of taking exception to the printed record. Still others took up the challenge with enthusiasm.

Colonel Bullard's impressions from his Virginia tour reveal how traditional interpretations of events in military history could be altered by a visit to the actual site. At Fredericksburg, the colonel's evaluation of northern generalship followed an unconventional path from the very start. Noting that his colleagues concurred entirely that Union general Ambrose E. Burnside was a fool, Bullard begged to differ. There is a difference, argued the colonel, between a "fool conception" and "an incapacity of execution." Burnside did indeed have a plan, Bullard was convinced. What he lacked was the ability to "tell how or show how to execute it."

A trip to the artillery positions on the Union right flank convinced Bullard of the fundamental soundness of Burnside's position. He concluded that fire from the federal guns indeed could have rendered untenable the southern stronghold on Marye's Heights. Burnside's decision to employ repeated frontal assaults on the heights, Bullard concluded, was not really a bad plan. The faulty artillery support was the real culprit. Bullard left Fredericksburg with an unusually high opinion of the much maligned general: "This day's study of the *ground leaves me less patience with those* who on a map study are so ready *to condemn poor Burnside as a fool or an idiot.*[42]

By comparison, Bullard's views on Chancellorsville were more traditional. Not surprisingly, he praised Lee's leadership profusely. He was not at all convinced, however, by his colleagues' most frequently offered explanation for Gen. Joseph Hooker's poor showing. He rejected their notion that the North's defeat at Chancellorsville stemmed from Hooker's loss of confidence following his pledge to abstain from alcohol for the duration of the campaign. Bullard decided that Hooker was merely a publicity hound so determined to go "on to Richmond" that he lost his zeal for high command when he was told to focus on Lee's army instead.[43]

A surprising diversity of opinion arose when the students considered the generalship of Ulysses S. Grant in the Virginia campaigns of 1864. Few of the officers held high opinions of Grant's ability. After a visit to the battlefield of The Wilderness, Colonel Bullard summed up Grant's tactical philosophy succinctly: "I have the greatest hammer."[44] In Bullard's eyes, Grant's reliance on brute force, not finesse, made his generalship suspect. The colonel also found Grant guilty of playing favorites and fomenting feuds among his subordinates.[45]

Bullard was also among those who refused to give credit to Grant for any revolutionary change in Union strategy. He believed Grant's main objective was the same that a long line of Union generals before him had coveted: Richmond.[46] Bullard misunderstood Grant because he failed to see the campaigns of 1864 in Virginia as one part of the North's newly unified grand strategy under the general's control.

Colonel Bullard's views of Grant fit well into the professional opinion of a generation of officers who often seemed to find Robert E. Lee's artful leadership more to their liking. Bullard's entire Army War College class suffered from an "I don't care: he-won-any-way" attitude toward Grant.[47] Even a move that generally reflected well on the northern leader—the crossing of the James River on the way to Petersburg in June 1864—came under harsh criticism from these student officers. In 1911 Captain Moseley's critique raked Grant over the coals for fatiguing his cavalry, interfering with troop dispositions, marching his tired infantry too far too fast, overloading them with food and ammunition, failing to provide accurate maps, and mishandling his supply effort. True, Moseley criticized Lee for failing to intercept Grant, but, as part of his responsibility to compare fighting in the 1860s with combat after 1900, he also stressed that if the southern general had possessed a single airplane, the crossing of the James could have been an incredible disaster for Grant.[48]

Despite Bullard's and Moseley's comparatively few negative comments about Lee, many of their classmates did not look uncritically upon the generalship of the southern leaders. Still, the military reputations of Lee and his chief lieutenant, Stonewall Jackson, were so strong that Steele was gratified to note during a visit to Manassas that praise for the two Confederate leaders came from northern- and southern-born officers alike.[49] Bullard typically described Lee's leadership as "a wonderful performance."[50]

Slowly, the more sophisticated and objective students of Lee's generalship began to separate the man from the myth. Col. Joseph Gaston, for one, asserted that Lee's dispositions for the Battle of Gettysburg were faulty from the beginning. In blaming Lee for many of the problems that led to the South's defeat in the Pennsylvania campaign, Gaston offered an interpretation of events quite unlike the more typical narratives that blamed other southern leaders for the loss.[51]

At least partly because Swift impressed upon his students the distinction between Lee the model of Civil War generalship, and Lee the military maverick whose greatest success came "when he departed the furthest from the established rules," professional opinion about the southern commander began to change.[52] Committed to the army's desire to inculcate officers with the spirit of safe leadership, Swift tried to point out occasions when Lee took unacceptable risks—as at Antietam—but he did not succeed in tempering his charges' deep admiration for Lee and Jackson.[53]

If improving the students' military decision-making ability, their capacity for staff work, and their appreciation of terrain features were the chief professional benefits of the historical rides, the participants also discovered other, unexpected advantages. First, they greatly strengthened their common bond as professional officers when men of earlier generations of soldiers joined the tour. Former Confederate cavalry colonel Thomas T. Munford joined the Army War College Class of 1911 on a tour of Virginia battlesites and provided a detailed, on-going commentary about southern cavalry operations. His presence so inspired the class that the officers—northerners, southerners, and westerners alike—stopped in The Wilderness long enough to rebuild a rock monument marking the spot where Confederate general John M. Jones was killed.[54] During a tour of the Shenandoah Valley, another class was joined by Ohio congressman Warren Keifer, who, as a young brevet brigadier general in 1864, had led a brigade under Gen. Philip H. Sheridan.[55]

The students not only enjoyed the company of veterans of the 1860s but also got to rub shoulders with the army's top leaders in their own time. On several occasions, army chief of staff Leonard Wood motored down to join the class at Manassas, a short ride from his headquarters in Washington.[56] Secretary of War Henry L. Stimson joined the Army War College classes of 1911 and 1912 for several days of touring around the Richmond battlefields.[57] The captains, majors, and colonels also got to know important staff department heads such as Col. Jefferson Kean of the Medical Department, Gen. William Crozier of the Ordnance Bureau, and Gen. Enoch Crowder, the judge advocate general.[58] The Army War College Class of 1913 even entertained Maj. Gen. Colin Mackenzie and Col. George Paley of the British army for two weeks.[59]

Not all the guests were current or former military men. Two special non-military guests were Thomas Nelson Page, the noted southern author,[60] and Robert M. Johnston of Harvard University. The latter was especially well received by the officers because he sought their professional comments on the battlefield of Second Manassas for a projected companion volume to his widely praised history of First Bull Run.[61]

Another benefit of the battlefield tours was that the participants were able to study elements of civilian society that might otherwise have escaped the awareness of career officers. Bullard and Steele, for instance, became percep-tive social critics and observers of the human condition during their tours. Steele deplored the living conditions he found among the Georgia "crack-ers," who watched sullenly as the neatly dressed officers rode by on well-fed horses.[62] Steele, Bullard, and Moseley all seemed to feel more comfortable with gentlemen of the landed upper classes, who frequently offered water, wood, and tent sites to the tour groups. Moseley noted that his instructors had a knack for approaching owners of large homes who happened to have attractive daughters sitting on the front porch.[63] An excited twelve-year-old girl who helped entertain Marshall's tour group later became a secretary at the Pentagon and Marshall's receptionist.[64] On Bullard's visit to the Virginia battlefields, after debating whether or not to buy a coon dog pup from some poor Virginia blacks who visited their camp, he relaxed in the yard of one antebellum mansion, musing that he believed he was indeed "to the manor born."[65]

Bullard and Steele also learned, to their dismay, that their years in na-tional service had hidden from them the sectional hostilities that still ran deep between northerners and southerners even after 1900. Since both men were Alabamians and had kinsmen who had worn Confederate gray during the Civil War, they were sensitive to riding through their native South wear-ing the uniform of the U.S. Army.

When Steele first arrived at Chattanooga in 1907, he probably feared that his contingent would be met by opposition. Only the year before, protesting southerners had petitioned President Theodore Roosevelt to recall the con-tingent of U.S. troops traveling with Father Thomas Sherman, who had wanted to follow the path from Chattanooga to Atlanta that his famous father had taken in 1864.[66] Nothing untoward happened to Steele's group then, but the next year at Winchester, Virginia, he was bothered again by the failure of the local people to come out and visit their camp. "I fear they look upon us as the Yankee army and they haven't much of joy to recall of that army," Steele surmised. "And can you blame them after what they, or their parents and grandparents passed thro?"[67]

Bullard seemed even more convinced than Steele that sectional hostility was still strong and remained a divisive, even dangerous, problem for the United States. When a northern-born classmate criticized as sentimental, trite, and forced, the inscription on the monument marking the spot where Stonewall Jackson was mortally wounded at Chancellorsville, Bullard shiv-ered with disgust. Noting that the speaker was a man marked for high com-mand in event of war, Bullard doubted whether he could serve under "a man so devoid of human feeling."[68] He decided that his colleague's aloofness was typical of "men from the colder north." Southerners might be "more bombastic and verbose," the colonel wrote, "but they were also warmer, more human, and personally responsive."[69] Despite the colonel's increasingly open fondness for his fellow southerners, however, he did not question his own career choice. "I could hardly control my voice & emotions as I looked & moved among these things," Bullard recalled after viewing the relic displays at the White House of the Confederacy. "One can but grieve that they were given for a *principle of disunion and disintegration*, but they were nevertheless sublime."[70]

As Bullard learned at Chancellorsville, the battlefield trips offered military students an outstanding opportunity to observe their colleagues outside the formalities of the classroom in settings approximating field service. The impressions forged during a two-to-four week historical ride were important to officers who might someday be assigned to active duty with these classmates.

A significant commentary on some officers' views on the prerogatives of high rank was made when Major Swift ran into an unexpected problem on the Army War College staff ride in 1909. Two officers who outranked Swift usurped his leadership. Swift sent off a telegram to General Wotherspoon: "[Lt. Col. Charles] Chubb has assumed command by virtue of rank. To avoid complications I request that both Chubb and [Lt. Col. David] Rumbough be ordered to return at once." Wotherspoon recalled the two men and "had quite a talk with both of them and they now understand my position in this affair of command in the staff rides." Since the "primary reason for this ride and others like it is for instruction," it was only logical that "the senior officers charged with instruction must conduct the exercises." Only in the event of "a serious emergency, such as a shooting affray between the enlisted men of the command, say, and a civilian" should the senior officer present take over the responsibility of command. The example made of Chubb and Rumbough was sufficient; no similar problems emerged on later trips.[71]

Steele decided that nearly all the members of his 1908 tour group "size up splendidly," but he also made clear that it did not take a perceived gross lapse of professionalism to evoke the harsh judgment of a colleague.[72] Always a gentleman and an optimist, Steele rarely lost his composure and genuinely enjoyed the camaraderie of the trip. Nevertheless, he came down hard on Capt. Howard Hickok for stealing tent pegs and monopolizing the best tent sites.[73] Although Colonel Bullard wrote himself reminders to curb his excessive profanity and his readiness to provoke arguments, he was much tougher on Capt. Ezekiel Williams, the "loudmouth," Col. Willard Holbrook, the "bootlicker," and especially Col. John Fair, whose ardent support of Republican Teddy Roosevelt's Bull Moose campaign for president offended Bullard, a loyal Democrat.[74]

Additionally, after a year or more confined to classrooms, the officers looked upon the historical ride as a wonderful opportunity for physical reconditioning and for releasing restless energy before they returned to field duty with troops.[75] Their rustiness was sometimes all too apparent. In 1909 Maj. W. D. Connor dislocated an elbow when his horse threw him,[76] and almost every Army War College trip lost officers to illness brought on by the unpredictable spring weather of Virginia or pulled muscles from the un-wonted exertion. On occasion, the officers took advantage of the infor-mality of the trip to enjoy the outdoors. Even the normally businesslike Bull-ard took a break from serious reflection on a rare unregimented day in the middle of his class trip and "went fishing."[77]

Still others released their pent-up energies in a barrage of practical jokes. During an evening encampment near Antietam, Steele and some of his friends took one of their party on his first snipe hunt. After allowing the victim to squat in the dark for two hours while the conspirators went back to camp, Steele realized that their prey never understood the joke. When the young man returned to report that he had captured no snipe and that he had never even heard one coming in his direction, Steele concluded, with a logic that only he understood, that the target of the prank showed about as much promise of becoming a soldier as "a baby boy."[78]

As the battlefield tours became a standard instructional procedure in the army's postgraduate schools, participants on the Army War College's tours of the Civil War battlefields finally attempted to live up to Wagner's promises that in the long run the trips would benefit the entire officer corps. Trips to the battlefields of the 1860s became part of the research program for the Army War College's first comprehensive historical project.

By the time the Class of 1913 took its spring historical rides in Virginia, Maryland, and Pennsylvania, its members had already spent much of March in a concentrated study of the printed literature on individually assigned aspects of a Civil War campaign.[79] Upon arriving at the appropriate bat-tlefield, each officer followed the usual procedure and distributed a mimeo-graphed outline of the forces involved in the affair, delivered a lecture on the historical events at that site, and suggested ways in which technological advances would affect a fight if it took place on the same ground in the early twentieth century.

After returning from these rides, however, each student in the Class of 1913 and the next few succeeding classes submitted a typewritten profes-sional evaluation of his campaign, based on both his research in the histori-cal literature and his on-site examination of the battlefield.[80] The General Staff hoped that after several years, the faculty could find suitably sophisti-cated essays on each campaign to put together an Army War College history of the Civil War for use at all levels of the officer education system. If this first project went well, future classes might produce official histories of other American wars.[81]

Despite their popularity and their potential long-range contributions to the army's growing professional literature, trips to Civil War battlefields by students from the Army War College and the Leavenworth schools alike were discontinued in 1915. When problems with Mexico heated up and President Woodrow Wilson ordered American troops to the Rio Grande, many officers on detached duty at the postgraduate schools were needed on active service with their regiments. When the academic year at the Army War College and the Leavenworth schools was shortened to meet the new emergency, historical studies in general, and the historical rides in particular, were early casualties.[82] Even if staff rides were to be continued, Maj. W. D. Connor, now of the new U.S. Army Historical Section, argued, they should "be undertaken in areas which could become critical on our own borders and coasts."[83]

The outbreak of World War I suspended the trips entirely. When the army schools reopened after the armistice, a few historical rides were attempted, but the practice was not given its former prominence in the curriculum. At least for the immediate postwar years, the shock of World War I convinced many that the army needed to prepare for the future, not look to the past. Although they enjoyed a brief resurgence in the 1930s, battlefield tours would not become a standard part of officer education again until the army's revival of historical studies in the 1970s.[84]

Still, during its brief life, the historical ride served the army well. In addition to exercising their military minds and military eyes, students increased their confidence in using their analytical abilities to look beyond textbook solutions to military problems. The staff problems conducted between historical sites offered fresh perspectives and lasting lessons on the vagaries of army paperwork and the importance of cooperation, personal endurance, and initiative in active campaigning. Gen. Hunter Liggett, commander of the U.S. First Army in the American Expeditionary Force and a veteran of numerous Civil War battlefield tours as a student and instructor at the Army War College, probably summed up best the opinion of many of his professional colleagues when he recorded simply but eloquently that "no officer who took these staff rides failed to appreciate their immense advantages mentally and physically."[85] Such instructional techniques, which offered both practical and theoretical peacetime training, persuaded increasing numbers of officers to agree with Liggett that "much can be learned from an intelligent study of military history, and no one can be too well prepared for the great responsibilities of war."[86]

5

A MODEL AND A MUDDLE: TWO
HISTORICAL RESEARCH PROGRAMS,
1908–1917

Gen. M. M. Macomb, president of the Army War College just before World War I, borrowed a quotation from British historian Thomas Carlyle and installed it as the unofficial motto of his school: "In a certain sense all men are historians."[1] During the decade before American entry into the war, Carlyle's sentiment became a familiar theme to officers who attended the army's chief postgraduate schools. At both the Staff College at Fort Leavenworth and the Army War College, military educators greatly improved upon the traditional applicatory method of instruction in the art of war and taught their students the principles of scientific historical research.

By applying the source method to the study of past campaigns, a small number of progressive soldier-scholars, especially those at the Staff College, established a specialized program in military history that had no peer at any civilian American university. In 1915 Harvard University history professor Robert M. Johnston, the chairman of the American Historical Association's short-lived Special Committee on Military and Naval History, was so impressed with the model instructional program at the Leavenworth school that he hoped civilian institutions would emulate it.[2]

Advocates of military professionalism scored a substantial, if incomplete, victory when they secured a place for the scientific study of military history in the army's postgraduate schools. The strongly theoretical course work, designed chiefly to improve analytical and critical skills, used the methods of the new scientific history to promote the spirit of safe leadership in ways the more traditional map problems or even the novel historical rides did not. The high quality of the Staff College program, in particular, confirms that the army was interested in military history for more than its immediately useful and practical lessons.

After a promising start, and despite many signs of a bright future, the army's pre–World War I historical research program did not flourish. Budgetary restraints, increasingly frequent disruptions in the academic schedule, marginal institutional support in such important matters as the retention of uniquely talented faculty, and, probably most important, continuing questions about the appropriate content of professional education all became obstacles in the path of army historians.

The source method turned the traditional applicatory method on its head. When the Staff College Class of 1908, the first group to undertake source-method instruction, was introduced to the new technique, they found that a campaign studied in this way could provide much more than historical illustrations of correct or incorrect applications of a predetermined rule of the art of war. They no longer dissected a campaign merely to see which a priori axioms surfaced from an in-depth examination.

Instead, in a source-method course, the instructor incorporated after-action reports and other original documentation into classroom exercises to force officers to reconstruct the key events and then decide for themselves which factors had precipitated the result. There was no preplanned "proper" solution. After thorough examination of many campaigns, students became aware of the wide variety of conditions that somehow had contributed to wins and losses in the past. This knowledge, then, would enhance a commander's confidence in his ability to analyze the complex military situations he might face.

Analytical investigation from this new perspective required far more intellectual flexibility from students than did other instructional methods. Instructors hoped to wean their students from rote memorization. The new course work in historical methodology was one sound way to combat the gibes of critics of the army school system who argued that many of the faculty's instructional practices produced only "pol parrots."[3]

Although formal instruction in the source method was not introduced in army schools until 1908, precedents for such study had existed in many major American universities since the 1880s. In the seminars that lay at the center of their professional training, a new generation of scholars had embraced the standards for historical scholarship practiced in the great European universities. Objectivity replaced moralization, analysis eclipsed mere narrative, and—many would argue, unfortunately—a passion for detail overwhelmed literary artistry. Like the trend away from romanticism and toward realism in the arts, science, and literature in American society, the new scientific history was compared favorably to the new art of photography. As scholar Justin Winsor argued, history, like a camera, "catches everything, however trivial," just as it is, without disguise or elaboration.[4]

Not blind to the General Staff's growing need for accurate, objective studies on a wide variety of professional topics, the army's advocates of "the new history" quickly made their case. Research-methods courses like those taught in civilian universities, if added to the curriculum of the postgraduate officer education system, would produce soldiers trained in the investigative and analytical skills the War Department needed. Not only would the army as a whole benefit from the work of its trained researchers, but also each officer who passed through a course in historical methodology and source evaluation learned important, useful skills that improved his ability to analyze complicated military questions, even in the heat of battle.[5]

A few progressive young officers, especially those who had been exposed to historical seminars in civilian schools, recognized that it was time to break away from total reliance on the applicatory method; despite their knowledge of military affairs, men such as Arthur Wagner, Eben Swift, and Matthew Forney Steele had no formal training in up-to-date research methods. The new source method of the civilian historians promised more than their predecessors' outdated conceptions of original research, which centered on providing "examples of the study of principles [of war] by their application."[6] The introduction of the source method into the Staff College reveals that soldiers, at least, did not perceive Professor Hart's history gap as an unbridgeable chasm.

Much of the credit for the army's shift to source-method study of military history belongs to Capt. Arthur Latham Conger, who received his initial appointment to the faculty of the Department of Military Art at the Staff College in the fall of 1907. Unlike Wagner, Swift, and other officers who were drawn to the study of history as a measure of military professionalism, Conger approached the study of the past from a perspective that was nearly unique among turn-of-the-century U.S. Army officers. His special talents ultimately made him the army's single most influential advocate of scientific history.

Conger was always a bit of a military maverick. Indeed, in his youth, Conger did not seem to be headed toward an army career at all. He traveled widely in Europe and the Near East as a teenager, and by the time he entered Harvard University, he showed evidence of rather eclectic interests in philosophy, classics, music composition, and Oriental religions. After graduating in 1894, he resisted family pressure to enter the ministry, joined the Theosophical Society instead, and gave serious consideration to a career in music.

But for the outbreak of the Spanish-American War in 1898, Conger probably would not have entered the army at all. At loose ends when the war began, Conger enlisted as a private in the Twelfth New York Volunteer Infantry before accepting a lieutenant's commission in the Regular Army. Assigned to the Philippines, Conger later recalled that he learned the art of war from his captain, but he learned the science of strategy from Gen. Robert P. Hughes, whom he remembered as "the most scholarly of our generals."[7]

Conger's special talents surfaced a few years later when he became a member of the School of the Line Class of 1906 and the Staff College Class of 1907. The young officer's penchant for scholarly attainments and his newfound enthusiasm for military affairs attracted the attention of Col. John F. Morrison, the guiding light of the Department of Military Art. The colonel recognized Conger's unique qualities and arranged for his assignment to the faculty of the Leavenworth schools immediately after graduation from the Staff College.[8]

Until Conger's assignment to the Leavenworth schools, instruction in military history, exclusive of the illustrative approach used in map exercises and map maneuvers, centered on Captain Steele's lecture course and the newly introduced staff rides taken by selected officers to the battlefields of the Civil War. Conger immediately began to restructure the Staff College's history course around the research techniques he had learned in his seminars at Harvard. From 1907 until American entry into World War I, except for a three-year period (1910–1913), Conger remained on the faculty of the Leavenworth schools.

Conger's innovations introduced during his first year at the Staff College revised the army's approach to the study of history. He initiated the seminar method of instruction for his classes. He controlled the content and the level of sophistication of the research course by carrying most of the instructional responsibilities himself. Although not a sterling classroom teacher — one student recalled that when the captain began to lecture "everyone goes to sleep" — he enjoyed the moral support of his superiors at Fort Leavenworth and set the standards for army historical study until the outbreak of World War I.[9] A former student described Conger as "a man of brilliant, if sometimes eccentric genius [who] inspired me to more real thought than any other teacher at the school."[10]

For the Staff College Class of 1908, Conger decided to introduce his students to the source method through a detailed study of a single Civil War campaign. After deciding that Gen. George B. McClellan's 1862 Peninsula campaign offered a wide variety of historical questions for analysis, Conger warned his students of the intellectual rigor of his course of instruction. Advising them not to bother memorizing the events of the campaign, he announced that he chose McClellan's unsuccessful drive on Richmond because there was no comprehensive book that might sway the students' own analysis of important command decisions.

The captain then required his class to reconstruct the campaign for themselves from the original orders and after-action reports printed in *The Official Records of the Union and Confederate Armies in the War of the Rebellion*.[11] Using the source method, the students traced day-to-day movements on a large-scale map prepared for Conger by the Staff College's engineering department.[12] After members of the class charted each day's move, they explained the reasons behind each march, accounted for discrepancies in reports by different participants, and weighed the credibility of each source they used.

Conger pushed his students to search for answers beyond the raw material they found in the official reports. He encouraged them to look for unexplained lapses in the documentary record. The captain was convinced, for instance, that McClellan had held back from the War Department a number of important reports from the Peninsula campaign. "From the fact that *McClellan's Own Story* gives a number of documents never turned in to the W[ar] D[epartment] for file and the evident circumstance that many of these reports if known would have made Gen. McClellan's position still more embarrassing than it was, suggests—though it does not prove—that he either kept these reports in his private file or caused them to be destroyed," Conger argued.[13]

He also encouraged his students to seek out credible published eyewitness accounts, although he also demanded that they find corroborative evidence in the documentary record to substantiate the claims made in each secondary source.[14] He would accept no arguments based on the "everyday popular histories" that seemed to "multiply like flies in a summer cavalry camp."[15] Colonel Morrison was so pleased with the outcome of the initial offering that he recorded in his annual report, "One campaign so studied is more valuable to a military man than many more superficially studied."[16]

For the Class of 1909, Conger made still greater strides when he expanded his course to include intensive analyses of a wider variety of campaigns. Early in the academic year, his students spent twenty half-days dissecting the capture of Fort Donelson in February 1862, General Grant's crossing of the James River in June 1864, and the Peninsula campaign. Later in the year, the students spent nineteen additional half-days analyzing Austerlitz and Waterloo, the Prussian victory at Metz in 1870, and the Battle of Paardeberg during the Boer War.[17] Morrison noted the improvement in the quality of the students' papers and the attention to detail that carried over to the officers' preparation for their battlefield tour in Virginia: "I have never seen [the student officers' battlefield lectures] excelled for a clear concise exposition of military movements."[18]

Still, neither Conger nor Morrison explained why, after such a promising start with the Class of 1908, the intensive study of a single campaign gave way so rapidly to less comprehensive investigations of seven battles. Possibly, they were preparing for the time when Conger would be reassigned to field duty and the instructional responsibilities would be delegated to a faculty member less capable of handling either the minute details of a single campaign or the intellectual demands of the source method. Even so uniquely qualified a faculty member as Conger was vulnerable to army regulations that restricted the number of years a line officer could be absent on detached duty from his regiment. Despite the protests of Leavenworth administrators, Conger was relieved at the end of the academic year in the spring of 1910.[19]

With Conger's guiding hand removed, the quality of the Leavenworth history program could well have taken a sharp nosedive. But the captain had decided to do all he could to prevent it. Before his reassignment, Conger took an unusual step to help guarantee the continued success of the Staff College's historical studies. In 1908, when he first put his course together, Conger had invited Prof. Frederick Morrow Fling, a member of the History Department at the University of Nebraska, to visit the Staff College.[20] The captain asked him to inspect the content of the curriculum and advise the faculty on the latest advances in historical methods, a task Fling agreed to continue even after Conger was reassigned.[21]

Fortunately for the future of the army history program, Fling enjoyed his connection with the Leavenworth schools. The efforts of this energetic and committed civilian scholar capably filled the gaps the army's rotation system sometimes left open. In addition to his informal advisory duties, Fling, a specialist in European history, became a popular "inspirational" lecturer to the Staff College classes.[22] Even more important, Fling also arranged for Capt. Stuart Heintzelman, Conger's associate and successor as instructor of the methods course, to be admitted as a special student in the Department of History at the University of Nebraska. Under the professor's close direction, Heintzelman was trained in the historical methods required to maintain the standards that Conger had established.[23]

Fling, the civilian, remained the constant steadying influence needed to maintain high standards in the Leavenworth history program. By the time Conger returned to the Staff College in 1913, Fling had contributed so much time and effort to the history program that the school's assistant commandant offered to repay the University of Nebraska by detailing soldiers from the Fort Leavenworth garrison to assist the land-grant institution's military science department.[24]

Upon his return in the summer of 1913, Conger quickly proved that he had spent his free time during his three-year absence looking for ways to improve his methods course. After being relieved of duty in 1910, he immediately requested and received an extended leave of absence to travel to Germany for a firsthand look at history instruction in its universities.[25] (Interestingly enough, he does not seem to have spent much time visiting the famed officer schools to observe their military history courses.) After attending *Sommer-Semester* at the University of Heidelberg, he planned to spend the winter term at the University of Berlin to take "several courses of unusual military value," including, apparently, studies with noted German historian Hans Delbrück.[26] Once exposed firsthand to the most up-to-date historical methodology of the German universities and steeped in nineteenth-century European military history, Conger returned to the Staff College inspired to increase the sophistication of his research course.

During his absence, Conger became convinced that reconstructing Civil War battles and campaigns solely from the orders and after-action reports printed in the *Official Records* and a random smattering of secondary accounts did not sufficiently challenge his students' analytical abilities. To increase the level of difficulty, Conger redesigned the course around a wider variety of material to test each man's capacity to judge evidence, to discern true principles of war, and to "see right through the sources, however contradictory they may seem on the surface, and to discover the real facts."[27]

The Fort Donelson campaign suited his purposes well. The relatively small number of troops involved on each side, the availability of nearly all important official reports and excellent maps, and the lack of any reliable secondary work to sway unduly his students' opinions all fit into his plans. To supplement the *Official Records*, Conger gathered together contemporary northern and southern newspaper reports, postwar reminiscences by participants, biographical sketches of key leaders, previously unpublished documents, and correspondence from wartime residents of the Fort Donelson area who recalled the events of 1862. He then arranged with the Staff College Press to print and bind this additional source material in a separate book, *Donelson Campaign Sources*.[28] In combination with the materials already printed in the *Official Records*, students were confronted with sufficient contradictory or misleading information to test their intellectual mettle.

Also during his second tenure at Fort Leavenworth, Conger further extended the army's history program by pushing for the relocation of the Fort Donelson campaign study into Capt. Farrand Sayre's first-year class in the School of the Line.[29] Since only the top graduates of that school continued on to the next year's work at the Staff College, the captain hoped that when the advanced class entered his upper-level history seminar, the students would be prepared for even more sophisticated historical study and high-quality individual research.

Conger continued to produce his own instructional materials for his methods courses. He was not entirely satisfied with his first efforts. Harboring serious misgivings about his slim volume of Fort Donelson sources, Conger believed by providing his class even with these few additional sources, he had allowed them to begin their studies "at the second round of the ladder of historical research, and not at the first . . . the 'search for documents.'"[30] Moreover, he had come to realize that many of his students possessed at least a passing knowledge of the Civil War.

The captain therefore sought out more unfamiliar battles. He used his European schooling to advantage to compile a volume of original sources on the Battle of St. Privat (also known as Gravelotte), a Prussian victory over the French in August 1870. The distinctiveness of this documentary collection stemmed from Conger's successful efforts to track down many German sources that few American officers had ever seen. Better still, from Conger's perspective, those few of his colleagues who had studied the campaign at all invariably had relied upon the narratives from the French army's official histories. With the cooperation of Harry Bell of the foreign languages department, Conger selected and organized the translated documents for publication. Although he was again ordered away from the Staff College for temporary duty with a Texas maneuver brigade just as *St. Privat: German Sources* went to press in 1914, his wife, Margaret Guild Conger, completed the proofreading and footnotes.[31]

Plagued by increasing disruptions of the school schedule as affairs on the Texas border heated up, Conger did not try to publish another such elaborate collection of documents in book form. Nonetheless, by 1915 he had gathered and collated mimeographed copies of appropriate sources for a detailed study of Napoleon's battle at Marengo in June 1800.[32] He also began to collect documents for a more complex source-method study of McClellan's Peninsula campaign; completion of this work, however, fell to one of Conger's successors in the post–World War I historical section of the Army War College.[33]

Still, Conger's first goal was not to write textbooks but to produce soldiers capable of independent historical research. He gave increased attention in his classroom to writing military history essays. Each officer must learn "to deal with historical sources intelligently" and express his findings in artful prose. If a soldier developed this ability to the fullest, he stood to profit personally and professionally, intellectually and practically. "Not only does he need it if he is to profit from the experience of others in gaining a mastery of his profession but he needs it every day in war time in penetrating the fog of war, sifting all the erroneous and fragmentary information which comes to his ears, and finding out what is really the tactical and strategical problem confronting him," he argued.[34]

Conger's high standards and his emphasis on historical writing did not go unnoticed among his peers and superiors. The army's professional journals, especially the *Infantry Journal*, sought his students' historical essays for publication.[35] Conger turned down the editors, however, responding that he considered the essays merely classroom exercises, not finished projects.[36] Conger's superiors voiced their interest in obtaining the services of graduates of his seminars whenever they confronted the subject of writing official histories of American wars.[37] When in 1914 Chief of Staff Leonard Wood established a small historical section for the General Staff, Conger's name was among the first suggested—by a civilian scholar—as an appropriate appointee to the new office.[38] A former commandant of the Staff College summed up Conger's contribution succinctly: "[His] course teaches a student in one year the things it took me thirty years of largely wasted reading to find out for myself about military history."[39]

More impressive, Conger had also established a solid reputation among civilian historians. In 1912 he was one of three army officers sent to the important American Historical Association annual convention in Boston where Hart described the history gap. In 1914 he was asked to chair the AHA's special committee to award a prize for writing military history.[40] An enthusiastic Professor Fling, while reviewing the captain's *Donelson Campaign Sources* for the *American Historical Review*, used the opportunity to praise profusely the quality of instruction in Conger's classes. After observing a Staff College class critique McClellan's siege of Yorktown in 1862, Fling recalled the experience:

> It was a genuine graduate seminar in which the best kind of critical training was being given and the most satisfactory results obtained. Here, I thought, is the training school for the future military historians of this country. Two years of the severe critical training in historical research given at Leavenworth ought to equip a man for independent research.[41]

Conger's performance at Leavenworth suggested a bright future for the study of history in the professional education of the officer corps. But the study of military history at the army's capstone educational institution, the Army War College, followed a far less promising path. Although the Army War College was supposed to be the pinnacle of a progressive system of professional education, in the years before World War I graduation from the Staff College at Fort Leavenworth was not a prerequisite for assignment to the senior school. Not every officer at the Army War College had passed through one of Conger's history seminars. Nonetheless, the school's administrators fashioned a history program that was rigorous, ambitious, and assumed a working knowledge of the source methods taught by Conger and Heintzelman. The Army War College's plans for its history program simply demanded too much of the students, some of whom were ill prepared to implement them.

The fundamental flaw in the Army War College's historical research program lay in its close adherence to Gen. Tasker H. Bliss's original injunction that the student officers should "learn by doing."[42] When the school's administrators unveiled their plans for the students to conduct research on the campaigns of 1861–1865 for an official Army War College history of the Civil War, they hoped that the officers could learn the historian's craft and contribute to professional military literature at the same time. Earlier classes had seemed to tackle with great enthusiasm other ambitious projects for which they had little advance preparation, such as the creation of war plans. When it came to writing sound history, however, the Classes of 1913, 1914, 1915, 1916 and 1917 found Bliss's injunction difficult to follow.

There were four major problems. First, even if the students had completed the historical research course at the Staff College, they had learned only the process of reconstructing a battle from a limited number of sources, most of which were provided to them. Despite Conger's best intentions, his students had gained little experience in original investigation using the sources of a research library. At the Staff College, students had tended to seek only corroborative evidence in the post's specialized library to back up the sources they had already been assigned to use; their experience with independent research was not extensive, even for the narrow topics they investigated for term papers.

Second, the soldiers soon discovered that familiarity with the intellectual processes for evaluating source material did not mean they could transfer their ideas to paper in well-organized and pleasing prose. Just as Conger's course did not stress independent research, Staff College instruction also had not provided sufficient experience in writing history for graduates to claim exposure to more than a fraction of the historian's art.

Third, until the school closed in 1917, Army War College classes continued to include officers who had not passed through any kind of advanced professional education at all. As late as 1911, and perhaps later, conservative senior officers received appointments to the Army War College primarily to try to convert them to the cause of professional education. For such officers, several of whom retired before World War I, the need for theoretical education or the writing of history still seemed the height of folly, and, accordingly, they approached their tasks with indifference.[43]

Finally, and contemporary evaluations deemed this crucial to the failure of the Civil War project in particular, the Army War College faculty lacked an Arthur Conger. No single instructor at the Washington school came close to exerting the control that the captain held over the intellectual standards and the quality of instruction at the Staff College.

Army War College administrators were not unaware of the problems, but they also could not push through the War Department bureaucracy the changes in personnel policy that would resolve them. In the end, the faculty offered merely a partial solution to only one of the major obstacles that blocked the progress of their history program. Since they could not find another Conger, the Army War College faculty did the next best thing. They attracted the interest of a civilian scholar who already had demonstrated a great interest in military history and held strongly to an unusual view that soldiers and academicians could cooperate to write it. Prof. Robert M. Johnston of Harvard University became the Army War College's Fred Fling.

Johnston sympathized with the problems of the Army War College because he had faced similar frustrations in attempting to interest academic scholars in the study of military history. He first discovered a curiosity about military affairs during his academic training in the seminars of British and German universities where the discipline enjoyed far greater professional respectability than it did in the United States. When he took a teaching position at Bryn Mawr College in 1908, he began a one-man crusade to change American perceptions about his specialty. His efforts largely inspired the special military history session at the AHA's annual convention in 1912.[44]

Johnston's first introduction to army officers who shared his interest in military history stemmed from his successful attempts to solicit official War Department representation at the Boston meeting. He welcomed the participation of the three army officers assigned to attend—Conger, of course, along with Maj. James W. McAndrew of the Army War College Class of 1913 and Capt. George H. Shelton of the Twenty-ninth Infantry. In repayment for their invitation to the AHA meeting, McAndrew invited Johnston to join the Army War College staff ride to the Virginia battlefields in late May and early June 1913.[45]

These initial contacts between Johnston and Army War College students and faculty led to more lasting cooperation. Army War College administrators turned to Johnston when they discovered their students' great need for instruction in the fundamentals of historical research and writing. Invited by McAndrew, who by late 1913 was an instructor at the Army War College, Johnston addressed the Class of 1914 before they began their Civil War essays. In clear and simple language, he delivered a lecture entitled "The Functions of Military History."[46]

The best military history, Johnston believed, held both theoretical and practical values: "What we are concerned with in reality is not science, but applied science; not military history, but applied military history." He recognized four aspects of the soldier's art where military history would be "of direct utility" because it could suggest important questions worthy of investigation: organization, tactics, strategy, and national policy. Johnston abhorred a superficial study of military history that would merely reinforce standard lessons on the principles of war. Only the "minuteness of study" that promoted an officer's "critical sense" produced useful and accurate history.[47]

To instill this spirit of critical analysis, Johnston impressed upon his audience that the documentary record of the military event under study must be each officer's first stop. No doubt the graduates of Conger's Leavenworth seminars in the source method found Johnston's words familiar, but the point was too important to slight. Like Conger, Johnston believed, although official reports were "frequently written in the stress of field operations or even in battle, and they are sometimes even worse for being written six months after the event," there was still no better starting point. They key to producing accurate history lay in "the whole matter of the criticism of military documents," which presented so many more problems than sources for non-military events that "it is a great business in itself." Despite the great challenges, thorough critical analysis was absolutely necessary to remedy what Johnston perceived to be the biggest problem of contemporary Civil War historical literature: "The event is so interesting that we are always trying to get a view of what the whole Civil War was without any minuteness of study."[48]

Johnston demanded that the officers adhere to academic historians' standards for source evaluation to avoid the errors that plagued the previous generation of Civil War authors, who wrote "in terms of rhetoric and literature." For Johnston, history was "the art of presenting facts with methodical clearness," an especially useful skill that technical expertise in military matters alone could not supply. The best long-term result of writing military history "on the most close, technical and minute lines," he emphasized, was its ability to influence larger works, so that the information of a few specialists would ultimately "permeate down to the understanding of the many" and "in time educate the nation."[49] The latter became a common theme of soldiers who hoped the study of military history could arouse an interest in martial affairs among civilians during the pre–World War I preparedness movement.[50]

Johnston's single lecture to the Army War College Class of 1914 was one more than the previous year's students had received, but it was soon clear that the fledgling historians required considerably more guidance. To reinforce the lessons Johnston impressed upon the class, Conger was ordered east from Fort Leavenworth to spend several weeks in late February and early March 1914 talking informally with the students on the finer points of historical research.[51]

Even this did not help. When the year's curriculum underwent its annual evaluation, Army War College administrators concluded that it was "clear to almost everyone that results of permanent value could not be obtained unless the work was directed by an expert in approved historical methods."[52] Little progress was made during 1914 on the Army War College's history of the Civil War, and faculty members had to be satisfied with recognizing that "each individual was at least able to improve his own knowledge of the history of that period."[53]

Nonetheless, until the Class of 1917 set aside its historical studies to give greater attention to mobilization plans on the eve of the U.S. entry into

World War I, Army War College students struggled to meet the ambitious program set out for them. Although administrators recognized that most officers' previous academic work had not prepared them for independent research and that the addition of several more inspirational talks each year from Johnston could not make up for this deficiency,[54] the goals of the history program were not reduced to more realistic levels. For all the positive assessments of the Staff College research program, both within the army and from members of the American Historical Association, the Army War College history program bred only frustration.

The intellectual burden placed on the Class of 1916 by Army War College president Macomb revealed just how ambitious the ideal attainments of the history program had become. As the students prepared to begin their Civil War research projects, the general lectured them on the importance of "The Scientific Study of Military History." Modern soldiers, Macomb believed, needed to know the methods of historical research. Most important, of course, officers would "materially enhance their value to the government in time of war" if during peacetime they strengthened their knowledge of the art of war. Properly prepared histories of the Regular Army, the militia, American wars and campaigns, and the evolution of national military policy, written by soldiers who understood institutional problems and priorities, would also be "a boon" for swaying legislators in Washington. Moreover, the army schools, and especially the Army War College, should lead by example to induce "our universities, colleges and secondary schools to establish upon a firm foundation the correct teaching of military history, which in itself would be a great step toward national preparedness."[55]

At a time when camps on the Plattsburgh model popped up all over the United States, when Regular Army officers were detailed to indoctrinate civilian volunteers, when the possibility of American involvement in the European war loomed like a dark cloud on the horizon, Macomb saw both necessity and opportunity in his students' study of military history. When he argued that "no nation that persists in neglecting the study of its own military history will know how to maintain 'its place in the sun,'" Macomb put the army in the intellectual front lines of the fight for the defense of the American way of life. The study of American military history, especially the blunders and near disasters, would convince officers to accept as a primary professional responsibility the eradication of "jingoistic" attitudes inside and outside the army that had stymied the development of a realistic military policy.[56]

Despite Macomb's high-sounding rhetoric, however, the Army War College's students took no great inspiration from his words. Historical studies at the army's senior educational institution continued to flounder. Charged with overseeing the Civil War studies of the Classes of 1915 and 1916, Lt.

Col. Clement A. F. Flagler, an engineer officer with no advanced training in history, finally destroyed much of the spirit of independent research with his talk entitled "Historical Research."[57]

Perhaps Flagler merely attempted to get to what he considered to be the heart of the historical method—selection and evaluation of sources—but in doing so, he effectively diluted the researchers' objectivity and gutted the course of much of its intellectual rigor. The colonel outlined the precise method he expected each student to follow: select an up-to-date secondary work as a guide; collect source material; evaluate, authenticate, and interpret the data; prepare an outline or "working analysis"; resolve discrepancies; write the narrative; write the military analysis.

To his credit, Flagler's greatest concern was for the evaluation of sources. In terms reminiscent of Conger's warnings about McClellan and the documentation of the Peninsula campaign, Flagler warned his students to beware of officers whose "desire for promotion, for reputation, for credit, either for themselves or their command, envy of or antipathy to others, and personal vanity, are frequently in evidence."[58] To this point, Flagler's warnings were useful; Johnston, too, had offered the students similar admonitions.

Unfortunately, Flagler's students seldom needed to make decisions about the authenticity or accuracy of a source they wanted to use. The colonel concluded his comments with a long list of available sources, summarizing the material that could be found in them. More important, he obviated his students' need to analyze them critically by offering his own blanket praise or condemnation.

Flagler's assessments of individual works often revealed his own weaknesses and predilections. He dismissed the Surgeon General Department's excellent five-volume *Medical and Surgical History of the War of the Rebellion* as "too technical for a general historian." Flagler accepted other works uncritically, such as former southern general E. Porter Alexander's *Military Memoirs of a Confederate*. He labeled the former artilleryman's work "one of the best, if not the best, and most accurate history from the southern side," an assessment that, although probably true in general, also deserves to be limited to the events to which Alexander was a direct observer. He did not trust William Swinton's early works on the Union armies because "historical fact is sacrificed to literary effect," never mentioning, if indeed he knew, that the author was among the first postwar writers to interview important northern and southern participants concerning a number of controversial events.

Flagler was equally adept at heaping praise or condemnation on whole classes of literary works. He deemed the entire set of the *Southern Historical Society Papers* "extremely useful" but offered no warning about their intense pro-Virginia and pro-Lee bias. In another generalized evaluation, Flagler dismissed corps and regimental histories as "almost universally worthless. They are made to sell, and are incomplete, biased, and inaccurate if not worse." He also warned his students to avoid biographies and what he called minor histories, because "they are not worth expenditure of the short time at their disposal."[59]

Perhaps this last dictum was the key to the whole problem. Flagler, possibly unintentionally, subordinated the spirit of independent research to the General Staff's desire to make progress on an official history project in the time allotted for the work. Not surprisingly, he did not consider the possibility of sending his students to do research in unpublished sources, even those readily available in Washington. Perhaps he himself did not know of the valuable historical sources within a short walk of the Army War College building. Still, the lack of a professional historian to guide the day-to-day work of the officers was rarely so obvious.

When the army schools closed down for the war years, in sharp contrast to the success of Conger's high-quality history course at the Staff College, Army War College administrators had little to show for their efforts to establish a strong historical research program. In addition to, or possibly as a consequence of, the unavailability of professional guidance, only two years into the Civil War project, the annual review of the curriculum concluded that much duplication of work had already occurred.[60] After three years of work by three separate classes, the year-end review reported that "no material progress" had been made on the Civil War project.[61] By 1916 military leaders had concluded that the one month allotted for independent research during each academic year was simply insufficient to transform officers into historical scholars.[62]

Conger's presence lessened the impact of these problems at the Leavenworth schools, but even there, not all of military history's problems could be resolved by curricular reform. The army schools' adoption of the source method was an admirable and progressive experiment, but like many other innovations in the American military establishment in the pre–World War I years, it was vulnerable to institutional priorities. Three problems, especially, plagued the army's history program. Budgetary constraints, disruptions in the school system, and a continuing lack of consensus about the role of history in officer training loomed constantly over the heads of these progressive education reformers.

The same financial conservatism that prevented several officer classes from participating in Civil War battlefield tours afflicted classroom teaching. At Fort Leavenworth, Colonel Morrison tried in vain to convince The Adjutant General to provide copies of the necessary volumes of the *Official Records* for Conger's class. He was told peremptorily that he was "asking the impossible."[63] The Adjutant General's refusal stemmed partly from the unavailability of the volumes Morrison requested. The War Department's bizarre distribution system in the 1880s and 1890s had scattered the books among individual officers and backwater posts where they were said to be propping open doors and windows.[64] Rather than assist the Leavenworth schools actively, the War Department took no steps except to suggest that the Staff College Press reprint the needed volumes at its own expense, a cost manifestly too high for the institution to bear.[65] Funds for maps, library accessions, printing subventions, and the like were equally difficult to obtain from a tight-fisted War Department.

Disruptions to the school system came in two forms: faculty assignments and schedule changes caused by international crises. The constant loss of experienced faculty members to the army rotation system had caused problems throughout the schools since they were established.[66] For the army history program, the situation was desperate simply because so few officers were qualified to teach the courses that used the new source method of instruction. In addition to Conger, only his successor, Heintzelman, and a handful of other officers, such as Capt. Oliver L. Spaulding, who had been educated to the methodology at the University of Michigan before he was commissioned, were capable of teaching the courses properly. Although every academic department at every army school lost valued faculty from time to time, the War Department's view that suitable replacements were always available was not quite accurate in this case.

The appointment of faculty to Conger's own department at the Staff College revealed the scope of the problem. After service on the faculty from 1907 through 1910, the captain was routinely relieved for line duty. Heintzelman carried on until he, too, was ordered back to his regiment in 1912. In his annual report of 1913, the acting commandant of the Staff College, Lt. Col. W. P. Burnham, complained that the rotation system left him in the awkward position of starting the next academic year with an entirely new faculty in the school's most important section, the Department of Military Art.[67]

The departing senior instructor, Maj. Farrand Sayre, echoed his superior's criticism. He warned the War Department that its personnel policies were at least partly responsible for the growing number of talented officers who refused to accept details to the faculty of army schools. Younger officers now seemed to look at teaching assignments as disruptions to their careers rather than positive upward steps. If the War Department needed evidence of poor morale among its instructors, Sayre argued, it needed only look at the recent sharp decline in the number of officers writing textbooks and developing other professional instructional tools.[68]

An eclectic scholar who later completed a doctorate in classics at Johns Hopkins University after his army career ended, Sayre found his fears for the future of the military art department considerably relieved when he learned that Conger had been reassigned to the Staff College faculty.[69] To establish a sense of continuity in the curriculum and administration of the department, Sayre invited Conger to visit in April 1913 to present a one-month course in historical research methods.

When Conger applied for leave to go to Kansas from his station in Texas, however, his commanding officer turned him down. Ironically, Conger's superior was Gen. W. H. Carter, for several decades a staunch advocate of officer education. Carter was not unusual in not recognizing the special skills that made Conger so important to the school system. When he rejected the application for leave, Carter wrote: "The army can supply another officer capable of delivering a month's instruction at Fort Leavenworth upon any subject."[70]

In this case, Carter was wide of the mark. A quick look at the captain's orders for the previous six years would have demonstrated just how unusual Conger was: Not only had he been delivering regular lectures at the Staff College and visiting the Army War College on occasion, but also he had become, in effect, the army's traveling spokesman at the other army schools and National Guard encampments. If the army was to remain committed to a top-flight history program at either the Staff College or the Army War College, it needed to take into account the special talents of officers such as Conger, Heintzelman, and the handful of like-minded soldiers.

In addition to faculty assignments, other disruptions of the academic year caused further problems for the history program at the army's senior officer schools. Beginning in 1914, in response to the problems on the Mexican border, the academic year at the Leavenworth schools was shortened and restored as affairs seemed to warrant. The shortened curriculum not only quickened the return of students to their regiments, an important concern for units serving along the Rio Grande, but also required the instructors to report for temporary field duty instead of allowing them to plan for the following academic year.

At the Army War College, the course of instruction was not reduced in length, but priorities shifted. The Class of 1917, for instance, spent March—the month usually allotted for historical studies—engaged in special projects and studies ordered by the War Department and General Staff that related to mobilization and war plans. In May 1917 the students finally received their historical research assignments, but they were ordered to "take advantage of spare time resulting from necessary delays and interruptions in the strategic maneuvers [exercises]" to complete the projects.[71]

Although they were told to finish their research assignments during July 1917, the wide variety of distractions that followed U.S. entry into the European War in April diluted much of the officers' interest in and attention to their literary tasks. It was difficult for many officers anticipating overseas duty to work within the confines of a library when they could take advantage of an Army War College dictum to "spend time in the open air" to prepare for active service.[72]

Finally, and most important, even though many senior officers had been convinced of the merits of historical instruction, as late as 1914 few could agree why soldiers should study history and what benefits each man could expect to gain from it. The negative attitudes toward intellectualism that existed when the debates over education reform began in earnest in the 1880s were still around in 1914. Gen. Hugh L. Scott found little to praise in the army school system. "Youth is the time and school is the place for schoolboys. Officers over 35 years of age should not be subject to anything like scholastic recitations . . . [that] will interfere with their duties, narrow their minds, and retard their progress."[73] The comments of Macomb, Johnston, and Flagler, however, suggest only some of the roles military history was supposed to play in the education of an army officer, at least in the minds of some of its strongest advocates.

The army's historical research program before World War I produced a confusing puzzle of intellectual ups and downs for historians in and out of uniform. Although military history was not the only discipline to suffer through such peaks and valleys—instruction in modern languages and military law faced similar problems—its increasing acceptance as the key to the professional study of military art and science seemed to act as a magnet for advocates and critics of the new standards of professionalism. Its prominent place in officer education made historical study especially vulnerable to the crosscurrents of intellectual and practical requirements in the modernizing American army. Until the General Staff could decide on the best way to realign the army schools into a truly progressive educational system and make its authority stick, each institution operated independently of the others. The cumulative nature of history could not flourish under this disjointed organization.

During the pre–World War I years, the army's most capable historians spoke with no greater authority than other education reformers, who found less intellectually rigorous uses in the study of the past to justify changes for the future. As a result, the positive achievements of the unprecedented Leavenworth military history seminars lay nearly forgotten amid a mass of less noteworthy efforts. The brief ascendancy of the source method at the Staff College and the ambitious, if mishandled, applications intended for this technique at the Army War College proved again that military reformers who were deeply committed to officer education were not blind to intellectual trends in mainstream American society. What they could not solve immediately was how to balance the spirit of the new methods of historical research, which demanded objective and independent inquiry, against the practical requirements of their profession that the discipline was supposed to serve, all the while operating under the close scrutiny of partisans on both sides.

PART 2
MILITARY HISTORY AND AN AMERICAN LITERATURE ON THE ART OF WAR

Not all American officers could attend the Leavenworth schools or the Army War College. For soldiers in isolated garrisons or officers whose penchant for discussing important questions was not satisfied in the classroom, additional ways to promote the professional study of the art of war seemed necessary. Garrison schools and lyceums filled some of this void. Military writing offered still another outlet for many officers in the Old Army. By World War I, American soldiers of all ranks—progressives and conservatives, graduates of postgraduate schools and anti-intellectuals—enjoyed an open interchange of ideas on important military questions through an impressive body of theoretical literature on the art of war. Military writing by American officers before World War I took four primary forms: professional journals, military monographs, army school textbooks, and "official history." Only the first three can be termed successful experiments, but all opened up new fields for the intensive study of professional questions.

American military writers, although they addressed many topics of professional importance, emphasized two major themes in their literature. First, the United States needed to cast off its reliance on the lessons of European military theorists. Military science varies "with the topography, the organization of the army, national characteristics, and the nature of the enemy," wrote one prominent author. "A text-book . . . might be admirably adapted to the requirements of European officers and at the same time be in some respects quite unsuited to our needs."[1] Few writers in this first literary blossoming in the U.S. Army broke new ground in military theory; nearly all, however, based their analyses of the principles of war and their practical applications on examples drawn from the annals of American military history. The pressures of professionalism and nationalism combined to create a uniquely American military literature where one had not existed previously.

The second theme that many American military authors shared centered on the U.S. Army's need for "a national conception of war." The army needed "*a common doctrine* as to the purposes and end of training, the means to be employed, and the results to be attained," argued the editors of the *Infantry Journal.*[2] Most soldiers believed it was impossible to set down a national military doctrine until officers understood the lessons of American wars and knew something of the history of the U.S. Army and its relation to the political institutions that controlled it. To fill the need for studies of the American military past, some officers, such as Capt. Matthew Forney Steele in his *American Campaigns*, provided not only a military history of important battles but also suggestions for important institutional reforms.

Other army intellectuals held high hopes for an "official history" written by army officers and bearing the sanction of the War Department (or after 1901, the General Staff). Only a work produced by the best minds in the army would fulfill "the need to have our military history correctly recorded." Promulgating this official view on military theory and practice promised to promote safe leadership and meet the army's need "for military efficiency and national well-being."[3]

No comprehensive American military doctrine emerged from the army's literary efforts before World War I. Still, American soldiers no longer felt bound to foreign doctrine, and they learned considerably more about their own military and political institutions. Until the General Staff agreed upon an appropriate military doctrine, *Infantry Journal* editors wrote, "discussion is a good thing."[4] The various forms of military literature offered suitable arenas for many officers to continue these debates.

6

THE PEN RIVALS THE SWORD: WRITING
ABOUT THE AMERICAN WAY OF WAR

"The army is ever astride a hobby," complained Lt. Matthew Forney Steele in 1895. "It rides them one at a time, and a new one has been saddled and brought forth—the cult of literature. The whole service seems to have gone to letters."[1] During the late nineteenth century, an unprecedented number of U.S. Army officers took pen in hand to produce an important, if embryonic, body of work that attempted to impose an American perspective on the professional study of the art of war.

Unlike Continental writers who drew their inspiration from the important military contests of major European armies, the American army's fledgling theorists grew increasingly interested in the battles and campaigns in their own institution's past. They did not expect to uncover different principles of war, but they did question whether or not European applications of those axioms were appropriate to an American army fighting in North America. This emerging professional literature on the art of war, with its growing emphasis on the campaigns of the U.S. Army, opened debate about the need for a national military doctrine that did not rely on traditional European theory.

American military authors of the late nineteenth century faced numerous challenges. The army's writers, like its educators, represented a trend toward intellectualism that many traditionalist or practical soldiers resisted and resented. To complicate matters considerably, the War Department did not quite know how, or even whether, it should encourage its writers-in-uniform. Until 1901 when Secretary of War Elihu Root's demand for reform led to the creation of the General Staff, no office in the War Department's old bureaucratic system was responsible for overseeing the army's intellectual affairs. Military writers had to overcome strong institutional and personal biases for their literary plans to succeed. Often thrown back on their own resources, the army's first writers had to be a tenacious lot. Fortunately, crosscurrents of change in the American armed forces occasionally opened unexpected opportunities. American officers who joined the army's cult of literature found a ready audience among the growing numbers of their colleagues who advocated a better-trained military establishment.

The army's writers contributed to the cause of military professionalism in important ways. They wrote a large body of theoretical literature on the art

89

of war designed to demonstrate their authority in this specialized field.[2] By promoting a greater understanding of the peculiarities of American warfare in the past, they forged a bond of shared tradition that strengthened in all members of the officer corps a powerful spirit of professional identity. By addressing in detail the glories and mistakes of past U.S. wars, they suggested a wide variety of constructive institutional, personnel, operational, and professional changes. In the end, the public and intraservice discussion generated by the work of these writers proved just how healthy the intellectual and professional climate in the Old Army was at the turn of the century.

Military authors were swept up in the vibrant spirit of nationalism that engulfed much of American society during the 1890s. Like the histories of James Schouler and other contemporary historians, much of their writing was designed "to foster love of and loyalty to [the United States] by depicting its common sufferings, fears, joys, achievements, and triumphs, and by showing how their own nation was different."[3] They were willing to take the first tentative steps toward developing a philosophy of warfare more appropriate to the army of the American republic. Nonetheless, the efforts of military writers, just like the increasing influence of army educators, inspired the wrath of less progressive soldiers. The army's new hobby did not sit well with many army bureaucrats or with traditionalists who lamented the passing of the increasingly outmoded philosophy that "only war teaches war."

The mere suggestion that generalship could be learned from books struck many conservative soldiers as the height of folly. No officer, Capt. James Chester believed, understood Napoleon's methods, "or what to purblinded mediocrity appear to be his methods," sufficiently well to write them down for students of the art of war. Napoleon "had no system. He acted thus and so because the conditions of the problems were thus and so."[4] To Chester, the best school of war was the battlefield.

The resistance of traditionalists to military writers who tried to reduce to a formula the methods of successful commanders hid deeper concerns for the future of the American army. Their criticisms would have been unexceptional if they followed from a contemporary Clausewitzian emphasis on the importance of the intangibles of war or the effects of "friction" on military campaigns. But many of these officers were either reactionaries or romantics. They held on to an increasingly outmoded, romanticized notion of the importance of the military genius, the individual who wielded the power of an army as if it were his personal weapon. Writing or reading professional military literature, Chester argued, was wasted on "real commanders, who stand out clear and distinct on the pages of history, [who] were captains by spiritual commission. They could command, even their enemies, and be obeyed."[5]

Not all who resented the officer corps' increasing interest in the activities of the "book men" in its ranks were as eloquent as Chester. "I fully believe and am convinced that the system of theoretical instruction, education, evangelization, and reformation, now so eagerly sought by some few among us, is not needed," Lt. C. D. Parkhurst complained bluntly.[6] Although many reformers looked back upon the follies of the Civil War to justify officer training in peacetime, Lt. E. H. Plummer believed the conflict taught just the reverse:

> Until recently the majority of the officers of the regular army had received, during the Civil War, practical experience in campaigning and fighting which would have proved invaluable to the country had another war occurred soon thereafter, and did serve to give to those entering the service after the war, a training based on that experience; it was given, however, so quietly and unobtrusively that it has not been duly appreciated. The conspicuous absence of technical text books from this source is strongly suggestive that their experience led these veterans to believe that theories and books cannot make efficient or capable officers.[7]

Against such determined and short-sighted critics of military writing, the army's authors waged a constant battle.

Obstacles that plagued military writers often took forms other than the recalcitrance of traditionalist officers. Institutional conservatism and the War Department's lack of awareness about the needs of—or the need for—authors of professional military studies caused considerably greater and more fundamental problems. Change came slowly. Only after the constant complaints of the faculty at the army postgraduate schools that they could not find suitable textbooks for their theory-based courses in the art of war did the War Department decide to investigate the weak state of American military writing.

The War Department's hesitation to commit itself to the army's authors, either with official endorsement or financial assistance, frustrated many writers, discouraged others, but surprised few. Even if he did not realize it, each individual who sought support reminded the War Department of a lingering nightmare: the compiling and publishing of the official record of the Civil War.

Although it had started out with such promise, the Civil War project had quickly become a case study in poor management. Congress in May 1864 first passed appropriations for the publication of this history, but the final volumes did not appear until 1901. Plagued by cost overruns, political interference, lack of trained archival personnel and office space, difficulty in collecting records outside of Washington, and numerous other problems, the *Official Records* project left a sour taste in the mouths of many War Department decisionmakers and congressmen who had been asked repeatedly for additional funding.[8] This debacle overshadowed the successful publication of the surgeon general department's medical history of the Civil War and the army's routine printing of technical manuals and official reports.[9] It also cast doubt on the War Department's willingness to take on responsibilities for new literary projects.

To counter Washington's official silence, soldiers found alternative methods to promote the efforts of their colleagues who wanted to write about the art of war and share their opinions with their fellow officers. The establishment of four major military journals and the willingness of writers to obtain the services of private publishers for book-length monographs went far toward filling the army's immediate need for a professional literature. Once the paths had been blazed, more and more officers followed these routes into the army's literary circle.

The first influential professional military periodical to win the support of army officers was the *Journal of the Military Service Institution of the United States (JMSIUS)*, established in 1879. Facing substantial competition only from the *Army and Navy Journal*, which since 1863 had kept soldiers, sailors, and interested civilian observers apprised of national military developments in a chatty newspaper-style weekly format, the editors of *JMSIUS* hoped to foster a spirit of professionalism in the officer corps.[10] The primary obligation of the journal's parent organization, proclaimed Gen. John M. Schofield in his inaugural address, was the "preservation of the vital military germ from which your country expects great armies to spring." The journal contributed to the development of this professional spirit by printing "real, exact, and extended knowledge. . . . The military student must intently study the history of military contests and endeavor therefrom to learn the facts."[11]

From its inception, the journal printed timely articles on practical questions, debated significant professional issues, and reviewed important books on the art of war and on military history to help "bring together on common ground all branches of the army."[12] Not every issue carried an article that dissected an American campaign, but, probably more important, the journal served as an influential advocate of progressive reform causes, and its authors frequently turned to the experience of the past to make their pleas for future change. Although it adopted no single agenda and advanced no single view on the American way of war, the periodical became so important to the professional culture of the U.S. Army that in 1913 Chief of Staff Leonard Wood seriously considered extending War Department recognition to the publication by naming it the official journal of the General Staff.[13]

In 1888 the *Journal of the U.S. Cavalry Association*, followed shortly in 1892 by the *Journal of the United States Artillery* and in 1904 by the *Infantry Journal*, set similar goals. The editors of each new journal hoped their specialized articles would not only promote technical expertise but also help to instill a deeper spirit of military professionalism, especially in readers who had not yet been inculcated with this new philosophy at the army's schools.

Lt. John W. Ruckman, one of the founders of the artillery journal, expressed concisely the hopes and sentiments of its editors: "To have a professional magazine appearing regularly . . . is a most desirable end and will fill a place, so far unfilled in our instruction." The junior officer continued in the same vein: "If we can found an independent Artillery Journal we believe it will do as much if not more than any one thing to solidify and improve our arm[,] resurrect it from its present death and transform it into an efficient body of men."[14]

Regular readers of the new journals not only were able to keep current on the technical advances in their profession as never before, they also gained a greater sense of historical awareness. Illustrations of bungled performances during any of the wars of the United States served well the reformers' long-term intentions to refine the officer education system, to promote an increase in the peacetime force, and to argue for promotion based on merit or for any one of a myriad of other causes. Even if few of the journal articles cultivated a genuine appreciation of the intellectual elements of the study of the past, history-as-advocate in pre–World War I literature played a role similar to that of history-as-illustration in leadership training in army classrooms.

The subjective and utilitarian use of the past so apparent in numerous articles in these journals has often created the impression among twentieth-century academicians that military history, at least in the hands of the army, was little more than self-serving.[15] Such an assessment obscures more than it enlightens. The use of historical example served purposes more constructive than mere hero worship.

For many contributors to the new American literature on the art of war, the path to a more professional officer corps followed two tracks, and the study of military history offered reliable guideposts along each route. First, each officer had to understand his role as a soldier, as a professional trained in the principles of war and their applications on the battlefield. This required him to transcend his own sense of nationalism to learn all he could from the past experiences of others, even those of potential enemies. Second, each American officer needed to understand the relation between his army and his government in order to comprehend his nation's conception of the proper conduct of war. Both goals placed great demands upon the record of the past.

This rise of literary fever, then, like many of the demands for progressive reform and professional standards, evolved from a grass-roots interest among the officers themselves. Many of the soldiers to first take pen in hand had served overseas as special observers and wanted to share their experiences and insights with their colleagues. They found a ready audience.

Lt. Francis V. Greene's extended report on the Russo-Turkish War of 1877–78 and Lt. Tasker H. Bliss's detailed article on the battle at Plevna offered American soldiers firsthand views of a war they would not have known about if they had waited for War Department information. Both works have stood the test of time and still rank as the most useful military literature on the topic written by American authors. Although they stressed the methods by which the Russians and Turks applied the accepted principles of the art of war, Bliss and Greene offered pre–World War I American officers lessons that were more than immediately practical. From their narratives on the conduct of the campaigns of 1877–78, a serious student could catch a glimpse of the warfare of the future.[16]

Without considerable personal effort, however, neither Greene nor Bliss could have informed American soldiers about this small but important war in a distant part of the world. Bliss, for instance, applied to the War and State departments for useful governmental documents, only to learn that "the only information in their possession was contained in a few letters which these departments considered confidential [such as] the reports of our attaches."[17]

Bliss's and Greene's interest in the Russians and Turks did not herald a new age of broadening international perspectives in the officer corps. For much of the remainder of the nineteenth century, if they chose to look outside North America, most U.S. Army officers were drawn almost exclusively to the rapid and decisive battlefield successes of the Prussian army in its wars against Austria and France. Since the American army had already copied parts of the curriculum of the Prussian officer schools, adopted translations of Prussian textbooks for classroom use, and accepted the *pickelhaube* as the helmet for its dress uniform, it is not particularly surprising that many officers entered the ranks of the military author corps by sticking with traditional practice to promote professional knowledge by analyzing Prussian campaigns.

The impact of Prussian military thought on the American army cannot be dismissed lightly. However, it was not nearly so overpowering as it has sometimes been portrayed.[18] As nationalistic fervor ran high, American officers grew increasingly sensitive to the impact of national character on military affairs. It quickly became apparent that Prussian historical example alone could no longer satisfy the intellectual needs of American soldiers.

The military history of the United States—and the inapplicability of the Prussian past for the American future—increasingly commanded the attention of the U.S. Army's officer corps.

The nineteenth-century literary careers of two American officers illustrate well the kinds of intellectual changes military authors faced and the institutional challenges they had to overcome. Even as junior lieutenants, both John Bigelow and Arthur Wagner believed European military professionals could teach important lessons. But they also believed Americans had to be able to decide which lessons were appropriate to combat in North America or to the army of a republic. They also learned that getting their views into print required luck, money, and the tenacity of a pit bull.

In 1880 when Bigelow of the Tenth U.S. Cavalry published a brief volume entitled *Mars-la-Tour and Gravelotte*, he helped to begin the revolution in American military thought. The lieutenant claimed that even the vaunted Prussian military establishment was not the master of all professional practice in the art of war. Its performance in battle proved that its leaders did not understand the proper use of skirmishers or the importance of artillery bombardment preliminary to infantry charges. The Prussians also misunderstood the use of cavalry as scouts or mobile infantry.[19] Although Bigelow thought well of Moltke's basic plans, his open dissatisfaction with certain Prussian methods inspired other American soldiers to challenge the German stranglehold on the military thought of the U.S. Army.

In 1889 when Lt. Arthur L. Wagner published *The Campaign of Königgrätz: A Study of the Austro-Prussian Conflict in the Light of the American Civil War*, he argued even more convincingly than Bigelow that Prussian military doctrine did not provide the yardstick by which American warfare should be judged. The Austro-Prussian War began the year after Appomattox, but instead of searching for lessons from the Civil War, the Prussians had "studiously ignored or despised them," even especially helpful ones such as the use of "hasty entrenchments" on the battlefield.[20] American soldiers, Wagner believed, should not be compelled to follow blindly the methods of the Prussian General Staff, which had committed a gross breach of professionalism when it denied the importance of the lessons of the Civil War.

At the same time Wagner, Bigelow, and other American soldiers began to express their doubts about the Prussian way of war, they found a new source of professional inspiration closer to home: the experiences of the heroes of the Civil War. "From every war there arises a vast mass of literature, especially in the way of personal memoirs, containing much that is valuable, together with much more that is of no value at all, and long years of patient study have in many cases failed to separate the one from the other," noted Bliss about the growing mountain of Civil War histories and memoirs.[21]

Nonetheless, increasing numbers of American officers agreed with Wagner that "scarcely a feature of the tactics of the present day . . . did not have its germ, its prototype, or development in that great contest."[22] They were convinced that the Civil War, not the Prussian experience, would provide the best examples to teach American officers the fundamentals of the art of war.

In the hope of laying a strong foundation for discussing the art of war from an American perspective, Lieutenant Bigelow in 1890 published *The Principles of Strategy, Illustrated Mainly from American Campaigns*. In his preface, Bigelow set high goals for his work. He intended to discuss "the subject of strategy in the light of American warfare, and thus furnish instruction for Americans, not only in the theory of the subject, but also in the military history and geography of their own country."[23]

Bigelow's work illustrates the first tentative steps in the transition of American military literature. The lieutenant shied away from the use of Continental examples, but he continued to rely upon European theory. When he wrote about the importance of strategic points and operations from a base, and, most notably, when he considered the "strategic chess board" and the "geometrical discussion of strategic movements," he drew heavily upon the military thought of Swiss theorist Henri Jomini.[24] But Bigelow did not follow tradition and illustrate Jomini's maxims from Napoleonic campaigns; he chose examples from American wars instead.

The history of the Civil War provided the fodder for Bigelow's theoretical discussion of three of the most important elements of any officer's professional knowledge: regular, political, and tactical strategy. Regular strategy—he sometimes called it strategy proper—aimed to defeat the enemy indirectly by depriving him of his supplies, a concept curiously out of step with the general turn-of-the-century view that wars of the future would be decided by quick, successful offensive battles. In 1864 when Gen. William T. Sherman cut the railroads and roads leading into Atlanta, Confederate general John Bell Hood's army evacuated the city. Sherman's maneuvers convinced Bigelow that an army could win if it could guarantee its own supply of men, ammunition, and provisions while denying them to the enemy. Once Sherman had forced the withdrawal of Hood's men, the way was open for the famous and decisive March to the Sea.[25] No well-read soldier could miss the impact of Jominian ideas on Bigelow's notion of strategy proper.

The lieutenant's discussion of political strategy, on the other hand, relied upon some of the more sophisticated ideas of Prussian theorist Karl von Clausewitz. Although Clausewitz believed most strongly in the need for each army to develop a military strategy that held the destruction of the enemy force as its ultimate goal, he also recognized that modern war was an extension of politics.

A more advanced concept than the geometrical conformations of regular strategy, political strategy aimed to embarrass the enemy's government. By destroying the enemy's governmental machinery, as with the capture of his capital city, or by eroding confidence in the government so completely that it no longer could assert its authority over its citizens, successful execution of a political strategy carried the war home to the enemy's people.[26] As demonstrated by Sherman's March to the Sea or Gen. Philip H. Sheridan's torching of Shenandoah Valley farms in 1864, political strategy as executed by the Union army contributed decisively to the defeat of the Confederacy.

Of the three concepts, tactical strategy was the most familiar to American soldiers at the turn of the century. Bigelow postulated that defeating the enemy on the battlefield was the aim of tactical strategy. Through elaborate diagrams, he dutifully demonstrated the benefits of interior lines and concentration, his keys to success in combat. Nonetheless, he did not reveal much enthusiasm for recent applications of tactical strategy in modern warfare. It bothered him that "the most common use, in fact, of regular and political strategy is in such subordination to tactical strategy."[27] When Union general Joseph Hooker planned his Chancellorsville campaign, he decided to attack Lee rather than cut him off from Richmond. After Lee attacked first and routed the Army of the Potomac, the Union's campaign ended in "total failure," a fate that might have been different if Hooker had chosen instead to go after the Confederate capital, a more important and decisive political goal.[28]

Devoting considerable attention to the Vicksburg and Atlanta campaigns, Grant's movements from The Wilderness to Petersburg in May and June 1864, and Stonewall Jackson's marches up and down the Shenandoah Valley in 1862, Bigelow remained true to his intention to write primarily of American military affairs. Although he could not entirely avoid the example of European armies, he severely limited his favorable comments on foreign military practices. The Prussians, once the model of military professionalism, garnered only a few words of praise for their methods of protecting supply lines and the efficiency of their military railroad system.[29] Bigelow contributed considerably to loosening the grip of Prussian doctrine on American military practice and inspired other officers to continue cultivating the disfavor of U.S. officers for European methods.

Not surprising for a book that attempted to break with tradition, Bigelow's work received mixed reaction. Critical reviews revealed that substantial elements of the officer corps were not yet prepared to break their reliance on European theory. Lt. John P. Wisser genuinely believed Bigelow's book would "appeal to everyone who admires honest effort and true patriotism," but he did not see any new insight on the principles of war. Wisser admitted only offhandedly that Bigelow's inclusion of incidents from the Civil War and the Indian wars was a commendable innovation and that other authors would do well to follow the path he had blazed.[30]

On the other hand, some officers viewed Bigelow's rejection of European military history as a dangerous precedent. "Not only are American campaigns as yet too few to furnish the best obtainable illustrations in every case; it is also true that the American Napoleon has yet to appear," a reviewer for the *Cavalry Journal* complained. By centering much of his discussion on U. S. Grant's campaigns of Shiloh and Vicksburg, Bigelow had "denied himself the free use of the great abundance of material available from European cases."[31] Lt. Carl Reichmann agreed: "Some striking exemplifications of strategic principles which are shown in the campaigns of Napoleon and Moltke have not yet been illustrated in our own wars."[32]

Nonetheless, most officers appreciated Bigelow's efforts to offer American soldiers useful applications of military principles drawn from the wars of the U.S. Army. Reviewers for the *Journal of the United States Artillery*, especially, were proud "that an American officer . . . had placed before the military student . . . certain important principles of strategy [that] have been exemplified in our history, which have been the subject of criticism by European writers, and have found a place in foreign standard works on this subject."[33]

These anonymous reviewers raised a point that embarrassed U.S. Army officers who were pushing for increased attention to the military lessons of American wars. By the 1890s, British officers, especially those in Col. G. F. R. Henderson's classrooms at the Staff College at Camberley, were devoting more attention to the campaigns of the American Civil War than were their counterparts in the U.S. Army.[34]

The publication of Bigelow's *Principles of Strategy* illustrates more than just the changing nature of professional military thought in the United States. The tortuous path that the author followed from manuscript to bound volume offers a complex case study in the institutional problems facing late-nineteenth-century U.S. Army officers who hoped to publish books on military history and theory.

Since his first successful literary effort (his book on Gravelotte), Bigelow had contemplated committing much more of his time to military writing. He found little encouragement. On a trip to New York City's newspaper and magazine editorial offices, he could find no market for his article on Khartoum. He visited the Van Nostrand publishing house to ask "what the prospects were for a military writer." He received "no encouragement to believe that I could make any money from writing."[35] Van Nostrand's feelings mirrored those of most of the publishing world. Therefore, finding no public audience and no War Department policy extending official endorsement to writers of military texts, the publication of Bigelow's book became largely a family affair.

The lieutenant was fortunate to be the son of one of New England's most prominent citizens. John Bigelow, Sr., a Boston Brahmin who had served in a variety of high appointive governmental posts, belonged to many of the best-known learned societies in the Northeast. The younger Bigelow grew up in a household where education was taken seriously; his brother Poultney became a widely respected expert on German culture, well known for his knowledge of European political affairs.[36] Apparently the lieutenant's family ties sufficiently impressed G. P. Putnam's Sons of New York City, which published the first edition of *The Principles of Strategy*. But family name only went so far. Putnam's agreed to print only five hundred copies because the publisher was simply not willing "to predict for the book a very rapid sale."[37]

The Bigelow family maintained their high hopes for the lieutenant's book, however, and they refused to accept Putnam's opinion. They believed John's name "should be identified with military writing of the best kind."[38] To gain a wider audience for his brother's work, Poultney Bigelow offered T. Fisher Unwin, a prominent London publisher, the rights to print and distribute *The Principles of Strategy* in Britain and on the European continent.

Unwin demanded a contract far more favorable to the publisher than to the author. Before he would allow the presses to roll, he required a guarantee from The Adjutant General of the U.S. Army that the War Department would purchase two hundred copies. He also set down as a condition of publication that purchasers of Bigelow's book would be required to pay shipment and insurance costs. The lieutenant or his family had to put up £30 before Unwin would sign the contract, and the author was limited to twelve free copies.[39] (Putnam's, at least, had honored Bigelow's request that fifty-six complimentary copies be sent to American military schools.[40])

Bigelow's problems did not end with Unwin's agreement to print the lieutenant's book. The publisher's royalty settlement was also far from generous; he refused to award Bigelow any remuneration from the copies that the War Department was committed to buy. The only bonus, exacted at Poultney Bigelow's insistence, was Unwin's agreement to provide specially bound "substantial, but not gaudy," copies of the book for presentation to "the best leaders of Europe," including two of the most influential German military writers, Count Alfred von Schlieffen and Count August von der Goltz.[41]

Finally, in September 1891, Lieutenant Bigelow looked forward to the delivery of the completed work. Stationed at Fort Grant in Arizona Territory, he wrote to thank his father for all his efforts and to reflect upon his feelings now that his ten-year project was complete. He had just learned that Putnam's was sending him a copy of his book, and after nearly two years of

the "strain of waiting and hoping from day to day to hear something encouraging," he could not restrain his excitement. "My present sensations
carry me back to the morning of my wedding day," he wrote.[42]

Bigelow followed an unusually complex path to publication, but his efforts
were not without reward. Others followed his lead. Increasingly, progressive
army officers saluted their colleagues who took financial risks to publish
their ideas with no guarantee of War Department remuneration. "Owing to
the irregular and spasmodic demand for military books . . . every work of
a purely historical character . . . represents a literary struggle in which the
author finally triumphs by dint of patience, industry, and perseverance,"
commented Col. T. F. Rodenbough, a Civil War cavalry veteran who was
pleased with these new trends toward military professionalism.[43]

Not all American officers lured into the cult of literature felt obliged to
follow Bigelow's difficult route through private publishers and limited cir-
culation. By the 1890s, faculty members from many different parts of the
army postgraduate school system complained about the lack of suitable
texts.[44] The lure of a ready market inspired a new tactic that, if successfully
pressed, promised army authors maximum professional rewards with minimum expenditure of time and effort. In search of an official imprimatur—
ideally The Adjutant General's designation that the book was required reading for promotion examinations or classroom work—each hopeful author
who approached War Department officials with his literary plans spurred
still others to try, too. In a few years, chaos surrounded the process by which
the army searched for authoritative texts.

By 1895 the question of granting official sanction to newly published
books or to works that had not yet been printed had become so thorny that
The Adjutant General felt compelled to address the issue. There had been
no need to explore the question while the small "reading military public"
in the United States relied upon the works of foreign writers. Now that the
audience for American authors of "military history and biography" was growing, he believed the time had come to set departmental policy.

In the end, The Adjutant General's policy was no policy at all. He was
not convinced that War Department sanction should be thrown behind the
works of American authors when so many soldiers themselves seemed content to buy and use the works of better-known European writers. "I have
generally found every officer to possess something of a library relating to the
military subjects in which he was most interested," he asserted. "Unfortunately, there are other authors besides American ones . . . [who] have acquired a special prestige in the treatment of such vital questions as modern
grand tactics, troop-leading, organization, etc. . . . [Our officers] therefore

buy the works of foreign authors of known reputation in preference to equally good ones by unknown American authors."[45]

The Adjutant General recommended an extremely conservative approach to granting official sanction to books submitted for War Department consideration. He not only believed American officers still preferred foreign military literature, he also had become convinced that "there should be no standard text books, obligatory for the [promotion] examination [or school use]." Once a work on a military topic was labeled "sanctioned," The Adjutant General continued, "it kills off future investigation for a while." He also believed it was "not professional" for the War Department to sign a contract with an army officer to write a military monograph.[46]

The question of government-sponsored publications also bothered The Adjutant General. In each major European army, the texts that received the official sanction of the army were issued in the name of its General Staff. The Adjutant General was uncomfortable with the notion of developing a similar arrangement in the U.S. Army. He believed a prepublication contract between army officials and a member of the officer corps might compel the author to write what he thought his superiors wanted to read. He deemed it best that literary endeavors remain a matter of individual initiative. "There is no standard but the truth . . . and there should be no restriction placed on its expression." Instead of a list of mandatory, sanctioned readings for promotion examinations and classroom use, The Adjutant General suggested the creation of a list of recommended readings that "will encourage thought, publication and equal sales."[47]

The question of financial responsibility was also an important part of the army's problem with its authors. Even the most respected American military writers expressed deep concern about finding a publisher and arranging a suitable financial agreement. Only in unusual cases, as with Bigelow's *Principles of Strategy*, would the War Department guarantee in advance to purchase a designated number of volumes for distribution to post libraries.[48] As a result many superb studies remained nearly unknown and unread. Van Nostrand had told Bigelow back in 1884 that an "excellent little work lately published on Sea Coast Defences" had sold not "more than 20 copies. . . . [I]t was not even taken by the government for the post libraries," and a "history of the 5th Cavalry was likewise not bought by the government."[49] Except in rare cases when it purchased extra copies to offset a publisher's postpublication losses on books the department deemed important, the policy did not change. During this era of War Department fiscal conservatism, the burden of finding a publisher—and the financial risk—fell on the author's shoulders.

The hands-off attitude of the War Department certainly kept it free of costly commitments, but The Adjutant General preferred to explain it differently. He argued that the official policy really provided a safeguard for the future of military writing. Professional perspectives on the art of war constantly underwent changes that generated serious debate, and these issues should be open for free discussion. If the department stepped in and gave financial assistance or official sanction to any one author, then the debate would be closed, perhaps prematurely, and the prevailing interpretation would be that of the man who first gained Washington's ear. No good could come from a policy that seemed to give "the race to the swift, not the strong."[50]

The most committed of the army's authors by and large remained undeterred by the conservative language of the 1895 nonendorsement policy. Long before the army decided against granting official sanctions, officers with literary aspirations had sought ways to obtain favorable concessions from the War Department without entangling their books in the bureaucratic red tape of formal policy. Army writers flooded influential friends in Washington with outlines and manuscripts, hoping their colleagues could wangle some special arrangement. An active "old boy network" flourished. A soldier with access to the commanding general, whose office oversaw much of the education system — and by extension, the textbook question — found himself in a position to help friends who had good ideas for useful volumes or to offer advice to colleagues who hoped to break into the author corps.

During the 1890s, Maj. Tasker Bliss, now an aide to commanding general John Schofield, observed firsthand how greatly his access to the commander had increased his influence in matters of professional education and literature. One fruitful connection kept Bliss in constant contact with Lt. Arthur Wagner of the Infantry and Cavalry School faculty. Both men benefited from their professional relationship. Although the lieutenant frequently offered his perceptive insight and sound advice to Bliss on the specific textbook needs of army schools, he also made sure to apprise the major of the progress of his own literary endeavors.

Wagner encouraged Bliss to push especially hard for publication of textbooks on the art of war written from an American perspective. "The best foreign text books on the subject of minor tactics, while perhaps admirable in the main, generally contain something at variance with the lessons of our own wars, and contrary to the military ideas of our own people," Wagner explained.[51] The lieutenant, like other progressive reformers in the army, demanded an end to the day of the "Ireland army," led by "men whose military education was acquired in following the company swill cart."[52]

Wagner himself, of course, planned to contribute some of the new texts on the American way of war, but even an officer as well placed as he required great personal initiative and badgering to see his works in print. Shortly after completing his essay on the Battle of Königgrätz, and at Bliss's suggestion, Wagner turned his prodigious energies to a small book on minor tactics.[53] Both men recognized the need for a text that not only examined important applications of the principles of war but also took into account the geographical conditions that made North American warfare different from fighting in Europe. Wagner realized that in 1890 the concept was still a novel one. "Some enthusiastic Prusso-maniacs would have us draw all our tactical lessons from '66 or '70, instead of allowing us to take at least *some* from '64–'65," Wagner groused to Bliss.[54]

By attracting the interest of influential officers such as Gens. Thomas Ruger and Wesley Merritt, Wagner was guaranteed formal War Department acceptance of his work upon its publication in 1892.[55] Formal endorsement did not mean, however, that the War Department underwrote the cost of publication. Wagner was informed that the press at the Infantry and Cavalry School could not print the book; working with a civilian publisher, Col. Edward Townsend explained, would allow Wagner greater control over binding, typeface, and other fine details.[56] The lieutenant received little but moral support for his important work, even though he had announced his intention to sign over the copyright of his book on minor tactics to the War Department. Wagner was not writing for personal reasons: "If I can produce a satisfying work, I do not care even to consider the question of financial gain."[57]

Wagner is far better known today for two additional books that also became standard works throughout the U.S. Army school system. Both *The Service of Security and Information* (1893) and *Organization and Tactics* (1895) were updated by the author every few years, and the periodic revisions were continued by some of Wagner's students after he died in 1905. The two texts replaced European works on those subjects, and, additionally, they stressed the American military experience over that of Continental armies.

In *The Service of Security and Information*, Wagner sought only to "select the best established theories of European tactical authorities, illustrate them by a reference to events in our own military history, and to apply to them the touchstone of American practice in war."[58] Wagner viewed the two elements of security and information as essential aspects of safe leadership. A commander needed to know about the geography, topography, and resources of a theater of operations. He also needed reliable information about the strength, composition, movements, and morale of the enemy forces. American military history revealed many instances when officers of the U.S.

Army erred badly in security matters, Wagner argued, and such carelessness was no longer compatible with the new command philosophy adopted by its officer corps. Peacetime military planning, the hallmark of a modernized professional army, rested on a serious commitment to gathering information at all times.

Like much army professional military literature in the late nineteenth century, Wagner's books were as much a plea for the future as they were an analysis of the past. During the Mexican War, the United States was so short of fundamental information on Mexico's geography that one of Zachary Taylor's missions on the march to Monterrey was to find out whether or not the resources of the region could support a force of six thousand men. Even during the Civil War, accurate maps were so rare that "reconnaissances, frequently under fire, proved the only trustworthy sources of information."[59]

Wagner hoped the specter of past mistakes would force the U.S. Army to take its information-gathering service more seriously. The War Department was not entirely blind to the army's organizational shortcomings and was already taking steps to remedy the problem. In the 1890s, the Military Information Division became an integral part of The Adjutant General's Office.[60]

Wagner used a great deal of imagination in his work. Unlike Bigelow, who stressed the importance of strict adherence to the principles of war, Wagner used illustrations from American campaigns to demonstrate the importance of an army officer's personal initiative in the applications of military axioms. He liked to present the full range of options open to a commander. Depending on his mission, an officer conducting a reconnaissance might use an infantry or cavalry patrol; again, under specific circumstances, a patrol of cyclists or even an observation balloon might be a better choice. Balloons, in particular, intrigued Wagner because of their ability to intimidate an enemy as well as to gather information. He agreed with Confederate general E. Porter Alexander that the Army of the Potomac had made a serious mistake when it gave up its balloons just before the Gettysburg campaign.[61]

Specific guidelines bothered Wagner so much that he refused to give them in some cases. In any special reconnaissance, "a good rule in one case might be a fatal guide in another."[62] In stressing the intangibles of war and the uniqueness of events, Wagner, far more than Bigelow, adopted the literary pattern of many Continental writers who preferred not to set down maxims but to allow principles to emerge from the historical narrative.[63]

For many American officers, Wagner's books offered a treasure trove of information about American military history. Wagner gave considerable attention to the genuine security blunders in American military history. He could not fathom the surprise of Grant's Union forces at Shiloh; to Wagner, it was really little more than common sense to keep heavy patrols well ahead of the main body of an army while marching in enemy territory. He also devoted considerable space to the recruiting and handling of spies—"A spy must always be well paid"—and made some preliminary comments on the special nature of scouting by Indians, contrasting the infantry-style tactics of the Apaches with those of the well-mounted Sioux.[64].

Organization and Tactics, if anything, had a more wide-ranging historical focus than Wagner's other writings. "If an officer would prepare himself to be of service to his country, he must attentively consider the recorded experience of those who have learned war from the actual reality, and must accumulate by reading and reflection a fund of military knowledge based upon the experience of others," he wrote in his preface.[65] Again he stayed away from hard rules. Terrain and circumstances dictated decision making, and he believed the best-prepared soldier was he who studied wars that had been fought under geographical conditions most like those under which an American army was likely to fight.

As with most of his written work, in *Organization and Tactics*, Wagner strode away from traditional historical and military literary practices. He wanted to teach lessons with the didactic history-as-illustration methods of the army schools, but he did not want to compress into the pages of his books a pat system of rules and regulations and principles that always "worked."[66] He also developed a considerable awareness of those intangibles of war that caused friction or affected morale, and he investigated logistical and security concerns in their strategic applications beyond the battlefield.

As its title suggests, Wagner's second major work was an advanced, one-volume synopsis of army organization, including combat and auxiliary troops and the proper proportions of each. He devoted individual chapters to infantry, cavalry, and artillery in attack and defense. Coordinated actions involving artillery, cavalry, and infantry as well as the special problems of convoys also received Wagner's attention. Most unusual, however, were his three chapters devoted to historical sketches of infantry, cavalry, and artillery from the Middle Ages (or earlier) through the Russo-Turkish War. These essays were designed for individual perusal, not for formal classroom use, but Wagner was convinced that they were "a valuable feature of the book." The progress of his military thought in seeking "from the experience of the past a guide for the future" was undeniable.[67]

Unlike the professional resistance Bigelow's theoretical volume had met from army conservatives a few years earlier, both of Wagner's major books were greeted with nearly unrestrained praise by military men. *Organization and Tactics* was so popular that the *Cavalry Journal* printed most of its chapters verbatim.[68] Interpreting the demand for American textbooks as a good sign, Capt. W. A. Kobbe's comments in the *Journal of the U.S. Artillery* revealed the degree to which American professional opinion was turning against traditional European interpretations of the art of war. The captain was certain that Wagner's works would help officers "understand that the details of our profession vary as greatly with 'national characteristics' as do those of commerce and jurisprudence. Europe used to send us her castoffs. Fortunately we had men of cool head and stout heart who saw the lack of tradition meant absence of trammel [which] was clearly to our advantage."[69]

Wagner was the significant exception to the army's rule against granting official prepublication endorsement to an author's work. Although the War Department's financial commitment to his books remained minuscule, Wagner's scholarly reputation and his ties to Bliss and other important officers in Washington assured him special consideration, especially extended leaves of absence from his duty station, so he could complete his writing projects. Despite the War Department's ambivalence toward its military writers, however, sufficient numbers of army officers agreed that the development of a professional literature was too important an issue to wait for Washington to become more favorably disposed toward cultivating the art. They continued to publish with private firms and to take the financial risk themselves.

Not all officers who sought out private publishers for their works on the art of war fit the pattern that Wagner or Bigelow had helped to shape. Some soldiers who sympathized completely with the general goals of the military progressives did not feel comfortable with the army's trend toward the analysis of American campaigns and away from the traditional study of European battles. Capt. Herbert H. Sargent, in particular, felt such a strong commitment to the importance of studying all types of military history, not just the history of the U.S. Army, that he published at his own expense several important works on Napoleonic campaigns.[70] Although he did ask the War Department to guarantee a purchase of two hundred copies, Sargent also recognized that he was bucking the trend toward American military history, and so he was not surprised when he was refused official support.[71]

Sargent resented, but understood completely, one important aspect of the U.S. Army's growing interest in military history. American officers were increasingly well disposed to dissect past campaigns if lessons of immediate utility on the battlefield emerged at the end. Recent campaigns—those from 1861 to the present—seemed to offer the best opportunity for useful lessons.[72] Sargent disagreed. He believed Napoleon's operations demonstrated the proper use of military principles more clearly than any more modern campaign.[73]

Sargent's American reviewers expressed strong doubts about the captain's views on military history. They challenged him to stress Napoleon's "conspicuous luck" and not merely discuss "the supposed strategy."[74] As the more "scientific" among American officers agreed, Sargent's Great Man approach to military history was not particularly useful if the author only intended to describe Napoleon's "helter-skelter hits" and call those that succeeded "strategy." Such an approach clashed with the philosophy of safe leadership, which discounted the importance of personal genius in generalship.

Sargent, for his part, never ceased his crusade to resurrect the spirit of Napoleon. In 1907 he wrote to his friend Capt. Matthew Forney Steele to complain, "I think it is strange that Napoleon's Campaigns should be entirely neglected at Leavenworth. There is still, I think, more to be learned from a strategical point of view from the study of one of his masterly campaigns than from any other single campaign in history."[75]

Ironically, European military critics, unlike their American colleagues, greeted Sargent's little histories with rave reviews. British author William O'Connor Morris, a biographer of Napoleon, congratulated Sargent: "You beat us easily in military history." The *Army and Navy Gazette* of London ranked Sargent with Lord Wolseley, one of the most noted British military authors of the turn of the century, who, in a case of turnabout-is-fair-play, attracted considerable notice in the United States for his studies on the American Civil War.[76] On the strength of his reputation in Europe, Sargent's status as a military theorist grew so considerably from his works on Napoleon that shortly after the Army War College was established, a congressional delegation visited the War Department with a plan to create a chair of military strategy, on condition that only Sargent could fill it.[77]

By the outbreak of the Spanish-American War, several literary traditions coexisted among the army's growing corps of theorists. A small minority of traditionalists, like Sargent, found it difficult to break from the attraction of the European military experience. Many more, like Wagner and Bigelow, had been weaned from European military history to examine the principles of war as practiced in the United States. No matter whether an author was an "Americanist" or a "Europeanist," he invariably used historical example to illustrate a larger point. If much of their early work cannot stand up to the rigors of modern historical methods, they were no more guilty of abusing canons of objectivity than the American historians of the "nationalist" school, which also flourished in the 1890s.

For now, the various traditions were able to live together in peace and no one school of thought about the utility of the past won out over the others. When the War Department decided to allow American officers to write authoritatively about the performance of the U.S. Army in the Spanish-American War, even granting them access to official records not open to civilian scholars, the two officers whose works attracted the greatest official notice were Wagner, the Americanist, and Sargent, the Europeanist. Bigelow also helped to keep his literary reputation alive by writing his reminiscences of campaigning near Santiago.[78]

By the turn of the century, military writing on the art of war had become much more than the army's hobby. Although the War Department had not yet implemented organizational changes to facilitate and encourage the work of its authors, committed writers had found ways around the bureaucratic red tape to share their ideas on the art of war with their colleagues.

Most American soldiers were pleased to note that for the first time in their professional lives interest in the American military experience far outstripped more traditional European topics. The increased emphasis on the use of historical examples and on the detailed study of past events underscored to the army's advocates of professionalization, to educational reformers, and to postgraduate students that an important positive change was taking place. "American military methods of today as evinced in discussion, papers, essays, and periodicals are aggressive and independent, as we have finally cut off alien tutelage," Captain Kobbe asserted.[79] The new hobby, this cult of literature, heavily flavored with events from the annals of the American military past, helped to define both the theoretical basis for the professional status of the U.S. Army's officer corps and the corporate identity that follows from traditions held in common.

7

AMERICAN CAMPAIGNS:
THE U.S. ARMY'S FIRST
MILITARY HISTORY TEXTBOOK

"Military history has never been included in the general scheme of professional culture for officers of the military service. It never can be until . . . a textbook shall become available," wrote Capt. Matthew Forney Steele in 1908.[1] Intent on filling that gap, Steele wrote *American Campaigns*, the first military history textbook to be adopted throughout the U.S. Army postgraduate school system. From the time of its publication in 1909, *American Campaigns* stood the test of time so well that it was still in use in army classrooms well into World War II. Indeed, some Army Reserve and National Guard training centers did not give it up until the 1950s.[2]

The durability of *American Campaigns* as a textbook overshadows two of the work's important, but mixed, legacies for the fortunes of military history in officer training. Steele's project helped to overturn the conservative War Department publication policies that had discouraged many army authors from trying their hand at writing about the art of war. But in its tendency to use American military history to illustrate predetermined principles of warfare, Steele's book helped to perpetuate the deductive applicatory methods of teaching the art of war. Even at the time of its publication, *American Campaigns* represented a type of history rapidly falling into disfavor among disciples of the new scientific history, and the work's endurance implied to scholars in and out of uniform that the army was not entirely committed to meeting the standards of the modern historical methodology.

For all its drawbacks, *American Campaigns* filled a great need in American military literature. To complement the translations of European works that composed much of the professional reading in the army's postgraduate schools, U.S. Army officers desperately needed accurate studies of American military events to help them understand the distinctions between the styles of warfare on the Continent and in North America. American military historical literature was so thin that a list of recommended books for military libraries compiled in 1895 included only general histories of the United States written by civilians who had briefly considered military affairs in their broad-brush narratives. Francis Parkman and John Bach McMaster elicited great praise for their work on American colonial wars.[3] For officers who wanted to study the Civil War, Century's Battles and Leaders series, Scribner's Campaigns of the Civil War series, *The Official Records of the Union and Confederate Armies in the War of the Rebellion*, and the memoirs of Gens. Ulysses S. Grant, William T. Sherman, and Joseph E. Johnston received qualified recommendations.[4] Only John Codman Ropes won significant praise for his *The Story of the Civil War*, a work rated as one of the "highest excellence."[5] None of these volumes, however, offered soldiers who needed an objective, comprehensive account of American military affairs the kind of detailed information they had to have to evaluate command decisions. From its inception, *American Campaigns* was designed to fill this important void in "professional culture."

Matthew Forney Steele was typical of many reform advocates among the junior officers during the late nineteenth century. Steele admitted that his interest in attending the U.S. Military Academy at West Point was inspired solely by the opportunity for a free education. He graduated in the middle of the class of 1883, claiming years later, "I was mediocre in everything."[6] Although it is not clear exactly when Steele developed his strong interest in military history, his early career assignments forced him to give more than superficial attention to it. After an initial assignment at a post where "sobriety was not entirely the order of the day," Steele was reassigned to Fort Yates, where he found his inspiration to take his professional studies seriously: a commanding officer who required it. Once started down that path, he never turned back.

Buoyed by his tour at Fort Yates, Steele was quick to take up many causes important to army reformers. Several in particular seemed important to him. He endorsed setting rigorous entry requirements for officers commissioned directly from civilian life, the establishment of a postgraduate school system for officer education, and promotion based on merit instead of seniority.[7] He seemed especially interested in the creation of a professional military literature, and he frequently contributed short articles or editorial rejoinders for publication in the army's several service journals.[8]

Steele firmly believed "skillful and efficient men in the military profession, like the skillful and efficient man in any other profession, must know the theory and practice of his profession."[9] Like many of his contemporaries, he admired the Prussians, who had convinced him of the benefits of peacetime training. Although the Prussians had fought no major campaign for almost a half-century after Waterloo in 1815, the professionalism of the new generation of army officers, educated in the art of war in the classroom, had contributed decisively to victory in the wars of 1864, 1866, and 1870–71.

To Steele, the ambivalence of the American people and many in the military itself toward "booklearning, as they contemptuously call it," was not

only dangerous but also a major obstacle to the development of a professional spirit in the U.S. Army.[10] He had little use for officers who criticized
their colleagues for falling victim to "the fever for rushing into print" or for
those who wished that "the Cavalry Journal and all the other service magazines were in the place where it never freezes."[11] Such officers, Steele concluded, were "like rhumatism, they are one of the ills of the military service,
which one can escape only by an early death."[12] His heroes comprised a dis-
tinguished list of literate soldier-authors, including Xenophon, Caesar, Frederick the Great, Napoleon, and Grant, all of whom were ideal officers because they had learned to "think when they write."[13]

Steele's philosophy on military reading and writing emerged long before
he started *American Campaigns* and strongly influenced his approach to that
project. Despite his commitment to promoting the intellectual ability of the
officer corps and his enthusiasm for the army's "new hobby," he also worried
about the potential dangers if the new trend was embraced excessively. "Will
captains be reduced if they can't write an essay if the literary craze con-
tinues?" he wondered.[14] Steele did not believe that reading Jomini and Ham-
ley should alone declare a soldier suitable for high command "whether he
can ride his own horse over a ditch, or no, whether he can command his
troop or platoon at squadron drill or no."[15] For Steele, time spent in professional reading must be profitable; it must either provide definite information
or offer recreation. Idle reading beyond these objectives was time wasted and
could turn "recreation into dissipation. That is true whether his dissipation
takes the form of overindulgence in reading or overindulgence in strong
drink."[16] Steele was determined to write a book that met his idea of the
model military text, one that presented briefly and concisely both the theories of military art and science and their practical applications.

The army's recognition of its need for a book like *American Campaigns* surfaced even before Steele received assignment to the faculty of the Department of Tactics at the Leavenworth schools in the fall of 1904. He joined
an academic department undergoing a rigorous self-evaluation designed
to improve the quality of theoretical instruction in its courses in military
strategy. The centrality of military history to the new curriculum seemed con-
firmed when Commandant J. Franklin Bell wrote in his 1904 annual report:
For a "serviceable and adequate idea of strategy . . . [m]aps are requisite to
the subject, and it is so interwoven with military history that the two are
inseparable."[17]

The faculty's inability to find an appropriate text troubled them, however.
Col. Arthur Wagner, acting as Bell's assistant commandant, believed even
Jomini and Clausewitz would approve of the new course of instruction, be-
cause "the plain fact of the matter is that . . . [the old course] is taken *verbatim*

et literatim from the chapter headings of a small book on strategy which is at the same time too brief and too advanced to use as a satisfactory text-book." He wanted a book to suit a new course of instruction that would be "less abstruse and more practical than before."[18]

Other officers had more precise demands for the new textbook. Many education reformers believed it was wrong to teach American officers more about European military history than about the campaigns of their own armed forces. Students in the Class of 1904, for example, had studied only about Vicksburg, Atlanta, and the 1862 Peninsula campaigns from the Civil War, while devoting considerably more time to dissecting Novara, Ulm, Napoleon's 1796 Italian campaign, Königgrätz, Messena's retreat at Torres Vedras, Metz and Sedan, and Plevna.[19] Writing on behalf of the faculty of the Tactics Department at the Leavenworth schools, Maj. Eben Swift argued that officers in the U.S. Army must learn the history of American wars first and only then the developments in world military history since 1866.[20]

With Wagner's blessing, Swift implemented his plans to Americanize the offerings of the tactics department. For his part, Steele developed a series of lectures on American military campaigns originally slated for delivery to first-year students in the School of the Line. By 1906 he had developed a series of stereopticon views of the successive stages of battles and campaigns to accompany the lectures.[21] Until Swift succeeded in introducing historical research methods into the advanced curriculum of the Staff College, Steele's lectures served students in both the School of the Line and the second-year course.

After the plans for a source-method research course received formal approval, Swift's successor, Col. John Morrison, remained sufficiently impressed by Steele's ability to explain the basic events of American military history that he did not want to discard the captain's lectures. In early 1908 he suggested that Steele publish his lectures so that officers who did not attend the more prestigious professional army schools could enjoy the benefits of his concise explanations of major events in American military history.[22] The result of Morrison's suggestion was the writing of *American Campaigns*.

The support and sponsorship of so influential an army educator as Morrison, however, did not smooth the path to publication. Steele fell prey to many of the Old Army's attitudes toward all but the most technical military writing by its officers. Throughout much of the publication process, even for a book deemed so necessary by army educators, the degree to which Steele himself handled each aspect of the printing and illustrating of *American Campaigns* recalled the dogged efforts of John Bigelow and other military authors who had personally underwritten the costs of their works.

In the end, however, Steele's book became a landmark in the army's encouragement of its authors. When the General Staff and the War Department finally accepted primary responsibility for the publication of *American Campaigns*, the army's substantial financial commitments to the project went far beyond a promise to buy a predetermined number of copies from a private publishing house. Unlike Wagner, Bigelow, and other earlier writers, Steele did not need to worry about taking a steep personal financial loss if his book did not sell well. Moreover, since his work filled an acknowledged need and could count on a ready audience at the service schools, the War Department's risk was equally small. Still, Washington's official interest in Steele's work was an important test of the War Department's commitment to officer education and military professionalism.

Steele originally intended to publish in one volume all thirty-four of his lectures from the School of the Line's strategy and military geography and history course, but his plans underwent many important alterations along the way. At Colonel Morrison's suggestion, Steele first decided to limit his book to the twenty-six lectures on American military campaigns he had already prepared and to add one original chapter on the Santiago campaign of the Spanish-American War.[23] Even with the deletion of eight lectures, Steele estimated his book would reach 243,000 words, or 675 pages.[24] The elimination of several lectures on recent African and Asian conflicts in which American troops were not involved and for which complete data were unavailable made for a tighter final product: a book suitable for classroom use that addressed the single theme of American campaigns.

Cutting back on the number of lectures allowed Steele to give substantially more attention to a special feature that nearly every military student considered essential: the inclusion of maps for every stage of each campaign. Steele determined that to explain the twenty-seven campaigns he had chosen, he needed at least 355 separate plates.[25] His decision to include so many maps forced him to make a second major departure from his original plan. In its final form, *American Campaigns* comprised two volumes—one for the text and one for the plates—to make it easy to read about the battle and to see the appropriate maps at the same time.

In early 1908 Steele received the go-ahead to proceed with his writing.[26] Working at "high steam pressure," he buried himself in his writing even before final official permission was granted by the War Department.[27] But he could not foresee how rocky the path to final publication would become in the next year. Since previous authors had been able to write without interference from Washington, Steele apparently did not expect his project to attract the unprecedented attention of the War Department. For the better part of a year, to his displeasure, the captain found himself attempting to reconcile the department's decisions with his own ideas on how best to handle the publication of his book.

Initially, Steele apparently intended to follow the practice of other army authors and find on his own a reputable publishing house to handle his work. He decided to do this to guarantee his ability to remain objective in his writing, not because he felt he had no other options. "Since no one can discuss any of our wars without cri[ti]cizing our wretched military policy, and as no one can discuss the operations of the Civil War without saying something uncomplimentary of certain high functionaries, like Halleck and Mr. Stanton—that is, no one can unless he shuts his eyes to the truth of history," it was probably "better that any publication involving any suspicion of criticism of a public official or department, even though it referred to a time already passed into the National history, should not be issued as a public document."[28]

The major drawback to contracting with a publishing house to print a work like the one Steele envisioned was the high price of production. This bothered him. He stood firm in his desire that every officer should be able to afford his book.[29] Indeed, his severest headaches during the publication of *American Campaigns* arose from the economic side of the project, when either he or the War Department attempted to keep the work's cost down while maintaining its high quality and utility.

As Steele quickly found out, the plates for the maps accompanying the text, not the lectures themselves, provided most of the economic stumbling blocks. If a publishing house itself had designed the necessary maps, the price of the final volume would have been prohibitive. Moreover, Steele was not sure a civilian mapmaker could be counted on to include all the necessary terrain features that might be crucial for an audience of military men.[30] Although the services of a draftsman from the Corps of Engineers was available to him, Steele did not have time to order a specially executed set of maps.

To resolve his dilemma, Steele wrote to the publishers of the histories that contained the best maps he could find and asked for permission to use them in *American Campaigns*. He flattered, cajoled, and tempted G. P. Putnam's, the Century Company, and Houghton Mifflin, among others, to grant him permission to use the plates of maps from books they had published.[31] When they balked and asked payment for the privilege of using their maps, Steele tried to convince the publishers of the long-term benefits they would enjoy if they cooperated with him. "I feel sure that the publication of these lectures, and the use that is to be made of them in the educational scheme of the army, will, in the end, be the means of returning to you a far greater amount than you ask for the privilege of reproducing your illustrations."[32] Steele hoped the potential for increasing the sales of other books to the army service schools might convince the publishers that granting permission to use their maps was good business.

His tactics worked. By May 1908 Steele had received authorization to use the maps he wanted from all but one or two publishers.[33] By June he believed finding the heirs of Cadmus Wilcox to get permission to use maps from his history of the Mexican War was the only major obstacle still facing him.[34] He had reason for optimism. His attempts to polish his essays had progressed so well that except for the original chapter on the Santiago campaign, he was able to send off the bulk of the text to the War Department for review by the General Staff.[35]

To his dismay, Steele found his problems were far from over. Early in June, Capt. M. F. Davis informed Steele that the General Staff wanted *American Campaigns* to be published by the government to keep the price down. The War Department had rejected as too high a prepublication estimate by Scribner's, the New York firm with whom Steele had apparently struck a deal.

When Davis informed Steele of the General Staff's decision, he outlined the special problems the army faced when dealing with the works of its authors in uniform. If the General Staff distributed Steele's book at no cost as it did other public documents, it could not guarantee an adequate supply to meet the demands of the schools. On the other hand, if Steele's work were to be printed by a private concern and then adopted as an official textbook by the General Staff, Davis could not guarantee the number of copies the War Department would buy. In the past, the department had ordered books as needed in lots of one hundred to five hundred. Only in rare cases, as with Wagner's *Security and Information*, did the government buy as many as two thousand copies.[36] Since Wagner's books were used both in army service schools and by the National Guard, the department did not lose money by purchasing so many copies. On other occasions, however, it had not been so lucky; thus the War Department was searching for a new way to finance the publication of necessary texts.[37]

While Steele tried to fit indexing and writing a preface into his regular schedule of duties, including a staff ride to the Civil War battlefields in the eastern theater, the War Department believed it had found a tentative solution to the publication problem.[38] First, it decided that the department should pay the printing costs. As "the only suitable text-book on the subject," *American Campaigns* was deemed "absolutely necessary in [the] military education of officers in the army and National Guard," and as such, it should be seen as part of the "ordinary business" of the War Department.[39] When the Government Printing Office estimated that printing five thousand copies of *American Campaigns* would cost $9,327.85, however, the chief of staff discovered that the high price prohibited the War Department from printing the book without congressional approval. This was a restriction imposed by the General Deficiency Act of March 3, 1905.[40] The project had run into yet another unexpected snag.

The War Department would not be undermined so easily, however. When the secretary of war asked the comptroller of the Treasury Department to look for alternative funding paths, he was told that Steele's project might be considered to be the business of the General Staff instead of the War Department.[41] The distinction was a subtle one, but it could resolve the funding problem. If a request for funds was forwarded to the White House from the army itself rather than from an executive department, the president of the United States could order the printing of the book through the Emergency Fund, War Department Act, approved on March 3, 1899. When President William H. Taft signed the necessary papers, the next hurdle to publication had been conquered.[42]

With the funding problem resolved, the War Department next considered who actually should print the volumes. The Government Printing Office could print only official public documents, and the department preferred not to grant Steele's volumes such status before they were in use in the schools. Moreover, if the book was designated a public document, the printing office would be required to make it available to any citizen who requested a copy. The War Department then would have no guarantee that the printer's supply would meet the army's demand.

To maintain greater control over the work's distribution, the War Department decided to accept bids from private firms to print and bind one thousand copies of *American Campaigns*. In October 1908 the department finally signed a contract with Byron S. Adams, a local printer, who offered to provide the needed bound copies for $5,400.[43] As a final show of support for the author, the War Department delayed Steele's transfer to active duty in the Philippines and assigned him to the Army War College to allow him to complete the proofreading, indexing, and other details while in close contact with the printer.[44]

American Campaigns's complicated route from lecture notes to printed book heralded a significant departure in army publishing. Authors in uniform who followed Steele had a War Department precedent that, although not guaranteeing support for any specific project, at least offered them encouragement to prepare manuscripts that filled specific needs in the army's school system.

For a book described as "absolutely necessary," however, the postpublication history of *American Campaigns* is a checkered one. Although many officers greeted the volumes with genuine approval, a significant few noted that the captain's work represented the narrative and applicatory approaches to military history that faculty at the Staff College and School of the Line were already trying to transcend. Nonetheless, for the first time, American officers had readily available chapter-length treatments of the colonial wars, the Revolutionary War's northern and southern campaigns, the War of 1812, Taylor's and Scott's campaigns in Mexico, nineteen Civil War campaigns, and the Spanish-American War, all designed specifically for a military audience.

As a history textbook, *American Campaigns* has been described as a "tossed salad."[45] Steele espoused no single historical philosophy. In fact, he often fell under the sway of historians who attracted him primarily because their arguments were different from those appearing in many standard histories. He stayed away from much important primary source material, most notably the one hundred twenty-seven volumes of *The Official Records of the Union and Confederate Armies in the War of the Rebellion*, ostensibly because he feared he "might yield to the temptation to read on, from one report to another, far beyond the time I have had to spare."[46]

The captain's eclecticism led him down some unusual, and seldom traveled, intellectual paths. When he wrote about the campaigns of the American Revolution, for example, he found himself drawn to the works of Sydney George Fisher, a scholar of the emerging "empire school" who broke out "of the usual rut of American historians, and gives us a view of the quarrel from the Englishman's side as well as from the American's."[47] He viewed the traditionally slighted southern campaigns of Gen. Nathanael Greene during the American Revolution as "more brilliant, from a strategic point of view, than any other operations of Americans or British in this war."[48] When he considered Lee's performance at Gettysburg, Steele again tried to buck tradition; he was among the first to accept many of the critical assessments suggested by former Confederate artilleryman E. Porter Alexander, whose "most scientific and scholarly" memoirs presented a strong challenge to the postwar southern apologists for the defeat of the Lost Cause.[49]

In just as many cases, however, Steele merely reiterated uncritically the interpretations of other historians or used their arguments to make a pitch for a special cause he advocated. His beliefs in the need for a professional officer corps and military preparedness and his disdain for the inefficacy of political interference in army affairs often lay just under the surface of his historical narratives. George Washington, for one, thoroughly amazed Steele. "Our history has chosen well in making Washington the hero of the war. . . . It is not hard, however, to point out mistakes made by Washington; it is strange that he made no more," Steele wrote, in a plea for more intensive officer training. If the general had been a student of military history, Steele argued, he would not have split his forces so frequently around New York City. Only British general Howe's timidity prevented disaster.[50] Steele attributed the poor American military performance during the War of 1812 to "lack of preparedness, – to bad legislation," and reminded American citizens that "the man that votes and makes the legislators" must heed the lessons of this war.[51]

Steele devoted the bulk of *American Campaigns* to the Civil War, and in these commentaries he made his most pointed critiques. The essays reveal, however, the fundamental problem that plagued students who later relied so strongly on Steele's book. The captain generally did not provide a set of principles of war to guide or provide comprehensiveness to his chapters. He referred casually to a specific Napoleonic maxim when it helped him to make a point, but even this he did sparingly. Only once, in discussing Stonewall Jackson's generalship, did he outline as many as six maxims, and then he admitted there was nothing magical about any of them. He had drawn three of them from an article by former Confederate general John D. Imboden and three from Jackson's military biographer, G. F. R. Henderson.[52] Each essay, then, tended to illustrate one or two fundamental points that Steele wanted to drive home. In no case did he attempt a comprehensive analysis in which he demonstrated correct and incorrect applications of all the interrelated principles of war.

Steele's treatment of the Battle of Shiloh offers a case in point. "The campaign and battle of Shiloh are the hardest of all the campaigns and battles of the Civil War for the student to solve. . . . It is not hard for the student to find abundant faults. It is only hard for him to fix the responsibility for them."[53] In response to the U.S. Army's new interest in inculcating a spirit of safe leadership among the members of its officer corps, Steele focused almost exclusively on mistakes in tactical and strategic decision making at Shiloh. Union generals Henry W. Halleck and U. S. Grant failed to maintain the momentum that followed the victories at Forts Henry and Donelson and threw away another chance to defeat the South after the Confederate army retreated from Shiloh. Grant seriously neglected his troops' security arrangements, and his men were surprised and nearly defeated as a result of his oversight. The most severe problem, Steele argued, was "that neither hostile army on that day was *commanded* in fact." Grant was not even on the field for the first few hours of the battle, and Confederate commander Albert Sidney Johnston was killed in the front lines "doing the work of a brigadier."[54]

What was rarely clear in Steele's critiques, however, was exactly which lesson he intended to impart. Although informing his readers that he blamed poor generalship for the conduct of the Battle of Shiloh, he did not tie in the impact of other important tangibles and intangibles over which the generals had no control. Each side suffered from poor maps, rough terrain that limited the use of cavalry and artillery, confusing command structures and other organizational problems, severe straggling, and—most important— green troops. When Steele concluded that Shiloh showed what happened when a raw army was put into action too soon, he had changed his focus completely to stress one of the intangibles of war that the best tactical generalship in the world could not overcome.[55]

Students in the various army schools who were among the first to try to untangle Steele's sometimes convoluted and confusing narratives still seemed to appreciate the captain's efforts. In January 1910 students at the Leavenworth schools received paperbound copies of American Campaigns, which they were supposed to turn in at the end of the course. An administrator later reported that so many of the students had rebound their paperback copies to make them more substantial and had written and taken notes in them that they had to be charged for altering their books in an unauthorized manner.[56] From the Army War College in Washington, Capt. Malin Craig wrote to Steele that the members of the Class of 1910 had taken American Campaigns on their tour of Civil War battlefields. "We have finished the Virginia ride, had a bully good time, and to a man have tested out your 'American Campaigns' with the result that we all wonder how in the dickens you ever were able to produce it."[57]

The military preparedness movement that preceded World War I further enhanced the popularity of Steele's book. By 1913 Regular Army officers and the National Guard had exhausted the original printing of American Campaigns, and the War Department received authority to spend $6,299.00 for three thousand more copies.[58] The War College Division of the General Staff received so many requests from congressmen for copies of Steele's work that by December 1913 it simply referred such requests directly to Byron Adams, who continued to hold the contract for the book.[59]

The printer knew a sound business venture when he saw one. He asked the War College Division for a list of all military and patriotic organizations and colleges so he could send out a circular to advertise American Campaigns to an even wider audience.[60] When he received a list of schools with professors of military science and a suggestion that he contact the adjutant generals of each state, Adams went one step further and designed an advertisement to be placed in selected professional journals and popular publications.[61]

By November 1914 American Campaigns was in such short supply that Gen. M. M. Macomb began to refuse congressmen's requests for copies. "If the Army is too generous there wouldn't be enough left for its needs." After September 1, 1914, Macomb decided, no more than one copy would be furnished to each congressman on the ground that army appropriations were not to be used to fund publications for nonmilitary personnel. Macomb encouraged Congressman J. W. Bryan, one of the officials who was refused additional copies of *American Campaigns*, to introduce a bill in Congress to fund the printing of twenty thousand additional copies to be scattered throughout the nation.[62] By 1916 it became necessary to limit the distribution of the work even more severely; only officers on active duty could receive a copy of Steele's book unless special instructions to the contrary were issued by the War Department.[63]

Despite the great demand for *American Campaigns*, reviewers from the army's professional journals greeted the work with measured, if not effusive, praise. The *Cavalry Journal* thanked Steele for his book, noting that "the service needed a text to ferret out the facts, written by a military man, with lessons in a compact form that can be carried to the Philippines or Alaska." Admitting that "the study of our own military experiences can hardly be termed our favorite professional pursuit," the reviewer believed time, not indifference, had been the primary obstacle to historical study. Steele's book was "tangible evidence" that an officer's "veil of ignorance" could be lifted, especially if the volumes were used in garrison schools and not just at the army's senior schools. If *American Campaigns* could "awaken a spirit of inquiry among the younger officers" and stimulate independent investigation, "it would accomplish its highest mission."[64]

Like the *Cavalry Journal*, the editors of the *Journal of the United States Artillery* and the *Infantry Journal* lauded Steele's work. The separate volume of maps was its "most valuable and unusual feature." The artilleryman who reviewed the work for his branch's journal commented that "Major Steele has done for American Campaigns what Colonel Dodge has done for Alexander the Great, Hannibal, Caesar, and Gustavus."[65]

A disquieting note, however, came from the *Army and Navy Journal*, which noted that Steele showed insufficient acquaintance with documentary records, especially regarding the Spanish-American War.[66] For his brief supplementary essay on the conflict of 1898, Steele had relied heavily upon the work of his friend Capt. H. H. Sargent while paying less attention to equally important works by Arthur Wagner and John Bigelow. Sargent's book had been widely criticized for its repetition and excessive historical illustration, and Steele fell into the pit dug by his friend.[67]

For the small number of officer-educators who advocated teaching historical methods to students in the postgraduate schools, the *Army and Navy Journal*'s criticism pointed out the most nagging problem of traditional history instruction in professional training. A work like Steele's reinforced overreliance on deductive reasoning and memorization. More useful to the service were officers who were trained to use their analytical abilities and who would react more intelligently to new situations than those soldiers who only memorized their textbooks for an exam. For these well-educated officers, the publication of Steele's *American Campaigns* was best viewed not as an end but as a beginning toward even greater intellectual development. With the availability of a reference book such as Steele's, some army educators predicted a time when the lecture format of the military history course in the School of the Line could be abandoned and replaced by independent projects based on intensive, original research that adhered to the standards of historical scholarship at civilian universities.

In his 1908 annual report, issued before Steele's book was printed, Colonel Morrison recommended that in the future, each candidate for the School of the Line must pass an examination on the battles discussed in *American Campaigns* before he would be admitted. Junior officers could master the material in Steele's book while still in the garrison schools at their duty stations, which Morrison believed would not cause them undue stress. "There are a few things in the course that one can learn as well at his station as here and this should be required."[68] If this recommendation was approved, the School of the Line's history lectures could be replaced by additional theoretical course work in the art of war.

Morrison continued to advocate an end to the history lecture course for the class of 1910–11 once the material became generally available with the publication of Steele's book.[69] By 1911 *American Campaigns* had been relegated to the reference shelf at the Leavenworth schools, especially at the Staff College, where course work in military history had turned to the source method of instruction. Almost as soon as Steele's book appeared in print, then, its chief slot in the army's school system was eliminated.

American Campaigns contributed far less to the professional education of officers in the U.S. Army than Steele and his War Department backers had originally hoped it would. When trouble broke out along the Mexican border and affairs in Europe boiled over into World War I, historical studies were among the first courses dropped from the army school curriculum to allow officers to return to their active duty stations. What the army now needed was information on the recent developments in European military and diplomatic affairs, subjects that had been relegated to the scrap heap since American officers had demanded greater attention to the study of the history of the United States.

The needs of the army had changed so suddenly and so dramatically that when in 1917 printer Byron Adams asked the War Department if it was likely to need more copies of *American Campaigns* for the army's expanding officer corps, he was told that "French warfare is the leading study at present." He was encouraged, however, to fund the printing of a new edition himself. Although the War Department would consider it "a matter of serious consequence to the military establishment from a military stand point-of-view, were this valuable work to become unavailable," it was apparent that it had terminated its financial commitment to *American Campaigns*.[70]

The War Department's stand only reflected *American Campaigns's* dwindling value in the eyes of Regular Army officers. After its highly touted beginnings, the work failed more and more frequently to live up to the standards of the historical scholarship taught in the army schools. At the Army War College, the Class of 1915 heard *American Campaigns* damned with faint praise as "a valuable skeleton for any work on the Civil War. The fact that a few errors and inaccuracies have crept into it does not detract from its value."[71] Future critics would not be so kind. In 1922 Maj. Conrad Lanza of the Historical Section of the Army War College recommended formally that *American Campaigns* be replaced by a more accurate work.[72] "A republication of this volume would not be suitable to modern methods of the scientific teaching of history," he reported to The Adjutant General after he represented the army at the American Historical Association's national convention.[73] Throughout the 1920s the Historical Section considered writing a new general history of American military affairs specifically to replace Steele's book.[74]

American Campaigns enjoyed far more lasting appeal among the many American civilians interested in military preparedness and among those who served as part-time soldiers in the National Guard. Capt. M. H. Taulbee of the First Infantry Regiment of the Oklahoma National Guard was among the first to adopt Steele's volumes for use in the correspondence school for its citizen-soldiers; he wrote Steele that he had been unsuccessful in finding such a useful treatise until the War Department provided him with copies of *American Campaigns*.[75] John F. McGee, a self-proclaimed student of military history, praised Steele for remedying the most common problems contained in the majority of writing on army affairs. Military history, wrote McGee, "is made up largely of fulsome eulogy resting on a foundation of falsehood."[76] Steele must have been pleased when McGee promised that from then on, whenever he wanted the truth about American military affairs, he would rely not only on his old standby, John Codman Ropes, but on the captain's work as well. Since Ropes was one of Steele's own favorite historians, he must have enjoyed being ranked with such august company.

The popularity of *American Campaigns* in military organizations outside the active service extended through World War II. Late in 1939, Farrand Sayre, one of Steele's former colleagues on the faculty of the Leavenworth schools, wrote him that "I have found many militia and reserve officers are acquainted with your book 'American Campaigns,' which is still a standard authority."[77] The U.S. Infantry Association thought highly enough of the work to finance its republication in 1943 so it would be available to instruct officer candidates during World War II.[78]

Steele also found vehement critics among his civilian readers, some of whom took exception to the captain's version of historical events. Nowhere was this more true than in cases when Steele passed harsh judgment on an ancestor of a family sensitive to such slights. In 1937 Confederate general John C. Pemberton's grandson tried to convince Steele that he had judged the southern commander's actions at Vicksburg far too harshly. After the Vicksburg National Military Park was opened in 1937, the younger Pemberton discovered that the official interpretation of events was drawn from Steele's text. Providing copies of family papers, including a letter from Jefferson Davis in which he accepted personal responsibility for the loss of Vicksburg, Pemberton's grandson asked Steele to reconsider his original views. He hoped the evidence he supplied would get Steele to change "the opinions you set forth in 1909 in your cruel and brutally damning study of General Pemberton."[79] Steele was sympathetic to the man's strong feelings, but he would not budge from his initial opinions.

The importance of this single book, one of hundreds of volumes authored by soldiers in that first great flowering of professional literature, stems from both its unique contribution to the U.S. Army's intellectual development and the War Department's institutional response to its publication. In its narrative form with commentary designed to illustrate standard principles rather than to discover new ones, American Campaigns exemplified the first strand of historical consciousness to emerge in the U.S. Army. In many ways, it also culminated the pre–World War I expression of that intellectual strand. In its time, it was the only comprehensive work available to officers or academic scholars who desired an analysis of American military affairs from a professional soldier's perspective. In that respect, it deserved the prepublication financial consideration the War Department gave it. Warts and all, it filled an important gap in the professional literature of the time and provided soldiers with an unprecedented source of basic military information to lay the groundwork for their advanced studies in the art of war.

The War Department's considerable involvement in the publication of American Campaigns revealed an important change in its attitude toward professional military writing. In its handling of the printing of Steele's work, the department set a precedent that enhanced the role of military history in professional education. Few would equal Steele's success, but it was important for military authors to know that if they could interest the War Department in a high-quality project that met a perceived army need, a procedure existed to consider its publication without granting it official status and a long-term commitment to its use.[80]

American Campaigns and the army's commitment to support works of this kind also help to explain the scholarly community's poor image of the intellectual quality of much military history. Steele's volumes appeared precisely when civilian academicians rejected the subjective historical narrative for in-depth, objective studies based on primary research and high standards of scholarship. Still, Captain Steele provided a factual account that was both fairly accurate and full of useful history-by-illustration for soldiers who frequently had neither time nor inclination to learn the academics' methods. For an army that for years had held deep-seated suspicions of book learning—indeed, still held them to some degree—the publication of *American Campaigns* was a far more important step than its brief and sometimes stormy history suggests.

8

A FIRST ATTEMPT
AT OFFICIAL HISTORY

"Can we afford to continue any longer to neglect the use of History as a means of teaching American War?" asked the editors of the *Infantry Journal* in 1912. Progressive soldiers realized that the study of past campaigns could do more than illustrate principles of strategy and tactics in the classroom. They believed American military history could also provide the foundation of a badly needed national conception of war, a common military doctrine that permeated the army "through and through with the teaching of the general staff."[1] For many advocates of military reform, "official histories" of the nation's past wars, sponsored by the General Staff, could fill this gap in the professional development of the officer corps.

Never had the American army so desperately needed its General Staff to take a strong stand on the myriad of professional controversies. Since the reform impulse began in the late 1870s, the army's authors had produced such a rich and sizable literature on important military issues that some foreign observers were astonished by the quantity of solid work emanating from the small peacetime American officer corps.[2] Before the turn of the century, at least, the War Department encouraged these literary debates by refusing to extend its formal approval to any single author's ideas. By the second decade of the twentieth century, however, the flood of military literature had rendered nearly impossible the task of separating the wheat from the chaff. To find a way out of this literary chaos, the U.S. Army's General Staff decided to follow the practice of the Germans, the French, and, most recently, the British, and experiment with writing its own official histories of the wars of the United States. This would give the General Staff a stronger hand in inculcating its officers with an American philosophy of warfare.[3]

Although the General Staff entered into the work with enthusiasm in 1912, the U.S. Army's first attempt to produce an official history failed. Both institutional resistance and intellectual questions about the validity of the concept of "official history" plagued the project from the start. The institutional problems offered genuine challenges to the successful completion of this ambitious project. The General Staff could not extend its solid support to the research effort so long as its own future remained vulnerable to the whims of a vacillating Congress.[4] The army's personnel policy requiring officers to return to active troop command after a maximum of four years of staff duty worked against continuity in the research and writing efforts required for sound historical studies. As international affairs heated up in 1914, the few overextended officers on staff duty had little time to take on historical research.

The writing of official history raised other questions as well. Even in army circles, the potential for tampering with objectivity and accuracy in government-sponsored history drew fire even from some who ranked among the service's strongest advocates of studying the past. The availability of only a small number of officers who had more than cursory training in historical methods bothered many critics of the project. More important to the failure of the official history project, however, were the great number of historical and intraservice questions that remained unanswered. Until the General Staff settled these issues, there would be no intellectual or doctrinal framework for an official history of any American war.

Although it was the General Staff's responsibility to decide these important questions, the officers it assigned to oversee the writing of official histories did not know the dimensions of the challenges facing them. They frequently came to their staff assignments from different arms of the service, and their diverse backgrounds in education and experience gave them widely varying perspectives on key army controversies. Thus, they were unlikely to reach consensus easily on important strategic and tactical issues that had to be resolved before those views could be included in an official history. When the General Staff proved unable to find the common ground on which to build a comprehensive American military doctrine, the army's initial plunge into official history faltered and then died prematurely in 1916.

The life of the army's first official history project might not have been so short if it had not generated so much controversy in army and civilian circles. Many progressive officers recognized the need for an authoritative voice in military matters, but even they could see only limited uses for official histories. "The professional fitness of our officers is best advanced by a study of a correct history of our past campaigns in war," Maj. James W. McAndrew asserted, but he believed these studies sponsored by the General Staff were best restricted to use in army classrooms. Still, he hoped well-trained civilian historians would gain confidence in the accuracy of the army's official histories and would use them carefully in their own works. In that way, the American people were more likely to come to understand military affairs.[5]

Other American soldiers harbored doubts about official history because they knew how the historical sections of foreign armies had abused the concept. Even those American officers most inclined to support the project found much to criticize in the histories produced by foreign armies. Capt. Arthur L. Conger lambasted the vaunted German General Staff for its pronounced tendency to publish historical works that "displayed the strongest partisanship, as well as every pretext . . . for justifying the German military system," even when analyzing foreign conflicts in which it had not participated such as the Boer War. The bias in the German historical section's works was so well known, he continued, that "[Germany's] high officers understand quite well the lack of value of the official history and look elsewhere when they wish to study their own wars."[6]

The door against official history was not entirely closed. Conger, for one, seemed confident that American soldiers would avoid the objectivity problems that marred the Germans' historical works. The "best safeguard" against incompetent officers or men assigned to the duty "for political reasons" lay in forging a close alliance with professional historians in the American Historical Association.[7] Academicians who had helped to build the American army's history program in its postgraduate schools agreed with Conger's assessment. As long as the General Staff did not totally ignore the suggestions of seminar-trained scholars, Profs. Frederick Morrow Fling and Robert M. Johnston agreed that American official history could be markedly better than the European version.[8]

Not all interested observers held even these hopeful, if conditional, views of official history. Oswald Garrison Villard, editor of the *New York Evening Post*, was convinced that if the General Staff tried to write American history, it "would invariably lead to the writing of history from one particular point of view, perhaps from a predetermined point of view." A self-proclaimed pacifist who nonetheless had supported the formation of the General Staff, Villard praised the army for improving the quality of its officer education, especially in its efforts to teach them how to write. Just the same, if the army's official literature started off "with the theory that we have got always to carry on war or that we must demonstrate that present conditions are not what they ought to be," the end result would be no more valid than if he himself attempted to write history from his pacifistic point of view.[9]

Villard and other critics also pointed out, quite correctly, that the army's rotation policy caused the membership of the General Staff to change so frequently that "continuous scientific historical production" was impossible.[10] The editor of the *Nation*, who supported many other army reforms, feared that any official history would of necessity be "the machine-made kind—written to demonstrate, not the truths of history, but the necessity for that national military policy which might happen to be advocated by the temporary personnel of the War Department."[11]

Even Theodore Roosevelt, the great advocate of military preparedness and professionalism, took a dim view of the merits of official history: "[T]he general staff can't with propriety tell the whole truth about the government and about the people to the government and to the people." With considerably less enthusiasm than Conger had expressed, Roosevelt believed any plan for army officers to write military history must rely upon collaboration with civilian historians who could teach some of the "most important lessons . . . that the military men can't with propriety teach."[12]

Damned by faint praise at best, the writing of official history nonetheless attracted sufficient support from War Department officials to be included in the General Staff's projected agenda for 1912. Since the responsibility for the entire army education system fell to the War College Division, this branch of the General Staff initially served as the center for the army's historical work. Still imbued with former president Tasker Bliss's philosophy to "learn by doing," Army War College students set to work on an official history of the Civil War. In doing so, they finally accepted Matthew Forney Steele's challenge to the War Department in 1895: "Now that the *Official Records* is nearly done, I hope that the War Department will appoint a board of competent officers to write a history of this war. Such a history would be the most perfect one ever written of any war, because both sides are well represented and there are qualified officers, by reason of literary attainment, patience and industry, and ability to be impartial."[13]

The initial plan of 1912 built upon technical studies of Civil War battles that had been incorporated into the Army War College curriculum several years earlier. Before visiting the Civil War sites in Virginia, Maryland, and Pennsylvania, each student in the Classes of 1910, 1911, and 1912 had familiarized himself with a portion of a campaign or battle so he could lead an on-site discussion of the historical events. Each officer also suggested the manner in which a modern army would fight on the terrain of the Civil War battlefield he had studied. As part of his formal classroom assignment, each officer combined both his historical narrative and his professional commentaries into a typewritten copy of his field notes, complete with citations from the historical sources he used to prepare his talk.

Although many students in the first few classes strayed little from a strict narration of events, they demonstrated solid potential for contributing useful essays to an official history. Nearly all the officers had reconstructed their narratives from the raw after-action reports in the *Official Records* and from reputable secondary sources frequently used by their contemporaries among civilian historians. The first essays, produced with no outside advice from academic historians, indicate that with greater direction and stronger emphasis on analysis, the compilation of an official history of the Civil War that was not "something of fiction for our officers to read" was a feasible project.[14]

An even greater emphasis on historical research at the Army War College during the 1912–13, 1913–14, and 1914–15 academic years hinted at the depth of the General Staff's commitment to the project. Professor Johnston agreed to Major McAndrew's request that he share his expertise and enthusiasm with the Army War College Class of 1914.[15] During the next few years, Johnston visited Washington each spring to lecture to the students on sound historical methods and the importance of accurate military history.[16]

The War Department extended its cooperation to the project, too. Captain Conger was ordered away from the Staff College for three weeks to offer an intensive review of research techniques for the Army War College Class of 1914.[17] The future of the project received what seemed to be a special boost when army Chief of Staff Leonard Wood ordered the establishment within the General Staff of a three-man Historical Section in January 1914.[18] With the entire month of March usually set aside for historical studies in addition to the staff and historical rides in the spring, the success of the project seemed guaranteed.

At the same time the War College Division expanded its efforts to create a conducive atmosphere for sound historical research, it also planted the seeds of the project's ultimate demise. In addition to greatly improved analytical historical essays, Army War College faculty expected their students to increase their attention to two special supplements added to the factual narrative. These two addenda—a detailed professional analysis of the opposing generals' command decisions in light of the so-called principles of war, and an informed speculation as to how the Civil War battle would unfold if it were fought by the American army of the early twentieth century— quickly became as important as the historical narrative itself.

These innovations help to explain why the army threw its support so completely behind this project when just a few years before it had granted semiofficial status to Matthew Forney Steele's *American Campaigns*; Steele had offered only incomplete professional analyses and had made no comment on modern fighting. With this demanding new format, however, few Army War College students could live up to the historical section's expectations.

When in 1916 Maj. William D. Connor of the Historical Section recommended the termination of the Civil War project, he told only half the story in blaming the failure on the unwieldy writing style and shoddy historical research techniques of some of the Army War College students.[19] True, Connor would face genuine challenges if he were forced to endorse an official army stand on the controversial historical events of the 1860s. The professional soldiers proved themselves no more likely to share a common interpretation of historical events than did civilian scholars.

The major was in for far greater problems, however, in attempting to reconcile the officers' views on how to fight a modern battle on the ground where the Blue and the Gray had slugged it out fifty years earlier. The officers of the Historical Section seemed to expect a comprehensive statement of American military doctrine to emerge from the Civil War studies. When no consensus on doctrinal questions appeared, Connor misunderstood or refused to admit the real cause for the project's failure: the Historical Section's own inability to resolve intraservice debates.

Connor placed the blame on the Army War College students. The Class of 1915, "like its predecessors, had no clear vision of the proper path to follow in historical research and did not understand how history should be written," an early Army War College chronicler reported.[20] What he did not add, and what is just as important, is that the three members of the Historical Section charged with editing the student essays for publication were as inadequately trained in the methods of history as the officers attending the Army War College. Faced with an incomplete concept of the historical art and conflicting doctrinal views, they saw only evidence of poor research techniques, and for this they must accept a large part of the blame for the project's demise.

If the officers overseeing the official history's progress had looked closely, they would have found much to praise as well as much to condemn. In a number of respects, these initial essays, many of which were filed in their unpolished or unrevised forms, show the author's potential to view the Civil War as far more than a "drums and trumpets" affair.[21] In one particularly important clue to their historical perspectives on the war, the Army War College students did not ignore the political parameters of military strategy. The mere one hundred miles that separated Washington from the Confederate capital of Richmond suggested to them that political implications had to be considered in nearly all major military moves in the Virginia theater.

The officers' insights on the campaign of First Bull Run in July 1861 showed their intellectual sophistication. Indeed, Lt. Col. A. P. Buffington prefaced his comments on the battle with his assertion that the key to understanding the entire military campaign lay in recognizing the interrelatedness of political priorities, army organization, and geography.[22] The cry of an impatient government and pressure from the public and the press for Gen. Irvin McDowell to move "on to Richmond," the expiration of the terms of service of thousands of Union volunteers who had enlisted for only ninety days, northern hopes of disrupting the first session of the Confederate Congress on July 20, and a road and rail center at Manassas all lured an ill-prepared army into action too quickly.[23]

Identifying the political reasons behind the Army of Northern Virginia's two invasions of the North attracted special notice and revealed the kinds of problems the editors from the historical section faced. Although the officers deserve credit for looking beyond purely military explanations, they failed to establish precise goals for each of the unsuccessful campaigns and tended to avoid setting priorities when they suggested multiple reasons for Lee's invasions. Lt. Col. B. W. Atkinson argued convincingly that Lee's primary goal in the Antietam campaign was to gain Maryland's allegiance for the South, an aim that neatly illustrated John Bigelow's concept of "political strategy."[24] Maj. Hanson Ely insisted, however, that Lee's invasion served not one but three primarily nonmilitary purposes: encouraging Maryland's secession, increasing northern war weariness, and improving the Confederacy's chances for foreign recognition.[25]

The decisiveness of the Gettysburg defeat, especially, inspired a deep search for justification of the risks that Lee had taken in his "extremely bold and dangerous, if not desperate, move," comparable to "playing the last card."[26] Lt. Col. Joseph Gaston attempted a complex line of argument, asserting that Lee had no choice but to invade the North to capture supplies for his army, to influence Confederate diplomatic efforts, to try to force the lifting of the blockade, to inspire the Union's peace party to greater activity, and to stab at Washington if the Army of the Potomac marched on Richmond.[27] This morass of intriguing, confusing ideas illustrates the ability of at least some officers to consider important factors outside the purely military sphere, even if they were not uniformly successful.

Historical Section editors also failed to appreciate the frequency with which Army War College students criticized governmental policies in their proper historical contexts. Like Emory Upton's historical treatment of the *Military Policy of the United States*, these essays provided a forum for any author who wanted to use key events from the Civil War to argue for necessary changes in the twentieth century. The Battle of First Bull Run, like most first battles, offered many lessons for those concerned with the state of American military preparedness. McDowell's attempt to fight a battle with green troops on the brink of being mustered out showed "the inexpediency of sending a boy to mill."[28] At Second Bull Run, when elements of Gen. John Pope's Army of Virginia combined with portions of Gen. George McClellan's Army of the Potomac, the ensuing confusion and decisive defeat offered an important lesson in the "futility and danger of hurriedly collecting together an aggregation of military units, however well trained and equipped the individuals composing them may be, and calling them an army."[29] A zealous reformer could adapt these arguments, like Upton's examples, to his cause. The students, however, succeeded in keeping past and present in their separate spheres, no mean feat during an age of constant reform and rampant advocacy.

Still another clue to the quality of many of these essays was the authors' willingness to take stands on important historical controversies. Indeed, in some notable cases, their refusal to take part in a whitewash of either northern or southern leadership challenged the predominant arguments of civilian historians and Civil War veterans whose views held sway in much of the contemporary literature of the conflict.

The actions of Civil War generals who allowed a defeated enemy to leave the battlefield especially attracted the professional wrath of Army War College students, who generally embraced the spirit of the offensive and who vehemently disagreed with traditional historical interpretations. After the Union rout at First Bull Run, "the Confederates did not reap the full benefit of their victory as, no matter how much the troops were exhausted, a pursuit that night would have added terribly to the Federal disaster even if Washington had not been taken," argued Lt. Col. Alfred Hasbrouck.[30] Colonel Buffington agreed.[31] To reach this conclusion, both officers examined and then rejected the traditional excuses offered by Gens. J. E. Johnston, P. G. T. Beauregard, Jubal Early, and artillery captain and future general John Imboden, who argued that the Confederate troops were too disorganized, outnumbered, or undersupplied to continue.[32] The Army War College students sided unanimously with the lesser-known minority view of Confederate artilleryman E. Porter Alexander, who protested that "never did an enemy make a cleaner escape."[33]

In an equally unresolved historical controversy, however, Army War College students' differing verdicts on Gen. George Meade's inaction after his victory at Gettysburg landed them right in the center of a heated debate. After crediting Meade with a fine defensive effort, Capt. George P. Howell argued that it was "inexcusable" for the general to become "too solicitous about supplies" when Lee was still trapped with his defeated army north of the flooding Potomac River.[34] Maj. W. W. Harts agreed: "He could not have used his army to better purpose than to attack General Lee in his unfavorable and disheartening position."[35]

Col. Charles Noyes, however, did not agree with his colleagues' sharp criticism of Meade. In his view, the retreat of Lee's army had been deliberate, not a disorganized or demoralized rout. Meade's need for supplies was genuine, Noyes believed, and, like the Confederates at First Bull Run, the Union army was as disorganized by victory as the southerners were in defeat.[36] Such disagreement among army officers made it difficult to determine the proper course of action that would satisfy the new command philosophy of safe leadership.

In his time, Noyes voiced one of few opinions that did not attack Meade's conduct. Except in the works of family and friendly biographers, vindication of Meade's Gettysburg performance became the prevailing interpretation in

Civil War literature only after World War II.[37] Moreover, Meade's Gettysburg conduct did not mar his reputation completely in the eyes of Army War College students, who exonerated him completely for protesting the insubordinate conduct of Gen. Philip H. Sheridan when Grant's handpicked cavalry chief disrupted the Army of the Potomac's line of march to Spotsylvania in May 1864.[38]

Probably the single most important historiographical skirmish in which the soldiers took part swirled around the military abilities of Robert E. Lee. During the full flower of the Lost Cause and the so-called Lee cult, the Virginia-based Southern Historical Society neatly tailored an image of Lee as a flawless "marble man."[39] Even the defeat at Gettysburg had not been his fault, Lee cultists argued, deftly turning responsibility for the loss onto one or another of his subordinates, most likely non-Virginians such as James Longstreet. Among those who dared to challenge that image of Lee before World War I were Army War College students. The officers' effusive praise for Lee's generalship in such resounding victories as Second Bull Run or in his tough, last-ditch fight against Grant in 1864 surprised no one. They raised perceptive questions, however, concerning the general's command decisions in two of his most pivotal battles, Antietam and Gettysburg.

At Antietam, the officers agreed, Lee took far too many unnecessary risks when he decided to stand and fight. Their visits to the battlefield had convinced them that the terrain was ill-suited to a sound defensive effort. The undulating ground and scattered woodlots blocked his view of large parts of the battlefield, his troops were exposed to Union artillery on higher ground that outflanked parts of his line, and he was backed against the Potomac River with only one usable ford near a vulnerable right flank.[40] They rejected the views of one of Lee's most prominent biographers, Armistead Long, who had called the southern line "a strong defensive position" and even the assessment of so careful a scholar as G. F. R. Henderson, who had found the battleground of Antietam "well adapted for Lee's purposes."[41] The Army War College students threw their support instead behind the dissenting views of enemies of the Lee cult such as Longstreet and artilleryman Alexander, who bluntly wrote that the position "was by no means so strong as it is often said to be."[42] With Lee's political purposes for invasion already foiled, Maj. Hanson Ely stated—and other officers concurred—the South fought only for "prestige and morale," which were not worth the risk of defeat.[43]

The officers' assessment of Lee at Gettysburg was not quite so free of the taint of the Lee cult. Captain Howell released Lee from responsibility for bringing on the battle on July 1; A. P. Hill's men had disobeyed orders, and Lee had to come to his subordinate's relief. But he also bemoaned Lee's failure to take Little Round Top at sunrise on July 2 when the hill was still un-covered and the Union supply lines still vulnerable. Still, the only indica-tion that Howell was not a member in good standing of the Lee cult was his refusal to blame Longstreet's slowness for the failure to take Little Round Top.[44] Other officers, too, attempted to parcel out the blame to Lee's subor-dinates, especially to cavalryman J. E. B. Stuart and Second Corps com-mander Richard Ewell, two frequent victims of the molding of Lee's flawless image.[45]

Still, in important ways the Army War College students began to close ranks against a whitewash of Lee's conduct at Gettysburg. They openly criti-cized his discretionary orders to Stuart and to Ewell as dangerous when operating in enemy territory; Lee's friends only blamed his subordinates for failing to carry out the orders.[46] The Army War College students tended to agree that Longstreet's plan to break off the engagement after July 1, maneuver around the Union left, and take up a solid defensive position where Meade would have to attack the southern forces was a better course of action than the frontal assaults Lee had ordered on July 2 and 3 at Gettys-burg.[47] Overconfidence and dispersion in the face of an enemy and in hos-tile territory were foolhardy.[48] Pickett's Charge, in their eyes, was utterly inexcusable.[49]

If Major Connor of the Historical Section could not understand the gen-uine strides the Army War College students had made, he was correct in noting certain historical shortcomings of the project. First, it was far from comprehensive. The only campaigns for which the students prepared profes-sional studies were located in the eastern theater. Moreover, although some officers wrote about important Virginia battles, such as Stonewall Jackson's running fights up and down the Shenandoah Valley in 1862 and Jubal Early's 1864 raid against Washington, they had not always visited these bat-tlefields and, therefore, they could not write with the same authority as they could of fights whose sites they had toured.[50] Campaigns that held profound implications for modern warfare, such as Petersburg, had received only a superficial glance. The classes accorded scant attention to supply efforts or other auxiliary services, except when they directly contributed to defeat.

Connor also faced the challenge of eliminating a myriad of minor factual inaccuracies. In an otherwise perceptive essay on Antietam, for instance, one officer praised the strategic employment of both the Union and Con-federate cavalry. He missed completely the fact that the northern horsemen had spent September 17 behind McClellan's battlelines, failing to spot the approach of A. P. Hill's men, who quick-marched seventeen miles from Har-per's Ferry to launch the surprise attack that secured Lee's buckling right flank.[51]

Although Connor's disappointment over the frequency of factual errors convinced him of his colleagues' poor research techniques, he apparently did not realize that many of the Army War College students' analytical problems stemmed from a different source. Their failure to agree consistently on the soundness of Civil War generalship was not entirely a lack of intellectual rigor but rather an inability to break from the influence of contemporary trends in professional military literature at home and abroad. For more than a generation, officers had been weaned slowly from the lists of raw maxims or principles of war that had marked the much older military literature that oversimplified the keys to Napoleon's generalship.

In the place of long lists of axioms, a more sophisticated approach to warfare had emerged in the last half of the nineteenth century, one that gave far greater significance to the intangibles of war.[52] One important element of this new military literature sprang from the works of French military writers such as Ardant duPicq, whose stress on the importance of morale and other human factors placed new qualifications on the long-accepted military maxims of Napoleon.[53] The growing influence of the works of Clausewitz in French and German military literature also forced officers to look both for sources of friction that might undermine the standard rules of war and for ways to overcome them.[54]

Although these new directions in professional military literature had softened the tendencies of a generation of authors to list formal, unbreakable laws of war, they also bred ambiguity and confusion. To be sure, certain principles emerged repeatedly in any discussion of military events, but by the beginning of the second decade of the twentieth century, Army War College students could find no single, comprehensive, War Department–approved list of axioms to provide an analytical framework for their professional evaluation of Civil War events. Unable to turn to a single authoritative source, they relied instead upon various compilations of general principles such as those in the U.S. Army's *Field Service Regulations* and in the drill regulations for each arm of the service. Because they drew inspiration from the different sets of guideposts available to them, it is not surprising that confusion reigned. For engineer, infantry, cavalry, and field artillery officers and coast artillerymen, each of whom interpreted nineteenth-century battles from the unique perspective of his own specialty, consensus was impossible.

Not until 1921 did the War Department formally codify a list of nine principles of war that embraced the concepts of the offensive, the objective, mass, economy of force, movement, surprise, security, simplicity, and cooperation.[55] Still, none of these axioms would have struck pre–World War I Army War College students as new. Even without a comprehensive list of maxims, students discovered that the greater problem stemmed from the knowledge that these principles could be applied to nineteenth and twentieth century military situations in many different ways. Just as when they attacked their map exercises, they sought – but did not always agree upon – a "correct" solution.

The students themselves recognized the sizable challenge they faced. As Maj. Charles Gerhardt observed: "The principles of war were the same then as now but details have changed and it was for a good commander then as now to separate details from principles."[56] In the end, the officers' zeal both for illustrating the diverse applications of these "unchanging" rules and for finding exceptions that cast doubt on the validity of the principles justified Major Connor's decision to postpone further work on any history project that carried the official sanction of the War Department until the confusion and contradictions could be eliminated.

For the pre–World War I generation of U.S. Army officers, the nine concepts codified in 1921 simply refined and elaborated two key points they had particularly stressed in their historical essays. American officers, like their European counterparts, deliberated upon the strengths of offensive warfare and the proper methods to ensure the success of offensive manueuvers.[57] Also, responding to the challenges of technological advances and intraservice debates that raised questions about the future role of the cavalry, the officers paid considerable attention to reconnaissance and communications and other important issues that fell under the principle of security. Army War College students did not ignore the other seven axioms, but they did tend to treat them as means to carry out successful offensive or security operations.

Nowhere was the American officers' lack of doctrinal conformity more apparent than when they attempted various applications of the concept of the offensive. They did not entirely comprehend the European idea then so much in vogue, a concept that held important implications on many levels, from grand strategy and campaign planning to battlefield tactics. Moreover, the European concept had evolved from a complex network of interrelated elements. Technological capabilities, geography, foreign diplomacy, national strategic goals, domestic politics, economic priorities, the institutional biases of the warring countries' professional military men, and the lessons of European military history all needed to be considered.[58] Because they were sensitive to the peculiar course of American history and most comfortable when evaluating these axioms as operational principles, Army War College students did not embrace nearly as broad and cohesive a concept of the offensive.

When American soldiers adapted their ideas about the offensive to issues of grand strategy, their findings sometimes clashed sharply with European views. For many of the same reasons that Europeans adopted grand strategic

plans for offensive war, American officers recognized conditions that enhanced the value of the defensive. At the end of a century of "free security,"
and as reflected by the officers' duty to review war plans, American soldiers
took seriously their responsibilities for national defense. Some officers viewed
the defensive as the equivalent of taking the high moral ground. Such soldiers agreed that the Confederacy had been absolutely correct in 1861 in
its initial adoption of a defensive strategy.[59] If the Confederacy had attempted
a quick strike on northern forces, anything less than a crushing victory
would have destroyed one of the most important of the South's strategic
goals: rallying international opinion to support a nonaggressor with a formal
alliance or at least with military and economic aid.[60]

In contrast, when Army War College students considered the offensive
strictly as the key concept in planning a military campaign rather than national strategy, they tended to concur almost too quickly in its superiority
over the defensive. Maintaining a strategic initiative while depriving the
enemy of its freedom of action was such an article of faith for these officers
that when Capt. Duncan Major critiqued Gen. Joseph Hooker's performance on May 1 at Chancellorsville, he strongly, and correctly, condemned
the Union general for halting an effective strategic turning movement, becoming "wedded to the defensive," and losing a prime opportunity to destroy
the vastly outnumbered southern army.[61]

Not all claims for the superiority of the strategic offensive were equally
convincing, however. Maj. W. W. Harts, for one, so deeply believed in its
superiority over "a purely defensive and waiting campaign" that he could
understand Lee's disastrous 1863 invasion of Pennsylvania as the kind of "aggressive movement" the South "imperatively needed," even if Harts could not
justify it.[62] His failure to weigh the risks of a massive defeat or even to consider the logistical problems of such a campaign on an overstretched Confederate economy severely weakened Harts's argument. His essay was not the
only one that suffered from too unqualified an allegiance to the spirit of the
offensive.

To add further to the confusion, the offensive as a tactical concept thoroughly confounded Army War College students. For some officers, the Civil
War taught much about the strength of the defensive, and they tried to swim
against the current of professional European and American military writing.
For those officers who held to the offensive philosophy, victory in attack
rested on no single factor but rather relied upon the successful application
of any of a wide variety of tangibles and intangibles. The variety of arguments made for good debate; it created equally poor prospects for official
history. American proponents of the tactical offensive offered several hints
for success. First, they agreed that the strength of the defensive had so

greatly improved with the use of entrenchments, weapons such as the machine gun, and obstacles such as barbed wire entanglements, that plans for frontal assaults should be rejected in favor of flanking or turning movements.

The Civil War had offered considerable evidence of the impact of these new trends on modern war, and Army War College students harshly criticized generals who refused to accept the new realities. The Union divisions that lost most heavily at Second Bull Run suffered needlessly in their frontal assaults against the embankment of an unfinished railroad that protected Stonewall Jackson's men, and Army War College critics roundly condemned Gen. John Pope for refusing to try instead to turn the vulnerable Confederate left flank.[63] In contrast, Confederate general James Longstreet's massive flank assault at the same battle that swept the Union left from the field and triggered a wholesale northern retreat toward Washington drew considerable praise as a properly executed offensive measure.[64] Unimpressed by Grant's performance at Spotsylvania where northern troops pierced the Confederate trench lines twice and still came away without a decisive victory, Capt. Howard Hickok convincingly concluded:

> The battle illustrates a principle—a principle which, due to a lack of skill on the part of the defenders in the Austro-Prussian campaign of 1866 and of those in the Franco-Prussian War of 1870–71 was not utilized, but which was strikingly illustrated in the Manchurian campaign of 1904–05—that properly placed and defended entrenchments are unattackable frontally and that turning movements best be resorted to.[65]

Beyond this one bit of consensus, American officers revealed wide splits in professional opinion on the necessary preconditions for a successful tactical offensive. Several officers, for example, noted the importance of gaining fire superiority before attempting an infantry charge. If Col. Emory Upton had to repeat against the longer-range weapons of 1914 the charge he had made at Spotsylvania in 1864, Maj. DeRussy Cabell argued, the colonel would not have made the assault in one dead run but instead had his men use the "run and stop" method of gaining and then regaining fire superiority throughout the advance.[66]

Not all officers were convinced that the new longer-ranged weapons necessitated substantial changes in traditional infantry tactics. Maj. F. K. Fergusson noted that Upton's men at Spotsylvania had charged across only two hundred yards of open ground, well within the accurate range of Confederate rifles all the way. The longer range of new weapons alone would bring no changes to a battle fought in forested and uneven terrain like that in Virginia.

In Fergusson's view, however, the greatly increased volume of fire from the newly introduced machine gun would indeed force a different method of advance until the offensive found a way to regain fire superiority.[67] The link between the machine gun and the power of the defensive was not lost on many Army War College students. Equally apparent, however, was their hesitance to make concrete recommendations for the employment of the new weapon or even to comment upon the appropriate place for machine-gun units in army tables of organization. The vagueness of the U.S. Army's position on machine guns finally resolved itself through trial and error on the western front during 1917–18.[68]

Additional artillery support offered one obvious solution to the attacker's need for achieving fire superiority, but American officers gave in only slowly to the notion that the long arm could be much more than a mere auxiliary to the infantry. Some officers who appreciated the greater firepower of modern artillery and its high-explosive shells saw drastic changes if Civil War battles should be refought under twentieth-century conditions. At Gettysburg, Gen. John F. O'Ryan believed, well-placed Confederate artillery with converging fire on the Union position on Cemetery Ridge would have made the northern army's defensive position so completely untenable that Pickett's Charge would not have been necessary at all.[69] Major Fergusson also believed the modern heavy-explosive artillery shell would have wrecked the "frail, hastily prepared log breastworks" that Lee's men defended at Spotsylvania before the northern infantry attacked.[70] The addition of indirect fire systems and forward spotters also would have improved the potential contributions of the artillery on terrain like that around Spotsylvania, where heavy woods had restricted the use of Civil War field pieces.[71]

Still, not all officers were convinced that artillery held the key to the fire superiority problem. Colonel Gaston criticized the Union army at Gettysburg for carrying too much artillery with it. Agreeing with 1912 tables of organization that allotted one regiment of artillery—24 field pieces—to each infantry division, Gaston argued that the Army of the Potomac's 362 guns were a burden, not an asset. A properly organized force the size of the Union army needed only 204 guns—276 if an optional artillery reserve was added—and "each piece more than is required is a detriment, and takes up road space which should be used for a better purpose."[72]

Major Cabell shared his colleague's view. The Union artillery's experience at Spotsylvania had helped to convince him that the modern tendency to increase the proportion of field artillery in the army was "inherently wrong."[73] In these officers' defense, both men based their assessment on terrain conditions and logistical problems. Still, both seemed blind to the potential for artillery to take a larger role in support of offensive operations.

To complicate further the Historical Section's attempt to bring order out of doctrinal chaos, Army War College students offered a variety of additional significant factors, all of which, in one situation or another, had contributed to the major success or massive failure of a Civil War tactical offensive. Key among these lessons was the importance of concentrating force at a vulnerable point on the enemy's line. First Bull Run and Antietam taught the folly of "fighting by detachments"; a concerted push by concentrated Union forces might have crushed the Confederate left near Manassas or broken through Lee's thin lines on the ridges outside Sharpsburg.[74] The new philosophy of safe leadership forced Lt. Col. Thomas B. Dugan to criticize Lee for violating the rule of concentration by "rashly" splitting his outnumbered force in the face of a larger Union army at Chancellorsville,[75] a move that most previous observers, especially Southerners, had interpreted as undeniable proof of the Confederate commander's military genius.[76]

For potential readers of the army's official history of the Civil War, the list of important concerns continued on and on and, unfortunately, hit or miss. Improperly conducted staff duties contibuted to Union defeats at First Manassas, where Gen. Irvin McDowell tried to direct the entire battle with the help of just three staff officers, and at Chancellorsville, where a shortage of supply officers led to ammunition problems at crucial times.[77]

Breaking the rule of unity of command also courted disaster. The Union army's failure to unite the Army of Virginia and troops from the Army of the Potomac and the Washington defenses under a single commander (even one so prone to bungling as John Pope) had so undermined the North's efforts at Second Bull Run that "the result might well have been for[e]seen."[78] Jackson had invited disaster for the Confederates on May 2 at Chancellorsville when he advanced his three attacking divisions closely behind each other. Not only did the units become intermixed, they were left that way in the confusion that followed Jackson's mortal wounding and the accession to command of a stranger, cavalryman J. E. B. Stuart.[79]

The soldiers' reaction to allowing subordinate commanders to take the initiative and press local advantages was mixed. In some cases, initiative wisely used promoted the likelihood of offensive success. Jackson's active maneuvering and attacking during the Second Bull Run campaign wrested a victory from John Pope before the Union general realized that Lee's army was divided and success was within his grasp.[80] Initiative misused brought unacceptable losses. A. P. Hill's assault on John Buford's Union cavalrymen on McPherson's Ridge on July 1 at Gettysburg triggered an all-out Confederate advance without reliable information about the Union army, thereby committing Lee to a battle on ground of the northern commander's choosing.[81] Thus, taken together, the students' essays revealed that much about the

American way of war remained unresolved. Until the Historical Section of the General Staff untangled the different views on these fundamental points, any discussion of an appropriate American military doctrine generated more cacophony than consensus.

Second in importance only to maintaining the spirit of the offensive for American soldiers of the pre–World War I years was the concept of security. Although secrecy, surprise, and celerity contributed directly to the success of both strategic and tactical offensives, the security issue inspired especially sharp controversies among American soldiers because it directly impinged upon one of the thorniest doctrinal questions of the day: the future of the cavalry.

The proper employment of cavalry had prompted frequent serious discussions in the United States and in Europe between the Civil War and World War I.[82] Some American officers maintained that the days of the cavalry charge on the battlefield was not yet over; the combination of man, horse, and cold steel had stood the test of time as a mounted shock force against infantry or other cavalry, and it was still unequaled as a pursuit force. Long before his assignment to the Army War College, then-captain James G. Harbord, the future chief of staff of the American Expeditionary Force, had come to believe the Civil War's great lesson for his arm was that "the cavalry on either side progressed in efficiency in proportion to its willingness and ability to engage mounted – the most successful command was that which was most skillfully handled as mounted."[83]

Many others, however, saw cavalry's role on the battlefield diminishing as the firepower of the infantry and artillery increased in range and volume. Some cavalrymen, drawing upon selected events from the Civil War experience, believed the future of the arm lay in a more versatile role as mounted infantry, an effective blend of firepower and mobility.[84] Still others argued that the great Confederate raiders, such as John Hunt Morgan and Nathan Bedford Forrest, had anticipated the proper role of modern cavalry when they launched their independent strategic raids in Tennessee and Kentucky against Union supply lines, railroads, and communications networks.[85] Still another group of military observers believed the cavalry's day as a combat arm was nearly over; its responsibilities for reconnaissance and security would limit it in the future to the status of an auxiliary service.[86]

Most American cavalrymen credited their arm with sufficient flexibility to take on all these duties as well as an old-fashioned mounted charge if it became necessary. Most of the modernists agreed, however, that the days of cavalry as a shock force were numbered: "The dread of flashing sabers retain[s] its hold only upon the uncultured mind, hence a rush of a body of horsemen has a terrifying effect upon European infantry; but our system of free schools has so enlightened the masses that our thinking bayonets can estimate it at its true value . . . and they can take [a horseman] at a disadvantage."[87]

The Army War College student's extraordinary attention to the role of the cavalry in Civil War campaigns was triggered by what many of them perceived to be the reactionary reforms in the *Cavalry Service Regulations* of 1912. For years, American cavalry officers had extolled the successful "detached actions" of Morgan and Forrest, the delaying actions of John Buford's dismounted northern cavalry at Thoroughfare Gap or the work of Fitzhugh Lee's advanced guard at Spotsylvania, and the bold reconnaissance work of J. E. B. Stuart, all important innovations that Civil War horsemen had introduced to the mounted arm.

The new regulations seemed to them a throwback to a distant past. Principle 1 stated: "Mounted action is the principle method of fighting of cavalry. Animated by an aggressive spirit, it will seize every opportunity to attack with the horse and saber." So that the thrust of the new regulations would not be misconstrued, principle 7 stated pointedly: "Habitual reliance on dismounted action will weaken and eventually destroy initiative; difficulties of terrain are likely to be overestimated. Cavalry imbued with the true spirit of the arm does not remain inactive, waiting for a more favorable opportunity for a mounted charge."[88]

The positions of both schools found their way into the official history of the Civil War. The modernists found plenty of ammunition to argue a case against the more traditional approach to cavalry employment. The charge of the South's vaunted Black Horse Cavalry at First Bull Run contributed little to the outcome of the battle, but if it had been posted to screen the Confederate flanks, it might have spotted McDowell's turning movement before the battle had even started.[89] The failure of Union horsemen to locate either Jackson's or Longstreet's men during the Second Bull Run campaign, exclusive of Buford's successful delaying action at Thoroughfare Gap in the early stages of the maneuver, "illustrates the way cavalry should never be used; its supreme importance in strategic operations is pushing forward, keeping in touch with the enemy."[90] The excellent work done by the dismounted Confederate cavalry and its horse artillery at Nicodemus Hill at Antietam contrasted with the inactivity of the Union cavalry that remained unemployed behind the center of McClellan's line, waiting to pursue a defeated southern army after a breakthrough that never materialized.[91] The bold action of Fitzhugh Lee's four hundred horsemen at Hartwood Church, where they penetrated the northern cavalry screen of eight thousand troopers with a loss of only fourteen men and returned with important intelligence, "proves the possibility of good cavalry properly handled in a reconnaissance against any cavalry improperly handled."[92]

More tradition-bound cavalry enthusiasts, however, found a special target of criticism in the strategic raids that modernists found so appealing. "Hooker's whole disaster" at Chancellorsville, Lt. Col. John McDonald argued, "was due to the absence of his cavalry corps on a practically boot[y]less raid."[93] General Stoneman's "exploding bombshell" tactics during that campaign, when small bands of his raiders peeled off into the Virginia countryside, lost the Union approximately one thousand horses for no good reason.[94] Stuart's independent operations against Union supply lines at the expense of his intelligence duties on the march to Gettysburg was "unjustified by the result."[95] Most pointedly, Phil Sheridan's independent cavalry raids in May and June 1864 were "at variance with accepted views then and now."[96] His raid on Richmond during the Spotsylvania fighting, "like most others of the war, redounded to the personal glory of its commander, but was without commensurate results to the Union army" because Stuart's mortal wounding at Yellow Tavern on May 11 was not the object of the raid.[97]

To complicate still further the future of the cavalry, technological innovations, especially the airplane and wireless telegraphy, seemed to have more direct implications for the mounted service than for any other. Army War College students resisted the urge to predict a revolutionary impact by the airplane. Indeed, those few who mentioned the airplane at all did not seem to know quite what to expect from it. Colonel Gaston recommended its use, along with the wireless and a specially trained corps of military cyclists, in open terrain like that of Gettysburg to maintain open lines of communications.[98] Major Harts was sure the airplane and the wireless would prevent a movement such as Lee's invasion of Pennsylvania, because "now every move would be known almost as soon as [it was] made."[99] Major Cabell, on the other hand, discounted the usefulness of the airplane in the Spotsylvania campaign, because the heavily wooded terrain could hide much from an airborne spotter.[100]

The airplane was not the only poorly understood novelty that affected the future of the cavalry. Only Major Gerhardt gave more than superficial consideration to the motorized truck, which, in combination with scientific management, could be a boon to supply efforts.[101] All in all, the cavalry doctrine problems alone were probably sufficient to convince Major Connor that completion of an official history with an approved War Department interpretation of the military conduct of the Civil War was not possible at that time.

In the end, War Department expectations for an official history to take the first steps toward explaining a national philosophy of warfare were simply unrealistic. Neither Army War College students nor the General Staff appreciated the complex process through which military doctrine evolves. A nation's philosophy of war is not a static entity; it was the height of folly to hope it would leap in full flower off the pages of American history.

With the rapidly altering face of war, decisions concerning changes in strategic and tactical doctrine could not afford to remain solely a sterile classroom pursuit. As the Germans quickly realized in 1914 and the Americans slowly found out once they were in combat in 1917–18, the making of doctrine had evolved into an active process that required constant reassessment of accepted practices in light of combat experience, consideration of suggested revisions, testing and evaluation of new methods, retraining of men and officers, and modification of equipment and organization.[102] An official history of the scope the War Department planned was not merely ambitious; it was also doomed to be obsolete on the day it was published.

In a small peacetime army that had seen comparatively little combat since 1865 — especially in large-unit actions — no single set of shared experiences provided a basis for reaching consensus on a philosophy of war. Each officer's perspective on strategic and tactical doctrine reflected his own limited service, the benefits of whatever postgraduate schools he had attended, the prejudices of his arm, and his personal efforts to keep current with important technological developments. The state of military professionalization in the U.S. Army early in the twentieth century had not yet instilled in each officer the spirit of kinship that evokes a common philosophy of warfare. The General Staff's turn to official history proved its readiness to accept its responsibility to speak with authority on questions of doctrine. The unfinished Army War College history of the Civil War stood as silent testimony to the sizable dimensions of the challenge.

PART 3
THE SOLDIERS
VERSUS THE SCHOLARS

Until the decade before World War I, the U.S. Army's intellectual authority over military history remained largely unchallenged. Its monopoly ended, however, when the American Historical Association mounted a strong offensive to validate the historians' claim to that field. Both the soldiers and the scholars concluded that an important element of their professional identity was at stake, and military history became a field of battle between the two groups.

Few soldiers or scholars were as perceptive as Prof. Albert Bushnell Hart, who had described the special burdens under which military history had labored since its emergence as a specialized field of intellectual study. The discipline was a two-sided coin: On one side (the face most familiar to soldiers) was the study of military history as the principles of war and their application in past battles; on the flip side (the side scholars recognized as part of their own discipline) was the study of military history with the kind of scientific methodology that ensured objectivity and accuracy.[1]

The army held the upper hand in the battle from the start. It controlled most of the important documentary records needed to write a comprehensive military history of the United States. Moreover, army bureaucrats, especially The Adjutant General of the U.S. Army, had the power to determine who could use the rich archival material, and his office had not been sympathetic to the needs of scholars. Additionally, the army had taken the lead in publishing some of these records, the work of selection, arrangement, and editing being carried out by War Department clerks. The final results had not always been satisfactory, but with military history claiming a special place in advanced officer education, the War Department felt sure that appropriately skilled personnel would become available to improve and expand these efforts. Military history underpinned so many aspects of the professional culture of the officer corps that the Old Army welcomed no interlopers.

The civilian historical community, on the other hand, saw only the blemishes in the army's dealings with its past. Their criticisms had considerable merit, but they also left no middle ground to open the door to constructive

145

resolution of the shortcomings of the army history program. Scholars decried the strict, but never totally exclusionary, War Department policies governing access to its records. Others slammed the army's historical and editorial projects for their failure to meet the standards of modern scholarship. A strong sense of professional purpose inspired scholars to take measures to correct the course of the study of military history in the United States. As the challenger, the AHA could pick its fights, but the army usually found ways to avoid total defeat.

The most frequently suggested solution to this battle for intellectual authority called for the army and the AHA to share responsibility for writing American military history. Its chief proponent, Prof. Robert M. Johnston, believed:

> If we can get experts in scholarly methods and experts in military science to extend the friendly hand of cooperation; if we can obtain more recognition for historical work at army headquarters; if we can establish seminar work in our universities; if we can find or found a journal in which military history would obtain recognition; if we could found a national society for military history—by all or by any such steps we should certainly further the cause of this deserving study.[2]

The army and the AHA tried many of these ways to make the professor's designs come true. Few on either side, however, correctly gauged the strength of the other side's resistance to change or to challenge. Although it was heralded as the ultimate solution to the entire thorny problem of intellectual authority, the creation of a historical section in the army's General Staff that included representatives of the academic community as advisers seemed to prove that the interests of soldiers and scholars blended as well as oil and water. They could mix for the short term, but they always returned to their separate spheres.

9

THE ROOTS OF
INTERPROFESSIONAL TENSIONS

In academic circles during much of the twentieth century, the study of the military past of the United States has labored under the burden of a durable and undeserved canard. According to its detractors, military history had been so completely sacrificed to meet both the practical needs of soldiers and the political arguments for a strong national defense that its intellectual integrity had been compromised irreparably. Too many scholars had relegated the written record of American wars to the category of propaganda or polemics, not history.

Such a blanket dismissal, however, obscures a darker story. Tensions between professional historians and the army emerged before World War I and contributed greatly to the future unpopularity of military history among academic scholars. The quest to exert control over the study of military history forced both soldiers and scholars to define and refine their spheres of professional authority, and the priorities of the two parties fated them to clash.

The historical community was the aggressor in these early battles, but its offensives often brought less than the desired results. Especially after 1907, when academics wrested control of the American Historical Association from the antiquarians and genealogists who had been the staple of its membership since its founding in 1884, scholars with close ties to the professional association led the struggle.[1] Among the AHA's new goals was the determination of its leaders to live up to its congressional charter, which authorized the organization to improve the quality of the practice of history in the United States by imposing its own scholarly standards on all of the government's historical activities. When the AHA won only concessions and not unconditional surrender from the army after several attempts to fulfill the spirit of the charter, the historians became frustrated and ultimately resentful of War Department interference. The legacy of these poor relations helped to damage the image of military history in academic circles for years.

In stark contrast to the zeal of the newly reorganized AHA, the U.S. Army as an institution paid little attention to the study of military history beyond its various instructional uses in the classroom. The General Staff was slow to authorize an office (or officers) to oversee the study of this subject. The progress of historical studies in the service, therefore, remained largely in the hands of individual soldier-scholars scattered through the faculty of its advanced schools. Although army Chief of Staff Leonard Wood finally ordered the formation of a historical section in the General Staff early in 1914, no suitable permanent personnel could be found, and the three officers who were routinely rotated in and out of it found themselves too burdened with other staff duties to give the study of history the direction it needed. To historians, the army must have seemed ripe for the kind of assistance scholars could offer.

Academic historians did not seem to appreciate, however, that the army's interest in historical studies, as with all its educational endeavors, rested first on the discipline's ability to contribute to military efficiency. Although many scholars in and out of uniform shared common views about the need for accurate scientific history, their institutional priorities prevented complete agreement on how such studies should be carried out. Rather than working for gradual improvements in the overall quality of American military history with the support and cooperation of potential allies in uniform, AHA members, in their desire for quick success, chose instead to launch frontal assaults on War Department policies. Naturally, these tactics were greeted with indifference, bureaucratic conservatism, or outright hostility by the army, causing resentment to grow within the AHA.

Three interrelated incidents in the decade before U.S. entry into World War I illustrate particularly important questions of authority that the AHA tried—and, to their minds, failed—to resolve with the War Department. First, the AHA demanded free and open access to War Department documents under the control of The Adjutant General's Office. Second, the historians desired control of the department's ambitious plans to collect and classify the nation's Revolutionary War records. Finally, the AHA wanted to take direction of the War Department's historical publications projects to prevent a recurrence of the debacle surrounding the printing of *The Official Records of the Union and Confederate Armies in the War of the Rebellion*. In none of these cases did the professional historians understand that their demands threatened traditional spheres of War Department authority. In failing to comprehend the army's pragmatic and conservative attitude, its fiscal concerns, or its bureaucratic priorities, the AHA time and time again demanded more than the army could concede.

The problem of access to records was an especially thorny one for academic historians because it struck at the heart of their new professional standards. Detailed research in primary sources had become the core of scientific history, and in the first decade of the twentieth century, scholars found many important resources closed to them by the restrictive policies of The Adjutant General of the U.S. Army, Frederick C. Ainsworth.

Ainsworth's restrictions inspired particularly deep anger among historians because many of them recalled a time when they had been welcome to use the official papers of The Adjutant General's Office. Few scholars who worked in the 1880s and 1890s had been refused access to the military reports, Indian treaties, and other papers in that office.[2] In February 1897, however, at the suggestion of records and pensions branch chief Ainsworth, The Adjutant General's Office issued tight new restrictions on access to its records. From then on, only governmental officials, applicants for military pensions, and candidates for membership in patriotic hereditary organizations were entitled to the assistance of the clerks of The Adjutant General's Office.[3]

The War Department had not intended to throw obstacles in the path of historical investigators. The fiscal retrenchment that plagued the army during the 1890s had forced a reduction in the number of clerks available to help researchers. The War Department merely established priorities to attempt to provide quick service to those with the most pressing needs. Space problems, too, had forced the War Department to adopt a more restrictive policy for access to its archives. The mountains of military papers collected in connection with the ongoing publication of the *Official Records* had so crowded the quarters of The Adjutant General's Office that only two or three people could be served at any one time.[4]

The new War Department policy of 1897 was not intended to bar all researchers from access to the army's records. Historical investigators could still review many of the documents they needed if they sought, in writing, The Adjutant General's permission.[5] Still, after several decades of free and easy research, many scholars resented what appeared to be a new spirit of noncooperation in the War Department.

In April 1904, when Ainsworth became The Adjutant General, the doors to the War Department's archives slammed shut. His control of the office was nearly absolute. A physician-turned-army-bureaucrat, he acted like lord of the manor.[6] An opponent of recent modernizing changes in the army such as the creation of the General Staff, Ainsworth looked back fondly on the days when the bureau chiefs truly held positions of power and influence. He resented any interference with, or criticism of, his operation from War Department officials and outsiders alike. His well-known dismissal in February 1912 stemmed from charges of insubordination toward the army chief of staff, another doctor-turned-soldier, Leonard Wood.[7]

Ainsworth obviously was no ally to historians. Officials of the AHA such as J. Franklin Jameson had tried on many occasions to reopen The Adjutant General's Office to historical investigators by flattering Ainsworth and offering to work with him to assure that access to the records would not be abused.[8] But they made no progress with the strong-willed general. Finally, almost in defeat, scholars tried to solve their problems with The Adjutant

General by working around him. Instead of attacking his office, they argued in favor of depositing all the government's records in a centrally located, professionally managed national archives. This step not only would preserve and organize the documentary records of the United States but also would dislodge control of important papers from troublesome bureaucrats such as Ainsworth.

When he was named The Adjutant General in 1904, Ainsworth seemed to be a solid choice. As a colonel in charge of the Bureau of Records and Pensions in the 1890s, he had developed an index card system for the personnel and medical records of each soldier. By 1912 his office had compiled nearly fifty million cards, all filed and easily retrieved. Nonetheless, "when a man of ability has devoted his life to a single thing like a card-catalogue system, he is very apt to confuse the means and the end," one critic charged. Instead of sharing the wealth of information he had collected, Ainsworth seemed to view the departmental archives as "so many typhoid fever patients, to be nursed with tenderest care and to be seen only by the nurses and the doctors."[9]

Charges of Ainsworth's favoritism to congressmen and special friends inspired a flurry of responses by some of the most noteworthy historians who had suffered from his restrictive policy. Dunbar Rowland of the Mississippi Department of Archives and History supplied the editors of the *Nation* with a letter of rejection he had received from Ainsworth: "It is simply out of the question to permit any one not under the control of the Department and not trained in the use of card files to have access. . . . To make an exception in your favor would open the door to a flood of appeals from others." The Adjutant General had then concluded, "You must regard the decision as final."[10] Among the items that Rowland could not view were the papers of the president of the Confederacy, a prohibition that helped to delay until 1923 the publication of his ten-volume *Jefferson Davis, Constitutionalist.*

Paul E. More, editor of the *Nation*, hoped to enlist the most prominent men in the historical profession to comment upon Ainsworth's conduct. He solicited a response from Jameson, who in his position as former president of the AHA and a principal leader in the drive for a national archives, could present a sound and, the editor hoped, a pointed critique.[11] As director of the Bureau of Research of the Carnegie Institute and as a member of several important AHA committees, Jameson had decided that his best course was to try to stay on good terms with Ainsworth. Nonetheless, he continued to hope that More would not end his assault on The Adjutant General. "I should be happy to see him retired or transferred to the Philippines or to the stars at any time," Jameson wrote in encouragement.[12]

Although More could not secure Jameson's participation — the scholar was known as one of the most effective lobbyists for historians' interests in Washington – the editor received overwhelming support from other important academics. Prof. William E. Dodd of the University of Chicago suggested that a commission be appointed to render the policy decisions that Ainsworth alone had been making. Dodd was still stinging from Ainsworth's refusal to grant him access to departmental records while he was writing his *Life of Jefferson Davis*. "Certainly no one could object to having the files of valuable Southern newspapers opened to the use of all," he argued.[13] Moreover, Dodd noted, historians were not the only scholars suffering from Ainsworth's restrictive policy. The Adjutant General had become a frequent topic of conversation at the national convention of other professional associations as well, most notably the American Statistical Association.

Prof. Frederick Bancroft chastised the editor of the *Nation* for describing "too mildly . . . [Ainsworth's] gross offences against numerous long suffering historical scholars." He assured readers that most historians had fallen victim to "the Ainsworthesque policy" at one time or another and were all too "familiar with the great man's reputation as autocrat, profuse with discourtesies." The War Department's poor record of cooperation compared unfavorably with the good service Bancroft had been rendered by the Agriculture Department, the Library of Congress, and other federal offices.

To compound his offenses, Ainsworth had blocked Bancroft's plans, approved by other high governmental officials, to begin preserving and indexing the office's collections of southern newspapers. Bancroft believed the government's decision, at the conclusion of Ainsworth's court-martial, to promote him on condition he retire immediately was an "unmilitary burlesque." But, he concluded, "all hail . . . the valiant lieutenant general of the peaceful Card-Index! Let him be retired at once, so that outrageous injustice may cease forthwith."[14]

Frederic L. Paxson of the University of Wisconsin also became a convert to the principle of open records after Ainsworth treated him rudely. During many months of work at the British archives where he had received all the assistance and special favors he requested, Paxson was appalled by the lack of cooperation he received from The Adjutant General's Office when he asked merely for verification of the authenticity of a document. The same request channeled to the commissioner of pensions, outside Ainsworth's jurisdiction, brought the required confirmation in a courteous two-page letter.[15]

On February 12, 1912, historians celebrated Ainsworth's relief from command, but they realized that their recent protest would have served no good purpose if the new adjutant general shared his predecessor's views. Jameson's silence during the recent barrage of criticism against War Department policy now paid off. One week after Ainsworth's departure, Jameson requested an appointment with Secretary of War Henry L. Stimson to consider the adoption of "more reasonable and liberal regulations."[16]

When he first approached Stimson, Jameson complained that Ainsworth had made his office's archives "more firmly closed against historical investigation than any government archives in the world . . . except of the Inquisition in Rome." Ainsworth's policy not only had blocked the writing of military history but also had obstructed progress on any comprehensive civil history of the United States; The Adjutant General's Office controlled many nonmilitary records, including the reports of scouting and mapping expeditions that had paved the way for the great westward migration.[17]

Stimson was receptive to the scholar's suggestions. He ordered the new adjutant general, Henry P. McCain, to heed Jameson's advice in drafting a new access policy to replace the War Department's order of February 1897.[18] Jameson did his job well. He clarified the language of the proposed new order to allow greater numbers of scholars to gain access to the departmental archives. For one, he opposed the use of the word "historians" as meaning only those who had already written histories, preferring instead "historical investigators," which might also include authors of monographs and younger scholars. He also pressed for admission of the secretaries or librarians of state historical societies, who were likely to be trained scholars, while eliminating the state archivists, who tended to be patronage appointees. Jameson's changes were incorporated into the final War Department order of March 26, 1912, which repealed the 1897 rule.[19]

Not all historians were satisfied with the new concessions that Jameson had so carefully worked out. It still contained limitations on access to recent records and other groups of papers deemed sensitive to national interests, a stand that Jameson had approved.[20] Still others believed the new order was no guarantee that departmental policy would not change each time a new adjutant general was appointed. Hostile feelings toward the War Department did not end with the repeal of Ainsworth's restrictive policy.[21]

A better solution, many historians believed, would be the creation of a national archives. Controlled by a commission of trained historians and librarians, the staff of this new repository would preserve and classify the records of all governmental agencies and aid in the collection of scattered sets of important national documents. In 1908 the AHA had established an executive commission to direct its part in the campaign for a national archives building.[22] The recent tumult over access to the records of The Adjutant General's Office had given a considerable boost to the proposed national archives, and historians believed it was time to consolidate their gains and assert their authority over collection and classification of all governmental documents.

Just when it seemed that ill will between the historians and the War Department might abate, however, the first shots were fired in a new battle, this one over the collection and publication of the documentary records of the American Revolution. In 1913 twenty years of precedents were working against the historians. Congressional interest in the collection and publication of these records began in 1892, when all relevant documents preserved in the Treasury and Interior departments were ordered to be consolidated with those already held by the War Department. The Sundry Civil Act of August 1894 went one step further and ordered all Revolutionary War and War of 1812 documents from every executive department be sent to the War Department for "preservation, indexing, and preparation for publication."[23] After the Spanish-American War forced a halt in the gathering of a complete documentary record, however, the project's momentum and the War Department's interest seemed to die.

Indeed, by 1908, when the House of Representatives considered a new bill to fund the project, prospects for the passage of the legislation appeared dim. The House Committee on Printing returned an adverse report on a project far less comprehensive than the 1894 plan, the publication of George Washington's military orders. Still, the bill was passed, and since most of Washington's material was already deposited in The Adjutant General's Office, Secretary of War William Howard Taft and Librarian of Congress Herbert Putnam decided to leave publication under the control of the War Department. After all, its personnel were "experienced in military affairs and in the use of military records."[24] To assert successfully a claim of authority over this project, historians had to prove that the War Department staff did not possess the required expertise.

If the historical community had read the reports of the Senate Committee on Military Affairs when it considered additional funding requests for the Revolutionary War records project in 1910 and again in 1912, civilian scholars would have been forewarned of the kinds of problems they would face.[25] Not surprisingly, the chief obstacle to the Revolutionary War records project had been Adjutant General Ainsworth. He had in fact opposed publication, because the War Department's collection remained incomplete even after the large accessions of the 1890s and because it was too costly in both time and money to collect important documents from state and local repositories. Even if the department received a sufficient number of missing documents to warrant publication, Ainsworth recommended that the project be left to "the military officers under the control of the War Department and the employees of that department . . . [who] are especially qualified for this work."[26]

Ironically, in March 1913, when Congress finally passed a bill allotting an initial appropriation of twenty-five thousand dollars,[27] the historians' enthusiasm for the project had been raised and dashed so frequently that few were prepared to take action. "I am as surprised as yourself at 'the turn the matter took,'" Prof. Fred Fling wrote to Albert Bushnell Hart, a fellow participant in the archives crusade.[28] When neither of these two prominent scholars, nor any other prominent representative of the historical association, sallied forth to present the historians' case for a well-executed documentary project, Harvard University professor Robert M. Johnston, a relative newcomer to AHA affairs, took up the cause.

Johnston, whose interest in military history was all-consuming, worked tirelessly to rekindle his colleagues' support for the Revolutionary War records project. Acting alone and without notifying AHA officials of his intentions, he wrote to Secretary of War Lindley Garrison in early June to suggest that supervision of the War Department project be handed over to an advisory committee of historians, archivists, members of the Carnegie Institute, and "probably representatives of the Army and Navy War Colleges."[29] He worried that leaving the project in the hands of War Department clerks would ruin it. He launched a crusade to convince the War Department that the Revolutionary War records project could become "the most important of our national documentary monuments" if properly executed by trained scholars who were prepared to carry out the necessarily wide-ranging search for source material in foreign archives and in American repositories.[30]

Most of Johnston's professional colleagues would have recognized his plan for an advisory board as consistent with long-standing AHA goals, but the inclusion of military representatives was an interesting new twist. Perhaps he believed that greater success and less acrimony would result from asking for help from inside the military establishment, a tack not taken during the access issue.[31] He knew that the Army War College was "anxious to do the right thing in the right way even if they do not yet know all about historical methods."[32] Early on, Johnston sought support for his proposed soldier-civilian committee from the shining lights of his profession. As he explained to Jameson, one of the potential benefits of a joint commission of historians, archivists, and military men "surely would be getting in the thin end of the wedge [into War Department records] and would lead in time to the control of the national archives by scholars."[33]

Johnston's original plan for a supervisory committee of soldiers and scholars was sound, but he had not counted on the hesitancy, if not outright recalcitrance, of the War Department. Despite evidence of thawing relations after the resolution of the access question, the War Department's resistance to outside intrusions remained largely intact. Secretary of War Garrison considered Johnston's suggestions and immediately determined to disregard them. Adj. Gen. George Andrews convinced him that as long as the department's documentary collection remained so incomplete, there was no need for an advisory committee to guide the documents' publication.[34] Apparently a man of Ainsworth's stripe, Andrews also believed even when the time came to select the documents to be printed, The Adjutant General or members of his department could do the job. Garrison seconded Andrews's comments in a long letter to Johnston, no doubt hoping that his explanation closed the matter.[35]

Johnston was not one to give up quickly. Still, he did not know what to do next. Flattery had failed, so he took out his frustrations in letters "directed to destroying and ridiculing the puerile arguments of the A.G.'s office."[36] His concerns stretched far beyond the future of the Revolutionary War records project alone. As with most of Johnston's activities to promote military history, he had an important reason for staying his course. "The War College men want a Historical Section for the [General] Staff. I think there are many objections [inside the army]. . . . Whether the present [Revolutionary War records] plan fails or succeeds[,] a good argument may be built up for a historical section."[37] This was probably Johnston's primary goal all along, but to reach it he was willing to use any soapbox, including diatribes against War Department control over the Revolutionary War records project.

By September 1913 Johnston had discovered two other approaches to attack the War Department's position and to promote the views of the AHA. First, he solicited well-known history professors such as William A. Dunning to write or visit President Woodrow Wilson, who was also a scholar and thus bound to be sympathetic to the historians' cause.[38] Johnston then suggested to Jameson that the War Department be invited to send a delegate to the AHA's annual December convention to explain the department's views on archives and records.[39] If that did not work, Johnston wrote, he was prepared to rely upon his "mulish disposition" to "worry them indefinitely" until the historians got their way.[40]

Although Johnston's attempts to bring President Wilson in on the side of the historians made no headway, Garrison at least yielded a little to the professor's persistent badgering. He promised to send Assistant Secretary of War Henry Breckinridge to the AHA's convention in December 1913 at Charleston, South Carolina.[41] Breckinridge then became the target of the historians' appeals. When Albert Bushnell Hart tried to flatter him into considering a close cooperation between the AHA and the War Department, Breckinridge quickly took the defensive: "I am merely going to acknowledge these suggestions at this time and look into the matter carefully to see what can be done and how best to do it."[42] The historians were not optimistic that Breckinridge could be convinced of the merits of their plans.

Before the convention, however, Garrison and Adjutant General Andrews seemed to derail all of Johnston's designs. After a review of the holdings of all the army's document collections in preparation for Breckinridge's appearance at the Charleston convention, they reasserted their commitment to keep the Revolutionary War records project a War Department affair exclusively. They rejected again Johnston's idea for a commission of historians and archivists to oversee the army's project.[43]

By November, the War Department's control over the publication of the Revolutionary War records seemed guaranteed. Capt. Hollis C. Clark, a recently retired officer with no formal historical training, was appointed by The Adjutant General's Office to take over the project. He went to work immediately. By the end of the month, the energetic captain had resolved a variety of legal questions concerning the collection of documents, smoothed out financial problems with the comptroller of the Treasury, dealt with the Civil Service Commission to obtain the requisite staff, and set up his office in Room 259 1/2 of the State-War-Navy Building in Washington.[44]

Initially, however, Clark seemed satisfied to follow The Adjutant General's guidelines regarding the collection, authentication, copying, arrangement, filing, and, finally, publishing of its historical documents.[45] When Secretary of War Garrison reported that Clark would be assisted by the "local historians, librarians, archivists and antiquaries" that Johnston had hoped to avoid, historians recalled their earlier fears that Ainsworth's relief alone had not solved their problems.[46] Jameson's visit to Andrews's chief clerk around December 1 suggested that the cause was lost: "[I]t seemed evident to me that Professor Johnston's assaults upon the War Department had not convinced it that it needed to put the direction of this enterprise wholly or partly in the charge of civilians [historians]."[47]

In early December, when AHA participation in the Revolutionary War records compilation appeared to be a dead issue, the historians found unexpected allies. A group of professional military men, whose aid the AHA had not yet solicited, expressed support for the historians' goals. Capt. W. L. Rogers, president of the Naval War College, protested to the secretary of the navy against Garrison's decision not to appoint an advisory committee of historical and archival experts. He firmly believed the project directors "should have the advantage of advice and consultation with trained historians who have made it their business to become acquainted with the original sources of historical information." Assistant Secretary of the Navy Franklin D. Roosevelt also promoted the historians' efforts.[48]

Even more welcome to the historians was the unexpected support of Captain Clark himself. When the captain stopped by Jameson's office for a chat, the scholar was pleased that Clark admitted his own limitations in historical matters. "He seemed a very sensible and right-thinking officer, by his own avowal not at all an historical scholar but an executive person . . . [who] has been occupying himself with the physical questions of processes of photographic copying rather than with historical studies," Jameson wrote to Hart.[49] Jameson saw an opportunity to impress Clark with the importance of maintaining high standards of historical scholarship, and Clark apparently took the bait. He decided to attend the AHA convention at Charleston, where he knew that both the historians and Assistant Secretary Breckinridge would discuss the matter face to face.

Buoyed by Clark's visit, Jameson renewed his hopes for active AHA participation in the Revolutionary War records project. During the autumn of 1913, the AHA executive council appointed Jameson, Hart, and Prof. Andrew McLaughlin of the University of Chicago as a special subcommittee to consider the most appropriate way for the association to take an influential role in the War Department's project.[50] The three men decided, however, that if the AHA wanted smooth cooperation, the historians must moderate their demands. Johnston's original demands for control by a commission of civilian historians had met with substantial resistance. Jameson now believed perhaps a committee of noted scholars, a group that was solely advisory in nature and prepared to lend its expertise whenever the War Department requested it, offered the greatest chance for success.[51] McLaughlin agreed:

> If the men in charge of the records express a willingness at the outset to consult with and take advice from a committee of the Association, the committee confining itself to recommendations concerning the scope and character of the material to be collected, it is not unlikely that they will accept suggestions and advice given at a later time when organization and publication are about to begin. Could not a properly constituted committee dexterously insert itself into the confidence of the military Pou Bahs at Washington?[52]

Hart also believed Jameson's suggestion was sound, especially after consulting with Captain Rogers for a naval officer's opinion of the plan.[53]

To some historians who learned of the issue at the Charleston convention, an advisory committee provided only a partial victory. Johnston, who still wanted the project to be supervised by historians, agreed with the AHA stand only with great reluctance.[54] Still, Jameson had been entirely correct: An advisory committee offered the only option short of total defeat.

The executive council of the AHA accepted, with one slight change, the modest proposal Jameson, Hart, and McLaughlin presented. The president was authorized to appoint a five-member advisory committee only if the assistant secretaries of the army and navy attending the Charleston convention seemed to favor the idea.[55]

From the perspective of the historians, the Charleston meeting went well. Breckinridge and Assistant Secretary of the Navy Roosevelt "showed an excellent spirit and intelligence," and they accepted with enthusiasm the AHA plan for a publications committee that would remain strictly advisory. They also agreed to meet in Washington with a panel of scholars appointed by the AHA executive council.[56]

As the new AHA president, McLaughlin made judicious appointments to the new advisory commission.[57] The chairman, Maj. John Bigelow, now retired from the U.S. Army, had just published an outstanding work on the Battle of Chancellorsville and had gained firsthand knowledge of Revolutionary War manuscripts from his work on the Battle of Saratoga.[58] Retired rear admiral French E. Chadwick, one of military history's foremost proponents during his tenure at the Naval War College, represented the interests of his service.[59] Jameson, Frederick Bancroft, and Justin H. Smith—all noted academic scholars—filled out the committee.

On January 16, 1914, the committeemen—except for Smith, who was absent on a research trip to New Orleans—met in the office of the secretary of war. Captain Clark, C. W. Stewart of the Navy Department, and Prof. C. O. Paullin, a specialist on naval affairs, were invited to sit in. The first meeting seemed to offer hope for a fruitful collaboration.

The committee's agenda hinted at its ambitious hopes for the Revolutionary War records project. The men addressed a wide range of important topics. Most important, they accepted a broad definition of the term "military records of the Revolutionary War" to guide the agents who would undertake the actual searches for official, unofficial, and personal documents. In addition, they made rough estimates of the amount of material deposited in various repositories around the nation; set up formal liaison channels between the army and navy departments' assistant secretaries and Jameson's Washington office; voted to include relevant diplomatic and political materials; recommended that a poster or other publicity be circulated among historical and library societies to obtain copies of documents held by private citizens; considered the problems of locating documents in foreign archives; recommended that the departments request an additional twenty-five-thousand-dollar appropriation in the next year's budget; and suggested the names of reliable historical scholars to search the state repositories as War Department agents.[60]

After this promising first committee meeting, however, the collection of documents proceeded so slowly that the entire project soon found itself in jeopardy. The committee itself convened rarely after its initial meeting.[61] The project's progress relied upon an annual appropriation from Congress, and after renewed funding in 1914 and 1915, legislators demanded results by 1916.[62] State agents had completed the copying of documents in only three states—North Carolina, Massachusetts, and Virginia—when the House Subcommittee on Appropriations called the War Department to task.[63] When it was clear that publication was still far in the future, the project's funding was terminated, and both the enterprise and the advisory commission died.

The failure of the well-publicized Revolutionary War documents project helped to frustrate some of the historians' other immediate plans for asserting their authority over the nation's historical programs. Many AHA members, for example, hoped the mountains of official papers collected during the research phase of the Revolutionary War records project would justify a stronger push for the centralization of governmental documents in a national archives. In addition, many scholars hoped successful collaboration with the War Department would go far toward persuading other federal agencies to concede the AHA's right to coordinate their historical research projects as well. If either of these plans succeeded, the historians foresaw a bright future for a third important goal—the establishment of a special congressional commission, manned by scholars recommended by the AHA executive council, to oversee all federal historical publications programs.

The AHA had good reason to be concerned about the quality of government-sponsored historical publications. As early as 1908, the organization appointed a special standing committee to study the problem, but its members did little beyond issue annual formal statements favoring a congressionally appointed council to supervise these projects.[64] When the actual collection of Revolutionary War records first started, proponents of a publications commission found new enthusiasm.

On the one hand, relations between the War Department and the AHA improved after the army agreed to listen to the historians' advice during the collection of Revolutionary War documents. On the other hand, the scholars destroyed these bridges almost as soon as they were built. The historians grudgingly accepted their advisory role, but they adamantly argued that they must be accorded an increasing say when the documents were prepared for final publication. As if to warn the army of the cost of refusing their substantial professional expertise, the historians launched a concerted attack on an earlier War Department historical fiasco: the publication of *The Official Records of the Union and Confederate Armies in the War of the Rebellion.*

From Maj. Gen. Henry W. Halleck's first recommendations in 1863 to preserve and print the military records of the Civil War until the work was completed in 1901, the project had not gone smoothly.[65] The War Department had allowed the endeavor to drift aimlessly until 1877, when Capt. Robert N. Scott received the assignment to bring order out of chaos. Scott found no master plan to follow, a hostile Congress in a financially conservative mood, no trained staff members, and constant criticism of his objectivity, especially from southerners.[66] Nonetheless, he and his staff produced an impressive 128-volume record accompanied by a valuable atlas of maps drawn by the Corps of Engineers.

The first generation of writers to enjoy access to the compilation expressed a mixture of awe, intimidation, doubt, and confusion. For his *American Campaigns*, Capt. Matthew Forney Steele admitted that he had rarely used the volumes, relying instead on the works of others who "had given many years of their lives" to analyzing "this great mine of fact – and fiction."[67] Former Confederate general E. Porter Alexander, who frequently visited Washington to use the War Department's archives and confer with academic friends such as Jameson and Dunning, agreed that "it is very slow studying the different points out of the War Records & books published by six different authors all *specially* qualified to tell something."[68]

By 1912 many researchers' opinions had changed for the worse. When Thomas L. Livermore attempted to complete the history of the Civil War that John Codman Ropes had left unfinished when he died, the former army colonel expressed serious doubts about the usefulness of the *Official Records*. For researchers with no firsthand military experience, Livermore warned, "it is a common impression that the reports in themselves convey intelligible and detailed accounts . . . and that the historian has only to select . . . such material as he may need for his narrative." Unfortunately, the colonel lamented, "most of [the reports] . . . convey no definite idea of the position of the troops to any one but the officers to whom they were addressed; and many have by themselves no value whatever to the historian."[69]

Livermore was not the only researcher with serious reservations about the utility of the Civil War records. Capt. Oliver L. Spaulding, one of the most scholarly of the army's officers, argued that "probably no one has ever tried to follow out any point to its ultimate end in them without being vexed at their omissions and inaccuracies."[70] The size of the publication alone was so intimidating that in 1916, one American critic – probably Professor Johnston – argued that since the completion of the *Official Records* in 1901, only "one German, two English, and two American civilians" had been able to use them "intelligently."[71]

The "nonscientific" editorial policies applied to the printing of the *Official Records* quickly became the key to the historians' campaign to take over control of the publication of the Revolutionary War records. Again, Johnston took the lead and surrendered no opportunity to expose the scholarly flaws of the Civil War records project. Because its editors failed to satisfy standards of historical scholarship, the published volumes had become "notorious among competent judges."[72] When Douglas Southall Freeman published *Lee's Dispatches* in 1915, the author's strict attention to accuracy and detail, "in striking contrast to the unscientific methods followed in the editing of the official *War Records*," allowed Johnston "a rare pleasure to welcome a work on the Civil War."[73]

If Johnston appreciated that the Civil War project was well under way long before the new methods of modern historical scholarship set the standards for such work,[74] he did not admit it. Such qualification would have weakened his case for AHA participation in the publication of the Revolutionary War records. His attempts to discredit the *Official Records* took two different paths, either one equally well calculated to make a good case for editorial control by experts in the classification and analysis of historical documents. His scholarly criticism was not surprising, but he also unleashed economic arguments that helped to recruit support from a far larger audience of Americans who detested governmental waste in any form.

The *Official Records* "are a monumental example of how not to spend money and how not to do a piece of work," Johnston informed an *Infantry Journal* audience.[75] The War Department had supported "a botched job from beginning to end," he insisted. The lithographic plates for the atlas maps had been sold for zinc scrap metal, an estimated loss to the department of thirty-five thousand dollars. The government had wasted as much as three million dollars by distributing the completed sets of volumes not to research institutions, where students could find ready access to them, but to "political heelers," who immediately sold the volumes to secondhand-book dealers. Other sets had been sent to small backwater military posts, "where the volumes rotted on a back porch during a rough winter, shared the stall with a family's cow, or furnished lighting material for the furnace."[76] Such a fate would not befall a well-managed scholarly project, he was sure. The AHA, in its drive for a federal historical publications commission that its members would control, had to agree.

The controversies surrounding access to governmental documents, the collection and classification of Revolutionary War records, and control over all federal historical publications projects illustrate the intensity of the interprofessional conflict when the scholars tried to assert their claim to special responsibilities traditionally belonging to the soldiers. For the historians, who stood to win much from any War Department concessions, the potential for gain seemed to demand aggressive, confrontational tactics. The army, on the other hand, stood equally steadfast in its intention to fend off what it perceived to be the scholars' unwarranted interference with longstanding War Department prerogatives.

The historians set themselves up for defeat when they demanded the army's unconditional surrender. The access problem was a fundamental sticking point that had hampered many historians. As Bancroft noted: "[E]ach person [I talked to] knew of several victims of that policy of whom none of the rest of us had heard" and seemed sure that "a cloud of witnesses" would be willing to testify against Ainsworth's ruling.[77] The scholars did not take into consideration the incredible burdens under which the War Department labored. Limited space, mountains of unfiled and unpublished Civil War records not used in the official publication, and rapidly growing numbers of applications for military pensions as the war generation aged all combined to create overwhelming problems for the clerks of the Adjutant General's Office, whose highest priorities necessarily did not include cooperation with academicians.

The historians' closely related arguments favoring expert assistance in the collection of, and later the publication of, the Revolutionary War records also clashed with traditional army responsibilities. For historians, the *Official Records* experience was sufficiently convincing to demand reform. Except for Jameson, however, they seemed to consistently underestimate the strength of military pride and conservatism.[78] To the staff of The Adjutant General's Office, army paperwork was different from other kinds of written documents, and they railed against apparent interference from outsiders who lacked the military experience that might allow them to judge any particular paper's historical worth.[79] Such views did not leave room for compromise or easy middle-of-the-road resolutions.

The irony, of course, is that the War Department had not rejected out of hand the historians' demands. Not all soldiers found the historians' demands totally unreasonable. In due time, when the War Department found ways to accommodate the scholars' needs to army priorities, many of the desired changes became departmental policy.

The access issue offers a good example. When Secretary of War Garrison ordered a departmentwide survey of record holdings, the intradepartmental memorandums revealed considerable support for opening to public scrutiny as many documents as would be consistent with national interest.[80] As many historians already knew, Ainsworth had approached his job with autocratic fervor. They were not aware that the chiefs of other army bureaus did not feel the same way.

But sympathetic bureau chiefs also realized that space limitations restricted their ability to translate their opinions into action. The problems of limited office space encouraged a number of them to support the creation of a national archives, even if it meant their surrender of immediate control over back records.[81] The AHA, at Jameson's encouragement, had been deeply involved in the drive for a national archives for years, but the army became so strong a supporter of the move that a representative of the War Department routinely received appointment to the historical association's standing committee on archives.[82]

Nor did the army ignore totally the historians' demand for strict adherence to archival and editorial standards in the publication of the Revolutionary War records. Since Johnston's first concerted attacks on the *Official Records*, more scholars had cited major flaws with the governmental project. Annie H. Abel argued that research among the original documents in War Department archives revealed that Union and Confederate officers who worked with Captain Scott had conspired to omit embarrassing documents from the printed volumes.[83] Scholars also insisted that the *Official Records* had been the victim of too narrow conceptualization. Frederic Paxson decried the army's obsession with operational issues.[84] Charles Ramsdell concurred heartily when he noted that the *Official Records* project was "an abomination to anyone who is interested in the economic side of the Civil War."[85] Finally, in 1930, the Historical Branch undertook a comprehensive review of the *Official Records'* publication process, outlining the similarities and differences between record keeping during the Civil War and World War I.[86] When the Historical Branch finally began work on the World War I documentary record in the late 1920s, it had won grudging support, if not active participation, of the professional historical community.

Still, the timing of the AHA's confrontational tactics and its insistence on supervisory control of army projects doomed its immediate efforts to extend its sphere of authority over military history. Not merely the dictates of military professionalism but the administrative prerogatives of the War Department permitted soldiers to tolerate no challenge to their traditional responsibilities. Members of the historical community, not yet entirely secure in their professional identity either, resented the army's attempt to deny them authority over programs they believed belonged rightfully to them. If the historians, as the aggressors, realistically expected to resolve their disagreements with the army, they needed to find an avenue less likely to raise the suspicions and incur the hostility of the War Department. As this realization sank in, confrontation slowly gave way to a desire for cooperation with the army, a move that in some ways gutted the force of the scholars' demands for intellectual autonomy over military history and fed their frustrations further.

10

EXERCISES IN FRUSTRATION:
TWO AHA COMMITTEES
FOR MILITARY AND NAVAL HISTORY

Although many issues created friction between soldiers and scholars during the decade before U.S. entry into World War I, mutually shared interests held up the promise that ways could be found to resolve the differences that separated them. With the preparedness movement sweeping the United States, important defense issues facing congressional scrutiny, and tensions rising on the international scene, a small group of historians sought out interested army officers who had expressed their concerns about the quality of research and writing on American military affairs. Together, they attempted to find ways to improve the standards of professional study of military history in the United States. Both the soldiers and the scholars understood that much of what passed for American military history was little more than frequently repeated, ultranationalistic, sometimes apocryphal stories. Both recognized that serious errors and misconceptions about the prowess of the U.S. armed forces desperately needed revision, even if they did not quite know how to go about it.

At its annual meetings in December 1912 and 1913, the American Historical Association approved the formation of two new committees devoted entirely to the study of military affairs. In 1912 a provisional commission was authorized to examine the special needs of the study of military history. Based on this panel's findings, the AHA executive council in November 1913 moved to establish a standing committee on military and naval history. The membership's approval of the council's actions at the meeting in December 1913 demonstrated the historians' desire to lessen interprofessional rivalry sufficiently to create an atmosphere of cooperation in which scholars and army and navy officials might work together. A second committee of historians and military men, also named at the 1913 convention, took up a single, specific goal: to stimulate scholarly writing on American military history through an essay competition that offered a cash award.

Unfortunately, the strong commitment to intellectual and literary excellence shared by the civilians and military men who served on each committee did not prevail. From the start, a variety of obstacles threatened to undermine any fruitful collaboration. The small number of like-minded individuals from the military and historical communities simply could not resolve all the institutional and intellectual problems that had fostered adversarial relations between their parent organizations, the War Department and the AHA.

These problems would not be solved easily. Not all scholars, for personal or professional reasons, welcomed the increased attention given to a single area of historical study to the exclusion of other specialties. The enthusiasm of military men sympathetic to the goals of the AHA was tempered by a realization that for the time being at least, they followed their interests as individuals and not as official representatives of the U.S. Army who could effect the necessary institutional changes to promote the study of military history. Moreover, the cooperative and nonconfrontational spirit adopted by both military history committees ultimately obscured the lack of—and need for—official procedures to resolve future intellectual and institutional problems between the two groups. Despite high hopes for their success, the immediate impact of the two AHA committees on the study of military history was negligible.

The moving force behind the creation of both of the AHA's special military history committees was the ever-active historical gadfly, Prof. Robert M. Johnston. First establishing a scholarly reputation in Europe on the strength of several notable critical works on Napoleonic campaigns, Johnston returned to the United States to teach. His research and writing and his unrelenting advocacy of historians' interests against the resistance of the War Department seemed to some of his colleagues to be a one-man crusade to right the course of the study of military history in the United States. A zealot of boundless enthusiasm, Johnston appeared unconcerned whether or not other historians agreed with his actions. Regardless of the official stand of the AHA, or even if the association refused to support him, Johnston was not the sort to be easily swayed from his own goals.[1]

Johnston believed collaboration between soldiers and scholars was the most promising way to produce a true history of American military affairs. The idea was striking and not a little controversial from its inception. Even to officers and academicians who recognized the need for sound military history, the success of a cooperative venture between the army and academic historians appeared unlikely as long as the AHA and War Department officials could not even reach agreement on such fundamental issues as access to documents. Initially, at least, Johnston worked on the assumption that the advancement of military history in the United States required an authoritative voice *outside* both the AHA and the immediate jurisdiction of the bureaucratic offices of the secretary of war and the chief of staff.

Johnston considered two specific alternatives that could promote the technical study of American military affairs as well as relegate "drum and trumpets" histories to the intellectual scrap heap. Either the creation of a specially designed historical section in the U.S. Army General Staff or the establishment of a national society devoted to the study of army and navy affairs would smooth the way for scientific study of military history.[2]

Each approach offered important benefits that might help to correct the historical record on American military affairs, and Johnston intended to push for both measures. He recognized, however, that institutional change in the army came slowly, especially in a powerful bureaucracy such as that of the War Department. He apparently decided early on to devote his energies to what he viewed as a more easily achievable goal—the formation of a military history society outside the army and the AHA—with the hope that a historical section in the General Staff would follow.

A national society for the advancement of military history offered great potential benefits. Chief among them, in Johnston's view, was the increased likelihood of combining the technical expertise of professionally trained army and navy officers with the research and writing abilities of competent civilians schooled in the scientific methods of professional historians. "It is possibly by forming a small group of writers, uniting these various qualities, that the best results can be achieved," Johnston surmised.

Although many historical societies, including the Military History Society of Massachusetts, had been established since the end of the Civil War, Johnston believed they did not provide a proper atmosphere for the "cool, scientific, absolutely detached investigation of war as war." Their whole purpose, he argued, was "to echo a struggle, or rather one side of a struggle, in which their members were concerned, always to turn toward the local and personal interest rather than to the impersonal and national."[3] A new national society offered the best opportunity for objective investigation.

Although Johnston had no immediate intention of involving the AHA in his project, he realized that the success of his new organization required the approval and participation of interested, qualified scholars. To this end, he decided to arrange for a public meeting on the future of the writing of military history to coincide with, but not be a formal session of, the AHA's annual convention at Boston in 1912. Enlisting the assistance of fellow Harvard professor Albert Bushnell Hart, who maintained strong ties to the Military History Society of Massachusetts, Johnston reserved as the birthplace of his new group the armory of an organization whose partisanship he had criticized.[4]

Hart's interest in Johnston's ideas led to much more than a meeting place for a new military history society. As an active leader in the AHA, Hart believed Johnston's concerns about the need to improve the writing of mili-

tary history merited the consideration of the entire profession. With Johnston's approval, he arranged with the AHA executive council to put the military history session on the official program of the 1912 convention.[5] Hart,
therefore, forged a first noncommittal link between the AHA and the fortunes of military history. Even with the AHA's newfound interest in his
cause, however, Johnston did not abandon his plan for an independent national military history society.

With the public announcement in early December of the military history
session at the upcoming AHA convention, Johnston's two suggestions, first
printed in the pages of the *Infantry Journal* in September, now attracted a
much wider audience of friends and foes alike. Although most agreed that
a scientific approach toward American military history was worthwhile,
they could not decide which, if either, of Johnston's options provided the
better chance for success. The editors of the *Infantry Journal*, in recommend-
ing to their readers a serious consideration of Johnston's suggestions, had
already argued that a combination of the two alternatives—an army historical
section with authority to seek the aid of, and to collaborate with, civilian
historians—would produce the best results.[6]

Not all observers viewed Johnston's suggestions so constructively. The editors of the widely read *Army and Navy Journal* did not question the need for
Americans to understand the true course of their military past, but they
found little to their liking in Johnston's proposals. Although remaining noncommittal on establishing a historical office in the General Staff, they believed the professor had exaggerated the army's lack of historical awareness.
"Are U.S. military experts *that* much in the dark?" they asked. In a diatribe
against those Americans who did not subscribe to the growing drive for military preparedness, the editors believed it would take more than a new historical society to persuade citizens to take the proper safeguards. Moreover, they
were convinced that a single society could neither eradicate the differences
of opinion in the military establishment nor "make all military students
think alike."[7]

Discussion and criticism of Johnston's plans were not limited to journals
only of interest to military men. Oswald Garrison Villard, the pacifistic editor of the *New York Evening Post*, viewed the growing interest in military
history as part of a greater trend that was "hastening this peaceful nation
into militarism."[8] The editor of the *Nation* considered other problems. He
feared that any works of history produced by active army officers would "be
of the machine-made kind—written to demonstrate, not the truths of history, but the necessity for the national military policy which might happen
to be advocated by the temporary personnel of the War Department. History
of that kind is worse than no history at all."

Although the editor of the *Nation* could see a future for a national military history society, he was not nearly so sure that the cooperation of professional soldiers was either necessary or desirable. Apparently unfamiliar with advances in historical instruction throughout the military school system, the editor assumed that the army still held exclusively to its well-known penchant for history-as-illustration. "The military man . . . like many professional men . . . too frequently starts off with a thesis he is determined to prove," the editor cautioned. He much preferred to leave the writing of military history to men of literary and scholarly talent, men such as John Codman Ropes, who, despite being physically unable to serve in the army during the Civil War, still became the foremost military student in the United States.[9]

The interest generated by his proposals must have pleased Johnston. He did not let criticism sway him from his original intention: to push for some organization—either inside or outside the army—where soldiers and scholars could collaborate on the writing of American military history. He was gratified when the AHA executive council extended an invitation to include his public meeting on the official program for the annual convention in 1912.

The panel took shape quickly and to Johnston's liking. Professor Hart lent his name and scholarly reputation to the proceedings when he agreed to moderate the session.[10] After the AHA executive council extended an invitation to the War Department to send representatives to the meeting, Johnston was delighted when three army officers were ordered to attend.[11] Theodore Roosevelt, who not only was the president of the AHA but also was a proponent of many of Johnston's views, agreed to speak as well. Not insensitive to charges that his ideas promoted militarism, Johnston invited *New York Evening Post* editor Villard, one of the most vocal critics of his proposals.

The session on military history was a rousing success. A large and enthusiastic crowd listened as a panel that included Johnston, Maj. James. W. McAndrew of the Army War College, Roosevelt, Villard, Capt. Arthur L. Conger of the Staff College, retired colonel Thomas L. Livermore of the Military History Society of Massachusetts, Prof. Frederick Fling of the University of Nebraska, and Capt. George H. Shelton discussed "Who Shall Write Our Military History?"[12]

Not surprisingly, most members of the panel concurred on two points. First, the ideal center of an intensive, and overdue, study of American military affairs was a historical section within the army's table of organization. Second, a constant collaboration between this military history office and civilian scholars was absolutely necessary to maintain the intellectual quality of the work.[13]

Only Villard expressed serious objections. "I am a peace man and almost a peace-at-any-price man," he said, and he feared that an army historical section would "necessarily develop their history from the point of view of proving that the country needs to do this or that in order to defend itself, in order to avert this threatening degradation that may come to us if some other nation should impose its will upon our will."[14] Most others agreed with Johnston, however, who dismissed as uninformed the notion that the study of war "would make us accessories to putting back the clock of civilization."[15]

Johnston's speakers so convinced the audience of the need to improve the study of the military past of the United States that delegates to the AHA convention in 1912 approved resoundingly two important resolutions. First, a five-member provisional committee was charged with considering "the best method of furthering the study and presentation of military history and of bringing into common action professional and civilian students." Second, to share their conclusions with other interested parties, the committee members were authorized to call another special military history session at the following year's convention to present their recommendations.[16] Although not yet formally and permanently affiliated with the AHA, the provisional committee provided proponents of the study of military history an advocacy group linked closely to the mainstream of historical scholarship.

The initial membership of the provisional committee revealed just how convincingly Johnston had pushed the ideal of collaboration, not confrontation, with the U.S. Army. He, of course, was the obvious choice for chairman. The backgrounds of the remaining members assured Johnston of a group who shared his views.[17] Professor Fling had been helping army officers to improve historical instruction at the Staff College since 1908. Colonel Livermore had accepted the responsibility for completing the Civil War histories left unfinished at the death of civilian scholar John Codman Ropes. Major McAndrew and Captain Shelton, both on active duty, shared strong interests in and a talent for writing military history.

From the start, Johnston realized that he had only taken the first step toward persuading the AHA of the merits of his grand design. A maverick on many occasions, he understood that this time at least he might reap greater benefits if he could rally the nation's premier historical association behind him. The leaders of the AHA seemed wary of Johnston's independent spirit, despite naming him to the chairmanship of the provisional committee. To temper Johnston's zeal, the executive council also appointed three prominent scholars—Fling, Hart, and Prof. William M. Sloane—to review the panel's recommendations and to suggest modifications before Johnston's ideas became the sole basis for the AHA's formal position on the future of the study of military history in the United States.[18]

The caution of the AHA's leadership was well founded. At the meeting in Boston in December 1912, Johnston had already formulated a plan that combined War Department participation on an AHA military history committee with the association's formal support for a historical section in the General Staff, if that office had authority to collaborate with civilian scholars. These suggestions were too drastic for the executive council. Even after Hart, who formally presented Johnston's proposal to the AHA leaders, watered down the propositions by suggesting that the AHA merely recommend—rather than officially support—the establishment of an army historical section, the council was not pushed into hasty action.[19] It voted to take the whole matter under advisement until the AHA annual convention at Charleston, South Carolina, in 1913.

After his initial setback at Boston, Johnston decided to strengthen his hand before Hart, Fling, and Sloane reviewed his proposals for the 1913 convention. First, he rid his committee of its lone dissenter. Colonel Livermore had attended no meetings, had protested that he could not understand Johnston's draft report, and had refused to lend his support to any program that might antagonize the army or ignore fraternal military organizations such as the Grand Army of the Republic.[20] He was not replaced.

Johnston also found other ways to make a strong case for a permanent AHA military history committee. In September he gained additional influential military allies when he visited the Naval War College to discuss with Adm. French E. Chadwick and Capt. W. L. Rogers his ideas for the creation of a naval history committee and a Navy Department historical section.[21] He also sounded out Assistant Secretary of the Navy Franklin D. Roosevelt about his views on a naval history committee.[22] Observing the success of AHA competitions for the Justin Winsor and Herbert Baxter Adams Prizes, Johnston began soliciting donations and accepting contributions for a cash award to fund a competition, administered by his committee, that he hoped would stimulate higher quality research and writing in military history.[23]

Johnston's primary concern, however, centered on formulating a policy statement that would become the basis of the AHA's formal position on the study and writing of military history. The provisional committee's report, which shows only Johnston's hand, began with harshly critical words about the quality of military history in the United States. Johnston attacked the "rhetorical" and "institutional" schools of historians who had either neglected or created widespread false conceptions about American military history. Moreover, since no university in the United States regularly offered military history in its curriculum, the American historical community had few scholars able to follow the sound example of their European colleagues. French and German academicians had successfully combined their own intellectual talents with the technical expertise of army officers to write accurate accounts of European battles and campaigns that were suitable for use in both civilian and military schools. By contrast, the quality of writing and research on American wars horrified Johnston. Not only did he find the work of his civilian colleagues to be extremely uneven, but also he was appalled that no professional army, navy, or academic journal regularly published reputable articles on topics in military history.[24]

Still, not all of Johnston's findings were negative. He admitted there were a number of promising avenues the AHA might follow to promote the study of military history. He strongly approved of Captain Conger's history seminar at the Staff College and believed the AHA should encourage other army schools and civilian universities to develop similar courses of instruction. He supported a rather paternalistic tie to the nation's major patriotic and military societies, both to encourage greater use of their historical collections and to exert control over the preservation of materials that might otherwise suffer in the hands of uninformed local groups or private individuals. He believed the AHA should take advantage of Congress' annual scrutiny of the General Staff to press hard for the creation of a historical section.[25]

Johnston made clear that he viewed the establishment of the history office as only an important first step, not an end in itself. If the army gave in, the new historical section, especially if manned by graduates of Conger's seminars, might then be more amenable to cooperation with the AHA in matters of the use of the War Department's military archives and the publication of its historical documents. To complete its goals, the AHA should name a permanent committee that included soldiers from the historical section and civilian scholars to collaborate on the writing of American military history.

To reach these ambitious objectives, Johnston offered four tentative recommendations. First, he suggested that the executive council of the AHA replace his provisional panel with a permanent committee on military history. Second, he hoped the council would give his report its formal approval. Third, he requested the council to send copies of the report to President Wilson, the secretary of war, the presidents of leading universities, and the secretaries of patriotic and military societies. Finally, he inserted a cover-all recommendation that seemed to repeat the first three; in it he called for a statement welcoming War Department representation and participation at AHA meetings and a standing AHA committee of civilians and soldiers who would cooperate to write the nation's military history.[26]

Johnston's commitment and enthusiasm were not lost on Albert Bushnell Hart. When he looked over the draft of Johnston's report to the AHA executive council, he realized that much good could come from the historical association's adoption of the proposed plan. Hart feared, however, that some of

Johnston's more drastic demands might antagonize more conservative AHA council members.

Hart warned his Harvard colleague to expect to meet resistance on three fronts. First, he was sure the council members would view Johnston's recommendations as only a preliminary report on professional concerns about the state of military history. He doubted that they would be willing to go further and "be ready officially to subscribe to all of its statements and send them to the President and others." Hart also questioned the council's willingness to step beyond its sphere of authority to offer unsolicited advice to the War Department on matters such as the teaching of history in army schools. A third, more fundamental, problem bothered Hart: "I think there might also be objection to having the Association endorse specially a movement for military history, when we have not acted in this way for any other kind of history, economic, institutional, etc." He feared that a controversy over Johnston's report would create the impression that "military history is the one preeminent thing which at present needs attention in America before other kinds of history."[27] Hart hoped Johnston appreciated the need for moderation.

Despite these warnings, Johnston gambled and won. He presented to the AHA executive council a provocative report that was fundamentally unchanged from what he had submitted to Hart. He also came away with enough partial victories to satisfy him, at least temporarily, that the future of military history was indeed a bright one.

Johnston's timing was particularly good. In reviewing the draft reports of other committees and the agenda for the 1913 convention, the AHA executive council discovered an unusually high number of complex matters that related to the practice of military history. The printing of the Revolutionary War records, access to War Department reports, the establishment of a central national archives, the creation of a commission of professional historians to oversee federal documentary publications, among other issues, were slated for discussion at this convention.[28] To help resolve these questions, War and Navy department officials had already accepted invitations to attend.[29] In addition, Captain Conger and Capt. Oliver L. Spaulding were scheduled to deliver papers at the military history session to be held on the campus of The Citadel, the Military College of South Carolina.[30]

Johnston introduced another matter for the executive council's consideration when he revealed that his fundraising efforts to support a military history prize had already netted two hundred fifty dollars.[31] He pressed his case for the AHA to sponsor the competition. Indeed, questions concerning the study of military history generated so much discussion at the 1913 convention that Johnston's recommendation to appoint a group of men familiar with these specialized concerns seemed especially timely and welcome.

The executive council wasted little time in approving most of the general recommendations of Johnston's committee report. He won two points outright. The council granted Johnston's provisional panel full recognition as an AHA standing committee as he asked.[32] His fund-raising activities genuinely impressed the executive council and inspired the creation of a second committee responsible solely for conducting the military history prize competition.

Still, Johnston did not get all he wanted. As Hart had warned, the professor had to accept some partial successes. The executive council stopped short of a formal endorsement for the establishment of a Historical Section in the General Staff. Moreover, it refused to adopt any policy that might put it in conflict with the War Department. The AHA would not push its advice on the faculty of army schools unless the instructors solicited assistance from the association. The council also refused to submit to the War Department a formal demand for the establishment of an AHA-directed commission to oversee its historical publications projects.[33]

Johnston threw off his setbacks and determined to make the most of what he had gained. When he was asked to chair the permanent AHA committee, a high honor for a scholar who was little known by historians not especially interested in military affairs, he saw an opportunity to bring together precisely the sort of men who could further the spirit of cooperation between academicians and the War Department. The first AHA Committee on Military and Naval History included only three professional historians: Johnston, Fling, and naval historian and archives specialist C. O. Paullin.[34] Upon Johnston's suggestion, and at the request of the AHA president, the secretary of the executive council invited Assistant Secretary of War Henry Breckinridge, Assistant Secretary of the Navy Franklin D. Roosevelt, Army War College president Gen. Hunter Liggett, president of the Naval War College Adm. Austin Knight, and Major McAndrew of the Army War College faculty to join the committee.[35]

So tight was Johnston's control over the selection process that by threatening to resign and take the other members with him, he successfully turned back the executive council's short-lived desire to appoint Theodore Roosevelt to chair the committee. It was not merely Johnston's considerable ego at play here. He noted later: "With Colonel Roosevelt as chairman, the technical or professional standards which the Com[mi]t[te]e is anxious to reach would probably have been neglected."[36] It was more important to Johnston to bring together the best men for his long-term purposes than to court the instant visibility that prominent men such as Teddy Roosevelt would bring to the committee's work.

Unfortunately for the future of military history, the greatest irony to emerge from the formal affiliation of Johnston's committee with the AHA lay in the quickness with which it lost its sense of purpose. Instead of providing an open forum to discuss how best to write accurate accounts of American military affairs, the committee quickly lapsed into inactivity. When the secretary of the AHA executive council, Charles H. Haskins, asked Johnston about his immediate plans for the new committee, he learned that there was no set agenda for 1914.[37] In fact, Johnston seemed interested in only two minor issues. He continued to wonder about the advisability of pushing for a separate AHA committee to promote the study of naval affairs, and he considered organizing a naval history session for the AHA conference in 1914. When he asked Roosevelt for his opinion on these matters, the assistant secretary of the navy did not think it "essential that there should be a separate section meeting on naval history at the Chicago meeting next Christmas. In fact one of the needs at the present time is a closer cooperation and corollation [sic] between the students of military and naval history."[38] Without support from Roosevelt, Johnston's interest in pushing these causes faded quickly. After Johnston's great enthusiasm of 1913, his seeming indifference only one year later appears out of character.

Three factors help explain the surprising inaction of Johnston's new committee. First, influential members of the AHA executive council apparently made clear to Johnston that he did not have free rein to do as he pleased. Haskins, for one, assured a colleague that Johnston had been told that "nothing new should be attempted without consulting the council." "Johnston's [provisional] committee undoubtedly exceeded its function last year," Haskins wrote, not without a hint of praise. Nonetheless, he continued, "I do not believe there is any danger of their going too far this year."[39]

Johnston's personality also provides insight into his committee's lethargy. He was simply too much a maverick and an individualist to be comfortable in a situation that required diplomacy, willingness to compromise, and patience. His forte was an unrestrained sudden frontal attack, with or without reinforcements. He had often demonstrated this style in his frequent visits to persuade Secretary of War Lindley Garrison to appoint a civilian committee to oversee the publication of the War Department's Revolutionary War records and in his periodic conferences with Chief of Staff Leonard Wood to discuss the creation of a historical section for the army.[40] Johnston frequently used his chairmanship to endorse favorite projects, such as the continuation of appropriations for the printing of the Revolutionary War documents, that were not necessarily supported by his committee members.

The final problem faced by Johnston's committee resulted from its very diversity. Few of his committee members shared the professor's single-minded dedication to the future of military history. The appointment of the assistant secretaries of war and navy and the presidents of the two war colleges fulfilled Johnston's notion of the ideal committee to carry out his hopes for the future of the study of military history, but these men owed their first allegiance to other organizations. Indeed, Johnston's committee rarely met because he could not reach agreement on a time and place to fit the busy schedules of the military men and departmental bureaucrats whose appointments he had arranged.[41] After pushing so hard for its creation, Johnston used his committee primarily as a pulpit to publicize his own views.

In 1915 Johnston took up the kind of special cause that he believed justified his committee's very existence. At the height of the military preparedness movement, Johnston was convinced that the time was right to start teaching military history at civilian universities. Since few professors were qualified to teach courses in military history, however, he thought his AHA committee should issue a formal request to the War Department to assign graduates of Captain Conger's historical methods seminar to any American university that applied for one. He believed the odds for working out a suitable arrangement were good, especially because one of the key War Department figures with whom he would have to deal was his fellow committee member, Assistant Secretary of War Breckinridge.[42]

Johnston flattered the War Department officials, but when they did not respond immediately to his suggestions, the always impatient professor tried another tactic. In the name of the AHA committee, he sent a circular to the presidents of over twenty major American universities, advising them to ask the War Department for a Staff College graduate to teach military history at their schools.[43]

With recurring problems on the Mexican border already interfering with the army's academic year and the mounting pressure for Staff College graduates to take on more immediately important military assignments, the War Department flatly rejected Johnston's plan.[44] As usual, however, he did not walk away empty-handed. Johnston had hoped all along that the War Department would assign an army officer to his own institution. Moreover, he already had one in mind. He did not want just any Staff College graduate; he managed to land Captain Conger himself for Harvard University.

At Johnston's insistence, Dean K. G. T. Webster formally requested Secretary of War Garrison to assign Conger to Harvard to teach at a summer school session in 1915.[45] The War Department moved slowly, not wanting to set a precedent that Johnston could use to his advantage. Finally, The Adjutant General informed Conger that the War Department did not deem the plan advisable. If Conger wanted to go, however, he would be authorized to do so at his own expense, and he would not be required to request formal leave for the summer. This was as far as the War Department was willing to go.[46] In a unique experiment in soldier-scholar collaboration, the captain and the professor offered at Harvard that summer a well-received series of public lectures and a military history seminar for undergraduates, allegedly the only such program at a civilian university before World War I.[47]

After this very small personal victory, Johnston sought a way out of his AHA commitments. His chairmanship took time away from new projects, most notably the co-editorship of the *Military Historian and Economist*, which he and Conger established during the captain's stay in Cambridge during the summer of 1915. Still, he did not want to surrender entirely his influence over the AHA's policy toward the study of military history. Not surprisingly, he hoped to be replaced by an influential military man who shared his vision of cooperation between scholars and soldiers. After both Gen. John Morrison and the new Army War College president, Gen. M. M. Macomb, rejected the position, Johnston held out for the appointment of Gen. Tasker H. Bliss.[48] When this also fell through, Johnston agreed to retain the chairmanship for the immediate future. But in a surprise move and with no explanation, he also suggested that the executive council consider dropping the Committee on Military and Naval History from the AHA's list of standing committees.[49]

Johnston resigned his chairmanship in 1916, and, deprived of its driving force, the committee sat inactive for the next three years. From 1919 until the panel's demise, retired general Eben Swift chaired the committee and attempted to breathe life back into it. Unlike Johnston, he tried to convene regular meetings of its members.[50] From his office in Washington, he also organized popular seminars on military history for local AHA members and interested members of the general public.[51] Under Swift's direction, the committee attempted to arrange special sessions for AHA annual conventions and voted to support the preparation of AHA-sponsored volumes devoted to studies in military history.[52] At the annual convention of 1924, however, the AHA executive council voted to remove Swift's group from its list of standing committees.[53]

The council's action revealed nothing surprising. The old general did not fit the AHA ideal of seminar-trained scholars, and this "saturated solution of Civil War history" who had reigned for years over the army postgraduate schools no longer fit into the professional historical mainstream.[54] None of his committee members had gained sufficient professional status to salvage the group's reputation among AHA regulars.

More important, the intellectual climate of the historical profession had changed, and the study of military affairs found no comfortable place in it. As the belief grew in the academic committee that U.S. involvement in the Great War had been a mistake, Swift's nationalism—some would have argued militarism—worked against him and his committee. When the general complained about the flagging interest of the AHA in his group's activities and the increasing difficulty of calling together its members, the executive council decided to drop the committee.

If Johnston can be blamed for the poor showing of his own AHA committee, he still can take credit for the progress of another project he had inspired: the association's special military history prize committee. Although he had been considered for a dual chairmanship of the Committee on Military and Naval History and the panel to award the writing prize, Johnston refused the latter, because it would have overextended him.[55]

Johnston's contributions to the prize committee were nonetheless considerable. Through his own exertion, he successfully solicited one hundred fifty dollars from the Infantry Association and, with the assistance of Albert Bushnell Hart, collected an additional fifty dollars in personal contributions from members of the Military History Society of Massachusetts.[56] After Johnston added fifty dollars from his own pocket, the executive committee quickly accepted the two hundred fifty dollars and endorsed the formation of a special committee to conduct the competition for the writing prize.

Unlike the diverse membership of Johnston's committee, the scholars appointed to the award panel shared a common commitment to the goal of improving the writing of American military history. The chairman, Capt. Arthur Conger of the Staff College, represented well the interests of the military establishment, and his training in the best historical seminars in European and American universities guaranteed that the academicians on his committee would not question his qualifications to serve. Joining Conger were Professors Hart, Fling, Milledge L. Bonham of Louisiana State University, and Allen R. Boyd of the Library of Congress.[57]

Unlike Johnston's committee in another important way, the military history award panel did much more than serve the special interests of its chairman. Although Conger and Fling carried the burden of the immediate responsibility for laying out the conditions of the award, they consulted the other members of the committee, who fully concurred with their plans.[58] Since both the soldiers and the academicians on this committee channeled their efforts toward a goal they shared rather than wasting time squabbling on the issues that divided them, Conger's panel actually provided a more solid foundation for inspiring a collaborative spirit between the AHA and the War Department than Johnston's own committee had offered.

The award committee set about its duties with great diligence, intending to present the prize at the AHA convention in December 1915. It took great pains to publicize the competition in the *American Historical Review*, professional military journals, major newspapers in large cities across the United

States, and civilian and army and navy classrooms from coast to coast.[59] September 1, 1915, was the deadline for submissions. Most important, the committee agreed upon a stringent set of conditions for the manuscripts.

The tough requirements for the monographs demonstrated the entire panel's commitment to improving the quality of writing about American military affairs. They demanded original and independent research. Although not limiting competitors to any specific topic, the panel agreed with Fling that the Civil War offered the most promising opportunities for the high-quality research the members hoped the competition would inspire. Beyond that single hint, a monograph could deal with campaigns, battles, important controversial incidents that occurred during these actions, the fortunes of a corps or division in action, or such important general topics as mobilization, supply, the organization and training of volunteers, or national military strategy and policy. Each monograph submitted for consideration was expected to meet all the canons of historical criticism, contain references to all secondary literature used in its preparation, and be accompanied by a full critical bibliography. No author could exceed one hundred thousand words, and the committee made known that the neatness of the presentation and an artful writing style would also be taken into consideration.[60]

The first call for papers attracted a disappointing response. Only four authors contributed essays,[61] and the small number of competitors was only the first of a series of misfortunes to plague the committee. For all its good intentions to draw greater attention to the special problems of writing military history, the hopes of the award panel were dashed by events it could not control, some of which would actually have forced the committee to compromise the high standards it was specifically designed to promote.

The most embarrassing problem took the committee completely by surprise. In the best judgment of the panel members, not one of the four authors had achieved the high quality the historians demanded. Throughout the autumn of 1915, Fling and Bonham clashed with Hart and Boyd over whether to give the monetary prize at all. Fling, especially, stood firm against handing out the award to the best of what he considered to be a bad lot of entries, a sentiment in which Bonham concurred.[62] To award a prize under these circumstances would set a bad precedent as well as undercut the primary purpose of the competition.

Hart and Boyd, on the other hand, believed the award should be given to the author of the best paper regardless of the quality, if only to stimulate greater interest in and publicity for future contests.[63] Finally, Conger broke the tie by siding with Fling and Bonham. In explaining his decision to Hart, he pointed out that the prize given to the winner would be the entire sum collected, not the interest accrued from a permanent fund. Not knowing when another such cash award might be available to promote the writing of military history, Conger preferred to remain true to the spirit that had inspired the contest in the first place.[64]

Just as Conger and his committee prepared to reopen the competition for 1916, still other problems surfaced. First, Capt. H. L. Landers, the author of the paper that had been judged the best of the original four, accosted Conger and the other members of the committee and demanded an explanation for their decision not to present the award to him. Landers had been a promising student at the Staff College, and his criticism of Conger's handling of the contest left his former instructor vulnerable to unfounded charges of conflict of interest.[65] Moreover, before Conger could resolve the problems that this first competition had exposed, he was ordered from Fort Leavenworth to join his regiment on the Mexican border.[66]

Conger's departure signaled a long break in the effective work of the award committee. His replacement, the redoubtable Johnston, could not untangle the mass of unresolved questions and problems in time for the next contest.[67] Before the rules for a 1917 competition could be agreed upon, the United States had entered World War I and both Johnston and Fling were called into active service in the army's rapidly expanding historical office.[68] Another attempt to put together a contest in 1918 also failed.[69] The rough start and the long interruption between competitions effectively killed public and professional interest in the project and award.

Reviving the contest immediately after World War I became extremely difficult as the traditional sources for military history essays evaporated. In the Army Service Schools, the history seminars that might have produced award-winning essays were dropped for a time in favor of courses more immediately and practically related to the issues of leadership and strategy that had emerged from the great conflict.[70] In the liberal atmosphere of American universities, where only a few years earlier the preparedness campaign had generated considerable interest in military affairs, the study of war now smacked too much of Prussian militarism to hold any appeal.[71] The future of the military history essay competition appeared bleak.

Still, the historians on the award committee refused to give up. In 1920, as interest in military history began its slow decline in popularity, the members of a reconstituted award committee successfully concluded a competition that relied almost entirely upon the conditions first adopted by the original panel for the 1915 contest.[72] Selecting from eight entries, Bonham, Boyd, Hart, and Fling, now joined by Prof. F. M. Anderson of Dartmouth College, awarded the first—and only—AHA Military History Prize to Thomas Robson Hay of Pittsburgh for his essay on Confederate general John Bell Hood's 1864 campaign in Tennessee.[73]

Even then, the award was given reluctantly. After an emergency conference of the committee members, they decided to name a winner for fear that the funds would be returned to the AHA general treasury if the prize was not awarded. After the two hundred fifty dollars was presented to Hay, along with the recommendation that he make substantial revisions to his essay before he attempted to publish it,[74] the committee disbanded when no additional funds were appropriated to continue the competition.[75]

The bright, brief flash that marked the life of the AHA's Committee on Military and Naval History and its monograph competition left little mark on the mainstream practitioners of the historical profession. The spirit of cooperation between soldiers and scholars that Johnston had envisioned did not take root in the highly partisan atmosphere of AHA committee rooms. A successful collaboration demanded that the two groups reach agreement about the areas in which the officers' authority remained unchallenged and the matters in which the expertise of seminar-trained historians took precedence. The resolution of such questions required a neutral court. The AHA meetings attended by War Department functionaries did not provide such an environment.

In his zeal to promote the scientific study of military history, Johnston also failed to grasp the simple reality that few men in or out of uniform shared his special enthusiasm. By sheer dint of personal effort, he had succeeded in marching his colleagues down an unfamiliar path, but they had not always followed eagerly. Even so strong an ally as Hart admitted with chagrin: "I hardly know how I came into the military business except through the energy of Johnston."[76] True, the AHA had given in to Johnston's constant pressure, but the executive council's decision to create the two military history committees in 1913 is best interpreted as an attempt to deal with the AHA's specific and immediate problems with the War Department, not as a revolutionary departure to promote a special field of intellectual inquiry.

When Johnston took his crusade to the AHA, he temporarily gave up on his original plans to push immediately for either an army historical section or an independent military history society. Nonetheless, his fundamental notions were sound and ultimately proved successful. The establishment of an army historical section came first. In January 1914 Chief of Staff Leonard Wood took the initial step when he ordered the creation of a small, three-man historical section within the General Staff. During World War I, demand for the services of scholars expanded so greatly that Johnston accepted a major's commission to serve in the Historical Section of the U.S. Army despite growing heart problems that would kill him in 1920.[77] From his post with the American Expeditionary Force, he pushed for the establishment of both a National War Museum to provide a repository for military archives and a supporting association of AEF veterans that would underwrite the cost of educational programs to keep the American public informed about military affairs.

He changed his original proposition in only one significant way: At first, at least, he intended to leave administration of the museum in the hands of the army historical section alone.[78] At that, it was probably not a huge departure from his original plan for collaboration between soldiers and scholars. When he made the suggestion, considerable numbers of prominent academic historians were serving on active duty with the army historical office that would administer the new museum.

Johnston's idea of an independent military history society also caught on, but in a way he did not expect. In August 1912 Congress incorporated a naval history society that drew upon the talents of such diverse members as civilian historians Paullin and Charles F. Adams, Admirals Chadwick and George Dewey, and several former secretaries of the navy.[79] Its first two projects were precisely the kind that Johnston no doubt hoped the army would adopt: a serious search for important records and documents in private hands and a successful publication project that included the printing of important personal diaries and officers' letter books.[80]

Although he did not live to see it, Johnston's dream for an independent military history society was fulfilled in 1935 when the American Military Institute was established. Fittingly, he was eulogized by his old friend, Col. Arthur Conger, in the pages of the first issue of its professional journal, now entitled the *Journal of Military History* (previously *Military Affairs*).[81]

The AHA in the years before World War I seemingly extended its hand to the War Department in a spirit of cooperation. But the professional association's interest in promoting American military history was a fleeting one. The inspiration that Johnston supplied died when he removed his own boundless energy, the fuel that made it burn so bright. And, as with many experiments, the AHA in the long run could not sustain a commitment it did not genuinely feel.

11

A PYRRHIC VICTORY: THE U.S. ARMY'S
HISTORICAL SECTION, 1914–1920

As long as the Old Army's struggle for authority over the study of military history remained unresolved, any hope for successful collaboration between soldiers and scholars required a delicate balancing of institutional interests. The AHA with its confrontational tactics had created considerable friction by pressing the historians' protests against the traditional practices of overworked, protective, or conservative War Department bureaucrats. The AHA's Committee on Military and Naval History provided a more congenial environment for individual historians and interested army authorities to discuss shared concerns. Nonetheless, its members had failed to inspire the professional historical association or the War Department to make the kinds of policy changes that would encourage a lasting spirit of cooperation.

During these frustrating years, soldiers and scholars turned to a third option that, like the others, guaranteed total victory to neither side. It did, however, clearly favor the army's interests. In 1914, Chief of Staff Leonard Wood took the first steps toward the creation of a historical section within the General Staff that possessed authority to consult actively with professional historians. This intriguing approach blended an old idea with a relatively new one, and, as with other attempts to find common ground shared by soldiers and scholars, it met with mixed results. Interest in a War Department or General Staff historical office had emerged frequently since the 1870s. By comparison, the notion of American military officers collaborating with academicians was a recent one, popularized in large part by the special session at the AHA annual meeting in 1912 that led to the creation of the historical association's Committee on Military and Naval History.[1]

Although a small historical section was established in 1914, the national mobilization of 1917 provided the first genuine opportunity to explore the possibilities of soldier-scholar collaboration. The wartime experience satisfied neither side completely. For the historians especially, efforts to collaborate with the army did not produce the desired results. No foundation for a long-term postwar blending of the technical expertise of military men and the research and writing skills of scholars emerged from the Historical Section. Instead of resolving the differences between the War Department and professional historians, the operations of the wartime Historical Section so intensified some problems that the academicians temporarily left the field of the fight for authority over the practice of military history.

From the beginning of the army's reform agitation in the post–Civil War years, the creation of a historical section greatly interested a number of key progressive officers and military critics. Col. Emory Upton was among the first to see the potential contribution of such a section to the improvement of military professionalism in the United States. In the lengthy report he filed after his worldwide inspection tour of foreign military establishments in the mid-1870s, he recommended that one section of The Adjutant General's Office be set aside to "write the military history of our wars, both Indian and civilized, thereby enabling our future officers to become familiar with the peculiarities of American fighting."[2]

Equally as persuasive as Upton was the influential British military critic Spenser Wilkinson, whose famous study *The Brain of an Army* inspired Secretary of War Elihu Root to create an American General Staff at the turn of the century. The secret to the vaunted Prussian generalship lay in the historical work of its General Staff, Wilkinson argued. If an army sought the "most effective means of teaching war during peace," it must create an office capable of high-quality, critical examination of past military affairs.[3]

The seeds planted by Upton and Wilkinson in the late nineteenth century sprouted first during the 1890s, but they did not immediately mature into the independent historical department each had advocated. Until the eve of World War I, the new bureau found itself so completely entangled with other important organizational reforms that the early antecedents of the U.S. Army's historical section showed up in different forms and in different niches of the increasingly complex War Department.

Military history's first foothold in the U.S. Army emerged during the War Department's push for the creation of a Military Information Division. Another of Upton's cogent suggestions, this fledgling military intelligence agency was designed to gather useful information about the state of preparedness and professional practice in foreign armies.[4] After a small-scale start in 1885, the Military Information Division in 1890 took on the responsibilities of collecting the reports of American military attachés overseas. When these specially assigned officers received orders to "examine the military libraries, bookstores and publishers lists in order to give early notice on any new or important publications," the official works of the historical sections in foreign armies attracted considerable attention in the United States.[5] Even if the early Military Information Division did not carry out independent historical research on its own, with directors such as Maj. Arthur L. Wagner, translations of foreign historical works became an important part of the "monographs, books, papers, and other publications" that the agency distributed throughout the army.[6]

During the first rocky decade in the life of the General Staff, the study of military history drifted, anchorless, throughout the army's table of organization. Transferred in 1903 from The Adjutant General's Office to the so-called Second Division of the General Staff, the Military Information Section found among its specific duties the "collection, arrangement, and publication of historical, statistical, and geographical information . . . [and] the preparation from official records of analytical and critical histories of important campaigns."[7] With only six officers assigned to the entire Second Division, however, historical work took a backseat to satisfying the informational needs of the rapidly expanding attaché service and to in-depth observations of the Russo-Japanese War.

In 1908 the army's erstwhile military history office moved again when the entire Second Division of the General Staff merged with the Third, or War College, Division to bring together under one chief all the necessary tools for efficient war planning. The Military Information Committee in this newly reorganized Second Section of the General Staff retained the same historical duties it had been allotted when it was part of the old Second Division, but now its work on campaign studies took second place to providing direct assistance to Army War College planners. When the Military Information Committee's records were centralized with those of the entire section, the specific duties of the office disappeared and its historical functions were forgotten.[8]

In 1910, when the General Staff was reorganized into four divisions— Mobile Army, War College, Coast Artillery, and Militia Affairs—the War College Division took charge of the "preparation from authentic sources of histories of important military events." Unfortunately, the responsibility for historical studies lay buried among numerous other important duties, including the publication of technical military monographs and articles for service journals, direction of military education in the army schools, maintenance of military maps, and comprehensive administration of the Army War College Library.[9]

Little wonder, then, that its advocates desired a more well-defined place in the army's table of organization for the sytematic study of American military campaigns. To jolt the War Department into extending a measure of official institutional recognition to the professional study of military history, a move that would merely match a long-standing practice in the armies of other major nations, concerned army officers and their erstwhile allies in the historical community launched a combined assault to promote this intellectual specialty in the United States as well.

Although progress came slowly, when the final successful push began, Prof. Robert M. Johnston was again in the forefront. In the pages of the *Infantry Journal*, he made a strong case in support of a special army history office.[10] Johnston's assertive arguments stimulated considerable debate in both army and civilian circles. The wide array of notables drawn to his cause guaranteed that the creation of a historical office would receive the serious consideration of the highest officials of the War Department and General Staff.

Johnston's first allies came from the military press. Not surprisingly, officers close to the army's education system threw their enthusiastic support behind the establishment of a historical section. The editors of the *Infantry Journal* embraced Johnston's plan as a remedy for the critical shortcomings of the General Staff, especially its failure to provide army officers with a uniquely American military doctrine. "There is still no historical section of the general staff, and yet there can never be a general staff prepared to meet in full the obligations resting upon it until such a section is created and at work," they argued. Only a deep study of American wars would provide the basis for a "native doctrine" that "fit the facts of our national development."[11]

Not all of the reaction to Johnston's proposal was positive. Most stridently against it were committed pacifists such as *New York Evening Post* editor Oswald Garrison Villard, who protested that an army historical section would produce only self-serving works that sugarcoated American militarism and cloaked the nation's imperialistic designs under a mantle of respectability and morality.[12]

More surprising was the response of the editor of the popular *Army and Navy Journal*, so often sympathetic to army reforms; he doubted that American military experts were so poorly informed that they required the services of a historical office. He saw so little practical need for army officers to study history that he dismissed Johnston's plan curtly: "The trouble with this country is not that it does not know how certain things happened in our past, but that we have not had the sense to see that they do not happen again."[13] The connection between past policy and future reforms escaped him completely.

Johnston's proposal received its most comprehensive and well-publicized examination at the special AHA convention session in 1912 devoted to military history. In a most striking consensus, the historical section's strongest advocates, both in and out of uniform, agreed that the future of military studies required the collaboration of army officers and professional historians.

The participation of soldiers in the AHA's special session guaranteed that the quickly reached consensus did not merely hide a power play orchestrated by civilian scholars to wrench control of the historical resources and publication program from the War Department. Key military professionals genuinely agreed that cooperation with civilian scholars was more likely than government-sponsored history projects to promote an accurate and objective study of American campaigns.

The soldiers offered persuasive arguments. Capt. Arthur L. Conger of the Staff College asserted that military history in the United States needed to avoid at all costs the charge of adopting "a point of view promulgated by the government for its own purposes," a serious flaw that tainted the official publications of the Prussian army's historical section. If scholars combined their writing and analytical talents with an army office that would compile "certain fundamental work, such as the establishment of the basic data relative to the strength, organization and armament of armies as well as the preparation of reliable maps," Conger was sure that accurate narratives would follow. If the army history section concerned itself chiefly with this kind of technical detail, the historical profession might well discover a new interest in military affairs.[14]

Col. Thomas L. Livermore then bridged the gap between the soldiers and the scholars. "[M]any civilian historians all through the country . . . would be glad to write of the Civil War if they only knew what they were writing about, if they only knew where the troops were." Livermore's arguments were especially convincing when he explained the difficulties he himself had encountered in his painstaking study of troop deployments around Vicksburg.[15] Cooperation between civilian and army scholars seemed increasingly possible when such respected academicians as Prof. Fred Fling criticized his own colleagues for erring in believing "history cannot be written by the army man, because the army man has in mind the application of things."[16]

Although Johnston's session at the AHA convention in 1912 increased awareness of the problems of writing military history, the War Department still hesitated before creating an army historical office. Two not entirely unrelated events then turned around the prospects for such an office. First, at Johnston's insistence, the AHA's new military and naval history committee presented to the War Department a formal recommendation, adopted at the 1913 annual convention, endorsing the formation of a historical section. Coming on the heels of an amicable agreement to cooperate on the Revolutionary War records project, Johnston's timing was outstanding.[17] More immediately influential, however, was Johnston's lecture to the Army War College entitled "The Functions of Military History."[18] Army Chief of Staff Leonard Wood, who attended the talk, had already spoken with Johnston about the subject on earlier occasions and concurred with his arguments. On January 3, 1914, Wood ordered the establishment of a history office within the General Staff.

Wood understood the magnitude of the challenge before him. "We cannot arrange it so that [the historical section] will spring into action fully equipped and highly efficient, but we can at least start it and build as we go," he wrote to Col. John Biddle, the senior General Staff officer at the Army War College.[19] Biddle and Army War College president Hunter Liggett soon realized the truth of Wood's words. "In my opinion there is nobody now available – on the general staff – to commence this work," Liggett wrote Biddle when they tried to find men suited to the new office.[20] Even after all the discussion on the benefits of soldier-scholar collaboration, however, the army did not turn to civilian historians to offset the new bureau's initial personnel problems.

The two officers had correctly assessed the shortage of qualified manpower. Biddle and Liggett's list of suitable officers included only five names. Complicating matters further, not one of the candidates was a General Staff officer; these soldiers would have to be transferred to the history office from their line commands and thereby remained vulnerable to the army's restrictions on detached duty. Infantry major James W. McAndrew and captains John McAuley Palmer and Arthur L. Conger, cavalry captain Stuart Heintzelman, and field artillery captain Oliver L. Spaulding looked to be the most promising candidates until sufficient numbers of Staff College graduates of the new history curriculum could man the new office.[21]

Liggett and Biddle had further reason for concern. Of the five officers they named, only Conger and Spaulding had received university training in historical methods and only the former had proven himself in army classrooms. Indeed, Professor Johnston advised Wood that "Captain Conger is the only army officer with any competence whatever for the work." Perhaps trying to open a door for civilian scholars, Johnston modified his endorsement with, "It is only fair to add, however, that he does not appear qualified on the literary side and should therefore have collaborators."[22]

Despite the shortage of qualified personnel, Wood, Biddle, and Liggett agreed to man a historical section. When none of their original candidates could be spared from their military duties, Biddle and Liggett selected three General Staff officers for the new office: Maj. D. W. Ketcham, Maj. William D. Connor, and Capt. H. C. Smither. They were untrained in historical methods, although all had attended or served on the faculty of at least one of the army's postgraduate schools. "I am glad the committee has been appointed, and I think it can commence the work, even if it cannot make much progress at first," Wood wrote Biddle.[23] Wood was content under the circumstances to let the new office serve primarily as an advisory committee and not as an active research agency.

From its establishment in January 1914 until the United States declared war in April 1917, the fledgling history office made no greater progress than

Wood anticipated. In addition to personnel problems, affairs on the Mexican border diverted the committee's attention from its editorial supervision of the Army War College official military history of the Civil War. The three-man bureau initiated no other major projects and devoted itself to General Staff duties, chiefly gathering information for future reference on the duties and organization of the historical sections of the British, French, German, Austrian, Japanese, and other foreign armies.[24]

Professor Johnston, from his position as chairman of the AHA Standing Committee on Military and Naval History, kept a close eye on the progress of the office he had helped to create. In a letter to Wood shortly after the section's formal establishment, Johnston suggested a division of the historical office's prospective responsibilities under two headings: instruction and publication. Immediate needs included the development of a brief course in the army postgraduate schools that would analyze the interrelations between war and economics since the sixteenth century, the improvement of the Virginia battlefield tours, and the introduction of a regular seminar to teach officers assigned to the Historical Section the newest archival techniques and advances in bibliography, criticism, and methodology.[25]

Johnston hoped these instructional improvements would facilitate the rewriting of American military history, which was the section's second major responsibility. He tried to establish a pattern of military-civilian collaboration by offering to work with the new section and students at the Army War College on a campaign study of Second Manassas to complement his own earlier work on First Manassas.[26] Better educated personnel could also improve the quality of monographic studies and provide a pool of reliable authors for one of Wood's pet projects, a professional journal for the General Staff.[27]

When his prodding precipitated no rapid change, Johnston maintained his pressure on the War Department in the pages of the *Military Historian and Economist*. He tried insults. In the journal's policy statement, he bluntly ignored the army Historical Section to write: "We need the best opinion[,] not the best support. For that reason we shall turn to Europe for a considerable part of the collaboration we require."[28] When that did not trigger a response, he devoted space to the follies of the French army's historical section in the hope of stirring the Americans to greater action.[29] After several years of frustration, Johnston characteristically complained, "Our [current] danger, in its most extreme form, is the conception of a Historical Section presided over by a veteran of the Civil War and engaged, at the expense of the public, in writing accounts of all its heroes."[30]

Johnston had good reason to be concerned. After the United States entered World War I in 1917, any attempt to increase the size or responsibilities of the small prewar history section was fruitless until the War Department untangled the armywide organizational problems intensified by the massive national mobilization. As long as Secretary of War Newton D. Baker, AEF commander John J. Pershing, and three successive army chiefs of staff could not resolve questions of authority with the traditionalists among the bureau chiefs, Johnston's suggestions to improve the historical office's efficiency was bound to disappear in the maze of paperwork and red tape.[31] Not until August 1917 did the War College Division and the secretary of war begin to consider how the Historical Section could contribute to the war effort, and more important, what steps needed to immediately be taken to lay the groundwork for writing a postwar official history.

On the surface, the War College Division's initial scheme for an official history of American participation in World War I seemed to mesh neatly with the notion of collaboration between civilian scholars and military men. Over one-third of the General Staff officers who ordinarily would have been first in line for appointments to the Historical Section had already been assigned to active duty with troops or on army, corps, or divisional staffs in Europe. To take up the slack, the War College Division quickly announced the army's commitment to utilize the talents of "historians of established ability" and even earmarked newly promoted Major Conger and Professors Johnston and Neilson at Harvard University as the likely coordinators of a comprehensive history program.[32]

Unfortunately, War College Division officials in August 1917 took no action to carry out their plans. They made no move to increase the size of the history office, dismissing as impossible the addition of active-duty army officers and questioning the need for recalling retired or disabled soldiers for service in the Historical Section. The War Department also resisted the commissioning of qualified academicians for duty in Washington, and bureau officials opposed as "premature" the formal appointment of civilian scholars to the new agency.[33]

The War College Division's refusal to secure the services of civilian scholars in the fall of 1917 nearly killed any chance for an official history at all. When the chief of the division's Military Information Section reported that the burden of collecting historical data had grown so heavy that continuing the effort without more men was "impracticable," the overworked officers assigned to these duties were relieved and their project discontinued.[34]

During the autumn of 1917, the only promising sign for the future of an official military history emerged when Johnston, Pershing, and AEF Chief of Staff Gen. James G. Harbord agreed that each unit commander (or his chief of staff) should keep a "war diary." A longtime European practice then under consideration for adoption by the American army, a war diary "can secure your place in history and vindicate you from the injustices our country sometimes visits on her Generals," Harbord wrote Pershing.[35] Although not as useful to historians as predicted, the army, corps, and divisional war diaries became important sources for unraveling the American contributions to the complex military operations on the western front.

For nearly five months, the future of the army's history program languished in uncertainty. Just when things seemed gloomiest, army Chief of Staff Tasker H. Bliss, supporter of military history since his tenure as instructor at the Naval War College in the 1880s, recommended in January 1918 the formation of an enlarged historical section composed of "the most competent civilian and military personnel." This office, attached to the War College Division of the General Staff, revitalized the prospects for writing a sound official record of American participation in "one of the world's few important crises."[36]

In its final form, Bliss's new wartime Historical Section reflected the ideas of one scholar and one soldier. Col. Paul Azan of the French army's historical section, in an address to the American Historical Association in December 1917, had called for the Americans to adopt the practices of his own organization. He called for a bureau whose prime function lay in studying and analyzing military documents to bring out important lessons, "those points that are useful for establishing the theory which the General Staff must put into effect for the whole army."[37] The French army, like other European military establishments, had created long ago a separate administrative archives from which the historical section of its general staff could cull important documents without concern for the proper maintenance of routine paperwork.

No such central administrative archives existed in the American army, and this prevented the full implementation of Azan's plan.[38] Until the war ended and historically important documents could be separated from the mountain of wartime paperwork, the officially stated policy of the War College Division's acting chief, Col. D. W. Ketcham, was that the Historical Section's responsibilities extended only to collecting and arranging official papers for later study.

Colonel Ketcham and his colleagues held a much lower opinion of Johnston's ideas. The professor, of course, had submitted his own scheme for the new Historical Section. "Subject to the direction of the General Staff," officers assigned to the historical office would be empowered to "invade the confidential records of the Intelligence Section and reorganize the record system of The Adjutant General's Department and of the Army at large, as a part of its war activities."[39] Dismissing this plan as far too ambitious and hinting at his concerns over Johnston's challenge to traditional army bureaucracy, Ketcham charitably stated that he simply could not muster the manpower to carry out such broad responsibilities as the professor suggested.

The War College Division assigned four broad functions to its new Historical Section. Naturally, the collection and arrangement of historical sources, including maps, was an important responsibility. Operation of the War Department library and the preparation of histories and historical monographs were two additional functions that had to be shelved until after the surrender. In wartime, only the section's fourth function, the study of the events and the lessons of current military history for officer education, held prime importance to Ketcham and his colleagues. They realized that reviews of current military affairs written from only an American vantage point would "be more or less in the nature of propaganda." Nonetheless, War College Division officials believed the section could do no more important service in wartime. "It is safe to say that the real history of the present war will not be written during the lifetime of the men who are making history," Ketcham concluded.[40]

Limited to specific duties by War College Division directives, the wartime Historical Section received a complement of only thirteen officers, seven assigned from the General Staff and six detached from combat arms, to carry out its responsibilities. Ketcham and his subordinates considered the officers' responsibilities to be military duties, and two key personnel guidelines demonstrated the strength of their opposition to the inclusion of any but active-duty officers.

Ketcham's preferred policy left little room for civilian personnel. First, if the office were required to accept personnel from outside the active ranks, properly qualified retired and disabled officers were deemed the most desirable candidates for historical duties. Second, and more to the point, Ketcham asserted that the "unrestricted utilization of civilian historians in or by the historical section is open to objection." Civilian historians, he noted, "are accustomed to little restriction in their activities and are apt to be impatient of restraint." Without well-defined and limited duties, they "are capable of causing considerable friction."[41] It seemed that the collaborative spirit, as well as freedom of access and interpretation, became early casualties of the war emergency.

Although Washington bureaucrats seemed intent on burying the future of collaboration between military and civilian historians, Gen. John J. Pershing prevented a premature interment. Granted wide latitude by Secretary Baker to override War Department standing policies, the general asked for a special seven-man historical section to serve at his headquarters in France. Pershing desired the assignment of five qualified army officers, preferably Staff Col-

lege graduates who were disabled for active service. In addition to the officers, Pershing asked for two civilian experts to act as advisers. They were
to be chosen from among the historians in the United States "who have
established reputations in dealing with military history."[42]

The general's requests clashed with standing policies, but the War Plans
Division that superseded the War College Division in the army's reorganization in February 1918 quickly found a way to satisfy him. The army's new
centralized system of administration cut deeply into the traditional powers
of the bureau chiefs, who resented the interference of all outsiders.[43] Now
more concerned with efficiency and smooth functioning than with red tape,
War Department officials were able to justify an important change from
their original plans: Civilian historians and retired and disabled officers
were to be commissioned directly as officers in the National Army and assigned to the Historical Section.[44] The door for a cooperative effort cracked
open once again.

The list of retired or disabled officers who received orders to report for
duty in the new, expanded History Branch read like a roster of the army's
intellectual leaders of the past generation. Although the new branch chief,
Col. Charles W. Weeks, was a relative unknown, the first list of qualified
officers included retired majors John Bigelow, Matthew Forney Steele, and
Herbert H. Sargent, who was now nearly deaf.[45] The War Department hoped
the leadership of such men would help to lay the groundwork for an ambitious, comprehensive official history of American participation in World
War I along seven lines: American diplomatic relations, naval operations,
AEF operations, financial operations, industrial mobilization, military mobilization, and pictorial records.[46]

Many of these retired officers readily embraced their new duties. Bigelow
took over the military mobilization section of the Historical Branch in Washington, and Sargent prepared to join the history section of Pershing's staff
in France. Of the best-known officers, only Steele refused, citing important
family business in North Dakota, where he continued to drill cadets at the
state's university at Fargo.[47]

Pershing specifically asked Johnston for the names of civilian historians
suitable for assignment to AEF headquarters. When he appeared not to
mind the changes the army had made in his original scheme for a historical
section, Johnston himself was invited to Washington to join the new bureau.[48]
Commissioned a major in the National Army, Johnston soon took command of the historical contingent assigned to the Military Intelligence Section of Pershing's staff.

Other top academicians soon followed Johnston into the branch's ranks.
Prof. Frederic L. Paxson of the University of Wisconsin took on the respon-

sibilities of preparing studies on the nation's economic mobilization.[49] Newly commissioned major Frederick Fling relied upon his deep knowledge of European history to take on the duties of the diplomatic history section and immediately sought State Department cooperation to complete the historical record of the roots of the war.[50] Among younger historians who would become more prominent in the postwar generation of scholars, Pvt. Dexter Perkins received a commission as a lieutenant and an immediate reassignment from his National Army unit to serve as a research assistant.[51]

When Johnston, Fling, and other university historians accepted their commissions, the War Department had taken a giant step toward establishing a spirit of cooperation between soldiers and scholars. Equally apparent, however, this collaboration took place on the army's terms. Although the army could draw freely upon the scholars' talents, the academicians were also officers who were subject to army regulations, which would reduce the likelihood of "friction."

Nonetheless, by July 1918 the branch's new personnel policy needed further refinements, and Colonel Weeks was forced to address more directly the issue of cooperation with civilians. Officers in the Historical Branch, faced with a growing mountain of topics that required special expertise they did not have, considered a proposal to establish a five-thousand-dollar fund to pay the expenses of civilians who had information or talents the office needed.[52]

At first, Colonel Weeks and his staff could reach no consensus. Maj. R. M. D. Taylor saw little choice but to seek the assistance of qualified specialists. "[T]here is a wide range of subjects which must be treated which are beyond the training and habit of thought of the military members of the branch. . . . I believe that the precedent should be established now that if the Historical Branch needs assistance that it should recognize it and pay for it."[53] Col. Adna G. Clarke concurred. He noted that the cost of publishing the official records of the Civil War had cost over three million dollars, and he did not believe the Great War project could be carried off for any less.

It was not entirely surprising that major objections came from Sargent and Bigelow, the more traditional army intellectuals. Sargent doubted that any civilian could offer important information the branch could not discover for itself. "When money is being spent so freely I feel we should have an eye for economy in matters of this kind. If any one has anything valuable to impart, surely he can write it out and send it." Bigelow was more direct: "Do not see necessity for it. Might approve of it later."[54] The proposal was designed to encourage the special contributions of men such as Judge Alfred K. Nippert of Cincinnati, who held valuable firsthand knowledge of the Russian invasion of East Prussia.[55] Nonetheless, without full concurrence, the five-thousand-dollar fund was disapproved.[56]

The War Department's stand against paying civilians for useful information greatly increased the burdens of the young Historical Branch as the war continued. At its peak, the branch consisted of forty commissioned officers, six warrant officers, and thirty-five civilian clerks and stenographers.[57] Although consideration of naval affairs was dropped, the responsibilities of the branch expanded nevertheless. The office was divided into nine sections, each of which acted as an independent investigation team in one of a broad range of important areas: administrative and general military history, records keeping, newspaper clippings files, diplomatic relations, army operations, military mobilization, economic mobilization, pictorial collections, and motion picture collections.[58] An official history of the Great War developed along these lines would have been the kind of comprehensive collaborative study the scholars and soldiers both wanted.

After the armistice, when the real work of the Historical Branch was just beginning, storm clouds gathered. During the six months following the end of the war, soldiers and scholars could no longer ignore an assortment of nagging problems that in the interests of good relations had been hushed during hostilities. Initially, at least, the spirit of cooperation seemed to remain alive. Each side was convinced that sound solutions could be found to resolve the three most troublesome problems: the Historical Branch's proper position in the army's table of organization to guarantee it sufficient prestige and authority to carry out its work, the continuing manpower shortages, and the problem of unauthorized records pilferers, or "privateers." Although the soldiers and scholars of the Historical Branch considered many reasonable ways to solve these problems, they could not foresee or forestall the destructive impact on their office of Secretary of War Baker's postwar policies.

A leading complaint of army historians centered on the Historical Branch's lack of authority to carry out even its fundamental duty to collect noncurrent military documents. Its position as an adjunct of the War Plans Division of the General Staff had proven unsatisfactory. Especially in Europe, "Historical Section business is on the bottom of staff piles because of the stress of operations," Johnston complained.[59] At the end of the war, Pershing drew attention to the important duties of the AEF's Historical Section when he transferred the office from his Intelligence Section to a more prominent position under the immediate control of his chief of staff, a move that Johnston applauded.[60] Pershing extended no further assistance until March 1919 when he assigned the Historical Section to be the custodian of all army historical documents in France and ordered his subordinates to turn over "such files as you may designate" to Johnston "at earliest convenience."[61]

Johnston hoped the Historical Branch in Washington would follow the lead of the AEF and transfer the office to the control of the army chief of staff.[62] Although this move would make the Historical Branch considerably more visible, not all interested observers agreed that exchanging one bureaucratic master for another augured well for the future of the office. Now that the war was over, the army's historians wanted an opportunity to pursue their work with an objective spirit and a minimum of bureaucratic manipulation or interference. Two notions seemed particularly appealing: independent status and equality with the other divisions of the General Staff or a secure location in the army school system.

Independent status, although an attractive idea, was a pipe dream from the start.[63] Even before the National Defense Act of 1920 gutted the broad wartime powers of the General Staff, the bureau chiefs reasserted their authority and pushed successfully for a return to the traditional decentralized bureaucracy of the prewar years. Under the new table of organization, the General Staff would become just another more or less equal department with the other bureaus.[64] An independent historical section in this new Office of the Chief of Staff would no longer have the special authority it might have received under the wartime organization. Moreover, a newly instituted Historical Branch would face serious opposition from older agencies that might well resent what they perceived to be meddling in their affairs.

Resettling historical studies in the school system seemed to offer a more practical solution for those who sought a suitable atmosphere for objective work. Col. Oliver L. Spaulding, appointed in July 1919 to succeed Colonel Weeks as head of the history office, preferred that the Historical Branch become the foundation of the new Department of History for the postwar Staff College and School of the Line at Fort Leavenworth. Safely ensconced in the schools and out of bureau politics in Washington, the army's historians could serve as investigators, writers, and instructors, "precisely as is the case with professors in a college."[65]

Spaulding's intention to create almost a university atmosphere at the army postgraduate schools offers solid evidence that soldiers in the Historical Branch had not discarded totally the notion of some kind of collaboration with civilian scholars. As early as May 1919, before Spaulding became chief and at a time when the number of officers appointed to the Historical Branch actually increased, Colonel Weeks had begun to look for new ways to keep academicians involved in the branch's work after they returned to civilian life.

Spaulding, too, realized that the future of the Historical Branch would rely heavily on obtaining assistance from outside the army. He especially dreaded the passage of the National Defense Act of 1920, which would have drastically reduced the number of General Staff officers, the pool from which the Historical Branch drew its personnel. If the act passed, Spaulding would be re-

quired to carry on the ambitious official history program outlined by the
wartime Historical Branch with a staff of only three officers, three warrant
officers, and eight civilian assistants.[66]

Plans to maintain a postwar historical section that combined the talents
of soldiers and civilian scholars first underwent serious scrutiny in May
1919. Maj. R. V. D. Magoffin, a Quartermaster Corps officer assigned to the
economic mobilization section of the Historical Branch, offered two suggestions to relieve the bureau's postdemobilization manpower problems. First,
he suggested that the Historical Branch procure an appropriation of fifty
thousand dollars to build up a "civilian personnel of prominent historians."
He also supported the army's call for the establishment of a General Staff
Officers' Reserve Corps, which would make possible the short-term recall
of former officers or the temporary commissioning of trained specialists for
specific duties.[67]

Magoffin preferred the Reserve Corps option. He believed military service,
even on a temporary basis, offered men an opportunity to demonstrate their
patriotism. Regulations establishing pay and rank would reduce dickering
that might occur in dealing with civilians. The system would permit the appointment of reserve officers when it was convenient for them to serve, especially during university summer vacations. Moreover, Magoffin was sure, reserve officers liable for Historical Branch duties would be encouraged to keep
up with the professional literature in their areas of expertise to benefit both
their military and academic careers.[68]

Although the notion of soldier-scholar collaboration remained the ideal,
the prospect of hiring civilian scholars for the Historical Branch did not offer an entirely satisfactory alternative to the Reserve Corps proposal. On
the one hand, the army could ensure a far greater degree of continuity and
expertise by retaining the services of permanent civilian employees. On the
other hand, Maj. R. B. Patterson feared, the Historical Branch would be
able to select only from those civilian historians who would "not be the
foremost men of their profession," the men who held important civilian
academic posts.[69]

Magoffin also had serious practical doubts about the future of soldier-civilian collaboration now that the war emergency had ended. "Do they work
well together?" he asked. He was not sure a civilian scholar hired at an annual salary of five thousand dollars could work without friction under an
officer whose pay was considerably less. Most important, he doubted that
civilian historians would willingly subordinate their desires for "professional
advancement" to accept positions in the army's history office.[70]

Finding no easy solution to the manpower problem, a special panel that
included Cols. Spaulding and Conger and soon-to-be-demobilized Majs.

Johnston and Fling recommended the formation of an AHA committee of historians and archivists to advise the Historical Branch chief.[71] The plan threw the burden of responsibility for civilian participation in army history programs at least temporarily on the AHA. There probably was no other choice at the time. The War Department, in its postwar fiscal retrenchment, disallowed the fifty-thousand-dollar army fund to hire civilian scholars.[72] The reserve officer option also produced no immediate relief, although the section was able to use it to its advantage by the late 1920s.[73]

Magoffin's veiled suggestions of occasionally stormy relations between soldiers and scholars during the war pointed out a third major problem, one that revealed the conflicting priorities that hampered the flowering of a genuine spirit of cooperation: disagreement over the disposition of important military records. Even while in Europe, Major Johnston complained that some high-ranking unit commanders would not cooperate with the AEF Historical Section's attempts to collect all relevant operational records.

As Johnston saw it, the greatest threat to carrying out the section's duties came from Regular Army officers who made special arrangements with friends in important staff positions to obtain documents for their exclusive use. His special target was Lt. Col. John McAuley Palmer, whose well-known works on universal military training and the special problems of the army of a democracy were topics that did not interest the Historical Branch.[74] "There should not be the least occasion for crossing between Colonel Palmer and the Section," Johnston had written to Colonel Weeks. Nonetheless, Palmer's activities had already caused "a constant series of minor embarrassments."[75]

Although Pershing took steps to facilitate his AEF Historical Section's work in Europe, the collection of records from all the relevant army and civilian agencies in Washington and from French and British archives offered far greater challenges. Spaulding's response to an AHA survey of the historical work of governmental agencies concerning their wartime activities revealed the scope of his office's project. By late 1919, his office files included the official war photographs of the Signal Corps, the papers that Paxson had compiled on domestic economic mobilization, scattered records of the American supply effort in France, documents from the General Purchasing Board, considerable amounts of diplomatic material, and a small collection of operational reports from general headquarters.[76]

In February 1920 Col. William Lassiter of the War Plans Division surveyed the various bureaus to determine how many important records still lay outside the authority of the Historical Branch. The results shocked Spaulding. He found that twelve other army bureaus retained control over their war records. Moreover, he discovered he was competing with the Chemical Warfare, Ordnance, Transportation, Motor Transport, Engineer, and Air Service bureaus for publication of unit histories and technical studies.[77] In addition, the Medical Corps had already initiated work on its ten-volume official history of its wartime service to complement its Civil War volumes.[78] Before the Historical Branch could begin to write an official history of the Great War, it had to determine what competing agencies were doing so it could avoid duplication of effort.

Despite these substantial obstacles, the Regular Army officers of the undermanned Historical Branch continued to cultivate a spirit of cooperation with civilian scholars. Their War Department superiors, however, did not understand the purpose or the needs of the section and, in their fiscal retrenchment after the war, changed the Historical Branch's mission and undercut its efforts to maintain ties even with those academic historians who had served with the section in wartime. For the short term, at least, the effects would be devastating for army-AHA relations and for the professional study of military history.

In August 1919 Secretary of War Baker placed severe restrictions on the duties of the Historical Branch. "The work of the Historical Section should in my judgment be limited to the collection, indexing, and preservation of records, and the preparation of such monographs as are purely military in character and are designated to be of use to the War Department," he wrote.[79] Baker's order cut in half the Historical Branch's proposed official history. Much of the work already completed by Paxson on domestic industrial mobilization did not fit into the new scheme and was set aside; with the assistance of the Carnegie Endowment, some of his work would be independently published. Fling's diplomatic history also fell under the ax.

At least for the immediate future, the duties of the Historical Branch were limited to four areas: classification of all historical records received by that office; the publication of completed sets of documents; preparation of monographs on purely military topics such as battlefield operations or the supply effort; and service as the army's information center for historical questions.[80] The comprehensive history planned in 1918 was dead.

Baker's attitude toward official history nearly completed the destruction of any collaborative efforts between the Historical Branch and civilian historians. The secretary believed it was "impolitic and indiscreet" for the War Department to sponsor a narrative history that would discuss economic, political, and diplomatic questions and other matters outside the expertise of soldiers. The services of trained historians offered no solution to Baker's objections. "[A]n official historian would be but one of many historians and yet his philosophy and method would be stamped with approval while the deductions perhaps equally sound, of other scholars from the same facts would not be so approved." War Department responsibilities extended only to making records available to scholars so they could arrive at their own conclusions "unembarrassed by . . . an official interpretation."[81]

Baker's rulings of August 1919 produced precisely the kind of restrictions to independent intellectual investigation likely to place soldiers and scholars at cross-purposes. Civilian scholars were sufficiently put off by the War Department's new stand that for the next decade the army, not the AHA, initiated most of the contact between the two groups.

During the 1920s, army officers tried to rekindle close ties with the scholarly community. Historical Branch members attended AHA conventions, served on its committees, discussed ways of obtaining documents from foreign archives, and even offered to update Steele's *American Campaigns* to meet the current standards of historical scholarship.[82] Under the terms of the National Defense Act of 1920, eleven additional officers became specially qualified for duty in the Historical Branch by studying history at civilian universities.[83] Believing the recent war would inspire greater interest in military affairs than ever before, branch members offered to prepare for college use textbooks or pamphlets like those already adopted by ROTC classes.[84] In a stunning role reversal, the Historical Branch even volunteered to act as an advisory board to review the work of civilian scholars who wrote about American military affairs.[85] The army exerted its authority over military history in what it hoped was a show of good faith.

During the 1920s, civilian historians, for their part, surrendered rather gracelessly and unnecessarily much of their authority over military history. The lure of independent investigation free of governmental restriction attracted many historians whose academic careers had been disrupted by military service or wartime work in such information or propaganda agencies as the National Board for Historical Service or the National Security League's Committee on Patriotism through Education.[86] In addition, the strong historiographical currents of progressivism now undercut the traditional emphasis on nationalism, which was at the core of much military history. Moreover, the increasingly liberal and pacifistic atmosphere at American universities during the 1920s did not offer much promise for the future of the discipline in civilian circles, especially when dozens of historians who had justified American involvement in Europe during their wartime service discovered that their words now put their professional reputations under scrutiny.[87]

By 1928 military history was in such disrepute that when J. Franklin Jameson answered Gen. W. D. Connor's request for a list of scholars who might be willing to serve on a rebuilt advisory committee for the abbreviated World War I records project, he was able to scrape together just sixteen names. Only four of the men on his list—Fling, Paxson, Charles Ramsdell, and Samuel Eliot Morison—were fairly well established as scholars.[88] Jameson even

included naval historians on his list because "so few historical scholars oc-
cupy themselves much with military history in any technical sense."[89]

Paxson, for one, agreed to serve on the advisory committee, but the bad
feelings that had followed the tabling of his mobilization study remained:
"The nature of army life does not produce many research historians and it
is not worth while even to try to get useful historical studies out of of [sic]
busy military men, even if they are of general staff calibre," he warned Connor.[90]

The establishment and early life of the army's Historical Section was a
Pyrrhic victory for advocates of American military history. The new office
provided the long sought-after central organizational niche for the study of
the American military past. As an army agency, however, the section remained vulnerable to whatever limitations the War Department imposed
upon it. The Historical Branch, therefore, could not always surrender un-
conditionally to meet the standards, scope of studies, or methodology demanded by civilian scholars. Stung by only partial victories, academicians
dug in and refused those as well. The civilians' uncompromising attitude seriously hampered army attempts to lay firmer groundwork for a successful collaboration until the next national emergency, in 1941, created a more conducive atmosphere.[91]

For its efforts, the Historical Branch received little more than a modicum
of official support, interest, or recognition outside the army schools, and it
was as frustrated as the civilian scholars at its helplessness to undertake
important projects without War Department endorsement, additional manpower, or funding. Although the study of military history remained largely
on the army's terms, it was, at the same time, trapped between the intellectual and institutional priorities of the War Department and the AHA. The
U.S. Army Historical Branch found itself in the unenviable position of trying to serve two tough masters simultaneously, with little likelihood of pleasing either one.

12

EPILOGUE:
"THANK GOD FOR LEAVENWORTH"

World War I supplied the officer corps of the U.S. Army with its first great opportunity to apply the lessons learned in peacetime classrooms to the grim test of active campaigning. Once American forces were committed to the front lines in France, army educators and the General Staff could find out if the spirit of safe leadership expounded in school translated effectively to responsible command on the battlefield. The verdict was not long in coming. Shortly after his return to civilian life from service with Pershing's Historical Section, Prof. Robert M. Johnston wrote that "the fanaticism of the Leavenworth men" in the performance of their duties was perhaps "our greatest asset in the war."[1] Maj. James A. Van Fleet of the Sixth Division was more to the point: "Thank God for Leavenworth."[2]

Indeed, graduates of the army's postgraduate schools, the American officers best trained in the theory and practice of the art of war, had left a mark on the American Expeditionary Force far out of proportion to their numbers. When President Wilson asked Congress for a declaration of war in April 1917, the officer corps of the Old Army with at least one year of service numbered only 3,885. Just a little more than half were West Point graduates. Only 5.1 percent of the 3,885 had attended the Staff College and even fewer— a paltry 4.7 percent—had received appointments to the Army War College. The talents of these few highly trained soldiers might well have been lost in the great expansion of the officer corps during the war emergency; on Armistice Day, the U.S. Army included 188,434 active-duty officers.[3] Nonetheless, through design, chance, and necessity, graduates of the army's advanced schools found themselves holding many of the most sensitive and responsible positions in the AEF.

In 1923 Col. Oliver L. Spaulding of the Historical Branch compiled a statistical report about the military education of general officers who served in World War I. The contribution of the army school system to the army high command was unmistakable. All 3 full generals were West Point graduates, and 1 had attended the Army War College. Both lieutenant generals had graduated from West Point and the Army War College. Of 106 major generals, 99 were graduates of the Military Academy, and of those, 48 had attended at least one—and often more—of the postgraduate schools. Of 296 brigadiers, 249 had attended West Point, with 119 receiving some kind of advanced theoretical education.[4]

Although attention to professional studies in and out of the classroom had not made every graduate an unqualified success on the battlefield, unschooled officers all too often proved to be even greater liabilities in combat. Johnston openly expressed his dismay in one particular case in which an officer "marked out for speedy promotion to the highest rank" who had not attended the army's advanced professional schools had revealed a tendency "to think that you can solve the problems of modern war as you can those of insurrecto warfare by a judicious combination of force, horse sense, and a little ingenuity." As a result, he had "needlessly butchered his brigade during several weeks, not knowing what orders to issue or how to issue them." Although he later performed creditably in a position that did not carry command responsibilities, this officer had become "a wasted man under our system; and all for lack of a few months' staff course at Leavenworth."[5]

Graduates of advanced army schools also filled important staff positions in combat commands and in the Service of Supply, which were equally important in an army committed to the teamwork essential to safe leadership. Of the 123 most important staff positions in the AEF—especially the chiefs of staff on the army, corps, and division levels—64.2 percent were graduates of one or more of the advanced service schools.[6] In the eyes of some observers, these staff officers, whose duties brought them into constant contact with each other, formed a "magic inner circle" in the AEF.[7] The effective service of the graduates of the advanced schools notwithstanding, it would be shortsighted to accept Major Van Fleet's effusive commentary on the army education system too literally. "Thank God for Leavenworth" suggests praise not only for the army schools but also for the spirit of professionalism they were designed to advance.

The senior officers of the Old Army who served in World War I had seen their profession change greatly during their careers. Many had begun their military service as frontier pacifiers. But they had then shucked off the "island community" mentality of garrison soldiers. They had been encouraged— and coerced—to read and write and reflect about their profession. They had come to acknowledge the complexity of command in modern war and had become disciples of safe leadership. They had become, in fact, the first commanders of the "New Army," led by a new kind of officer who was—as Matthew Forney Steele had urged years earlier—equally comfortable in the classroom and in the saddle.

Younger officers whose careers began in the decade before the Great War experienced far fewer doubts than their immediate superiors. They had discovered that they could not ignore their studies of military subjects if they expected to advance in their profession. Even officers who had not attended any of the postgraduate schools had begun to feel the influence of the schools' practices on their own careers as Leavenworth graduates returned to teach the new ideas in the garrison schools. The map problems, specialized text-books, staff rides, and other instructional methods developed at the senior army schools trickled down to officers stationed not only at posts all across the United States but also as far away as the Philippines.[8] Junior officers increasingly took advantage of the resources of the post libraries to keep current on the latest developments in all fields of military affairs. Maintaining a program of professional reading had become such an important part of professional culture that the *Officers' Manual* prepared for the newly commissioned lieutenants and captains of the World War I army devoted an entire chapter to a soldier's "personal military library." And it was impressed upon them that "all study of war, strategy, tactics, military supplies and transport, and every other branch, brings us sooner or later to the study of Military History."[9]

Serious young officers now eagerly embraced the new spirit of professionalism. As a newly commissioned second lieutenant, Omar N. Bradley recalled his first mentor after his graduation from West Point in 1915. Shortly after his arrival at Fort Yuma, he fell under the tutelage of Lt. Forrest Harding, "a man of rare wit, ability, intelligence and professionalism" who organized a weekly study group at his home to provide the younger officers with an opportunity to discuss practical small-unit tactical problems and other military questions.[10] Even with the creation of an entire officer education system, its grass-roots origins had not been erased entirely; sometimes the inspiration of personal example still worked effectively for the future leaders of the New Army as it had for Matthew Forney Steele and John Bigelow of the generation before.

If officer training proved its value in World War I, the conflict itself had a considerable effect on postwar professional education. Just as military history played an important role in inspiring a sense of professional identity in the Old Army, it found a place in the New Army as well. After postwar reassessments of army school curricula, however, it was given a more restricted role. During the 1920s and 1930s, the army's perception of military history for classroom use leaned almost exclusively toward the half of Professor Hart's "history gap" that included narrations of the events of wars and military science to teach practical command lessons.

At the Leavenworth schools, theoretical studies lost their central position in the curriculum. "The course in Military History and Strategy is scheduled to proceed hand in hand with the course in Tactical and Strategical Studies, Corps and Army, for the purpose of illustrating the actual workings of the principles discussed in the latter course."[11] Eben Swift's applicatory method had returned to center stage, whereas Arthur Conger's source-method courses practically disappeared. In the curriculum of the School of the Line in 1922–23, military history lectures constituted only 45 hours of a 553-hour schedule. By 1936–37, military history accounted for only 79 hours in an expanded curriculum of 1,309 hours of instruction.[12]

At the Army War College, instruction in military history initially followed prewar practices. The Class of 1921 even took its tour of Civil War battlefields, this time in a convoy of Cadillac touring cars instead of on horseback.[13] But curricular reform was under way at the senior school as well. Under the guiding hand of Commandant Edward F. McLachlin, Jr., the course of study was reconstituted around practical high-level command problems and mobilization questions of immediate import and not centered on theoretical instruction in the art of war.

The army's effort to have an accurate record of American military history written by officers at the senior postgraduate schools for the instruction of their juniors became a casualty of World War I. The Army War College's faculty did not resurrect the projected official history of the Civil War that prewar students had initiated. The small Historical Section, now a part of the Army War College's table of organization but not including the student body among its writers or investigators, took over responsibility for analyzing American participation in the Great War. Those elements of the army's prewar history program closest to the half of Hart's dichotomy that stressed methodology became the private reserve of the few officers assigned to the historical section.

To a great degree, World War I was a watershed for the professionalization of the officer corps of the U.S. Army. Graduates of the prewar schools who served overseas learned that their shared classroom experiences had created a special group of officers who "understood what you said and you understood what he said."[14] Although some high-ranking commanders resented what they viewed as a "Leavenworth clique," other officers saw "what Leavenworth *could* have meant to me" and sought assignment to the school after the war was over.[15] The course of instruction in the advanced schools, they were now convinced, made "a professional man out of a military officer; before Leavenworth he merely had a job."[16]

World War I also brought the U.S. Army's first great experiment in the use of military history to a close. Its results were mixed. In its contribution to the crucial intellectual component of military professionalism, the utility of the study of history for a soldier could not be questioned. Without a strong foundation in the practice of the profession of arms in the past, to use an analogy the Old Army's officers would recognize, the principles or laws of war existed only as the individual gears of a machine; military history provided the fuel, greased the wheels, shifted the gears, and showed all the different ways the machine could work, or, conversely, how it could break down. It could help to teach a soldier to think for himself, to be objective, to lift the fog of war a bit. It could help an officer perform his duties efficiently throughout his career, especially as his responsibilities grew.

But how well had officers really translated classroom work into practice in the field? Questions remained. Although many officers had come to accept military history as part of their prewar professional education, the evolution of American army doctrine during the Great War showed little evidence of the measured influence of the experiences of past wars. In the exigencies of war, the workable quick fix or trial and error seemed to displace the reasoning and analysis that the study of history was supposed to bring to military planning.[17] Postwar curricular reforms that reduced the time allotted to instruction in military history suggested that it had not redeemed many of the promises that its prewar advocates had made for it. It had to give way to the immediate practical problems of fighting a modern war.

Still, the officer corps of the Old Army deserves much credit for attempting to define military history's special niche in the education of a professional soldier. As with so many other elements of the Progressive Era's military reform movement, however, the subject inspired intense partisan debate. And in the end—despite history's impact on the curricula of all its advanced schools, the new theoretical literature on the art of war that was now based on American examples, and the formation of a history section in the General Staff—the Old Army had reached no consensus on several key questions about the utility of military history for the commanders of the future.

Nonetheless, although they could not have foreseen it, the officers of the Old Army left behind many perceptive insights about military history to hand down to future generations who would face similar questions. Three particularly difficult issues the Old Army grappled with hold special relevance to the modern generation of American soldiers. These three questions—Is military history important to the education of a professional soldier? If it is, what benefits could he expect to reap from such study? And at what point in a soldier's career would an understanding of military history do him the most good?—remain important because they are no closer to resolution now than they were in the days of World War I.

The clearest exposition of the dimensions of these three issues in the Old Army can be found in the results of an informal poll of army officers completed in early 1914, the last year of normal operations for the school system until after the war. The preceding December, Chief of Staff Leonard Wood had asked all brigade commanders, chiefs of posts, administrators of the army schools, and a cross section of alumni for their critical evaluation of the entire officer education system. He had come to recognize that the schools suffered from too much duplication of effort and had decided it was "time to coordinate and arrange for a progressive development" of officer education from West Point through the Army War College "with a raising of the standards both from professional attainment and general culture." Although Wood did not ask specifically for comment on military history, the subject could not be ignored in any comprehensive analysis of the extant course of study. Moreover, his suggestion that officers should pay more attention to such related fields as "international law, political geography [and] world politics" guaranteed that the study of military history would play a prominent role in the 1914 survey.[18]

The first and most fundamental concern, of course, was whether the study of military history was considered sufficiently important to merit a place in the professional education of army officers at all. The broad spectrum of opinion that still existed in 1914 reveals just how much this issue had splintered the officer corps. If the responses are an accurate reflection of the officers' views and not just what they thought Wood wanted to hear, support for theoretical instruction—and, therefore, for the study of military history at its core—had carried the day. But lingering reservations remained. Certainly there were still those who urged that the army officer avoid excessive "book work of which he already has a surfeit."[19]

Even Gen. John Morrison, for so long the guiding light of the Leavenworth schools, complained that there was "too much theory and too little practical work, not enough thoroughness and too much that is superficial," at the institutions he had helped to shape. He had not turned against officer education. Indeed, he still thought that the "officer who quits work in [his military studies in] a few years will be in the condition professionally that an up to date doctor told me is the condition of a medical man who had quit study ten years ago." But he also had begun to look at military history as "an elective" that should be used for its potential lessons in the importance of "training, fitness, arms, terrain, etc.," and other "practical applications."[20]

Still others continued to view the study of military history as "indispensable" to "the military man who is to become anything more than a tyro in his profession." Capt. Arthur Conger, the first instructor to use the source method of historical scholarship at the Staff College, remained committed to his belief that the study of history "trains the mind to deal intelligently with past events as well as with affairs of the present, to handle evidence, sifting the true from the false."[21]

Indeed, most respondents acknowledged in some way that military history deserved a place in their professional education. "There is no end to some lines of work such as Tactics, Military History, and kindred subjects," a committee from the Army Service Schools wrote.[22] But such comments rarely revealed the deep reflection or commitment to officer education of Morrison or Conger. Few soldiers had enjoyed anywhere near the degree of firsthand experience with the army school system that these two could claim. Perhaps it is not surprising, then, that many officers seemed content to validate the current curriculum rather than challenge it. Still, even if they could agree in general that a soldier should study military history, they could not reach consensus on a second key question: What benefits could he accrue by doing so?

The 1914 survey revealed the widely varying perceptions of the utility of military history that still surfaced in parts of the Old Army's officer corps. Some, such as Brig. Gen. James Parker, advocated the use of "treatises on the War of the Rebellion and the War of 1846" simply to illustrate practically "the method we are liable to make use of in war."[23] On the other hand, the study of military history might help teach an officer, especially a younger one, "to reason correctly," to "give him a broad point of view," and "to develop in him the desire to learn . . . with the fully awakened and maturing powers of a well balanced mind."[24] For still others, military history was integral to the army schools' mission "to introduce professional studies and familiarity with troops" to officers of all ranks.[25] Through the applicatory method, the study of past wars might break some army schools from their reliance on dated instructional methods that reward "memory, not judgment."[26] In as jingoistic an endorsement as any, Brig. Gen. Eli Hoyle desired "a course in history especially arranged to inculcate national & race pride—pride in the achievements of Americans from the beginnings of our history, & going back to our forebears. If we, as a nation, represent the best people now on earth and the best fighters (as I believe) the facts should be taught and the reasons therefore explained—blood, form of government, liberty, education, elements, freedom of the press, religious liberty, etc."[27]

A final area of disagreement was even more noticeable than the other two. This concerned the point in an officer's career when instruction in military history might be most beneficial to him. Probably because Wood had asked his respondents to evaluate each level of officer education, few made a case for extending the study of military history across the entire curriculum. Instead they offered arguments for and against teaching military history at nearly every level of the school system.

A number of officers believed it was best to begin an officer's exposure to the study of military history while he was still a cadet at West Point. It was important, they argued, to lay the groundwork for professional identity and responsibility at an early stage of a soldier's career, and the study of the great captains of military history provided just that kind of inspiration. Conger, as usual, offered his well-articulated views: A solid grounding in intellectually rigorous disciplines, which he described as "science, historical method, mathematics [and] logic," would develop in a young officer "the desire to learn by the employment of modern methods which make studies attractive." Conger cautioned, however, that the "study of history cannot be made profitable until the nature of history is understood. . . . [T]he student must be taught historical sources and their relation to events as well as to subsequently written history." Still, if he could construct his ideal West Point curriculum, he would include historical studies each year: modern European in the first year; American history in the second and third years; and military history, using "some simple source study," in a cadet's senior year.[28]

Still others thought that West Point was too early to introduce the army's future leaders to the study of military history. Morrison explained that a cadet is simply "not prepared" intellectually for course work in the art of war, and therefore he "acquires many false notions, he learns too many things that are not so, gets a false idea as to what he knows. He has to be untaught before he can be taught."[29] Maj. C. P. Summerall agreed in principle: "It is useless to expect any advanced ideas in military history, strategy or tactics, from men who have no experience with troops."[30] Capt. L. T. Richardson took the argument one step further: Until a young officer had obtained "a good foundation in tactics, [the] mere reading of military campaigns is of little value."[31] Still another captain saw no harm in teaching cadets both practical and theoretical elements of the art of war, including military history, but he believed they "should not be expected to obtain or retain much beyond a thorough grounding in minor tactics, camp sanitation, etc."[32]

The place of military history in the garrison school curriculum had many supporters and comparatively few detractors. To many, this was the ideal time for officers to take up this work. As Capt. Paul Malone noted, "History is placed in the course because it is really preparatory to the work at Leavenworth."[33] Morrison had already shown that he agreed with this assessment when he pushed for transferring the use of Matthew Forney Steele's *American Campaigns* to the garrison schools as one way to provide time at the Leavenworth schools for staff and supply work more appropriate to the mission of the advanced institution. Military reading programs at the garrison school level and the upgrading of post libraries would also improve history instruction, especially if the General Staff would pick one hundred to one hundred fifty titles "well selected from history, especially military history, political, physical, and commercial geography," and other relevant subjects.[34] Only a few officers, such as Capt. Oliver L. Spaulding, opposed the teaching of military history at garrison schools, but this was a reflection of his more general opinion that the poor quality of instruction at many post lyceums made them "an evil to be abolished."[35]

It was not at all surprising that if the army took no steps to include military history in the garrison school curriculum, few officers saw any reason to remove it from its long-standing place in the advanced schools at Fort Leavenworth. After all, the faculty of the Leavenworth schools had developed the applicatory method for use in army classrooms at all levels of officer education and had offered the only truly successful course work with the source method. If there were to be any improvements, one officer suggested, it might be best if Staff College students, at least, specialize in the "critical study of staff duties previously performed in our past wars."[36]

The Army War College, in light of its well-publicized attempt to write an official history of the Civil War, won both supporters and critics as a proper site for the army's historical instruction. Some believed its students had a special responsibility to complete such work as the Civil War history project with "special stress on performances of higher commanders."[37] But Capt. George Van Horne Moseley, a graduate of the school, still believed "part of the personnel was not ready" to do historical research. Instead of "putting the War College stamp on undeserving material," he hoped historical studies on the scale of the Civil War project would be postponed until classes could be filled by graduates of the Staff College who had taken a source-method course at Fort Leavenworth.[38] Conger agreed completely and added a codicil. Army War College students should devote their greatest attention to the study of campaigns that offered the most useful lessons about high command in modern war. He now ran against the intellectual current favoring the study of American campaigns, and he urged instead that the army's most senior students take up the study of the Franco-Prussian War after Sedan, the Manchurian campaigns of the Russo-Japanese War, and only then Grant's 1864 Virginia campaign.[39]

Wood could do nothing to implement most of this subordinates' suggestions. The Mexican border crisis and the Great War allowed little time to make the kinds of organizational changes that would provide army officers with an education system that was truly progressive and could be useful throughout their careers. At least most of their suggestions had been moderately conservative ones. Far more disquieting was the assessment of Capt. John McAuley Palmer, written from his far-off post with the Fifteenth Infantry in Tientsin, China, in which he complained that the "main defect in our system of professional training lies in the fact that it does not lead to any recognized professional goal. The General Staff is not a specialty here," and the "system won't work until we adopt this idea." Moreover, Palmer had found "no new military wisdom at Leavenworth or the War College" and believed any officer could learn the proper professional practice "if he would work out map problems, troop leading and military history under proper guidance at his own home." He concluded that the chief benefit of attending the army's advanced schools was limited to the practice a student received in "making decisions and issuing orders."[40] Clearly, he did not believe the professionalization process—either for efficiency in organization or for proficiency of personnel—had proceeded far enough.

The study of military history left a decided impression on the professionalization of the officer corps of the Old Army. But it was a curiously indistinct mark to any but the insider. On the surface, the performance of the officers of the Regular Army in the Great War had resolved the immediate question of professional recognition; few knowledgeable observers could challenge the importance of the Old Army's capable leadership in winning victory for American arms. "The Regulars have not been given anything like the credit they deserve," Professor Johnston asserted shortly after the war.[41] How many appreciated the contribution of military history studies to the Regular Army's show of professional proficiency is an open question.

Nonetheless, proven success in war did not spell the end of the Old Army's professionalization process. The postwar officer corps found itself reiterating the same concerns it had addressed before 1917. In 1919 Maj. Gen. William G. Haan, one of the very first Army War College graduates in the Class of 1905, offered some observations to a group of his subordinates at Camp Taylor, Kentucky, that would have sounded familiar in a frontier lyceum a generation earlier: "As the art of war develops, the training of the soldier becomes more and more complicated. A more liberal and technical education, a better coordinated mind, and a higher intelligence are required in order to succeed."[42]

Indeed, the experiences of the Great War had impressed upon the officers of the New Army that the complexities of modern war required much more of them than competency on the battlefield. They had discovered all manner of unexpected problems in conducting war in cooperation with allies, glaring gaps in tactical and strategical doctrine, great flaws in the supply system, and dozens of other problems that demanded immediately useful and practical solutions. Classroom work had not prepared them for all the challenges of high command. The emergence of army air power and the organization of armored, airborne, and mechanized forces required the talents of the army's most gifted theorists to develop appropriate doctrine for the employment of these new arms; innovation—not reliance on the past—was the order of the day. The army's experience with the massive mobilization of American industry in 1917–18 created a new demand for soldiers who could deal successfully with corporate leaders. Whole new military specialties in research and development of weapons and procurement of war matériel gave further notice that the specialization of function that had inspired the emergence of the officer corps as a unique profession in Progressive America would continue to exert its influence within the army.

Several generations later, we must wonder if the army's "search for order," as the process was understood at the turn of the century, was permitted to go too far after World War I. The organization of so many new kinds of troops within the army and the evolution of dozens of new technical and essentially nonmilitary skills undid much of the good of the army's first efforts to create a common bond that united all officers of the Old Army, regardless of branch, as specialists in the art of war. The dawn of the atomic age and the Cold War helped to recast the role of armies from fighting forces into armed deterrents, greatly eroding the "anticipation of war" that Lt. John Bigelow had described in 1883 as the source of a soldier's sense of purpose and professional pride. In its place grew a destructive spirit of personal and institutional self-interest. By the Vietnam era, military critic Richard Gabriel asserts, an erosion of the "perception of itself as a true profession" had set in. Officers and enlisted men alike had forgotten that their "reason for existence . . . is something higher than the pursuit of self-interest; namely, is the task of defending the freedoms of the Republic."[43]

Or, rather, they had been allowed to forget. In the army's post-Vietnam introspection, the "lack of an organizational memory" was held up as one of its most serious deficiencies.[44] After World War II, reforms in officer education shifted greater stress to management techniques, industrial relations, international affairs, research and development of weapons systems, intelligence and counterintelligence, and other studies that molded good managers or bureaucrats. The traditional avenues toward commissions and promotions had become so "deformed" that they could not "produce officers— planners and leaders—who are well versed in the art of war."[45]

As the war in Vietnam slogged to a close, the army's apparent lack of professionalism came under attack on many fronts. Careerism and "ticket punching," the eclipse of the "warrior" by the "war manager," and the intellectual stagnation that follows from what one observer called an all-too-common attitude "that no one has ever experienced difficulties quite like the ones they face"[46] showed just how far the army had strayed from the roots of its first great flowering of professional spirit. In its own way, the "island community" mentality had reasserted itself.

Soldiers and civilians alike appeared to realize the dimensions of the challenge facing the army. There was no lack of suggested reforms. To the ghosts of Schofield, Wagner, Swift, and other turn-of-the-century advocates of military professionalism, the new call to battle must have had a familiar ring. An Army War College study on military professionalism demanded that measures "be found to ensure that a climate of professionalism exists in the army. The attainment of such a climate is the essential prerequisite for genuine effectiveness."[47] A soldier must know that he is a soldier first and not a politician, a bureaucrat, or a manager. At the Command and General Staff College, the successor to Swift and Wagner's school, an army educator struck another theme once familiar to the Old Army's leaders: "Military excellence has always depended upon an officer corps which could think creatively about war—one which understood and practiced the Art of War."[48]

And the army has responded in much the same way as their professional antecedents did a century ago, by returning to the study of military history as one way to learn about the practice and theory of their profession. In 1971 the Department of the Army's Ad Hoc Committee on the Army Need for the Study of Military History reaffirmed the necessity for officers "to develop historical mindedness . . . to contribute individually to broadened perspective, sharpened judgment, increased perceptivity, and professional expertise."[49] The quality of instruction and instructors of history has improved at all levels of officer education. Selected officers attend civilian universities for advanced degrees in history; many then become instructors at West Point and, perhaps, after service with a troop command or other duties, they teach at higher levels of the army's school system. The staff ride and historical ride have been resurrected at all levels of officer training; soldiers still visit and learn from the battlefields of the Civil War just as Army War College students did before World War I.[50] The U.S. Army Center of Military History, the descendant of the Historical Section of the General Staff, now blends the skills of civilian scholars and army officers in ways that Professor Johnston could only dream about. The office readily supports the research of civilian scholars and serves the army's own needs as well. Despite all this, however, soldiers still raise the same questions about military history's continuing relevance to their professional practice that their ancestors asked years ago. It is a shame that the new historical awareness has not yet stretched back far enough to take advantage of the Old Army's experience in facing similar problems and professional concerns.

In 1984, with an almost eerie similarity to General Schofield's advice to his subordinates one hundred seven years earlier, army officers were told that "modern military endeavor consists of both science and art. Military science consists of the systematized knowledge derived by observation, study, and experimentation carried on to determine the nature, principles, means, methods, and conditions which affect the preparation for or conduct of war. The art of war is the application of this knowledge to a given situation."

A soldier can improve his understanding of the art of war by studying "the historical record of change in military methods" and the "impact of conditions on methods." Military history, after all, "is nothing more or less than the records of trial and error on which today's principles and methods are based."[51] It was a commentary that any of Eben Swift's students of the applicatory method would have understood.

NOTES

ABBREVIATIONS

AGO	Adjutant General's Office
AHA	American Historical Association
AWC	Army War College
JMSIUS	*Journal of the Military Service Institution of the United States*
LC	Library of Congress, Washington, D.C.
NA	National Archives, Washington, D.C.
RG	Record Group
USACMH	U.S. Army Center of Military History, Washington, D.C.
USAMHI	U.S. Army Military History Institute, Carlisle Barracks, Pa.
USMA	U.S. Military Academy, West Point, N.Y.
WCD	War College Division

CHAPTER ONE. INTRODUCTION

1. Memorandum of Maj. Gen. Kenneth G. Wickham, 28 January 1971, printed as Annex A, *Department of the Army Ad Hoc Committee Report on the Army Need for the Study of Military History*, 4 vols. [hereafter *Department of the Army Ad Hoc Report*] (West Point, N.Y., 1971), vol. 1: Annex, p. A-1.

2. Recommendations section, *Department of the Army Ad Hoc Report*, vol. 1: Report and Recommendations, p. 56.

3. "A retired general," *Department of the Army Ad Hoc Report*, vol. 4: Military History Questionnaire – Evaluation of Results, p. C-54.

4. Samuel P. Huntington, *The Soldier and the State* (Cambridge, Mass., 1957), p. 229.

5. See, for instance, the examples offered by John M. Gates, "The Alleged Isolation of U.S. Army Officers in the Late 19th Century," *Parameters* 10 (1980): 32–34.

6. A convincing argument for studying the common ground of reformers in both civilian and military circles at the turn of the century is offered by Jack C. Lane, "American Military Past: The Need for New Approaches," *Military Affairs* 41 (1977): 109–14.

7. Russell F. Weigley, "The Elihu Root Reforms and the Progressive Era," in *Command and Commanders in Modern Warfare: Proceedings of the Second Military History Symposium, U.S. Air Force Academy*, edited by William Geffen (Washington, D.C., 1969), pp. 11–27; James L. Abrahamson, *America Arms for a New Century: The Making of a Giant Military Power* (New York, 1981).

8. Useful essays on the key elements of the process of professionalization include Douglas Klegon, "The Sociology of Professions: An Emerging Perspective," *Sociology of Work and Occupations* 5 (1978): 259–82; and Harold L. Wilensky's durable article, "The Professionalization of Everyone?" *American Journal of Sociology* 70 (1964): 137–58.

9. See Burton J. Bledstein, *The Culture of Professionalism: The Middle Class and the*

Development of Higher Education in America (New York, 1976), for particularly useful historical insights and context on American society's perceptions about the professionalization
process during the Progressive Era.

10. A particularly outstanding study of the evolution of one part of the army education system as part of the professionalization process is Timothy K. Nenninger, *The Leavenworth Schools and the Old Army: Education, Professionalism, and the Officer Corps of the
United States Army, 1881–1918* (Westport, Conn., 1978). Also useful are the relevant sections of Harry P. Ball, *Of Responsible Command: A History of the U.S. Army War College*
(Carlisle Barracks, Pa., 1983), chapter 4; and Boyd L. Dastrup, *The U.S. Army Command
and General Staff College: A Centennial History* (Manhattan, Kans., 1982).

11. Maj. Eben Swift, who refined the technique, explained his methods to his new
students at the beginning of each academic year (see, for instance, "Remarks on the Applicatory System and the Course in Military Art," delivered at the opening of the fall
term at the Army War College on 1 September 1909, AWC Curricular File, 1909–10,
USAMHI).

12. The concept of "safe leadership" is a major theme of Eben Swift, *Remarks, Introductory to the Course in Military Art, at the Infantry and Cavalry School and Staff College, Fort
Leavenworth, by Major Eben Swift, 12th Cavalry, Instructor, September 1904* (Fort Leavenworth, Kans., 1904), but it can be found throughout instructional materials for the Leavenworth schools and the Army War College before World War I.

13. See, for instance, the comments of Prof. Fred Morrow Fling in "Who Shall Write
Our Military History?" *Infantry Journal* 9 (1913): 561–62.

14. Col. Theophilus Rodenbough to Capt. Tasker H. Bliss, 1 November 1889, Tasker
H. Bliss Papers, USMA.

15. See, especially, David D. VanTassel, "From Learned Society to Professional Organization: The American Historical Association, 1884–1900," *American Historical Review*
89 (1984): 929–56; and John Higham, *History* (Englewood Cliffs, N.J., 1965), pp. 6–50.

16. Jurgen Herbst, *The German Historical School in American Scholarship* (Ithaca, N.Y.,
1965), pp. 99–120.

17. "Who Shall Write Our Military History?" p. 547.

CHAPTER TWO. MILITARY HISTORY: "THE FOUNDATION
OF OUR ART, THE BASIS OF OUR PROFESSION"

1. Maj. Gen. John M. Schofield, *Introductory Remarks upon the Study of the Science
of War, from a Paper Read to the U.S. Military Science Institute, West Point, October 11, 1877,
by Major General Schofield, USA, Superintendent, U.S. Military Academy* (New York, 1877),
p. 6.

2. Two excellent studies that examine important aspects of the process of professionalization in the U.S. Army at the turn of the century are James L. Abrahamson, *America
Arms for a New Century: The Making of a Giant Military Power* (New York, 1981); and
Timothy K. Nenninger, *The Leavenworth Schools and the Old Army: Education, Professional-
ism, and the Officer Corps of the United States Army, 1881–1918* (Westport, Conn., 1978).
See also Edward M. Coffman, *The Old Army: A Portrait of the American Army in Peacetime,
1784–1898* (New York, 1986), chapter 5; Allan R. Millett, *Military Professionalism and Officership in America*, Mershon Center Briefing Paper 2 (Columbus, Ohio, 1977); Russell
F. Weigley, *A History of the United States Army* (New York, 1967), chapters 14 and 15; and
Peter Karsten, "Armed Progressives: The Military Reorganizes for the American Century," in *Building an Organizational Society*, edited by Jerry Israel (New York, 1972), pp.
196–232.

Especially useful is the conceptualization of Robert H. Wiebe's *The Search for Order, 1877-1920* (New York, 1967), which provided the analytical framework for Russell F. Weigley's important article "The Elihu Root Reforms and the Progressive Era," in *Command and Commanders in Modern Warfare: Proceedings of the Second Military History Symposium, U.S. Air Force Academy*, edited by William Geffen (Washington, D.C., 1969), pp. 11-27.

3. Capt. William E. Birkhimer in "Comment and Criticism" of an article about Artillery School instructional methods, in *JMSIUS* 19 (1897): 157.

4. Maj. Gen. John M. Schofield, "Inaugural Address," *JMSIUS* 1 (1879): 3.

5. Col. C. W. Larned, "West Point," reprinted from the *International Monthly* in *JMSIUS* 28 (1906): 412.

6. Wiebe, *Search for Order*, and Thomas L. Haskell, *The Emergence of Professional Social Science: The American Social Science Association and the Nineteenth-Century Crisis of Authority* (Urbana, Ill., 1977), are very enlightening on this issue.

7. Burton J. Bledstein, *The Culture of Professionalism: The Middle Class and the Development of Higher Education in America* (New York, 1976), offers useful historical insights on this topic.

8. Capt. T. A. Bingham, "The Prussian Great General Staff and What It Contains That Is Practical from an American Standpoint," *JMSIUS* 20 (1898): 667.

9. Prof. P. S. Michie, "Education in Its Relation to the Military Profession," *JMSIUS* 1 (1879): 154.

10. Ibid., p. 161.

11. 1st Lt. Arthur L. Wagner, "An American War College," *JMSIUS* 10 (1889): 287-88.

12. Col. James B. Fry, "Origins and Progress of the Military Service Institution of the United States," *JMSIUS* 1 (1879): 26-27.

13. Schofield, "Inaugural Address," p. 4.

14. Lt. John Bigelow, "Our Cavalry," *JMSIUS* 4 (1883): 406-7.

15. Capt. James S. Pettit, "The Proper Military Instruction of Our Officers," *JMSIUS* 20 (1898): 20.

16. Thomas E. Griess, "Dennis Hart Mahan: West Point Professor and Advocate of Professionalism, 1830-1871" (Ph.D. diss., Duke University, 1969), p. 46.

17. See Herman Hattaway and Archer Jones, *How the North Won: A Military History of the Civil War* (Urbana, Ill., 1983), pp. 12-13, for the impact of the study of military history on the Civil War generation.

18. The "island community" concept is discussed in Wiebe, *Search for Order*, especially chapters 2 and 3. See the concept adapted to the military establishment in Abrahamson, *America Arms for a New Century*, pp. 34-36.

19. Both John M. Gates, "The Alleged Isolation of U.S. Army Officers in the Late Nineteenth Century," *Parameters* 10 (1980): 32-45; and Andrew J. Bacevich, "Family Matters: American Civilian and Military Elites in the Progressive Era," *Armed Forces and Society* 8 (1982): 418-25, effectively challenge the notion of officer isolation.

20. Capt. Andrew J. Bacevich, "Progressivism, Professionalism, and Reform," *Parameters* 9 (1979): 66-71, reinforces the importance of viewing soldiers as both military professionals and members of a rigid bureaucracy.

21. Col. George S. Anderson, "Practical Military Instruction," *JMSIUS* 47 (1910): 331; see Bledstein, *Culture of Professionalism*, pp. 83-85, for the evolution of the professional schools in a historical context.

22. John Bigelow, "Military Education" manuscript, p. 147, Military Education File, Box 98-99, John Bigelow Papers, LC.

23. Matthew Forney Steele, "Obituary," p. 29, written in 1925 by Steele himself, Box 1, Matthew Forney Steele Papers, USAMHI. Steele wished that all graduates of West Point would review their careers this way.

24. Bigelow, "Military Education," p. 184.

25. See "Report of the General of the Army," in *Annual Report of the Secretary of War, 1881* (Washington, D.C., 1882), p. 38.

26. A summary of the reorganization at Fortress Monroe is contained in "Report of the Commanding Officer [Col. G. W. Getty] of the Artillery School," 4 November 1878, addendum G to *Annual Report of the Secretary of War, 1878* (Washington, D.C. 1879), pp. 197–207. For a history of the army's earliest efforts in advanced officer education, see Henry Schindler and E. E. Booth, *History of the Army Service Schools* (Fort Leavenworth, Kans., 1908), pp. 48–53.

27. This was Colonel Fry's sentiment in support of more advanced work in the employment of the combined arms (see Fry, "Origins and Progress of the Military Service Institution of the United States," p. 27).

28. "Report of the General of the Army," in *Annual Report of the Secretary of War, 1879* (Washington, D.C., 1880), p. 14.

29. Roger J. Spiller, "The Beginnings of the Kindergarten," *Military Review* 61 (1981): 2–12; and Nenninger, *Leavenworth Schools and the Old Army*, chapter 2.

30. Capt. W. H. Carter, "The Infantry and Cavalry School at Fort Leavenworth," *JMSIUS* 15 (1894): 759.

31. Gen. W. W. Wotherspoon to Maj. Eben Swift, 16 May 1904, Box 2, Eben Swift Papers, USMA.

32. The lyceum system was authorized by G.O. No. 80, Adjutant General's Office, 5 October 1891.

33. Elihu Root, "Address at the Laying of the Corner Stone, Washington, D.C., February 21, 1902," in *The Military and Colonial Policy of the United States: Addresses and Reports by Elihu Root*, compiled and edited by Robert Bacon and James Brown Scott (Cambridge, Mass., 1924), p. 126.

34. George S. Pappas, Prudens Futuri: *The U.S. Army War College, 1901–1967* (Carlisle Barracks, Pa., 1967), pp. 15–40; Harry P. Ball, *Of Responsible Command: A History of the U.S. Army War College* (Carlisle Barracks, Pa., 1983), chapter 4.

35. Fry, "Origins and Progress of the Military Service Institution of the United States," p. 29.

36. John B. Hattendorf, B. Mitchell Shipton III, and John R. Wadleigh, *Sailors and Scholars: The Centennial History of the Naval War College* (Newport, R.I., 1985), chapter 2.

37. Quoted by Gen. M. M. Macomb, "The Scientific Study of Military History: Opening Address in the Military History Course at the Army War College," 15 February 1916, USAMHI.

38. Maj. William Murray Black, "The Education and Training of Army Officers," *JMSIUS* 33 (1912): 8.

39. Capt. Campbell A. King, "The Peace Training of Armies," *Infantry Journal* 4 (1907): 98–99.

40. Bledstein, *Culture of Professionalism*, p. 134.

41. Lt. Hugh M. Kelly, "Progress and What It Entails," *Infantry Journal* 9 (1912): 300. For similar sentiments, see Comdr. Frank H. Schofield, "Military Character," *Journal of the United States Artillery* 46 (1916): 297–318, in which he stressed an officer's need for "knowledge of war based on historical study and interpreted experience."

42. Steele, "Notes for Essays," journal entry, p. 8, Box 21, Steele Papers, USAMHI.

43. Schofield, "Inaugural Address," p. 17.

44. Col. Henry W. Closson, "A Paper on Military Libraries," *JMSIUS* 15 (1894): 1125.

45. Schofield, "Inaugural Address," p. 6.

46. Closson, "Paper on Military Libraries," p. 1123.

47. Capt. A. W. Bjornstad, "Tactical Instruction of Line Officers," *Infantry Journal* 7 (1911): 687.

48. Schofield, "Inaugural Address," p. 13.

49. "The Scope of the War College Course," AWC Curricular File, 1909–10, 1:2, USAMHI.

50. "Scope of Course of Instruction," AWC Curricular File, 1911–12, 1:9, USAMHI; and Nenninger, *Leavenworth Schools and the Old Army*, pp. 83–84.

51. "Scope of Course of Instruction," 1911–12, 1:9.

52. Eben Swift, *Remarks, Introductory to the Course in Military Art, at the Infantry and Cavalry School and Staff College, Fort Leavenworth, by Major Eben Swift, 12th Cavalry, Instructor, September 1904* (Fort Leavenworth, Kans., 1904), p. 10.

53. "Scope of the War College Course," 1909–10, 1:2.

54. Swift, *Remarks, Introductory to the Course in Military Art*, pp. 9–10.

55. Col. Arthur L. Wagner, *Strategy* (Kansas City, Mo., 1904), pp. 51–52.

56. "Report of the Assistant Commandant of the U.S. Army Staff College, 1906," in *Annual Report of the Commandant of the U.S. Army School of the Line and Staff School, 1906* (Washington, D.C., 1907), p. 21.

57. Maj. Eben Swift, "Remarks on the Applicatory System and the Course in Military Art," 1 September 1909, AWC Curricular File, 1909–10, pp. 1–9, USAMHI; Nenninger, *Leavenworth Schools and the Old Army*, pp. 45–48.

58. Anderson, "Practical Military Instruction," p. 331.

59. Richard Hofstadter, *Anti-Intellectualism in American Life* (New York, 1963), p. 191.

60. "Too Much Book Learning for Soldiers," letter to the editor, *Army and Navy Journal* 49 (October 1911): 212.

61. Col. Charles B. Hall, "Address to the Student Officers of the Service Schools and Staff College, September 3, 1906," *Infantry Journal* 3 (1907): 60.

62. See, for instance, a popular article by Col. T. T. Munford, "A Confederate Cavalry Officer's View on American Practice and Foreign Theory," *Cavalry Journal* 4 (1891): 198, in which he argued that "soldiers are born and bred, but circumstances and opportunity do more than science, and wisdom far more than learning."

63. Capt. James Chester, "Some of the Artillery Difficulties Likely to Be Encountered during the Next Maritime War," *JMSIUS* 19 (1898): 557–58.

64. Duncan is quoted in Edward M. Coffman, "American Command and Commanders in World War I," in *New Dimensions in Military History*, edited by Russell F. Weigley, (San Rafael, Calif., 1972), p. 178.

65. Lt. John P. Wisser, "Practical Instruction of Officers at Posts," *JMSIUS* 9 (1888): 221.

66. Information on Wisser's service at the Naval War College is in a letter from Evelyn Cherpak, head of the Naval Historical Collection, Naval War College, to the author, 30 July 1985.

67. Wisser, "Practical Instruction of Officers at Posts," pp. 198–99.

68. Lt. E. H. Plummer, "Practice versus Theory in Army Training," *JMSIUS* 14 (1893): 1020.

69. Capt. Edward Field, "No Footsteps but Some Glances Backward," *JMSIUS* 6 (1885): 247.

70. Col. C. G. Morton to secretary, U.S. Army War College, 31 January 1914, WCD File 8213-24, RG 165, NA.

71. 1st Lt. Arthur L. Wagner, "The Military and Naval Policy of the United States," *JMSIUS* 7 (1886): 399.

72. For an early study that recognized the torn "loyalties" of army doctors, see Percy M. Ashburn, *A History of the Medical Department of the United States Army* (Boston, 1929). One example of a nonmilitary function taken over by a civilian agency occurred in 1912, when Congress granted the American Red Cross the right to raise volunteer hospital

units for the army in times of national emergency (see Brig. Gen. Jefferson R. Kean, M.D., "The Development of the Red Cross Medical Department Units," in *The Medical Department of the United States Army in the World War*, Vol. 1: *The Surgeon General's Office* [Washington, D.C. 1923], p. 92).

73. John Codman Ropes, *The Army under Pope* (New York, 1881), p. vii.

74. Tasker H. Bliss to John Codman Ropes, 30 January 1888, and Bliss to Ropes, 9 May 1892, in John Codman Ropes Papers, Military History Society of Massachusetts Papers, Boston University Archives, Boston, Mass.

75. Bliss to Ropes, 24 February 1893, ibid.

76. Haskell, *Emergence of Professional Social Science*, pp. 168–77; John Higham, *History* (Englewood Cliffs, N.J., 1965), pp. 6–50; David D. VanTassel, "From Learned Society to Professional Organization: The American Historical Association, 1884–1900," *American Historical Review* 89 (1984): 929–56; and Bledstein, *Culture of Professionalism*, pp. 85–87.

77. Jurgen Herbst, *The German Historical School in American Scholarship* (Ithaca, N.Y., 1965), pp. 99–128.

78. Prof. George E. Howard, "The Place of History in Modern Education," *Transactions and Reports of the Nebraska State Historical Society* 1 (1885): 202.

79. Typical of many soldiers' views on history is this revealing comment in a book review of Capt. John P. Wisser's *The Second Boer War, 1899–1900* in *JMSIUS* 27 (1905): 472–74: "It is unfortunate that the author was not satisfied with the role of historian; criticism . . . always detracts from the value of a book of this kind. What the military student desires, is an exact statement of what occurred; and it is exceedingly desirable that the relative importance of the various operations should not be colored, or be given any undue prominence, in consequence of the views of the author. Criticism immediately casts a shadow of doubt over the historical accuracy of the story."

80. See chapter 5.

81. For further development of this theme, see chapter 9.

82. "Our Military Propagandists," *Nation* 99 (July 1914): 63–64; see also chapter 10.

83. Many of these concerns are spelled out in "Who Shall Write Our Military History?" *Infantry Journal* 9 (1913): 545–78. For the World War I "official history" project, see chapter 11.

PART ONE. MILITARY HISTORY AND OFFICER EDUCATION

1. Elihu Root, "Extract from the Report of the Secretary of War for 1901," in *The Military and Colonial Policy of the United States: Addresses and Reports by Elihu Root*, compiled and edited by Robert Bacon and James Brown Scott (Cambridge, Mass., 1924), pp. 388–89.

2. William W. Wotherspoon, *Lecture to the Naval War College*, August 1910, quoted in George S. Pappas, Prudens Futuri: *The U.S. Army War College, 1901–1967* (Carlisle Barracks, Pa., 1967), p. 68.

3. Frederick Morrow Fling, Review of *Donelson Campaign Sources, Supplementing Volume 7 of* The Official Records of the Union and Confederate Armies in the War of the Rebellion, by Arthur L. Conger, in *American Historical Review* 19 (1914): 373.

CHAPTER THREE. MILITARY HISTORY AND
THE SCHOOL OF "SAFE LEADERSHIP"

1. Maj. Eben Swift, *Remarks Introductory to the Course in Military Art, at the Infantry and Cavalry School and Staff College, Fort Leavenworth, by Major Eben Swift, 12th Cavalry, Instructor, September 1904* (Fort Leavenworth, Kans., 1904), p. 14.

2. "Introductory Remarks by the President, 1 September 1910," AWC Curricular File, 1910–11, 4:15, USAMHI.

3. "A Lecture by Major A. L. Conger on Historical Research, the Engineering School, Camp A. A. Humphreys," n.d., p. 2, Arthur Latham Conger Papers, Theosophical Society Library, Pasadena, Calif.

4. John I. Alger, *The Quest for Victory: The History of the Principles of War* (Westport, Conn., 1982), chapters 3 and 4.

5. Maj. Gen. John M. Schofield, "Inaugural Address," *JMSIUS* 1 (1879): 9.

6. The standard biography of Upton is Stephen E. Ambrose, *Upton and the Army* (Baton Rouge, La., 1964); see also Andrew J. Bacevich, "Emory Upton: A Centennial Assessment," *Military Review* 61 (1981): 21–28.

7. Emory Upton, *The Armies of Asia and Europe: Embracing Official Reports on the Armies of Japan, China, India, Persia, Italy, Russia, Austria, Germany, France, and England* (Washington, D.C., 1878; reprint ed., Westport, Conn., 1972), p. 319.

8. "Report of the Commanding Officer of the Artillery School," enclosure G to *Annual Report of the Secretary of War, 1878* (Washington, D.C., 1879), pp. 201, 203.

9. "Report of the General of the Army," in *Annual Report of the Secretary of War, 1879* (Washington, D.C., 1880), p. 14.

10. Forrest C. Pogue, *George C. Marshall: The Education of a General, 1880–1939* (New York, 1963), p. 115.

11. Capt. Arthur L. Wagner, "Proper Military Instruction," *JMSIUS* 21 (1899): 205.

12. Pogue, *George C. Marshall*, p. 115.

13. Eben Swift, "An American Pioneer in the Cause of Military Education," *JMSIUS* 44 (1909): 67–72; and "Military Record of Captain Arthur L. Wagner with Extracts from Letters on File at the War Department with his Application for Major in the Adjutant General's Office," n.d., Appointments, Commissions, and Personnel File 2908, RG 94, NA.

14. Swift, "American Pioneer in the Cause of Military Education," p. 67.

15. Eben Swift obituary, *New York Times*, 26 April 1938, copy in Eben Swift Papers, USAMHI.

16. Commandant to Gen. W. W. Wotherspoon, 14 April 1904, Army Service Schools Documentary File 1281, RG 393, NA.

17. "General Swift Leads a 'Hike,'" *Atlanta Journal*, 9 September 1917, Swift Papers, USAMHI.

18. Timothy K. Nenninger, *The Leavenworth Schools and the Old Army: Education, Professionalism, and the Education of the Officer Corps of the United States Army, 1881–1918* (Westport, Conn., 1978), p. 36.

19. Eben Swift, "Remarks on the Applicatory Method and the Course of Military Art," AWC Curricular File, 1909–10, p. 2.

20. Ibid.

21. Ibid., p. 3.

22. On the importance of the use of Griepenkerl in the army schools, see Nenninger, *Leavenworth Schools and the Old Army*, p. 90; and Harry P. Ball, *Of Responsible Command: A History of the U.S. Army War College* (Carlisle Barracks, Pa., 1983), p. 101.

23. See, for instance, the comments of Hunter Liggett in *A.E.F.: Ten Years Ago in*

France (New York, 1928), pp. 291–92; and George Van Horne Moseley, "One Soldier's Story," p. 86, Box 1A, George Van Horne Moseley Papers, LC.

24. Nenninger, *Leavenworth Schools and the Old Army*, p. 141.

25. "Exercise No. 23 (Map Problem No. 19), Discussion by Major C. H. Barth, 12th Infantry, 9 December 1909," AWC Curricular File, 1908–09, Map Problems, pp. 282–88, USAMHI.

26. Arthur L. Wagner, "Report of the Military Art Department, 1893," quoted in Elvid Hunt and Walter E. Lorence, *History of Fort Leavenworth, 1827–1937* (Fort Leavenworth, Kans., 1937), pp. 147–49; see also Wagner, "An American War College," *JMSIUS* 10 (1889): 290–95.

27. Lt. Col. Smith S. Leach, "Memorandum for Information of Members of the Army War College in connection with Preparation of Tactical Problems," 14 November 1906, AWC Curricular File, 1906–07, Problems and Exercises, p. 2.

28. Capt. Malin Craig to Maj. Matthew Forney Steele, 28 May 1910, Box 19, Matthew Forney Steele Papers, USAMHI.

29. "Introductory Remarks by the President, 1 September 1910," 4:14, USAMHI.

30. "Supplement to Memorandum of LTC Smith S. Leach of 14 November 1906," 22 November 1906, AWC Curricular File, 1906–07, Problems and Exercises, p. 3, USAMHI.

31. Leach, "Memorandum for Information of Members of the Army War College in connection with preparation of Tactical Problems," Problems and Exercises, pp. 2–3, USAMHI.

32. Ibid., p. 2.

33. Maj. Eben Swift, *Orders, a Course in Tactics* (Fort Leavenworth, Kans., 1905), pp. 6–8.

34. Ibid., pp. 21–22.

35. "Army War College Course of 1909–10: The Scope of the War College Course," AWC Curricular File, 1909–10, p. 8, USAMHI.

36. "Tactical Problem No. 24," AWC Curricular File, 1907–08, Problems, p. 212, USAMHI.

37. "Tactical Ride No. 1," AWC Curricular File, 1907–08, Problems, p. 405, USAMHI, required the solution of map problems as well as on-site exercises.

38. For example, "Map Exercise No. 39," AWC Curricular File, 1908–09, 2:466–71, USAMHI, considers the location of dressing stations in an Antietam scenario; "Exercise No. 13," ibid., 2:189, is a Signal Corps problem in an Antietam scenario; "Map Exercise No. 60," ibid., 3:670, considers a division supply problem based on the Maryland campaign of 1862.

39. "Map Exercise No. 3," AWC Curricular File, 1909–10, 2:84, USAMHI, concerned the location of field hospitals.

40. "Problem No. 86," AWC Curricular File, 1909–10, 4: 934–37, USAMHI, considers consecutive problems based on the Gettysburg campaign. The Army War College Class of 1911 completed a series of problems that duplicated the moves of the First Bull Run campaign (AWC Curricular File, 1910–11, 2: Problems, pp. 1–13, USAMHI).

41. Maj. Eben Swift, "*Kriegsspiel* or Map Maneuvers," AWC Curricular File, 1908–09, Lectures, p. 324, USAMHI.

42. Ibid., p. 331.

43. Lt. C. A. L. Totten, "Strategos: An American Game of War," *JMSIUS* 2 (1880): 186–202; Capt. Charles Raymond, Kriegsspiel (Fortress Monroe, Va., 1881); William R. Livermore, *The American* Kriegsspiel: *A Game for the Practice of the Art of War* (Boston, 1882).

44. Swift, "*Kriegsspiel* or Map Maneuvers," p. 12, relates that the U.S. Army borrowed the celluloid method from the U.S. Navy.

45. Swift, *Remarks Introductory to the Course in Military Art*, p. 12.

46. Raymond, Kriegsspiel, p. 5.

47. Ibid., pp. 2-3. Rigid *kriegsspiel* is also called minor *kriegsspiel* (see Livermore, *American* Kriegsspiel, pp. 3-4).

48. Swift, "*Kriegsspiel* or Map Maneuvers," pp. 329-31. Swift also translated Verdy du Vernois's *A Simplified War Game* (Kansas City, Mo., 1897) (see Capt. Frank Edmund's review in *JMSIUS* 22 [1901]: 660).

49. Nenninger, *Leavenworth Schools and the Old Army*, p. 47; see also Farrand Sayre, *Map Maneuvers and Tactical Rides* (Fort Leavenworth, Kans., 1910), especially pp. 7-22.

50. Maj. DeRussy Cabell, "Talk on Map Maneuvers," AWC Curricular File, 1913-14, 4:2, USAMHI.

51. Ibid.; Swift, "*Kriegsspiel* or Map Maneuvers," p. 332.

52. "Map Maneuver No. 1," AWC Curricular File, 1912-13, 1:135-36, USAMHI.

53. "Map Maneuver No. 3," AWC Curricular File, 1908-09, 2:720-22, USAMHI.

54. "Army War College Course of 1909-10: The Scope of the War College Course," p. 12.

55. "Map Exercise No. 17," AWC Curricular File, 1908-09, 1:332, USAMHI.

56. Memorandum, Tasker H. Bliss to [The Adjutant General], 3 August 1903, in Lt. Col. George P. Ahern, "A Chronicle of the Army War College, 1899-1919," p. 18, undated typescript, USAMHI.

57. Bliss to The Adjutant General, 11 November 1903, p. 19, copy in Tasker H. Bliss Papers, USAMHI.

58. Capt. James Chester, "Military Misconceptions and Absurdities," *JMSIUS* 14 (1893): 502-18.

59. "Memorandum as to the Details of the Army War College Course, 1908-09," AWC Curricular File, 1908-09, 1:15, USAMHI.

60. Swift, "Remarks on the Applicatory Method and the Course of Military Art," p. 6.

61. Hunt and Lorence, *History of Fort Leavenworth, 1827-1937*, p. 148.

62. "Tactical Ride No. 1," AWC Curricular File, 1907-08, Problems, pp. 405-6, USAMHI.

63. Ibid., p. 407.

64. Maj. Guy Carlton, "Tactical Rides and Staff Rides," AWC Curricular File, 1910-11, Lectures, pp. 2-3, USAMHI.

65. "Field Fortification Problems 1-5," AWC Curricular File, 1910-11, 3:345-74, USAMHI.

66. Carlton, "Tactical Rides and Staff Rides," p. 2.

67. "Campaign Studies and Staff Rides," AWC Curricular File, 1906-07, Problems and Exercises, p. 422, USAMHI.

68. "Army War College Course of 1909-10: The Scope of the War College Course," p. 11.

69. Capt. Stuart Heintzelman to secretary of the Army War College, 31 January 1914, WCD File 8213-23, RG 165, NA.

70. "Who Shall Write Our Military History?" *Infantry Journal* 9 (1913): 547.

71. Swift, "Remarks on the Applicatory Method and the Course of Military Art," p. 1.

CHAPTER FOUR. CIVIL WAR BATTLEFIELDS: OPEN-AIR CLASSROOMS FOR MILITARY HISTORY

1. Robert L. Bullard Diary, Book 5, 5 June 1912, Robert Lee Bullard Papers, LC.

2. Lt. Elmer Hubbard, "The Military Academy and the Education of Officers," *JMSIUS* 18 (1897): 7.

3. Walter Goerlitz, *History of the German General Staff, 1657–1945*, translated by Brian Battershaw (New York, 1959), p. 24; see also Spenser Wilkinson, *The Brain of an Army: A Popular Account of the German General Staff*, 2d ed. (London, 1895), pp. 167–69.

4. Brian Bond, *The Victorian Army and the Staff College, 1854–1914* (London, 1972), pp. 137–38, 175, 255. On the introduction of battlefield trips to the Franco-German frontier, see Maj. Gen. Sir C. E. Callwell, *Field Marshal Sir Henry Wilson*, 2 vols. (New York, 1927), 1:13–14, 70–73.

5. Arden Bucholz, *Hans Delbrück and the German Military Establishment: War Images in Conflict* (Iowa City, Ia., 1985), pp. 3–6, 39–40.

6. Ibid., p. 4.

7. Ibid., pp. 19–22; Gordon A. Craig, "Delbrück: The Military Historian," in *Makers of Modern Strategy: Military Thought from Machiavelli to Hitler*, edited by Edward Mead Earle (Princeton, N.J., 1943), pp. 261–63.

8. Bucholz, *Hans Delbrück*, pp. 31–32; Craig, "Delbrück," pp. 265–66.

9. Craig, "Delbrück," p. 265.

10. Ibid., pp. 267–68; Bucholz, *Hans Delbrück*, pp. 32–33.

11. Bucholz, *Hans Delbrück*, p. 22.

12. "Military Record of Captain Arthur L. Wagner with Extracts from Letters on File at the War Department with His Application for Major in the Adjutant General's Office," n.d., Appointments, Commissions, and Personnel File 2908, RG 94, NA.

13. Lt. Arthur L. Wagner, *The Campaign of Königgrätz: A Study of the Austro-Prussian Conflict in the Light of the American Civil War* (Fort Leavenworth, Kans., 1889), p. 3.

14. Capt. Arthur L. Wagner to secretary of the Infantry and Cavalry School, 20 March 1895, AGO File 17317, RG 94, NA.

15. Ibid.

16. Gen. John M. Schofield, endorsement, 28 March 1895, with Wagner to secretary of the Infantry and Cavalry School, 20 March 1895, AGO File 17317, RG 94, NA.

17. Joseph R. Doe, endorsement, 1 April 1895, with Wagner to secretary of the Infantry and Cavalry School, 20 March 1895, AGO File 17317, RG 94, NA.

18. Arthur L. Wagner to The Adjutant General, 11 April 1895, AGO File 17317/A, RG 94, NA. Doe noted his disapproval in an endorsement, dated 27 May 1895, on this document. Funding problems plagued trip organizers even after the War Department approved in principle the usefulness of the trips. Because of the great distance from Kansas to the battlefields of Georgia, the Staff College faced an annual struggle to obtain authorization for mileage payments. When the authorization did not come through for the Staff College Class of 1910, twenty-one of its members and five instructors paid the cost themselves. See I. B. Holley, Jr., *General John M. Palmer, Citizen Soldiers, and the Army of a Democracy* (Westport, Conn., 1982), p. 192.

19. Arthur L. Wagner to commandant [J. Franklin Bell], 28 December 1903, reprinted as appendix H, *Annual Report of the Commandant of the General Service and Staff College, 1904* (Fort Leavenworth, Kans., 1905), p. 99.

20. "Annual Report of the Superintendent, United States Military Academy," in *Annual Report of the Secretary of War, 1902* (Washington, D.C., 1903), p. 47.

21. Report of the assistant commandant [Eben Swift], in *Annual Report of the Commandant of the Infantry and Cavalry School, 1906* (Fort Leavenworth, Kans., 1907), pp. 20–27.

22. "Campaign Studies and Staff Rides," AWC Curricular File, 1906–07, pp. 422–26, USAMHI; see also Lt. Col. George P. Ahern, "A Chronicle of the Army War College, 1899–1919," unpublished essay, pp. 61–64, USAMHI; and Harry P. Ball, *Of Responsible Command: A History of the U.S. Army War College* (Carlisle Barracks, Pa., 1983), p. 101.

23. Report of assistant commandant [Swift], 1906, pp. 20–24.

24. Ibid., p. 24.

25. "Campaign Studies and Staff Rides," AWC Curricular File, 1906–07, pp. 422–26, USAMHI.

26. Matthew Forney Steele to Mrs. Steele, 5 and 6 July 1907, Box 9, Matthew Forney Steele Papers, USAMHI.

27. Ibid.

28. Ibid., and Steele to Mrs. Steele, 7 July 1907, Box 9, Steele Papers, USAMHI. Capt. Richard H. McMaster was also impressed by the extensiveness of the Confederate earthworks at Resaca. (see Richard H. McMaster Diary, 7 July 1910, McMaster Family Papers, South Caroliniana Library, University of South Carolina, Columbia).

29. Steele to Mrs. Steele, 11 July 1907, Box 9, Steele Papers, USAMHI.

30. Steele to Mrs. Steele, 2 July 1908, Box 9, Steele Papers, USAMHI.

31. Forrest C. Pogue, *George C. Marshall: Education of a General, 1880–1939* (New York, 1963), p. 101.

32. Eben Swift, "Remarks on the Course of Instruction," AWC Curricular File, 1909–10, 1:12, USAMHI.

33. "Staff Ride 3," AWC Curricular File, 1909–10, 7:n.p.

34. "Staff Ride 4," AWC Curricular File, 1909–10, 8:n.p.

35. House Committee on Military Affairs, *National Military Parks*, 54th Cong., 1st sess., 14 February 1896, H. Rept. 273, p. 374.

36. Steele to Mrs. Steele, 11 July 1908, Box 9, Steele Papers, USAMHI.

37. Steele to Mrs. Steele, 5 July 1907, Box 9, Steele Papers, USAMHI.

38. Steele to Mrs. Steele, 14 July 1908, Box 9, Steele Papers, USAMHI.

39. Bullard Diary, Book 6, 11 July 1912, Bullard Papers, LC.

40. "Lecture by Major A. L. Conger on Historical Research, the Engineer School, Camp A. A. Humphreys," n.d., p. 2, copy of address found in Arthur Latham Conger Papers, Theosophical Society Library, Pasadena, Calif.

41. "How to View the Field at Gettysburg," *Army and Navy Journal* 52 (February 1915): 715.

42. Bullard Diary, Book 5, 4 May 1912, Bullard Papers, LC.

43. Ibid., 5 May 1912, Bullard Papers, LC.

44. Ibid., 6 May 1912, Bullard Papers, LC.

45. Ibid., especially entries for 9, 11, and 16 May 1912, Bullard Papers, LC.

46. Ibid., 7 May 1912, Bullard Papers, LC.

47. Ibid., 2 June 1912, Bullard Papers, LC.

48. "Notes on Grant's Movement across the Chickahominy and James, 1864," Box 8, George Van Horne Moseley Papers, LC.

49. Steele to Mrs. Steele, [?] July 1908, Box 9, Steele Papers, USAMHI.

50. Bullard Diary, Book 5, 4 May 1912, Bullard Papers, LC.

51. Lt. Col. Joseph A. Gaston, "The Gettysburg Campaign to Include the Fighting of the First Day," AWC typescript, 1912, pp. 63–64, USAMHI.

52. Eben Swift, "Discussion" to Map Exercise No. 65, AWC Curricular File, 1909–10, 4:881, USAMHI; Swift, "The Military Education of Robert E. Lee," *Virginia Historical Magazine* 30 (1927): 99–166.

53. See Swift's discussion of Map Exercise No. 65, AWC Curricular file, 1909–10, 4:878–84, USAMHI, and discussion of Map Exercise No. 92, ibid., 10:992. The officer who critiqued the latter problem cited a Union army officer, Francis W. Palfrey, who believed if Lee had commanded the northern army at Antietam, the southern army would have been defeated even if another Lee had been in command of it.

54. George Van Horne Moseley, "One Soldier's Story," Box 1A, Moseley Papers, LC; Hunter Liggett, *A.E.F.: Ten Years Ago in France* (New York, 1928), pp. 293–95. Mun-

ford was so overcome by the deference shown him that he thanked his hosts on his departure with "Gentlemen, you have broken my heart" (Moseley, "One Soldier's Story," p. 95).

55. Virginia battlefield trip itinerary, entry for 24 May 1909, AWC Curricular File, 1908–09, 2:787, USAMHI.

56. Diary of rides, entry for 30 May 1913, AWC Curricular File, 1912–13, 7:5, USAMHI.

57. Bullard Diary, Book 6, 9 June 1912, Bullard Papers, LC; Moseley, "One Soldier's Story," p. 95, Moseley Papers, LC; "Staff Ride No. 3: Diary of Historical and Staff Ride," AWC Curricular File, 1911–12, USAMHI.

58. "Campaign and Battlefield Studies," AWC Curricular file, 1909–10, 4:1151, USAMHI.

59. Diary of rides, entries for 1 and 12 May 1913, AWC Curricular File, 1912–13, 7:3–5, USAMHI; George S. Pappas, Prudens Futuri: *The U.S. Army War College, 1901–1967* (Carlisle Barracks, Pa., 1967), p. 75.

60. Moseley, "One Soldier's Story," p. 95, Moseley Papers, LC.

61. Diary of rides, entries for 30 May and 2 June 1913, AWC Curricular File, 1912–13, 7:5, USAMHI.

62. Steele to Mrs. Steele, 6 July 1907, Box 9, Steele Papers, USAMHI.

63. Moseley, "One Soldier's Story," p. 95, Moseley Papers, LC.

64. Pogue, *Marshall: Education of a General*, pp. 122–23.

65. Bullard Diary, Book 5, 14 May 1912, Bullard Papers, LC.

66. "South Wrathy at March," undated newspaper clipping, Box 26, Steele Papers, USAMHI. For the story of Father Sherman's intended journey and the South's response to it, see *New York Times*, 2, 4, and 7 May 1906.

67. Steele to Mrs. Steele, 8 July 1908, Box 9, Steele Papers, USAMHI.

68. Bullard Diary, Book 5, 5 May 1912, Bullard Papers, LC.

69. Ibid., 7 May 1912, Bullard Papers, LC.

70. Ibid., 20 May 1912, Bullard Papers, LC.

71. Swift to Gen. W. W. Wotherspoon, 21 May 1909, Box 3, Eben Swift Papers, USMA; Wotherspoon to Swift, 22 May 1909, ibid.

72. Steele to Mrs. Steele, 11 July 1908, Box 9, Steele Papers, USAMHI.

73. Ibid.

74. Bullard Diary, Book 6, 12 June 1912, Bullard Papers, LC.

75. Liggett, A.E.F., p. 295; Ahern, "Chronicle of the Army War College," pp. 83, 198–99.

76. Virginia battlefield trip itinerary, entry for 20 May 1909, AWC Curricular File, 1908–09, 2:787, USAMHI.

77. Bullard Diary, Book 5, 11 May 1912, Bullard Papers, LC.

78. Steele to Mrs. Steele, 11 July 1908, Box 9, Steele Papers, USAMHI.

79. AWC Curricular File, 1910–11, 2:5, USAMHI; AWC Curricular File, 1911–12, 1:5, USAMHI; Ball, *Of Responsible Command*, p. 111.

80. For an analysis of the content and quality of these essays, see chapter 8.

81. Ahern, "Chronicle of the Army War College," pp. 211–12, 237–39.

82. Ibid., pp. 191–92, 212, 239.

83. Maj. W. D. Connor to chief of staff, 25 August 1916, WCD File 7272-28, RG 165, NA, quoted in George James Stansfield, "A History of the Army War College at Washington, D.C. 1899–1940," typescript, 1964, pp. 8–9, USAMHI.

84. The resurging interest in historical rides is evident from the U.S. Army War College's new series of guides to Civil War battlefields, edited by Jay Luvaas and Harold W. Nelson. See also the October 1988 issue of *Army Historian* for a number of short articles on the importance of staff rides in the education of the modern officer corps.

85. Liggett, A.E.F., p. 295.

86. Hunter Liggett, *Commanding an American Army in France: Recollections of the World War* (Boston, 1925), p. 160.

CHAPTER FIVE. A MODEL AND A MUDDLE:
TWO HISTORICAL RESEARCH PROGRAMS, 1908-1917

1. Gen. M. M. Macomb, "The Scientific Study of Military History," p. 1, undated typescript, USAMHI.

2. R. M. Johnston to Assistant Secretary of War Henry Breckinridge, 5 January 1915, AGO File 2282637, RG 94, NA. As a member of the American Historical Association's Standing Committee on Military and Naval History, which Johnston chaired, Breckinridge submitted Johnston's comments to the secretary of war.

3. The nagging problem of officers who tried to pass their course work solely through memorization bothered army intellectuals before World War I. See, for instance, Lt. Matthew Forney Steele, "Military Reading: Its Use and Abuse," *Cavalry Journal* 8 (1895): 101; and Capt. L. T. Richardson to adjutant, Sixth Brigade [forwarded to secretary of the Army War College], 2 February 1914, enclosure to WCD File 8213-38, RG 165, NA.

4. Macomb, "Scientific Study of Military History," p. 8; Col. John F. Morrison, "Report of the Military Art Department," in *U.S. Army Staff College Annual Report, 1908* (Fort Leavenworth, Kans., 1909), p. 64; John Higham, *History* (Englewood Cliffs, N.J., 1965), p. 93.

5. See, for instance, the comments of Prof. Frederick Morrow Fling in "Who Shall Write Our Military History?" *Infantry Journal* 9 (1913): 562.

6. Capt. Eben Swift, "Report of the Department of Military Art," in *Annual Report of the Commandant of the U.S. Army Infantry and Cavalry School, 1905* (Fort Leavenworth, Kans., 1906), p. 3.

7. "Arthur Latham Conger," in *Harvard Class of 1894, Fiftieth Anniversary Report* (Boston, 1944), pp. 102–9.

8. Ibid., p. 104; Macomb, "The Scientific Study of Military History," p. 17.

9. "Arthur Latham Conger," p. 104; Timothy K. Nenninger, *The Leavenworth Schools and the Old Army: Education, Professionalism, and the Officer Corps of the United States Army, 1881-1918* (Westport, Conn., 1978), pp. 96–98.

10. Capt. Ola W. Bell, quoted in Nenninger, *Leavenworth Schools and the Old Army*, p. 96.

11. See Frederick Morrow Fling's comments on the conduct of Conger's class in his review of *Donelson Campaign Sources, Supplementing Volume 7 of* The Official Records of the Union and Confederate Armies in the War of the Rebellion, by Arthur L. Conger, in *American Historical Review* 19 (1914): 373.

12. Morrison, "Report of the Military Art Department," in *Staff College Annual Report, 1908*, p. 64.

13. Arthur L. Conger, "Lecture by Maj. A. L. Conger on Historical Research, the Engineer School, Camp A. A. Humphreys, Virginia," p. 5, undated typescript, Arthur Latham Conger Papers, Theosophical Society Library, Pasadena, Calif.

14. Morrison, "Report of the Military Art Department," in *Staff College Annual Report, 1908*, p. 64.

15. Conger, "Lecture by Maj. A. L. Conger on Historical Research," p. 4.

16. Morrison, "Report of the Military Art Department," in *Staff College Annual Report, 1908*, p. 64.

17. Col. John F. Morrison, "Report of the Military Art Department," in *U.S. Army Staff College Report, 1909* (Fort Leavenworth, Kans., 1910), p. 56.

18. Ibid., p. 59.

19. Morrison noted only that Conger was developing the course so "that it can be continued successfully," in ibid., p. 55; see also *U.S. Army Staff College Annual Report, 1910* (Fort Leavenworth, Kans., 1911), p. 44.

20. Robert E. Carlson, "Professor Fred Fling: His Career and Conflicts at Nebraska University," *Nebraska History* 62 (1981): 481–96.

21. Lt. Col. W. P. Burnham to Chancellor Samuel Avery of the University of Nebraska, 15 October 1913, Doc. 9245, Army Service Schools Documentary File 5240, RG 393, NA.

22. Burnham to Avery, 30 September 1913, filed with Doc. 9245, Army Service Schools Documentary File 5420, RG 393, NA.

23. Ibid. After his training at the University of Nebraska, Heintzelman requested and received leave to go to Europe to visit the battlefields studied at the Staff College (see Heintzelman to The Adjutant General, 21 April 1910, Army Service Schools Documentary File 3528, RG 393, NA; the approvals of department chairman Morrison and the commandant, dated 22 April, are appended to this document).

24. Burnham to Avery, 15 October 1913, Doc. 9245, Army Service Schools Documentary File 5240, RG 393, NA.

25. Conger to The Adjutant General, 30 July 1910, AGO File 1651176, RG 94, NA.

26. Ibid., and endorsement A by H. A. Smith with ibid.

27. Conger, "Lecture by Maj. A. L. Conger on Historical Research," p. 8.

28. Arthur L. Conger, *Donelson Campaign Sources, Supplementing Volume 7 of* The Official Records of the Union and Confederate Armies in the War of the Rebellion (Fort Leavenworth, Kans., 1913).

29. Macomb, "Scientific Study of Military History," p. 19.

30. Conger, "Lecture by Maj. A. L. Conger on Historical Research," p. 7.

31. [Arthur L. Conger and] Harry Bell, trans., *St. Privat: German Sources* (Fort Leavenworth, Kans., 1914), p. iii; Macomb, "Scientific Study of Military History," pp. 19–20.

32. Macomb, "Scientific Study of Military History," p. 20.

33. In 1922 Maj. Conrad Lanza of the historical section of the Army War College finally published a volume of sources concerning the Peninsula campaign to be used in the Army Service Schools.

34. Conger, "Lecture by Maj. A. L. Conger on Historical Research," p. 9.

35. G. A. Lynch [secretary of the Infantry Association] to A. M. Ferguson, secretary of the Army Service Schools, 7 December 1915, Doc. 3898, Army Service Schools Documentary File 3756, RG 393, NA.

36. Conger to Ferguson, [n.d.], ibid; Ferguson to Lynch, 13 December 1915, ibid.

37. Macomb, "Scientific Study of Military History," pp. 21, 28.

38. R. M. Johnston to Chief of Staff Leonard Wood, 31 January 1914, WCD File 8090-10, "Historical Section, Army War College, the General Staff," HRC 314.71, HS, WPD (1914–1919), USACMH.

39. Conger, "Lecture by Maj. A. L. Conger on Historical Research," p. 8.

40. See "Who Shall Write Our Military History?" and chapter 10.

41. Fling, review of Conger's *Donelson Campaign Sources*, in *American Historical Review* 19 (1914): 373.

42. Memorandum, Gen. Tasker H. Bliss to chief of staff [S. B. M. Young], 3 August 1903, quoted in Lt. Col. George Ahern, "A Chronicle of the Army War College, 1899–1919," pp. 17–18, undated typescript, USAMHI.

43. Capt. George Van Horne Moseley commented that as late as 1911, skeptical "irreconcilables" were detailed to the Army War College in the hope that the assignment

would "swell their heads" and convert them to the side of military education (Moseley, "One Soldier's Story," p. 92, Box 1A, George Van Horne Moseley Papers, LC).

44. See chapter 10.

45. See introduction to R. M. Johnston, *First Bull Run: Its Strategy and Tactics* (Boston, 1913).

46. R. M. Johnston, "The Functions of Military History," AWC Curricular File, 1913–14, Lectures, pp. 284–301, USAMHI.

47. Ibid., p. 286.

48. Ibid., p. 259.

49. Ibid., p. 298.

50. Similar sentiments were expressed by military men. See Maj. James McAndrew's comments in "Who Shall Write Our Military History?" p. 565, and Macomb, "Scientific Study of Military History," p. 7.

51. Memorandum, Brig. Gen. Hunter Liggett to Wood, 11 February 1914, WCD File 8090-11, copy in AGO File 2126426, RG 94, NA.

52. Ahern, "Chronicle of the Army War College," p. 239; Harry P. Ball, *Of Responsible Command: A History of the U.S. Army War College* (Carlisle Barracks, Pa., 1983), p. 111.

53. Ahern, "Chronicle of the Army War College," p. 212.

54. Since these additional conferences were considered "over the table" informal talks, the Army War College Curricular files contain no record of Johnston's comments. For a summary of his remarks, however, see Ahern, "Chronicle of the Army War College," pp. 238–39.

55. Macomb, "Scientific Study of Military History," pp. 5–7.

56. Ibid., p. 6.

57. Lt. Col. C. A. F. Flagler, "Historical Research," AWC Curricular File, 1914–15, 5:398–417, USAMHI.

58. Ibid., pp. 410–16.

59. Ibid.

60. Ahern, "Chronicle of the Army War College," pp. 198–99.

61. Ibid., p. 212.

62. George James Stansfield, "A History of the Army War College at Washington, D.C., 1899–1940," p. 11, typescript, 1964, USAMHI.

63. Morrison to Maj. E. E. Booth, [n.d.], included in commandant to The Adjutant General [Frederick C. Ainsworth], 25 November 1908, Army Service Schools Documentary File 5240, RG 393, NA; Capt. M. F. Davis to Booth, 9 January 1909, ibid.

64. Editorial comment [probably by Johnston], *Military Historian and Economist* 1 (1916): 199–200.

65. Col. Willard Holbrook to secretary of the Army Service Schools, 28 October 1913, Doc. 9246, Army Service Schools Documentary File 5294, RG 393, NA; Charles E. Wilson, foreman of the print shop, to secretary of the Army Service Schools, 23 October 1913, ibid.

66. The problem of retaining high-quality faculty members grew as Congress reduced the size of the General Staff in 1912, leaving a smaller pool of officers eligible for unrestricted appointment to school faculties. See Leonard Wood to Army War College president A. W. Mills, 10 April 1912, WCD File 7043-11, RG 165, NA; memorandum, Mills to Wood, WCD File 7043-15, ibid.; and memorandum, The Adjutant General to [Mills], 10 September 1912, WCD File 7043-118, ibid.

67. Lt. Col. W. P. Burnham, "Report of Commandant," in *U.S. Army Staff School Annual Report, 1913* (Fort Leavenworth, Kans., 1914), p. 4.

68. Maj. Farrand Sayre, "Report of the Military Art Department," in ibid., pp. 34–37.

69. Sayre was one of only three U.S. Army officers known to have received a Ph.D.

from a civilian university before World War II. The other two were Major Sauper of the Signal Corps and Q.M. Col. Mark L. Ireland. See Lt. Col. H. T. Aplington to Matthew Forney Steele, 17 February 1939, Box 19, Matthew Forney Steele Papers, USAMHI.

70. Conger to The Adjutant General [George Andrews], 16 March 1913, AGO Doc. 2021188, AGO File 127180, RG 94, NA, and third endorsement in ibid. by W. H. Carter, dated 18 March 1913.

71. Col. George H. Cameron, opening statement of scope of course, AWC Curricular File, 1916–17, 1:9, USAMHI.

72. Ibid., 1:26.

73. Brig. Gen. H. L. Scott to secretary of the Army War College, 24 December 1913, WCD File 8213-[no extension number], RG 165, NA.

PART TWO. MILITARY HISTORY AND
AN AMERICAN LITERATURE ON THE ART OF WAR

1. Capt. Arthur L. Wagner, *The Service of Security and Information* (Kansas City, Mo., 1895), p. 7.

2. "Doctrine, Conception, and History of War," *Infantry Journal* 9 (1912): 256–57.

3. "Our Military History," *Infantry Journal* 9 (1913): 382.

4. Ibid.

CHAPTER SIX. THE PEN RIVALS THE SWORD:
WRITING ABOUT THE AMERICAN WAY OF WAR

1. Lt. Matthew Forney Steele, "Military Reading: Its Use and Abuse," *Cavalry Journal* 8 (1895): 93.

2. The importance of authoritative literature to the professionalization of the officer corps is discussed in ibid., 93–105; Capt. Arthur L. Wagner, *Books for a Military Library* (Fort Leavenworth, Kans., 1895); Lt. R. E. Bebee, "Professional Reading for Infantry Officers," *Infantry Journal* 7 (1910): 33–45; and H. S. G., "Professional Reading," *Infantry Journal* 7 (1910): 330–37.

3. Boyd C. Shafer, *Faces of Nationalism: New Realities and Old Myths* (New York, 1972), p. 199.

4. Capt. James Chester, "Some of the Artillery Difficulties Likely to Be Encountered during the Next Maritime War," *JMSIUS* 19 (1898): 557.

5. James Chester, "Military Misconceptions and Absurdities," *JMSIUS* 14 (1893): 505–6.

6. Lt. C. D. Parkhurst, "The Practical Education of the Soldier," *JMSIUS* 19 (1898): 74.

7. Lt. E. H. Plummer, "Practice versus Theory in Army Training," *JMSIUS* 14 (1893): 1020.

8. See Dallas D. Irvine, "The Genesis of the *Official Records*," *Mississippi Valley Historical Review* 24 (1937–38): 221–29.

9. See, for example, U.S. Army Surgeon General's Office, *Medical and Surgical History of the War of the Rebellion*, 3 vols. in 6 pts. (Washington, D.C., 1877–1888), and the official reports of overseas observations by Emory Upton, Francis Vinton Greene, and William Hazen.

10. For the history of the most influential predecessor to the spate of professional military journals first published around the turn of the century, see Donald N. Bigelow, *William Conant Church and the* Army and Navy Journal (New York, 1952).

11. Maj. Gen. John M. Schofield, "Inaugural Address," *JMSIUS* 1 (1879): 1, 6.

12. Col. James B. Fry, "Origins and Progress of the Military Service Institution of the United States," *JMSIUS* 1 (1879): 28.

13. Chief of Staff Leonard Wood to Gen. Hunter Liggett, 3 January 1914, WCD File 8090-2, and memorandum, M. M. Macomb to Wood, 25 September 1914, WCD File 8090-24, both in "Historical Section, Army War College, the General Staff," HRC 314.71, HS, WPD (1914–1919), USACMH.

14. Lt. John W. Ruckman to Tasker H. Bliss, 26 November 1891, Tasker H. Bliss Papers, USAMHI.

15. See, for instance, Allan R. Millett, "American Military History: Over the Top," in *The State of American History*, edited by Herbert J. Bass (Chicago, 1970), pp. 157–59; and Walter Millis, *Military History*, American Historical Association Pamphlet 39 (Washington, D.C., 1961).

16. Francis Vinton Greene, *Report on the Russian Army and Its Campaign in Turkey, 1877–78* (New York, 1879) and Tasker H. Bliss, "The Campaign of Plevna," *JMSIUS* 2 (1880): 11–69. Excerpts from both works were used in army classrooms at Fort Leavenworth.

17. Tasker H. Bliss, "The Danube Campaign of 1877–78," undated typescript, Bliss Papers, USAMHI.

18. Peter D. Skirbunt, "Prologue to Reform: The 'Germanization' of the United States Army, 1865–1898" (Ph.D. diss., Ohio State University, 1983), discusses the influence of Prussian ideas on American military professionalism, but it does not give due credit to the impact of American nationalism on the intellectual development of the officer corps.

19. John Bigelow [Jr.], *Mars-la-Tour and Gravelotte* (Washington, D.C., 1880); Skirbunt, "Prologue to Reform," p. 106.

20. Arthur L. Wagner, *The Campaign of Königgrätz: A Study of the Austro-Prussian Conflict in the Light of the American Civil War* (Fort Leavenworth, Kans., 1889; reprint ed., Westport, Conn., 1972), and unsigned review of *The Campaign of Königgrätz* in *Cavalry Journal* 2 (1889): 429.

21. Bliss, "Danube Campaign of 1877–78," Bliss Papers, USAMHI.

22. Capt. Arthur L. Wagner, *Organization and Tactics* (Kansas City, Mo., 1895), p. 87.

23. John Bigelow [Jr.], *The Principles of Strategy, Illustrated Mainly from American Campaigns* (New York, 1891; reprint ed., Westport Conn., 1968), p. 6.

24. See, for instance, Lt. Carl Reichmann, Review of *The Principles of Strategy, Illustrated Mainly from American Campaigns*, by John Bigelow [Jr.], in *JMSIUS* 15 (1894): 861.

25. Bigelow, *Principles of Strategy*, p. 110.

26. Ibid., pp. 224–33.

27. Ibid., pp. 189–203.

28. Ibid., p. 205.

29. Ibid., pp. 114, 117.

30. Lt. John P. Wisser, Review of *The Principles of Strategy, Illustrated Mainly from American Campaigns*, by John Bigelow [Jr.], in *Journal of the United States Artillery* 3 (1894): 519.

31. W. A. S., Review of *The Principles of Strategy, Illustrated Mainly from American Campaigns*, by John Bigelow [Jr.], in *Cavalry Journal* 5 (1892): 102–3.

32. Reichmann, Review of Bigelow, *Principles of Strategy*, p. 861.

33. C. D., Review of *The Principles of Strategy, Illustrated Mainly from American Campaigns*, in *Journal of the United States Artillery* 1 (1892): 141.

34. Jay Luvaas, *The Education of an Army: British Military Thought, 1815–1940* (Chicago, 1964), pp. 219–25, 244–47.

35. Diary entry, 7 October 1884, John Bigelow Papers, USMA.

36. Margaret Antoinette Clapp, *Forgotten First Citizen: John Bigelow* (Boston, 1947), pp. 109–10.

37. G. P. Putnam to John Bigelow [Jr.], 21 September 1891, Box 98-99, John Bigelow Papers, LC.

38. Poultney Bigelow to John Bigelow [Sr.], 19 December 1890, Box 98-99, Bigelow Papers, LC.

39. [T. Fisher Unwin], draft of royalty scheme, n.d., Box 98-99, Bigelow Papers, LC.

40. John Bigelow [Jr.] to John Bigelow [Sr.], 11 September 1891, Bigelow, Jr., to G. P. Putnam's Sons, 24 September 1891, Putnam's Sons to Bigelow, Jr., 2 October 1891, all in Box 98-99, Bigelow Papers, LC.

41. Poultney Bigelow to T. Fisher Unwin, 27 August 1891, and Lt. Gen. Count von Schlieffen to Poultney Bigelow, 3 November 1891, both in Box 98-99, Bigelow Papers, LC.

42. Diary entry, 12 September 1891, Bigelow Papers, USMA; Bigelow, Jr., to Bigelow, Sr., 11 September 1891, Box 98-99, Bigelow Papers, LC.

43. T[heophilus] D. R[odenbough], Review of *The History of the First Regiment of Artillery, United States Army, from Its Origin in 1821 to January 1, 1876*, by Maj. William L. Haskin, in *JMSIUS* 1 (1879): 96.

44. The army schools suffered from a shortage of textbooks from the start. General Sherman donated his own copy of France James Soady's *Lessons of War* (London: W.H. Allen, 1870) to the Leavenworth schools. See Timothy K. Nenninger, *The Leavenworth Schools and the Old Army: Education, Professionalism, and the Officer Corps of the United States Army, 1881–1918* (Westport, Conn., 1978), p. 25; and Elvid Hunt and Walter E. Lorence, *History of Fort Leavenworth, 1827–1937*, updated ed. (Fort Leavenworth, Kans., 1937), p. 147, on the replacement of European textbooks with works by American authors.

45. Memorandum from The Adjutant General on "the adoption of official text books for examination of officers for promotion," 2 January 1895, copy in Letter Book, pp. 99–108, Box 7, Bliss Papers, USAMHI.

46. Ibid., p. 100.

47. Ibid., pp. 106–7.

48. Ibid., p. 100; Arthur L. Wagner to Bliss, 14 March 1890, Bliss Papers, USAMHI.

49. Diary entry, 7 October 1884, Bigelow Papers, USMA.

50. Memorandum from The Adjutant General on "the adoption of official text books," p. 100.

51. Wagner to Bliss, 11 February 1890, Bliss Papers, USAMHI.

52. Wagner to Bliss, 14 March 1890, Bliss Papers, USAMHI.

53. Wagner to Bliss, 12 December 1891, Bliss Papers, USAMHI.

54. Wagner to Bliss, 11 February 1890, Bliss Papers, USAMHI.

55. Wagner to Bliss, 12 December 1891, Bliss Papers, USAMHI.

56. Col. Edward Townsend to Bliss, 10 December 1892, Bliss Papers, USAMHI.

57. Wagner to Bliss, 12 December 1891, Bliss Papers, USAMHI.

58. Capt. Arthur L. Wagner, *The Service of Security and Information*, 2d ed. (Kansas City, Mo., 1895), p. 7.

59. Ibid., p. 9.

60. Bruce W. Bidwell, *History of the Military Information Division of the Army General Staff, 1775–1941* (Frederick, Md. 1986), pp. 51–63.

61. Wagner, *Security and Information*, pp. 161–64; E. Porter Alexander, "The Great Charge and Artillery Fighting at Gettysburg," *Battles and Leaders of the Civil War*, 4 vols., edited by Robert Underwood Johnson and Clarence Clough Buel (New York, 1888), 3:358.

62. Wagner, *Security and Information*, p. 111.

63. John I. Alger, *The Quest for Victory: The History of the Principles of War* (Westport, Conn., 1982), especially chapter 3.

64. Wagner, *Security and Information*, pp. 242–48.

65. Wagner, *Organization and Tactics*, p. x.

66. Maj. Michael D. Krause, "Arthur L. Wagner: Doctrine and Lessons from the Past," *Military Review* 58 (1978): 53–59.

67. Wagner, *Organization and Tactics*, p. xi.

68. Four chapters—"Organization and Discipline," "Space and Time Requirements," "Historical Sketch," and "Characteristics of the Three Arms"—appeared in *Cavalry Journal* 6 (1893), and "Cavalry in Attack and Defense" appeared in *Cavalry Journal* 7 (1894).

69. Capt. W. A. Kobbe, Review of *The Service of Security and Information* by Arthur L. Wagner, in *Journal of the United States Artillery* 3 (1894): 162.

70. Herbert H. Sargent, *Napoleon Bonaparte's First Campaign* (Chicago, 1895), *The Campaign of Marengo* (Chicago, 1897), and subsequent reprintings of both books, with revisions, helped to enhance the captain's reputation as a military writer before the Spanish-American War.

71. Sargent to The Adjutant General, 8 June 1895, AGO File 20982 and 20982/A, and Sargent to The Adjutant General, 2 October 1897, AGO File 63787, RG 94, NA.

72. Capt. Eben Swift, "Report of the Military Art Department," in *Annual Report of the U.S. Army Infantry and Cavalry School, 1905* (Fort Leavenworth, Kans., 1906), p. 16.

73. Sargent, *Napoleon Bonaparte's First Campaign*, pp. 15–17.

74. Sargent, in reply to E. F. Williams's review of Sargent's *Napoleon Bonaparte's First Campaign*, in *Cavalry Journal* 11 (1898): 494–96.

75. Sargent to Matthew Forney Steele, 25 March 1907, Box 11, Matthew Forney Steele Papers, USAMHI.

76. "Praise for Herbert H. Sargent's *Marengo* from Overseas," *Cavalry Journal* 11 (1898): 241–43.

77. Sen. William E. Mason to "the President," 30 June 1902, AGO File 443935, in Appointments, Commissions, and Personnel File 3474, RG 94, NA.

78. Herbert H. Sargent, *The Campaign of Santiago de Cuba*, 3 vols. (Chicago, 1907); Arthur L. Wagner, *Report of the Santiago Campaign, 1898* (Kansas City, Mo., 1908); and John Bigelow [Jr.], *Reminiscences of the Santiago Campaign* (New York, 1899). Although none of these works is an "official history" in the accepted sense, Sargent and Wagner had access to governmental documents that many civilian scholars did not have (see chapter 9). Wagner's work, in fact, is mostly a posthumous reprinting of his official report as chief of the Military Information Bureau.

79. Kobbe, Review of Wagner's *Service of Security and Information*, p. 163.

CHAPTER SEVEN. *AMERICAN CAMPAIGNS:*
THE U.S. ARMY'S FIRST MILITARY HISTORY TEXTBOOK

1. Matthew Forney Steele to Charles Scribner's Sons, 1 April 1908, Box 19, Matthew Forney Steele Papers, USAMHI.

2. Timothy K. Nenninger, *The Leavenworth Schools and the Old Army: Education, Professionalism, and the Officer Corps of the United States Army, 1881–1918* (Westport, Conn., 1978), p. 95. In 1938 the United States Infantry Association voted to give Steele a gift of five hundred dollars for his literary contributions to officer education.

3. Capt. Arthur L. Wagner, *Books for a Military Library* (Fort Leavenworth, Kans., 1895), p. 4.

4. Ibid., pp. 4–5.

5. John Codman Ropes, *The Story of the Civl War*, 3 vols. (New York, 1984, 1898, 1913), was the favorite historical work by an American author in the eyes of many soldiers, including Steele, Wagner, and Eben Swift, all instrumental to the army education movement.

6. See Steele's "Obituary," written by Steele in 1925, p. 8, Steele Papers, USAMHI.

7. In "The Evolution of Professional Culture in the American Army," typescript draft, Box 20, Steele Papers, USAMHI, Steele dated the beginning of military professionalism in the United States from the foundation of the Military Service Institution of the United States and its influential journal late in the 1870s. Although Steele wrote no major articles for this publication early in his career, he was a frequent contributor of rejoinders to essays about important policy questions and possible reforms.

8. Lt. Matthew Forney Steele, "Military Reading: Its Use and Abuse," *Cavalry Journal* 8 (1895): 93–104.

9. Steele, "Evolution of Professional Culture in the American Army," Steele Papers, USAMHI.

10. Ibid.

11. Steele, "Military Reading: Its Use and Abuse," p. 101.

12. Ibid.

13. "Military Reading – Its Methods, Its Uses, Its Abuses," draft typescript, "Notes for Essays" journal, Box 21, Steele Papers, USAMHI. Steele's *Cavalry Journal* article is heavily based on these notes.

14. Draft manuscript, untitled and undated journal, p. 8, Box 21, Steele Papers, USAMHI.

15. Steele, "Military Reading: Its Use and Abuse," p. 99.

16. Draft manuscript, untitled and undated journal, p. 13, Box 21, Steele Papers, USAMHI.

17. Gen. J. Franklin Bell to president of the Army War College Board, 31 January 1908, printed as appendix F to *Annual Report of the General Service and Staff College, 1904* (Washington, D.C., 1905), p. 73.

18. Memorandum, Col. Arthur L. Wagner to commandant [Bell], 28 December 1903, printed as appendix H in ibid., p. 91.

19. Maj. W. W. Wotherspoon, "Report of the Department of Tactics," printed as appendix B in ibid., pp. 27–28.

20. Maj. Eben Swift, "Report of the Department of Military Art," in *Annual Report of the Infantry and Cavalry School, 1905* (Washington, D.C., 1906), p. 16.

21. Maj. D. H. Boughton, "Report of the Department of Military Art," in *Annual Report of the Infantry and Cavalry School, 1906* (Washington, D.C. 1907), p. 14.

22. Col. John F. Morrison, "Report of the Department of Military Art," in *Annual Report of the Infantry and Cavalry School, 1908* (Washington, D.C., 1909), p. 32.

23. Steele to secretary of the Army Service Schools, 30 January 1908, Doc. 5476 in File 3069, Army Service Schools Documentary files, RG 393, NA.

24. Ibid.

25. Ibid.

26. Col. C. B. Hall to secretary of the Army Service Schools, 8 February 1908, enclosure to Doc. 5476 in File 3069, Army Service Schools Documentary files, RG 393, NA.

27. Hall to Capt. M. F. Davis, 31 January 1908, ibid.

28. Steele to Davis, 23 May 1908, Box 19, Steele Papers, USAMHI.

29. Davis to Steele, 3 June 1908, Box 16, Steele Papers, USAMHI. Steele explained that keeping the price down for army officers was the primary reason why his work was going to be published by the government and not by a major civilian publishing house (see Steele to the Century Company, 23 March 1908, Box 19, Steele Papers, USAMHI).

30. Matthew Forney Steele, *American Campaigns*, 2 vols. (Washington, D.C., 1909), 1:iv.

31. Steele to the Century Company, 23 March 1908, Box 19, Steele Papers, USAMHI; Steele to Houghton Mifflin Company, 23 March 1908, ibid.

32. Steele to Houghton Mifflin Company, 1 April 1908, Box 19, Steele Papers, USAMHI; Steele to the Century Company, 1 April 1908, ibid.

33. Capt. E. E. Booth to Davis, [May 1908], WCD File 5049-2, RG 165, NA.

34. Steele to chief of the Military Information Division, 10 June 1908, WCD File 5049-3, RG 165, NA.

35. Booth to Davis, 16 May 1908, WCD File 5049-1, RG 165, NA; Booth to Davis, 18 May 1908, Doc. 5476-A, in File 3069, Army Service Schools Documentary files, RG 393, NA.

36. Davis to Steele, 3 June 1908, Box 16, Steele Papers, USAMHI.

37. Ibid.: see also chapter 6.

38. Steele to chief of the Military Information Division, 30 June 1908, WCD File 5049-5, RG 165, NA.

39. Chief clerk [Schofield] of the War Department to chief of staff [Bell], August 1908, WCD File 5049-32, RG 165, NA.

40. [Schofield] to [Bell], 3 August 1908, WCD File 5049-30, RG 165, NA.

41. Comptroller of the Department of the Treasury to the secretary of war [Luke E. Wright], 26 August 1908, WCD File 5049-36, RG 165, NA.

42. Memorandum for chief of staff, 24 October 1908, WCD File 5049-36, RG 165, NA.

43. Ibid.

44. Secretary of the Army Service Schools to secretary of the General Staff, 21 October 1909, WCD File 5049-56, 28 October 1909, WCD File 5049-57, and 12 November 1909, WCD File 5049-58, all in RG 165, NA.

45. Jay Luvaas, "Military History: An Academic Historian's Point of View," in *New Dimensions in Military History*, edited by Russell F. Weigley (San Rafael, Calif., 1972), pp. 31–32.

46. Steele, *American Campaigns*, 1:iii.

47. Ibid., 1:vii; Sydney George Fisher, *True History of the American Revolution* (Philadelphia, 1902), and Fisher, *The Struggle for American Independence*, 2 vols. (Philadelphia, 1908).

48. Steele, *American Campaigns*, 1:53.

49. Ibid., 1:vii; E. Porter Alexander, *Military Memoirs of a Confederate* (New York, 1907).

50. Steele, *American Campaigns*, 1:39.

51. Ibid., 1:75.

52. Ibid., 1:511; John I. Alger, *The Quest for Victory: The History of the Principles of War* (Westport, Conn., 1982), pp. 85–87.

53. Steele, *American Campaigns*, 1:186–87.

54. Ibid.

55. Ibid., 1:190.

56. Unknown to secretary of the Army Service Schools, 17 March 1910, WCD File 5049-77, RG 165, NA; secretary of the Army Service Schools to unknown, 21 March 1910, WCD File 5049-78, ibid.

57. Capt. Malin Craig to Steele, 28 May 1910, Box 19, Steele Papers, USAMHI.

58. Memorandum for chief of staff [Leonard Wood], 24 September 1913, WCD File 5049-91, RG 165, NA.

59. W. H. K[eith] to Byron S. Adams, 9 December 1913, WCD File 5049-96, RG 165, NA.

60. Adams to Keith, 17 March 1914, WCD File 5049-100, RG 165, NA; Keith to Adams, 20 March 1914, WCD File 5049-101, ibid.

61. Adams to Maj. C. Crawford, 1 July 1914, WCD File 5049-104, RG 165, NA; Crawford to Adams, 2 July 1914, WCD File 5049-105, ibid.

62. Gen. M. M. Macomb to Congressman J. W. Bryan, 7 November 1914, WCD File 5049-109, RG 165, NA.

63. Memorandum for Macomb, 24 January 1916, WCD File 5049-113, RG 165, NA.

64. Review of *American Campaigns* in *Cavalry Journal* 20 (1910): 816–17.

65. Review of *American Campaigns* in *Journal of the United States Artillery* 34 (1910): 123–24; review in *Infantry Journal* 6 (1910): 772–73.

66. *Army and Navy Journal* 47 (March 1910): 804.

67. See, for instance, the unsigned review of H. H. Sargent's *Campaign of Santiago de Cuba* in *Infantry Journal* 4 (1907): 481–83.

68. Morrison, "Report of the Department of Military Art," in *Annual Report of the Infantry and Cavalry School, 1908*, p. 32.

69. Morrison, "Report of the Department of Military Art," in *Annual Report of the Infantry and Cavalry School, 1910* (Washington, D.C., 1911), p. 23.

70. A. W. Smith to Adams, 20 August 1917, WCD File 5049-X, RG 165, NA.

71. Lt. Col. C. A. F. Flagler, "Historical Research," AWC Curricular File, 1914–15, pp. 413–14, USAMHI.

72. Maj. Conrad Lanza to Lt. Col. Oliver L. Spaulding, 7 January 1922, Thomas File 2242, RG 165, NA.

73. Lanza to The Adjutant General, 5 January 1922, Thomas File 333, RG 165, NA.

74. Memorandum, E. F. McLachlin [commandant of the Army War College], to chief of staff [John J. Pershing], 8 February 1922, AWC File 216-17, in MISC 314.71 files, USACMH.

75. [Capt.] M. H. Taulbee [First Infantry, Oklahoma National Guard] to Steele, 16 February 1910, Box 19, Steele Papers, USAMHI.

76. John F. McGee to Steele, 27 October 1911, Box 19, Steele Papers, USAMHI.

77. Farrand Sayre to Steele, 10 January 1939, Box 19, Steele Papers, USAMHI.

78. See the title page and introduction to the 1943 reprint edition of *American Campaigns*.

79. John C. Pemberton [III] to Steele, 5 November 1937, Box 19, Steele Papers, USAMHI.

80. A similar situation occurred, for instance, when the War Department extended official encouragement to Capt. George H. Shelton, who desired to write a comprehensive history of the United States Army that would update Upton. In this case, however, the department's endorsement was not nearly so strong as the one given to Steele. Shelton was permitted to extend a duty assignment at Fort Jay, near New York City, to facilitate his dealings with the D. Appleton Company, which had asked him to undertake the work, but this was the army's chief concession. See memorandum to Chief of Staff Wood from Shelton, 27 March 1913, WCD File 7865, RG 165, NA; and memorandum by Gen. William Crozier to The Adjutant General, 30 June 1913, enclosed with ibid.

CHAPTER EIGHT. A FIRST ATTEMPT AT OFFICIAL HISTORY

1. "Doctrine, Conception, and History of War," *Infantry Journal* 9 (1912): 260.

2. Otto Grebtog, "A Chat on Military History and the Art of War" (translated from the *New Yorker Staats-Zeitung*, 12 May 1901), *Journal of the United States Artillery* 16 (1901): 171.

3. Ibid., pp. 167–68; "Who Shall Write Our Military History?" *Infantry Journal* 9 (1913): 548–53, 570–71.

4. James E. Hewes, Jr., *From Root to McNamara: Army Organization and Administration, 1900–1963* (Washington, D.C., 1975), pp. 15–17.

5. "Who Shall Write Our Military History?" pp. 562–66.

6. Ibid., p. 554.

7. Ibid.

8. Ibid., pp. 546–47, 560–61.

9. Ibid., pp. 555–56.

10. "Our Military History," *Infantry Journal* 9 (1912): 379–82.

11. "The Study of Military History," *Nation* 93 (December 1912): 557.

12. "Who Shall Write Our Military History?" p. 573.

13. Lt. Matthew Forney Steele, response to Capt. James S. Pettit's "The Proper Military Instruction of Our Officers," *JMSIUS* 20 (1899): 431; see also Lt. Col. George P. Ahern, "A Chronicle of the Army War College, 1899–1919," undated typescript, USAMHI.

14. Col. John Morrison to secretary of the Army War College, 29 December 1913, WCD File 8213-4, RG 165, NA.

15. Ahern, "Chronicle of the Army War College," p. 190.

16. Ibid., pp. 221, 237–38.

17. Ibid.; memorandum, Gen. Hunter Liggett to chief of staff [Leonard Wood], 11 February 1914, WCD File 8090-11, copy filed as AGO File 2126426, Records and Pensions 127180, RG 94, NA; A. L. Conger to Maj. W. H. Gordon, 17 February 1914, WCD File 8090-13, "Historical Section, Army War College, the General Staff," HRC 314.71, HS, WPD (1914–1919), USACMH; Maj. C. Crawford to Conger, 17 February 1914, WCD File 8090-14, ibid.

18. Chief of Staff Leonard Wood to Col. John Biddle, 3 January 1914, WCD File 8090-3, in "Historical Section, Army War College, the General Staff," HRC 314.71, HS, WPD (1914–1919), USACMH; see also chapter 11.

19. George James Stansfield, "History of the Army War College at Washington, D.C., 1899–1940," typescript, 1964, p. 11, USAMHI.

20. Ahern, "Chronicle of the Army War College," p. 237.

21. R. M. Johnston, "What Can Be Done for Our Military History?" *Infantry Journal* 9 (1912): 236.

22. Lt. Col. A. P. Buffington, "The First Battle of Bull Run," AWC typescript, Class of 1914, p. 1, USAMHI.

23. Ibid., pp. 1–2; Lt. Col. Alfred Hasbrouck, "The First Battle of Bull Run," AWC typescript, 1913, pp. 1–2, USAMHI.

24. John Bigelow [Jr.], *The Principles of Strategy, Illustrated Mainly from American Campaigns* (New York, 1891; reprint ed., Westport, Conn., 1968), pp. 224–27; Lt. Col. B. W. Atkinson, "The Battle of Antietam," AWC typescript, 1913, p. 54, USAMHI.

25. Maj. Hanson Ely, "The Antietam Campaign," AWC typescript, 1916, p. 30, USAMHI.

26. Maj. W. W. Harts, "Second Day of the Battle of Gettysburg," AWC typescript, 1912, p. 30, USAMHI.

27. Lt. Col. Joseph A. Gaston, "The Gettysburg Campaign, to Include the Fighting of the First Day, July 1, 1863," AWC typescript, 1912, p. 60, USAMHI.

28. Buffington, "First Bull Run," p. 93.

29. Maj. Edward Sigerfoos, "Campaign and Battle of Second Manassas," AWC typescript, 1915, p. 54, USAMHI.

30. Hasbrouck, "First Bull Run," p. 20.

31. Buffington, "First Bull Run," pp. 96–97.

32. Joseph E. Johnston, *Narrative of Military Operations* (New York, 1874), p. 59–66; Alfred Roman, *The Military Operations of General Beauregard*, 2 vols. (New York, 1884), 1:109, 114–19; Jubal A. Early, *Lieutenant General Jubal Anderson Early, C.S.A.: Autobiographical Sketch and Narrative of the War between the States* (Philadelphia, 1912), pp. 41–46; and John Imboden, "Incidents of the First Bull Run," *Battles and Leaders of the Civil War*, 4 vols., edited by Robert Underwood Johnson and Clarence Clough Buel (New York, 1888), 1:239.

33. E. Porter Alexander, *Military Memoirs of a Confederate* (New York, 1907; reprint ed., Dayton, Ohio, 1977), p. 50.

34. Maj. G. P. Howell, "Campaign and Battle of Gettysburg," AWC typescript, 1915, pp. 68–69, USAMHI.

35. Harts, "Second Day of the Battle of Gettysburg," p. 36.

36. Col. Charles R. Noyes, "Williamsport, Md.: Did General Meade Make a Mistake in Not Attacking?" (a paper read to the Officers Lyceum at Madison Barracks, N.Y., March 1898, attached to "The Gettysburg Campaign, Exclusive of the Battle," AWC typescript, 1914, USAMHI).

37. See Edwin B. Coddington, "The Strange Reputation of General George G. Meade: A Lesson in Historiography," *The Historian* 23 (1962): 145-66.

38. Maj. Robert S. Abernethy, "The Advance of Grant's Army towards Spotsylvania, May 7, and the Recontre Battle of May 8, 1864," AWC typescript, 1912, p. 79, USAMHI; Capt. Howard R. Hickok, "The Battle of Spotsylvania Court House, 9-12 May 1864," AWC typescript, 1910, p. 79, USAMHI.

39. Thomas L. Connelly, *The Marble Man: Robert E. Lee and His Image in American Society* (New York, 1977), especially chapters 2 and 3.

40. For a good description of the terrain around Sharpsburg and its suitability as a defensive position, see Stephen W. Sears, *Landscape Turned Red* (New Haven, Conn., 1983), pp. 185-88.

41. Atkinson, "Battle of Antietam," pp. 10-11, draws upon Armistead Long, G. F. R. Henderson, and at least three other respected authors to shape his evaluation of Lee's command decision to remain at Sharpsburg to fight.

42. Alexander, *Military Memoirs of a Confederate*, pp. 242-43, 246-48; James Longstreet, "The Invasion of Maryland," in *Battles and Leaders of the Civil War*, 4 vols., edited by Robert Underwood Johnson and Clarence Clough Buel (New York, 1888), 3:666-67.

43. Ely, "Antietam Campaign," p. 34.

44. Howell, "Campaign and Battle of Gettysburg," p. 67.

45. For a modern analysis of the various charges made against Stuart and Ewell at Gettysburg, see Glenn Tucker, *Lee and Longstreet at Gettysburg* (Indianapolis, 1968), chapter 12 (Stuart) and chapter 14 (Ewell).

46. Gaston, "Gettysburg Campaign," p. 74.

47. Ibid., pp. 74-75.

48. Harts, "Second Day of the Battle of Gettysburg," p. 34.

49. Ibid., p. 35; Brig. Gen. John F. O'Ryan [New York National Guard], "The Battle of Gettysburg, July 1-2-3, 1863," AWC typescript, 1914, p. 51, USAMHI.

50. Copies of many of these essays, prepared primarily for use in the official history and developed further from the students' Civil War battlefield assignments used here, can be found in WCD File 8525, RG 165, NA.

51. Ely, "Antietam Campaign," p. 35.

52. John I. Alger, *The Quest for Victory: The History of the Principles of War* (Westport, Conn., 1982), especially chapter 4.

53. See Edward Mead Earle, ed., *Makers of Modern Strategy: Military Thought from Machiavelli to Hitler* (Princeton, N.J., 1943), pp. 206-17.

54. Alger, *Quest for Victory*, pp. 60, 61, 183, 186-87.

55. Ibid., pp. 135-45.

56. Maj. Charles R. Gerhardt, "The Battle of Groveton and Second Bull Run," AWC typescript, 1913, p. 27, USAMHI.

57. See Michael Howard, "Men against Fire: Expectations of War in 1914," in *Military Strategy and the Origins of the First World War*, edited by Steven Miller (Princeton, N.J., 1985), pp. 41-57; and Jack Snyder, *The Ideology of the Offensive: Military Decision Making and the Disasters of 1914* (Ithaca, N.Y., 1984), chapter 1.

58. See Barry R. Posen, *The Sources of Doctrine: France, Britain, and Germany between the World Wars* (Ithaca, N.Y., 1984), pp. 13-33.

59. Buffington, "First Bull Run," p. 4.

60. R. M. Johnston, *First Bull Run: Its Strategy and Tactics* (Boston, 1913), pp. 15-16.

61. Capt. Duncan Major, "Battle of Chancellorsville, May 3, 1863, the Retreat of the Federal Army, May 5, 1863, the Federal Left in the Campaign of Chancellorsville, including the Second Battle of Fredericksburg, May 3, the Action at Salem Church, May 3 and 4," AWC typescript, 1912, p. 16, USAMHI.

62. Harts, "Second Day of the Battle of Gettysburg," p. 30.

63. Maj. Edward D. Anderson, "The Second Battle of Bull Run," AWC typescript, 1914, p. 40, USAMHI; Gerhardt, "Battle of Groveton and Second Bull Run," p. 29.

64. Gerhardt, "Battle of Groveton and Second Bull Run," p. 23.

65. Hickok, "Battle of Spotsylvania Court House," p. 86.

66. Maj. DeRussy Cabell, "The Operations about Spotsylvania, May 10–18, 1864," AWC typescript, 1913, p. 39, USAMHI.

67. Maj. F. K. Fergusson, "The Operations of May 10, 1864, at Spotsylvania," AWC typescript, 1912, p. 49, USAMHI.

68. James W. Rainey, "Ambivalent Warfare: The Tactical Doctrine of the AEF in World War I," *Parameters* 8 (Fall 1983): 36–37.

69. O'Ryan, "Battle of Gettysburg," pp. 49–51.

70. Fergusson, "Operations of May 10, 1864, at Spotsylvania," p. 49.

71. Hickok, "Battle of Spotsylvania Court House," p. 88.

72. Gaston, "Gettysburg Campaign," p. 77.

73. Cabell, "Operations about Spotsylvania," p. 48.

74. Hasbrouck, "First Bull Run," p. 17; Ely, "Antietam Campaign," p. 36; Atkinson, "Battle of Antietam," p. 55.

75. Lt. Col. Thomas B. Dugan, "Battle of Chancellorsville," AWC typescript, 1913, p. [43], USAMHI.

76. A good turn-of-the-century representative essay that praised Lee's conduct of the Battle of Chancellorsville is T. M. R. Talcott, "General Lee's Strategy at the Battle of Chancellorsville," *Southern Historical Society Papers* 34 (1906): 1–27. A modern source that reaches similar positive conclusions about Lee's generalship is Edward J. Stackpole, *Chancellorsville: Lee's Greatest Battle* (Harrisburg, Pa., 1958), pp. 367–72.

77. Hasbrouck, "First Bull Run," p. 17; Buffington, "First Bull Run," p. 92; Dugan, "Battle of Chancellorsville," p. [43].

78. Sigerfoos, "Campaign and Battle of Second Manassas," p. 55; Gerhardt, "Battle of Groveton and Second Bull Run," p. 29.

79. Dugan, "Battle of Chancellorsville," p. [43]; Major, "Battle of Chancellorsville," p. 16.

80. Capt. W. K. Naylor, "Second Battle of Bull Run," AWC typescript, 1910, p. 23; Gerhardt, "Battle of Groveton and Second Bull Run," p. 28.

81. Howell, "Campaign and Battle of Gettysburg," p. 67.

82. Jay Luvaas, *The Military Legacy of the Civil War: The European Inheritance* (Chicago, 1959), pp. 108–15, 125–30, 155–64, 193–97.

83. Capt. James C. Harbord, "The Cavalry of the Army of Northern Virginia," *Cavalry Journal* 14 (1904): 423–504; see also Lt. Hugh J. Gallegher, "Cavalry in Modern Warfare," *Cavalry Journal* 9 (1896): 38–47.

84. See, for instance, Moses Harris, "With the Reserve Brigade," *Cavalry Journal* 3 (1890): 20.

85. Lt. J. P. Ryan, "Some Cavalry Lessons of the Civil War," *Cavalry Journal* 8 (1895): 268–82; Lt. James H. Reeves, "Cavalry Raids," *Cavalry Journal* 10 (1897): 232–47.

86. See Harbord, "Cavalry of the Army of Northern Virginia," p. 423; and Gallegher, "Cavalry in Modern Warfare," pp. 38–40.

87. A. E. Wood, "The Proper Employment of Cavalry in War," *Cavalry Journal* 4 (1891): 114–36.

88. "Employment of Cavalry, General Principles," in U.S. Army, *Cavalry Service Regulations* (Washington, D.C., 1914), pp. 220–22.

89. Hasbrouck, "First Bull Run," p. 18.

90. Lt. Col. J. B. McDonald, "Operations of the Federal and Confederate Cavalry in the Chancellorsville Campaign," AWC typescript, 1912, pp. 1–2, USAMHI.

91. Atkinson, "Battle of Antietam," p. 55.

92. McDonald, "Operations of the Federal and Confederate Cavalry in the Chancellorsville Campaign," p. 90.

93. Ibid., pp. 93–94.

94. Ibid., p. 95; Capt. Charles S. Lincoln, "The Chancellorsville Campaign," AWC typescript, 1912, p. 52, USAMHI.

95. Gaston, "Gettysburg Campaign," p. 62; Harts, "Second Day of the Battle of Gettysburg," p. 33.

96. Abernethy, "Advance of Grant's Army towards Spotsylvania," p. 48.

97. Hickok, "Battle of Spotsylvania Court House," p. 79.

98. Gaston, "Gettysburg Campaign," p. 80.

99. Harts, "Second Day of the Battle of Gettysburg," p. 38.

100. Cabell, "Operations about Spotsylvania," p. 39.

101. Gerhardt, "Battle of Groveton and Second Bull Run," p. 30.

102. Rainey, "Ambivalent Warfare," p. 34; Capt. Timothy T. Lupfer, *The Dynamics of Doctrine: The Changes in German Tactical Doctrine during the First World War*, Leavenworth Paper 4 (Fort Leavenworth, Kans. 1981), pp. vii–viii.

PART THREE. THE SOLDIERS VERSUS THE SCHOLARS

1. "Who Shall Write Our Military History?" *Infantry Journal* 9 (1913): 547.

2. Ibid.

CHAPTER NINE. THE ROOTS
OF INTERPROFESSIONAL TENSIONS

1. John Higham, *History* (Englewood Cliffs, N.J., 1965), pp. 18–25 and chapter 2, uses 1907 as a pivotal year in the professionalization of American historians.

2. See Frederick Bancroft, letter in "Gen. Ainsworth and the National Archives," *Nation* 94 (February 1912): 180.

3. J. Franklin Jameson to Adj. Gen. Henry P. McCain, 21 March 1912, War Department File, Box 134, J. Franklin Jameson Papers, LC.

4. In the *Annual Report of the Secretary of War, 1898* (Washington, D.C., 1899), pp. 220–21, the need for more space in the Adjutant General's Office was called "very urgent," a condition that worsened as the official paperwork of the Spanish-American War flooded an already overwhelmed staff.

5. For the protests of men whose written requests had been turned down by Ainsworth, see letter by Virginia State Librarian H. R. McIlwaine in "Gen. Ainsworth and the National Archives," p. 180, and Brown University professor John MacDonald in ibid., p. 181.

6. Mabel E. Deutrich, *The Struggle for Supremacy: The Career of General Fred C. Ainsworth* (Washington, D.C., 1962), is the most complete biography of this controversial officer. See also Siert F. Riepma, "Portrait of an Adjutant General," *Journal of the American Military History Foundation* 2 (1937): 26–35.

7. For details of Ainsworth's court-martial, see House Committee on Military Af-

fairs, *Relief of the Adjutant General of the Army from the Duties of His Office*, 62d Cong., 2d sess., 8 April 1908, H. Rept., pp. 1–53.

8. As much as he disliked Ainsworth's policies, Jameson believed it was best to try to work with him (see Jameson to Paul E. More, 12 February 1912, War Department File, Box 134, Jameson Papers, LC).

9. "Withholding Public Records," *Nation* 94 (January 1912): 78–79.

10. Ibid., p. 79.

11. More to Jameson, 1 February 1912, War Department File, Box 134, Jameson Papers, LC.

12. Jameson to More, 2 February 1912, War Department File, Box 134, Jameson Papers, LC.

13. William E. Dodd, letter in "Gen. Ainsworth and the National Archives," p. 179.

14. Bancroft, letter in ibid., p. 180.

15. Frederic L. Paxson, letter in ibid., pp. 180–81; *Army and Navy Journal* 49 (March 1912): 815.

16. Jameson to More, 19 February 1912, War Department File, Box 134, Jameson Papers, LC.

17. Jameson to Secretary of War Henry L. Stimson, 21 February 1912, War Department File, Box 134, Jameson Papers, LC.

18. Stimson to Jameson, 26 February 1912, War Department File, Box 134, Jameson Papers, LC.

19. Jameson to McCain, 21 March 1912, War Department File, Box 134, Jameson Papers, LC.

20. Jameson to R. M. Johnston, 22 October 1913, War Department File, Box 134, Jameson Papers, LC.

21. Ibid.

22. *Annual Report of the American Historical Association, 1899* (Washington, D.C., 1900), pp. 24, 28, 32; and especially *Annual Report of the American Historical Association, 1900*, 2 vols. (Washington, D.C. 1901), 2:5–6.

23. F. C. Ainsworth to Sen. Morgan G. Bulkeley, 4 June 1910, printed in *Compilation of Revolutionary War Records*, 62d Cong., 2d sess., 15 January 1912, S. Rept. 176, pp. 3–4.

24. Secretary of War William H. Taft to Congressman C. B. Landis, 23 March 1908, printed in *Adverse Report to Printing of Complete Orders of Gen. George Washington during the Revolution*, in 60th Cong., 1st sess., April 20, 1908, H. Rept. 1568, pp. 2–4.

25. See *Compilation of Revolutionary War Records*, p. 1.

26. F. C. Ainsworth to secretary of war [Robert Shaw Oliver], 16 March 1910, printed in ibid., pp. 1–2.

27. Senate Bill 271, 2 March 1913.

28. Frederick Morrow Fling to Albert Bushnell Hart, 6 March 1913, Albert Bushnell Hart Papers, Harvard University Archives, Cambridge, Mass.

29. Johnston to Secretary of War Lindley Garrison, 6 June 1913, AGO File 2046689, filed in Records and Pensions File 420264, RG 94, NA.

30. Ibid., and Johnston's statement attached to memorandum from The Adjutant General [George Andrews] to Garrison, 10 June 1913, in ibid.

31. Johnston to Hart, 25 September 1913, Hart Papers, Harvard.

32. Johnston to Jameson, 6 June 1913, War Department File, Box 134, Jameson Papers, LC.

33. Johnston to Jameson, 13 June 1913, War Department File, Box 134, Jameson Papers, LC.

34. Memorandum, The Adjutant General to Garrison, 10 June 1913, AGO File 2046689, Records and Pensions File 420264, RG 94, NA.

35. Garrison ordered Andrews to prepare a comprehensive policy statement on the War Department's archives and to determine the extent of holdings in the different departmental agencies. See Andrews's "Memorandum relative to Historical Documents and Archives of the War Department," 10 December 1913, AGO File 2088403, RG 94, NA. Although not endorsing an open policy, Andrews did show much more flexibility than Ainsworth had.

36. Johnston to Jameson, 10 July 1913, War Department File, Box 134, Jameson Papers, LC.

37. Ibid.

38. Johnston to Jameson, 3 July 1913, War Department File, Box 134, Jameson Papers, LC; Johnston to Jameson, 7 September 1913, ibid; Johnston to Hart, 25 September 1913, Hart Papers, Harvard.

39. Johnston to Jameson, 7 September 1913, War Department File, Box 134, Jameson Papers, LC; Johnston to Jameson, 20 October 1913, ibid.

40. Johnston to Jameson, 7 September 1913, War Department File, Box 134, Jameson Papers, LC.

41. Johnston to Hart, 25 September 1913, Hart Papers, Harvard; Johnston to Jameson, 20 October 1913, War Department File, Box 134, Jameson Papers, LC.

42. Assistant Secretary of War Henry Breckinridge to Hart, 30 September 1913, Hart Papers, Harvard.

43. Garrison's hard-line stand against cooperation with, let alone supervision by, historians in army projects is apparent in his *Annual Report of the Secretary of War, 1913* (Washington, D.C., 1914).

44. H. C. C[lark] memorandum to [The Adjutant General], 8 December 1913, AGO File 2088403, RG 94, NA.

45. See Adjutant General Andrews's "Memorandum relative to Historical Documents and Archives of the War Department."

46. Lindley M. Garrison, extracts from *Annual Report of the Secretary of War, 1913*, in Hart Papers, Harvard.

47. Jameson to Hart, 8 December 1913, Hart Papers, Harvard.

48. Capt. W. L. Rogers [president of the Naval War College] to secretary of the navy, 3 December 1913, extract filed in Hart Papers, Harvard.

49. Jameson to Hart, 8 December 1913, Hart Papers, Harvard.

50. Charles H. Haskins [secretary of the AHA's executive council] to Hart, 2 December 1913, Hart Papers, Harvard; Jameson to Hart, 8 December 1913, ibid.; Jameson to Andrew McLaughlin, 8 December 1913, ibid.; Jameson to Hart, 22 December 1913, ibid.

51. Hart to Jameson, 12 December 1913, Hart Papers, Harvard; Jameson to McLaughlin, 8 December 1913, ibid.

52. McLaughlin to Hart, 11 December 1913, Hart Papers, Harvard.

53. Captain Clark visited Boston December 12–24, 1913, to interview scholars about the "War of Independence Papers Project." See Hart to Jameson, 12 December 1913, Hart Papers, Harvard; R. M. Johnston, Military Committee Record Book, 7, Box 459, AHA Papers, LC; *Army and Navy Journal* 51 (December 1913): 496.

54. Hart to Jameson, 12 December 1913, Hart Papers, Harvard, reveals that Hart and Captain Rogers, among others, finally convinced Johnston that a supervisory committee was much less likely to succeed with the War Department than a panel that was purely advisory.

55. Jameson to Waldo Leland, 8 January 1914, copy in secretary's file, Box 246, AHA Papers, LC.

56. Jameson to Hart, 6 January 1914, Hart Papers, Harvard.

57. Jameson to Breckinridge, 6 January 1914, Revolutionary War Documents File, Box 124, Jameson Papers, LC.

58. Jameson to John Bigelow, 5 January 1914, John Bigelow File, Box 60, Jameson Papers, LC.

59. Chadwick's appointment caused some temporarily serious protocol problems when retired army major Bigelow doubted that it was proper for retired navy admiral Chadwick to serve under him on the AHA committee, especially if they were to use their military titles. Jameson assured him that the admiral had served on many civilian committees and did not believe his title gave him any special status on these panels. Jameson to Bigelow, 12 Janaury 1914, John Bigelow File, Box 60, Jameson Papers, LC.

60. "Advisory Committee of the American Historical Association on the Military and Naval Records of the Revolution," Revolutionary War Documents File, Box 124, Jameson Papers, LC; Jameson to Garrison, 19 January 1914, ibid.

61. Johnston to Capt. Hollis Clark, 23 October 1914, Revolutionary War Records File, Box 98-99, John Bigelow Papers, LC; Clark to Bigelow, 23 October 1914, ibid.; Jameson to Bigelow, 7 May 1914, John Bigelow File, Box 60, Jameson Papers, LC; Bigelow to Jameson, 23 May 1914, ibid.

62. Hollis C. Clark to the secretary of war (through The Adjutant General), 7 June 1915, Thomas File 3819, RG 165, NA.

63. Ibid. Maryland congressman J. Harry Covington complained that although his state's adjutant general took special pains to prepare the appropriate papers for copying, Clark's workers never arrived to process them (see Covington to The Adjutant General, 21 April 1914, AGO File 2151057, Records and Pensions File 420264, RG 94, NA.

64. Higham, *History*, pp. 35–36; Clarence E. Carter, "The United States and Documentary Historical Publications," *Mississippi Valley Historical Review* 25 (1938): 3–24.

65. Dallas D. Irvine, "The Genesis of the *Official Records*," *Mississippi Valley Historical Review* 24 (1937–38): 221–29.

66. Ibid., pp. 226–28.

67. Capt. Matthew Forney Steele, *American Campaigns*, 2 vols. (Washington, D.C., 1909), 1:iii.

68. Quoted in Maury Klein, Introduction to E. Porter Alexander, *Military Memoirs of a Confederate* (New York, 1907; reprint ed., Dayton, Ohio, 1977), p. 10.

69. William R. Livermore, *The Story of the Civil War*, 3 vols. (New York, 1913), 3:v (under Ropes, John Codman, in "Bibliography").

70. Oliver L. Spaulding, Review of *First Bull Run: Its Strategy and Tactics*, by R. M. Johnston, in *Infantry Journal* 10 (1914): 722.

71. Editorial comment, probably by Johnston, in *Military Historian and Economist* 1 (1916): 200.

72. Johnston, statement attached to memorandum from Andrews to Garrison, 10 June 1913, AGO File 2046689, RG 94, NA.

73. Douglas Southall Freeman, *Lee's Dispatches: Unpublished Letters of General Robert E. Lee, C.S.A., to Jefferson Davis and the War Department of the Confederate States of America, 1862–1865* (New York, 1915); and unsigned review of *Lee's Dispatches* in *Military Historian and Economist* 2 (1916): 107–8.

74. Irvine, "Genesis of the *Official Records*," pp. 228–29.

75. R. M. Johnston, "What Can Be Done for Our Military History?" *Infantry Journal* 9 (1912): 236.

76. R. M. Johnston, "Records of the War of the Revolution," *Military Historian and Economist* 1 (1916): 83; editorial comment in ibid., p. 200; and "Our War Documents," *Military Historian and Economist* 3 (1918): 2–3.

77. Bancroft, letter in "Gen. Ainsworth and the National Archives," p. 180.

NOTES TO PAGES 162-168

78. Jameson to Hart, 8 December 1913, Hart Papers, Harvard.

79. See memorandum, Andrews to Garrison, 10 June 1913, AGO File 2046689, RG 94, NA.

80. Although Andrews took many positions unpopular with historians, he also agreed that many documents then closed to their use could be opened up to them (see Andrews, "Memorandum relative to Historical Documents and Archives of the War Department").

81. The chief of the Corps of Engineers and the quartermaster general, in particular, supported the idea of central archives. See addition G [quartermaster general], 14 November 1913, and addition H [chief of the Corps of Engineers], 20 November 1913, both contained in "Historical Documents in the War Department," AGO File 2088403, RG 94, NA.

82. Higham, *History*, p. 35; and memorandum, E. L. McLachlin to chief of staff [John J. Pershing], 8 February 1922, in AWC File 216-17, in MISC 314.71, USACMH.

83. Annie H. Abel, *The American Indian as Participant in the Civil War* (Cleveland, 1919), p. 361.

84. Frederic L. Paxson to Gen. William D. Connor, 1 April 1928, in "Correspondence re Initiation, Organization, and Report of the Advisory Board on Historical Work at the Army War College," AWC File 216-149/6, in MISC 314.71, USACMH.

85. Charles Ramsdell to Connor, 25 March 1928, in ibid.

86. "Study on the Project of Publication of 'The War of the Rebellion,'" RG 165, NA.

CHAPTER TEN. EXERCISES IN FRUSTRATION:
TWO AHA COMMITTEES FOR MILITARY AND NAVAL HISTORY

1. Alexander Baltzly, "Robert Matteson Johnston and the Study of Military History," *Military Affairs* 21 (1957): 26-30; Russell F. Weigley, *Towards an American Army: Military Thought from Washington to Marshall* (New York, 1962), chapter 11.

2. R. M. Johnston, "What Can Be Done for Our Military History?" *Infantry Journal* 9 (1912): 236-38.

3. Ibid., pp. 236-37; "Military History," *Infantry Journal* 9 (1913): 543-44.

4. Albert Bushnell Hart to Johnston, 21 November 1912, Albert Bushnell Hart Papers, Harvard University Archives, Cambridge, Mass.

5. Charles H. Haskins [secretary of the AHA executive council] to Hart, 7 December 1912, Hart Papers, Harvard; Hart to Haskins, 9 December 1912, ibid.

6. "Military History," p. 544; "Our Military History," *Infantry Journal* 9 (1912): 379-82.

7. *Army and Navy Journal* 50 (December 1912): 407.

8. "Our Military History," pp. 380-81. An examination of Villard's views on militarism can be found in Michael Wrezin, *Oswald Garrison Villard: Pacifist at War* (Bloomington, Ind., 1965), chapter 6.

9. "The Study of Military History," *Nation* 93 (December 1912): 556-57.

10. "Who Shall Write Our Military History?" *Infantry Journal* 9 (1913): 545.

11. Haskins to Hart, 7 December 1912, Hart Papers, Harvard; Haskins to Gen. W. W. Wotherspoon, 3 December 1912, AGO File 1981303, RG 94, NA; memorandum, Chief of Staff Leonard Wood to The Adjutant General [Brig. Gen. George Andrews], 2[?] December 1912, enclosed in ibid.

12. The full proceedings are recorded in "Who Shall Write Our Military History?" pp. 545-78.

13. [R. M. Johnston,] Military Committee Record Book, p. 1, Committee Miscellany

File (Military History Committee File), Box 459, AHA, LC [hereafter Johnston Record Book, LC]; *Army and Navy Journal* 50 (January 1913): 537–38.

14. "Who Shall Write Our Military History?" pp. 555–56.

15. Ibid., pp. 545–46.

16. Johnston Record Book, p. 1, LC.

17. Ibid.

18. Ibid.; Haskins to Hart, 9 January 1913, Hart Papers, Harvard.

19. Johnston Record Book, pp. 2–3, LC.

20. T. L. Livermore to Johnston, 27 September 1913, in Johnston Record Book, pp. 3–4, LC.

21. Johnston Record Book, p. 4, LC.

22. Johnston to Franklin D. Roosevelt, Assistant Secretary of the Navy Papers, Box 105, Franklin Delano Roosevelt Presidential Library, Hyde Park, N.Y.

23. Johnston Record Book, pp. 4–5, LC.

24. "American Historical Association, Christmas Meeting 1913, Report of the Committee on Military History," Executive Council, Secretary's File, Box 246, AHA Papers, LC.

25. Ibid.; also chapter 11.

26. "American Historical Association, Christmas Meeting 1913, Report of the Committee on Military History," Box 246, AHA Papers, LC.

27. Hart to Johnston, 14 October 1913, Executive Council, Secretary's File, Box 260, AHA Papers, LC.

28. See chapter 9.

29. Haskins to Assistant Secretary of War Henry Breckinridge, 10 November 1913, AGO File 2109322, RG 94, NA; Haskins to Franklin D. Roosevelt, 2 December 1913, Assistant Secretary of the Navy Papers, Box 103, Roosevelt Library; Roosevelt to Haskins, 19 December 1913, Box 66, ibid.

30. Memorandum, chief of staff [Leonard Wood] to The Adjutant General [Andrews], 17 December 1913, ibid.; memorandum, Office of the Chief of Staff to the judge advocate general [Enoch Crowder], 18 December 1913, AGO File 2109322/A, RG 94, NA; Crowder to [Wood], 20 December 1913, ibid.

31. Johnston to Hart, 24 November 1913, Hart Papers, Harvard; Johnston to Clarence Bowen [treasurer of the AHA], 30 November 1913, Secretary's File, Correspondence 1912–13, Box 21, AHA Papers, LC.

32. Johnston Record Book, p. 10, LC.

33. Evarts B. Greene [secretary of the AHA executive council] to Johnston, 17 January 1914, Executive Council, Secretary's File, Box 247, AHA Papers, LC; Greene to Haskins, 17 January 1914, ibid.

34. Greene to Breckinridge, 23 January 1914, Executive Council, Secretary's File, Box 247, AHA Papers, LC. Identical letters were written on the same date to Roosevelt, Admiral Knight, General Liggett, and Major McAndrew.

35. Breckinridge to Greene, 26 January 1914, Roosevelt to Greene, 27 January 1914, Knight to Greene, 27 January 1914, McAndrew to Greene, 27 January 1914, Paullin to Greene, 1 February 1914, and Liggett to Greene, 5 February 1914, all in Executive Council, Secretary's File, Box 247, AHA Papers, LC.

36. Johnston Record Book, p. 9A, LC.

37. Johnston to Greene, 2 November 1914, Executive Council, Secretary's File, Box 247, AHA Papers, LC.

38. Johnston to Roosevelt, [?] January 1914, Assistant Secretary of the Navy Papers, Box 105, Roosevelt Library; Roosevelt to Johnston, 27 January 1914, ibid.

39. Haskins to Greene, 5 February 1914, Executive Council, Secretary's File, Box 247, AHA Papers, LC.

40. Johnston Record Book, p. 10, LC.

41. Johnston to Greene, 2 November 1914, Executive Council, Secretary's File, Box 247, AHA Papers, LC.

42. Johnston to Breckinridge, 5 January 1914, WCD File 7425-8, RG 165, NA.

43. Johnston Record Book, p. 11, LC.

44. Memorandum, Gen. M. M. Macomb to chief of staff [Wood], n.d., enclosed with WCD File 7425-8, RG 165, NA; memorandum, Macomb to Wood, 28 April 1915, WCD File 7425-9, ibid.; Breckinridge to Johnston, 29 April 1915, AGO File 2282637, RG 94, NA.

45. Dean K. G. T. Webster to Secretary of War Lindley M. Garrison, 5 January 1915, AGO File 2284151, RG 94, NA; Garrison to Webster, 4 May 1914, enclosed in ibid.

46. The Adjutant General [Brig. Gen. Henry P. McCain] to Capt. Arthur L. Conger, 5 May 1915, AGO File 2284151, RG 94, NA; [McCain] to Conger, 15 May 1915, WCD File 7425-11, RG 165, NA.

47. Circular, "Military History," Harvard University Summer School (1 July–2 August 1915), enclosed with Conger to Allen R. Boyd, 28 June 1915, Miscellany File, Box 468, AHA Papers, LC; "Military History Course at Harvard," *Army and Navy Journal* 52 (May 1915): 1207.

48. Johnston to Waldo Leland, 10 December 1915, Secretary's File, Correspondence 1915, Box 28, AHA Papers, LC.

49. Greene to Conger, 23 November 1915, Executive Council, Secretary's File, Council Committees File 1915, Box 249, AHA Papers, LC.

50. *Annual Report of the American Historical Association, 1920* (Washington, D.C., 1921), p. 22.

51. AHA Program, Box 468, AHA Papers, LC; "Discuss War Tactics," *Morning Star,* (Washington, D.C.), 30 April 1921; "Officers Tell of Battles," *Washington Post,* 1 May 1921.

52. "American Historical Association, Committee on Military History, Meeting on April 30, 1921," Box 468, AHA Papers, LC.

53. *Annual Report of the American Historical Association, 1924* (Washington, D.C., 1925), p. 100.

54. Quoted in Timothy K. Nenninger, *The Leavenworth Schools and the Old Army: Education, Professionalism, and the Officer Corps of the United States Army, 1881–1918* (Westport, Conn., 1978), p. 45.

55. Johnston to Hart, 24 November 1913, Hart Papers, Harvard.

56. Hart to William Ropes Trask, 12 November 1913, Hart Papers, Harvard; Trask to Hart, 14 November 1913, ibid.; Trask to Hart, 19 November 1913, ibid.; Hart to Johnston, 20 November 1913, ibid.; Johnston to Hart, 24 November 1913, ibid.

57. Greene to Hart, 2 January 1914, Hart Papers, Harvard.

58. Conger to Hart, 2 March 1914, Hart Papers, Harvard; Conger to Boyd, 2 March 1914, Box 468, AHA Papers, LC; Conger to Boyd, 17 March 1914, ibid.

59. The competition was advertised in historical journals as well as professional military publications (see *Infantry Journal* 11 (1914): 86–87).

60. "Conditions of Award," copy in Hart Papers, Harvard.

61. Conger to Greene, 17 March 1916, Executive Council, Secretary's File, Council Committees File 1915, Box 249, AHA Papers, LC. The first four papers were Capt. H. L. Landers, "Lee's First Invasion of Maryland"; Maj. Irvin Hunt, "The Citizen Soldier"; Maj. Charles Gerhardt, "The Battle of Groveton and Second Bull Run"; and Audrey B. Colonna, "The Battle between the Merrimac and the Monitor."

62. Fling to Conger, 20 December 1915, copy in Hart Papers, Harvard.

63. Hart to [Conger?], 1 December 1915, Hart Papers, Harvard; Conger to Hart, 2 January 1916, ibid.

64. Conger to Hart, 21 December 1915, Hart Papers, Harvard; Conger to Hart, 2 January 1916, ibid.

65. Hart to Conger, 10 February 1916, Hart Papers, Harvard; Conger to Hart, 11 March 1916, ibid.; Conger to Boyd, 17 March 1916, Miscellany File, Box 468, AHA Papers, LC; Capt. H. L. Landers to Conger, 7 February 1916, ibid.

66. Conger to Hart, 14 May 1916, Hart Papers, Harvard; Conger to Boyd, 14 May 1916, Box 468, AHA Papers, LC.

67. Johnston to Boyd, 26 July 1916, Box 468, AHA Papers, LC.

68. Milledge L. Bonham to members of the Committee on Military History Prize, American Historical Association, 5 November 1918, Hart Papers, Harvard.

69. Conger to Hart, 24 May 1916, Hart Papers, Harvard; Bonham to Hart, 27 June 1918, ibid.; "Final Report of the Committee on Military History Prize Contest, American Historical Association," 21 December 1921, Box 468, AHA Papers, LC.

70. John Higham, *History* (Englewood Cliffs, N.J., 1965), pp. 48–49.

71. Ibid., pp. 47–50; Louis Morton, "The Historian and the Study of War," *Mississippi Valley Historical Review* 48 (1962): 605.

72. Memorandum, Bonham to members of the committee to award the Military History Writing Prize, 8 January 1919, Box 459, AHA Papers, LC; Bonham to Hart, 10 February 1919, Hart Papers, Harvard.

73. "Final Report of the Committee on Military History Prize Contest," Box 468, AHA Papers, LC.

74. Thomas Robson Hay to Boyd, 15 August 1921, Box 468, AHA Papers, LC; Hay to Gen. Eben Swift, 15 August 1921, ibid.

75. "Final Report of the Committee on Military History Prize Contest," Box 468, AHA Papers, LC.

76. Hart to J. Franklin Jameson, 12 December 1913, Hart Papers, Harvard.

77. Baltzly, "Robert Matteson Johnston and the Study of Military History," p. 30.

78. Memorandum, Maj. Robert M. Johnston to secretary of the General Staff, 5 December 1918, Thomas File 1718, RG 165, NA.

79. "Naval History Society," *Army and Navy Journal* 49 (July 1912): 1398; "Naval History Society," *Army and Navy Journal* 49 (August 1912): 1648.

80. "Naval History Society," *Army and Navy Journal* 50 (June 1913): 604.

81. Arthur L. Conger, "Robert Matteson Johnston, 1867–1920," *Journal of the American Military History Foundation* 1 (Summer 1937): 45–46.

CHAPTER ELEVEN. A PYRRHIC VICTORY:
THE U.S. ARMY'S HISTORICAL SECTION, 1914–1920

1. See "Who Shall Write Our Military History" *Infantry Journal* 9 (1913): 545–78. Many of these speakers' remarks are also contained in *Annual Report of the American Historical Association, 1912* (Washington, D.C., 1913), pp. 158–97.

2. Emory Upton, *The Armies of Asia and Europe: Embracing Official Reports on the Armies of Japan, China, India, Persia, Italy, Russia, Austria, Germany, France, and England* (Washington, D.C., 1878; reprint ed., Westport, Conn., 1972), pp. 328–29, 331.

3. Spenser Wilkinson, *The Brain of an Army: A Popular Account of the German General Staff*, 2d ed. (London, 1895), pp. 173–91.

4. Bruce W. Bidwell, *History of the Military Intelligence Division, Department of the Army General Staff, 1775–1941* (Frederick, Md., 1986), pp. 45–46, 51.

5. William C. Endicott to Maj. C. Post, 2 March 1889, WCD File 639-2, RG 165, NA.

6. Bidwell, *History of the Military Information Division*, p. 56.

7. Memorandum, chief of the Military Information Division to secretary of the General Staff, 27 August 1903, WCD File 639-20, RG 165, NA; memorandum, Office of the Chief of Staff, 3 February 1904, WCD File 639-22, ibid.

8. Lt. Col. George P. Ahern, "A Chronicle of the Army War College, 1899–1919," typescript, USAMHI, p. 91; Bidwell, *History of the Military Information Division*, pp. 82–83.

9. Memorandum, Office of Chief of Staff to Second Division, 26 September 1910, WCD File 639-5, RG 165, NA.

10. R. M. Johnston, "What Can Be Done for Our Military History?" *Infantry Journal* 9 (1912): 236–38.

11. "Doctrine, Conception, and History of War," *Infantry Journal* 9 (1912): 256–58.

12. Quoted in "Our Military History," *Infantry Journal* 9 (1912): 380–81.

13. Untitled editorial, *Army and Navy Journal* 50 (December 1912): 407.

14. "Who Shall Write Our Military History?" pp. 548–54.

15. Ibid., pp. 557–59.

16. Ibid., pp. 560–62.

17. R. M. Johnston to Secretary of War Lindley Garrison, 1 January 1914, Garrison to Johnston, 5 January 1914, and Chief of Staff Leonard Wood to Gen. Hunter Liggett, 5 January 1914, all in WCD File 8090-7, in "Historical Section, Army War College, the General Staff," HRC 314.71, HS, WPD (1914–1919), USACMH (hereafter Historical Section folder, USACMH).

18. R. M. Johnston, "The Functions of Military History," AWC Curricular File 1913–14, Lectures, USAMHI.

19. Wood to Col. John Biddle, 3 January 1914, WCD File 8090-3, Historical Section folder, USACMH.

20. Endorsement, Liggett to Biddle, 5 January 1914, added to Wood to Liggett, 3 January 1914, WCD File 8090-2, Historical Section folder, USACMH.

21. Biddle and Liggett to Wood, 6 January 1914, WCD File 8090-4, Historical Section folder, USACMH.

22. Johnston to Wood, 31 January 1914, WCD File 8090-10, Historical Section folder, USACMH.

23. Memorandum, Wood to Biddle (through Liggett), 9 January 1914, WCD File 8090-5, Historical Section folder, USACMH; memorandum, Biddle to [Maj. D. W. Ketcham, Maj. W. D. Connor, and Capt. H. C. Smither], 10 January 1914, WCD File 8090-6, ibid.

24. Maj. C. Crawford, secretary of the War College Division, to American military attaché [Lt. Col. George Squier], London, 17 January 1914, WCD File 8090-8, Historical Section folder, USACMH. A similar letter was sent to American attachés in Germany, France, Austro-Hungary, and Japan. Their replies are contained in WCD File 8090-15 [Britain]; 8090-16 [France]; 8090-17 and 8090-21 [Germany]; 8090-23 [Austro-Hungary]. A summary of the preceding reports is contained in "Notes on Historical Sections of General Staffs of European Armies, 1914," 1 September 1914, WCD File 8090-28, ibid.

25. Johnston to Wood, 31 January 1914, WCD File 8090-10, Historical Section folder, USACMH.

26. Johnston to Gen. M. M. Macomb, 9 October 1914, WCD File 8090-25, Historical Section folder, USACMH; Macomb to Johnston, 5 November 1914, WCD File 8090-26, ibid.; Johnston to Macomb, 7 November 1914, WCD File 8090-27, ibid.

27. Johnston to Wood, 31 January 1914, WCD File 8090-10, Historical Section folder, USACMH. For Wood's interest in a professional General Staff journal, see memorandum, Wood to chief of the War College Division [Biddle], 6 October 1913, WCD File 8090-1, ibid.; Wood to Liggett, 3 January 1914, WCD File 8090-2, ibid.; and Macomb to [Wood], 25 September 1914, WCD File 8090-24, ibid.

28. Statement of policy, *Military Historian and Economist* 1 (1916): 80.

29. Untitled editorial, *Military Historian and Economist* 3 (1918): 131. The follies of the

French historical section are discussed in detail in Lt. Col. René Tourrès, "Military History" (Paris, 1922). A typescript of this essay, translated by Sgt. Allen J. Doherty, is located in MISC 314.71 (Military History) File, USACMH.

30. Untitled editorial, *Military Historian and Economist* 3 (1918): 131.

31. James E. Hewes, Jr., *From Root to McNamara: Army Organization and Administration, 1900–1963* (Washington, D.C., 1975), pp. 24–25.

32. Memorandum, War College Division to secretary of war [Newton D. Baker], 21 August 1917, WCD File 10163-2A, RG 165, NA.

33. Ibid.

34. Memorandum, chief of the Military Intelligence Section, to chief of the War College Division, 25 August 1917, WCD File 10163-3, RG 165, NA.

35. Memorandum, Gen. James G. Harbord to Gen. John J. Pershing, 30 September 1917 [Historical Branch, War Plans Division File 177], Thomas File 333, RG 165, NA; memorandum, Frank McCoy to Harbord, 27 September 1917, ibid.

36. Memorandum, Gen. Tasker H. Bliss to secretary of war [Baker], 2 January 1918, enclosed with WCD File 8090-29, Historical Section folder, USACMH.

37. Lt. Col. Paul Azan, "The Historical Section in a General Staff," *Military Historian and Economist* 3 (1918): 87–91.

38. Memorandum, Col. D. W. Ketcham to [Bliss], 18 January 1918, WCD File 8090-29, Historical Section folder, USACMH.

39. Ibid.

40. Ibid.

41. Ibid.

42. Supplementary memorandum, Ketcham to [Bliss], 18 January 1918, WCD File 8090-30, Historical Section folder, USACMH.

43. Hewes, *From Root to McNamara*, p. 37.

44. Memorandum, Gen. William S. Graves to The Adjutant General, 21 March 1918, WCD File 8090-34 (enclosure 1), Historical Section folder, USACMH.

45. Memorandum, Graves to The Adjutant General, 28 February 1918, enclosure to WCD File 8090-30, Historical Section folder, USACMH; memorandum, Ketcham to [Bliss], 11 March 1918, WCD File 8090-31, ibid.; memorandum, Graves to The Adjutant General, 11 March 1918, enclosure to WCD File 8090-31, ibid.; memorandum, Gen. Lytle Brown to [Bliss], 13 May 1918, WCD File 8090-45, ibid.

46. Memorandum, Ketcham to [Bliss], 21 March 1918, WCD File 8090-34, Historical Section folder, USACMH.

47. Self-written "Obituary," pp. 67–72, Folder 1, Box 1, Matthew Forney Steele Papers, USAMHI. Steele remained professor of military science and tactics at the North Dakota State Agricultural College at Fargo.

48. Memorandum, Ketcham to [Bliss], 21 March 1918, WCD File 8090-34, Historical Section folder, USACMH; memorandum, Brown to [Bliss], 6 May 1918, WCD File 8090-41, ibid.

49. Memorandum, Brown to [Chief of Staff Peyton March], 12 July 1918, WCD File 8090-54, Historical Section folder USACMH; War Plans Division memorandum [by Paxson] for [March], 2 November 1918, WCD File 10163-16, RG 165, NA.

50. Lt. Col. C. W. Weeks to F. M. Fling, 7 March 1918, College of Arts and Sciences Record Group, History Department: Notes and Transcripts of Fred M. Fling Subgroup, University of Nebraska Archives, Lincoln; War Plans Division memorandum [by Fling] for [March], 12 June 1918, WCD File 10163-12, RG 165, NA; and secretary of state [Robert Lansing] to [Baker], 28 June 1918, WCD File 10163-14, ibid.

51. Memorandum, Brown to [March], [?] September 1918, WCD File 8090-56, Historical Section folder, USACMH; Dexter Perkins, *Yield of the Years* (Boston, 1969), pp. 57–61.

52. Memorandum, Brown to [March], 23 July 1918, WCD File 8090-55, Historical Section folder, USACMH.

53. Handwritten memorandum, Maj. R. M. D. Taylor to [Lytle Brown], 27 July 1918, enclosed with WCD File 8090-55, Historical Section folder, USACMH.

54. Memorandum, historical branch to War Plans Division [27 July 1918], enclosed with WCD file 8090-55, Historical Section folder, USACMH.

55. Memorandum, Brown to [March], 23 July 1918, WCD File 8090-55, Historical Section folder, USACMH.

56. Disapproval, dated 25 July 1918, noted on handwritten endorsement in ibid.

57. "Instructions on Editing Manuscripts, Historical Section, Army War College, October 23, 1939," AWC File 216-149/12, in MISC 314.71, p. 1, USACMH.

58. Ibid. This is the only source to mention the collection of motion pictures as part of the Historical Section's duties.

59. Maj. R. M. Johnston to Col. Charles Weeks, 21 November 1918, Thomas File 1718, RG 165, NA.

60. Ibid.; paragraph 1E, AEF Cable P-1914-S, Pershing to The Adjutant General, 20 November 1918, enclosure 1 in AWC File 216-374, in MISC 314.71, USACMH; historical branch [War Plans Division 70-16] to office of the secretary of the General Staff, 21 November 1918, enclosure 2 in AWC File 216–374, in ibid.

61. Paragraph 10, extract of AEF Cable 2997-R, 20 March 1919, enclosure 3 in AWC File 216-374, in MISC 314.71, USACMH.

62. Johnston to Weeks, 21 November 1918, Thomas File 1718, RG 165, NA.

63. Memorandum, J. W. D. Melvin to J. W. McAndrew, 26 November 1919, Thomas File 333, RG 165, NA.

64. Hewes, *From Root to McNamara*, pp. 50–53.

65. Memorandum, Lt. Col. Oliver L. Spaulding to [War Plans Division], 24 July 1919, WCD File 8090-102, Historical Section folder, USACMH.

66. "Instructions on Editing Manuscripts, Historical Section, Army War College, October 23, 1939," p. 1, USACMH.

67. Memorandum, Maj. R. V. D. Magoffin to Weeks, 10 May 1919, enclosure to WCD File 8090-99, Historical Section folder, USACMH.

68. Ibid.

69. Memorandum, Maj. R. B. Patterson to Weeks, 10 May 1919, enclosure to WCD File 8090-99, Historical Section folder, USACMH.

70. Magoffin to Weeks, 10 May 1919, in WCD File 8090-99, Historical Section folder, USACMH.

71. Col. A. L. Conger, Lt. Col. Oliver L. Spaulding, Maj. Fred Morrow Fling, and Maj. R. M. Johnston, "Proceedings of a Special Committee Convened at Washington pursuant to the Following [undated] Memorandum [Maj. Gen. W. G. Haan to 'the Executive']," 29 July 1919, WCD File 8090-102, Historical Section folder, USACMH.

72. Memorandum, Maj. Gen. Henry Jervey to War Plans Division, 20 May 1919, enclosure to WCD File 8090-99, Historical Section folder, USACMH.

73. In 1928, when the World War I official history project finally began in earnest, Gen. W. D. Connor desired the special commissioning of a number of academic historians, including Carlton C. H. Hayes, Wayne G. Stevens, and Thomas H. Thomas. See memorandum, Connor to Assistant Secretary of War Charles B. Robbins, attached to Wayne G. Stevens to Connor, 18 April 1928, AWC File 216-149/6, in MISC 314.71, USACMH.

74. I. B. Holley, Jr., *General John M. Palmer, Citizen Soldiers, and the Army of a Democracy* (Westport, Conn., 1982), pp. 711–13, discusses Palmer's weakness as a military historian.

75. Johnston to Weeks, 21 November 1918, Thomas File 1718, RG 165, NA.

76. Oliver L. Spaulding, "War Department," in Newton D. Mereness, ed., "Historical Activities during the War," *Annual Report of the American Historical Association, 1919* (Washington, D.C., 1920), p. 143. For the final disposition of these widely scattered records, see Garry D. Ryan, "Disposition of AEF Records of World War I," *Military Affairs* 30 (1966): 212–19.

77. Memorandum, Col. William Lassiter to [Maj. Gen. Enoch Crowder] the judge advocate general, 6 February 1920, printed in *Annual Report of the American Historical Association, 1919*, p. 150; results of the survey of the bureaus' holdings on pp. 150–55.

78. U.S. Army, Surgeon General's Office, *The Medical Department of the United States Army in the World War*, 15 vols. in 17 prts. (Washington, D.C., 1921–1929).

79. Memorandum, Baker to chief of staff [March], 4 August 1919, copy in "Instructions on Methods of Carrying Out the War Department Directive of August 14, 1929, and Correspondence re: Mission, Function, and Duties of the Historical Section, Army War College," AWC File 216-149/3, in MISC 314.71, USACMH.

80. "Instructions on Editing Manuscripts, Historical Section, Army War College, October 23, 1939," p. 2, USACMH.

81. Memorandum, Baker to March, 4 August 1919, in AWC File 216-149/3, in MISC 314.71, USACMH.

82. Spaulding to Maj. Conrad Lanza, 21 December 1921, Thomas File 2242, RG 165, NA; Lanza to Spaulding, 1 January 1922, ibid.; Lanza to The Adjutant General, 5 January 1922, Thomas File 333, RG 165, NA; memorandum, E. F. McLachlin, Jr., to chief of staff, 8 February 1922, AWC File 216-17, in MISC 314.71, USACMH; Assistant Secretary of War John W. Weeks to J. Franklin Jameson, [?] February 1922, enclosed with ibid.

83. Memorandum, McLachlin to [Pershing], 1 March 1923, AWC File 216-87, in MISC 314.71, USACMH. Section 127A of the National Defense Act of 1920 permitted the eleven officers to study historical methods at civilian universities.

84. Memorandum, McLachlin to [Pershing], 8 February 1922, AWC File 216-17, in MISC 314.71, USACMH; Lanza to The Adjutant General, 5 January 1922, Thomas File 333, RG 165, NA; memorandum, Spaulding to [Pershing], 20 March 1923, Thomas File 2383, RG 165, NA.

85. Spaulding to Prof. William E. Lingelbach, 20 March 1923, Thomas File 2383, RG 165, NA. Thomas File 2184, RG 165, NA, also contains book reviews and discussions on writing a War Department–sponsored manual on American military history.

86. George T. Blakely, *Historians on the Homefront: American Propagandists for the Great War* (Lexington, Ky., 1970), offers the best overview of academic historians' contributions to the war effort and the troubles they faced afterward.

87. See ibid., chapter 7; H. L. Mencken, "Star Spangled Men," *New Republic* 24 (September 1927): 119; C. Hartley Grattan, "The Historians Cut Loose," *American Mercury* 11 (August 1927): 414–30.

88. W. D. Connor to Fling, Paxson, Charles Ramsdell, and A. E. R. Boak, 7 March 1928, in "Correspondence re Initiation, Organization, and Report of the Advisory Board on Historical Work at the Army War College," AWC File 216-149/6, in MISC 314.71, USACMH.

89. Jameson to Capt. Leon Dessez, 16 April 1928, in ibid.

90. Paxson to Connor, 1 April 1928, in ibid.

91. See "An Adventure in Contemporary History," in Kent Roberts Greenfield, *The Historian and the Army* (New Brunswick, N.J., 1954), pp. 3–14.

CHAPTER 12. EPILOGUE: "THANK GOD FOR LEAVENWORTH"

1. R. M. Johnston, *First Reflections on the Campaign of 1918* (New York, 1920), p. 10.

2. Quoted in Lt. Col. William Geffen, "The Leavenworth Clique in World War I: A Military View," in *Command and Commanders in Modern Warfare: Proceedings of the Second Military History Symposium, U.S. Air Force Academy,* edited by William Geffen (Washington, D.C., 1969), p. 54.

3. Memorandum, Asst. Cmdt. George S. Simonds to commandant [Gen. E. F. McLachlin], 31 October 1923, AWC File 68-58, USAMHI.

4. Memorandum, Col. Oliver L. Spaulding to commandant [McLachlin], 22 October 1923, AWC File 68-58, USAMHI.

5. Johnston, *First Reflections,* p. 12.

6. Simonds to commandant, 31 October 1923, AWC File 68-58, USAMHI.

7. The "inner circle" concept was first introduced by Frederick Palmer in *Our Greatest Battle (the Meuse-Argonne)* (New York, 1919), p. 453.

8. Geffen, "Leavenworth Clique in World War I," p. 51.

9. Maj. James A. Moss, *Officers' Manual,* 6th ed. (Menasha, Wis., 1917), chapter 27.

10. Omar N. Bradley, with Clay Blair, *A General's Life: An Autobiography by General of the Army Omar N. Bradley* (New York, 1983), p. 38; Leslie Anders, *Gentle Knight: The Life and Times of Major General Edwin Forrest Harding* (Kent, Ohio, 1985), p. 37. Harding later became chief of the historical branch immediately after World War II.

11. *Annual Report of the Commandant of the U.S. Army School of the Line and Staff School, 1920–1921* (Washington, D.C., 1921), p. 23.

12. Elvid Hunt and Walter E. Lorence, *History of Fort Leavenworth, 1827–1937,* 2d ed. (Fort Leavenworth, Kans., 1937), pp. 157, 166–67.

13. George S. Pappas, *Prudens Futuri: The U.S. Army War College, 1901–1967* (Carlisle Barracks, Pa., 1967), p. 107.

14. Quoted in Edward M. Coffman, "The American Military Generation Gap in World War I: The Leavenworth Clique in the AEF," in Geffen, ed., *Command and Commanders in Modern Warfare,* p. 39.

15. Quoted in Geffen, "Leavenworth Clique in World War I," p. 54.

16. Ibid., p. 61.

17. See, for instance, the comments of Lt. Col. John McAuley Palmer, Pershing's assistant chief of staff for operations, on the AEF's ad hoc methods to solve problems quickly and practically (I. B. Holley, Jr., *General John M. Palmer, Citizen Soldiers, and the Army of a Democracy* [Westport, Conn., 1982], chapters 24 and 25).

18. Leonard Wood to president of the Army War College, 9 December 1913, WCD File 8213-1, RG 165, NA.

19. "Report of a Committee Appointed by Endorsement, HQ, USMA, Dec. 18, 1913, to Make Suggestions on the Education System of the Army," WCD File 8213-9 (enclosure), RG 165, NA.

20. Gen. John Morrison to secretary of the Army War College, 29 December 1913, WCD File 8213-4, RG 165, NA.

21. Capt. Arthur L. Conger to Maj. James McAndrew, 16 January 1914, WCD File 8213-26, RG 165, NA.

22. The committee's comments were included in acting commandant of the Army Service Schools to secretary of the Army War College, 19 January 1914, WCD File 8213-16, RG 165, NA.

23. Brig. Gen. James Parker to secretary of the Army War College, 3 January 1914, WCD File 8213-6, RG 165, NA.

24. Conger to McAndrew, WCD File 8213-26, RG 165, NA.

25. Maj. C. P. Summerall to [secretary of the Army War College], 2 February 1914, WCD File 8213-28, RG 165, NA.

26. Capt. L. T. Richardson to adjutant, Sixth Brigade, 2 February 1914, WCD File 8213-38 (enclosure), RG 165, NA.

27. Brig. Gen. Eli Hoyle to president of the Army War College, 12 February 1914, WCD File 8213-43, RG 165, NA.

28. Conger to McAndrew, WCD File 8213-26, RG 165, NA.

29. Morrison to secretary of the Army War College, WCD File 8213-4, RG 165, NA.

30. Summerall to [secretary of the Army War College], WCD File 8213-28, RG 165, NA.

31. Richardson to adjutant, WCD File 8213-38 (enclosure), RG 165, NA.

32. Capt. H. H. Tebbetts to [secretary of the Army War College], 24 February 1914, WCD File 8213-42, RG 165, NA.

33. Capt. Paul B. Malone to The Adjutant General, 15 December 1913, WCD File 8213-21, RG 165, NA.

34. "Report of a Committee Appointed by Endorsement," WCD File 8213-9 (enclosure), RG 165, NA.

35. Spaulding's comments are included in Conger to McAndrew, WCD File 8213-26, RG 165, NA.

36. Tebbetts to [secretary of the Army War College], WCD File 8213-42, RG 165, NA.

37. Ibid.

38. Capt. George Van Horne Moseley to secretary of the Army War College, 13 January 1914, WCD File 8213-13, RG 165, NA.

39. Conger to McAndrew, WCD File 8213-26, RG 165, NA.

40. Capt. John McAuley Palmer to [secretary of the Army War College], 19 February 1914, WCD File 8213-49, RG 165, NA.

41. Johnston, *First Reflections*, p. 37.

42. Maj. Gen. William G. Haan, opening address at the "Conference of Education and Recreation Officers Called by the Secretary of War at Camp Taylor, Ky., Dec. 9–11, 1919," copy in WCD File 8213, RG 165, NA.

43. Richard A. Gabriel, *Military Incompetence: Why the American Military Doesn't Win* (New York, 1985), p. 189.

44. Cincinnatus, *Self-Destruction: The Disintegration and Decay of the United States Army during the Vietnam Era* (New York, 1981), p. 175.

45. Gabriel, *Military Incompetence*, p. 187.

46. Cincinnatus, *Self-Destruction*, p. 175.

47. Quoted in ibid., p. 168.

48. Quoted in Gabriel, *Military Incompetence*, p. 187.

49. *Department of the Army Ad Hoc Committee Report on the Army Need for the Study of Military History*, Vol. 1: *Report and Recommendations* (West Point, N.Y., 1971), pp. 51–60.

50. See *Army Historian* 12 (October 1988) for a number of important articles on the utility of the staff ride in officer education in the modern U.S. Army.

51. Col. Huba Wass de Czege, "How to Change an Army," *Military Review* 64 (November 1984): 38, 44, 46.

SELECTED BIBLIOGRAPHY

ABBREVIATIONS

AWC = Army War College
JMSIUS = *Journal of the Military Service Institution of the United States*
USAMHI = U.S. Army Military History Institute, Carlisle Barracks, Pa.

PRIMARY SOURCES

MANUSCRIPTS

Boston University Archives, Boston, Mass.
  John Codman Ropes Papers, in Military History Society of Massachusetts Papers
Franklin Delano Roosevelt Presidential Library, Hyde Park, N.Y.
  Assistant Secretary of the Navy Papers
Harvard University Archives, Cambridge, Mass.
  Albert Bushnell Hart Papers
Library of Congress, Washington, D.C.
  American Historical Association Papers
  John Bigelow Papers
  Robert Lee Bullard Papers
  J. Franklin Jameson Papers
  George Van Horne Moseley Papers
National Archives, Washington, D.C.
  Record Group 94
    Adjutant General's Office files
    Appointments, Commissions, and Personnel files
  Record Group 165
    Thomas File
    War College Division files
  Record Group 393
    Army Service Schools Documentary File
South Caroliniana Library, Columbia, S.C.
  McMaster Family Papers
Theosophical Society Library, Pasadena, Calif.
  Arthur Latham Conger Papers
U.S. Army Center of Military History, Washington, D.C.
  "Historical Section, Army War College, the General Staff," HRC 314.71, HS, WPD
  (1914–1919)
  MISC 314.71 files

U.S. Army Military History Institute, Carlisle Barracks, Pa.
Tasker H. Bliss Papers
Matthew Forney Steele Papers
Eben Swift Papers
U.S. Army War College Curricular files for Academic Years 1904–05 and 1906–07 through 1916–17
U.S. Military Academy, West Point, N.Y.
John Bigelow Papers
Tasker H. Bliss Papers
Eben Swift Papers
University of Nebraska Archives, Lincoln
College of Arts and Sciences Record Group

BOOKS AND PAMPHLETS

Bigelow, John [Jr.]. *Mars-la-Tour and Gravelotte.* Washington, D.C.: Government Printing Office, 1880 (published first as an Ordnance Note).
———. *The Principles of Strategy, Illustrated Mainly from American Campaigns.* New York: G. P. Putnam's, 1891; reprint ed., Westport, Conn.: Greenwood Press, 1968.
———. *Reminiscences of the Santiago Campaign.* New York: Harper and Brothers, 1899.
Conger, Arthur L. *Donelson Campaign Sources, Supplementing Volume 7 of The Official Records of the Union and Confederate Armies in the War of the Rebellion.* Fort Leavenworth, Kans.: Army Service Schools Press, 1913.
[Conger, Arthur L., and] Harry Bell, trans. *St. Privat: German Sources.* Fort Leavenworth, Kans.: Staff College Press, 1914.
Greene, Francis Vinton. *Report on the Russian Army and Its Campaign in Turkey, 1877–78.* New York: D. Appleton and Company, 1879.
Johnston, R. M. *First Bull Run: Its Strategy and Tactics.* Boston: Houghton Mifflin Company, 1913.
———. *First Reflections on the Campaign of 1918.* New York: H. Holt and Co., 1920.
Liggett, Hunter. *A.E.F.: Ten Years Ago in France.* New York: Dodd, Mead and Company, 1928.
———. *Commanding an American Army in France: Recollections of the World War.* Boston: Houghton Mifflin Company, 1925.
Livermore, William R. *The American Kriegsspiel: A Game for the Practice of the Art of War.* Boston: Houghton Mifflin Company, 1882.
Michie, Peter Smith. *The Life and Letters of Emory Upton.* New York: D. Appleton, 1885.
Moss, Maj. James A. *Officers' Manual.* 6th ed. Menasha, Wis.: George Banta Publishing Company, 1917.
Palmer, Frederick. *Our Greatest Battle (the Meuse-Argonne).* New York: Dodd, Mead and Company, 1919.
Raymond, Capt. Charles. Kriegsspiel (Fortress Monroe, Va.: U.S. Artillery School Press, 1881).
Root, Elihu. *The Military and Colonial Policy of the United States: Addresses and Reports by Elihu Root.* Compiled and edited by Robert Bacon and James Brown Scott. Cambridge, Mass.: Harvard University Press, 1924.
Ropes, John Codman. *The Army under Pope.* New York: Charles Scribner's Sons, 1881.
———. *The Story of the Civil War.* New York: G. P. Putnam's, 1894 (vol. 1), 1898 (vol. 2); vol. 3, written by William R. Livermore, 1913.
Sargent, Herbert H. *The Campaign of Marengo.* Chicago: A. C. McClurg and Company, 1897.
———. *The Campaign of Santiago de Cuba.* Chicago: A. C. McClurg and Company, 1907.

————. *Napoleon Bonaparte's First Campaign*. Chicago: A. C. McClurg and Company, 1895.

Sayre, Farrand. *Map Maneuvers and Tactical Rides*. Fort Leavenworth, Kans.: Army Service Schools Press, 1910.

Schofield, Maj. Gen. John M. *Introductory Remarks upon the Study of the Science of War, from a Paper Read to the U.S. Military Science Institute, West Point, October 11, 1877, by Major General Schofield, USA, Superintendent, U.S. Military Academy*. New York: D. Van Nostrand, 1877.

Steele, Capt. Matthew Forney. *American Campaigns*. 2 vols. Washington, D.C.: Byron S. Adams, 1909.

Swift, Maj. Eben. *Orders, a Course in Tactics*. Fort Leavenworth, Kans.: Staff College Press, 1905.

————. *Remarks, Introductory to the Course in Military Art, at the Infantry and Cavalry School and Staff College, Fort Leavenworth, by Major Eben Swift, 12th Cavalry, Instructor, September 1904*. Fort Leavenworth, Kans.: Staff College Press, 1904.

Upton, Emory. *The Armies of Asia and Europe: Embracing Official Reports on the Armies of Japan, China, India, Persia, Italy, Russia, Austria, Germany, France, and England* (Washington, D.C.: Government Printing Office, 1878; reprint ed., Westport, Conn.: Greenwood Press, 1972.

Verdy du Vernois, Julius von. *A Simplified War Game*. Translated by Eben Swift. Kansas City, Mo.: Hudson-Kimberly Publishing Company, 1897.

Wagner, Capt. Arthur L. *Books for a Military Library*. Fort Leavenworth, Kans.: Infantry and Cavalry School Press, 1895.

————. (Lt.). *The Campaign of Königgrätz: A Study of the Austro-Prussian Conflict in the Light of the American Civil War*. Fort Leavenworth, Kans.: Infantry and Cavalry School Press, 1889; reprint ed., Westport, Conn.: Greenwood Press, 1972.

————. (Capt.). *Organization and Tactics*. Kansas City, Mo.: Hudson-Kimberly Publishing Company, 1895.

————. (Col.). *Report of the Santiago Campaign, 1898*. Kansas City, Mo.: F. Hudson Publishing Company, 1908.

————. (Capt.). *The Service of Security and Information*. Kansas City, Mo.: Hudson-Kimberly Publishing Company, 1895.

————. (Col.). *Strategy*. Kansas City, Mo.: Hudson-Kimberly Publishing Company, 1904.

Wilkinson, Spenser. *The Brain of an Army: A Popular Account of the German General Staff*. 2d ed. London: A. Constable, 1895.

JOURNAL ARTICLES

Anderson, Col. George S. "Practical Military Instruction." *JMSIUS* 47 (1910):328–40.

Azan, Lt. Col. Paul. "The Historical Section in a General Staff," *Military Historian and Economist* 3 (1918):87–91.

Bebee, Lt. R. E. "Professional Reading for Infantry Officers," *Infantry Journal* 7 (1910):33–45.

Bingham, Capt. T. A. "The Prussian Great General Staff and What It Contains That Is Practical from an American Standpoint." *JMSIUS* 20 (1898):666–76.

Bjornstad, Capt. A. W. "Tactical Instruction of Line Officers." *Infantry Journal* 7 (1911): 680–87.

Black, Maj. William Murray. "The Education and Training of Army Officers." *JMSIUS* 33 (1912):7–16.

Carter, Capt. W. H., "The Infantry and Cavalry School at Fort Leavenworth." *JMSIUS* 15 (1894):752–59.

Chester, Capt. James. "Military Misconceptions and Absurdities." *JMSIUS* 14 (1893): 502–18.

————. "Some of the Artillery Difficulties Likely to Be Encountered during the Next Maritime War." *JMSIUS* 19 (1898):556–73.

Closson, Col. Henry W. "A Paper on Military Libraries." *JMSIUS* 15 (1894):1121–42.

"Doctrine, Conception, and History of War." *Infantry Journal* 9 (1912):255–61.

Field, Capt. Edward. "No Footsteps but Some Glances Backward." *JMSIUS* 6 (1885):238–50.

Fling, Fred Morrow. Review of *Donelson Campaign Sources, Supplementing Volume 7 of The Official Records of the Union and Confederate Armies in the War of the Rebellion*, by Arthur L. Conger. *American Historical Review* 19 (1914):372–73.

Fry, Col. James B. "Origins and Progress of the Military Service Institution of the United States." *JMSIUS* 1 (1879):20–31.

Gallegher, Lt. Hugh J. "Cavalry in Modern Warfare." *Cavalry Journal* 9 (1896):38–47.

"Gen. Ainsworth and the National Archives." *Nation* 94 (February 1912):179–81.

Grebtog, Otto. "A Chat on Military History and the Art of War." Translated from the *New Yorker Staats-Zeitung*, 12 May 1901. *Journal of the United States Artillery* 16 (1901):165–71.

Hall, Col. Charles B. "Address to the Student Officers of the Service Schools and Staff College, September 3, 1906." *Infantry Journal* 3 (1907):60.

Harbord, Capt. James G. "The Cavalry of the Army of Northern Virginia." *Cavalry Journal* 14 (1904):423–504.

Harris, Moses. "With the Reserve Brigade." *Cavalry Journal* 3 (1890):9–20.

Howard, George E. "The Place of History in Modern Education." *Transactions and Reports of the Nebraska State Historical Society* 1 (1885):201–17.

"How to View the Field at Gettysburg." *Army and Navy Journal* 52 (February 1915):715.

Hubbard, Lt. Elmer. "The Military Academy and the Education of Officers." *JMSIUS* 18 (1897):1–24.

Johnston, R. M. "Records of the War of the Revolution." *Military Historian and Economist* 1 (1916):83.

————. "What Can Be Done for Our Military History?" *Infantry Journal* 9 (1912):236–38.

Kelly, Lt. Hugh M. "Progress and What It Entails." *Infantry Journal* 9 (1912):295–303.

King, Capt. Campbell A. "The Peace Training of Armies." *Infantry Journal* 4 (1907):88–109.

Larned, Col. C. W. "West Point." *JMSIUS* 28 (1906):412–16.

Michie, P. S. "Education in Its Relation to the Military Profession." *JMSIUS* 1 (1879): 154–79.

"Military History." *Infantry Journal* 9 (1913): 543–44.

"Military History Course at Harvard." *Army and Navy Journal* 52 (May 1915):1207.

Munford, Col. T. T. "A Confederate Cavalry Officer's View on American Practice and Foreign Theory." *Cavalry Journal* 4 (1891):197–203.

"Naval History Society." *Army and Navy Journal* 49 (July 1912):1398.

"Naval History Society." *Army and Navy Journal* 49 (August 1912):1648.

"Naval History Society." *Army and Navy Journal* 50 (June 1913):604.

"Our Military History." *Infantry Journal* 9 (1913):379–82.

"Our War Documents." *Military Historian and Economist* 3 (1918): 2–3.

Parkhurst, Lt. C. D. "The Practical Education of the Soldier." *JMSIUS* 19 (1898):72–75.

Pettit, Capt. James S. "The Proper Military Instruction of Our Officers." *JMSIUS* 20 (1899):1–54.

Plummer, Lt. E. H. "Practice versus Theory in Army Training." *JMSIUS* 14 (1893):1019–26.

"Praise for Herbert H. Sargent's *Marengo* from Overseas," *Cavalry Journal* 11 (1898):241–43.

Reeves, Lt. James H. "Cavalry Raids." *Cavalry Journal* 10 (1897):232–47.

Reilly, Lt. Col. J. W. "A Memoir of the Life of John Codman Ropes." *JMSIUS* 28 (1907): 147–48.

Ryan, Lt. J. P. "Some Cavalry Lessons of the Civil War." *Cavalry Journal* 8 (1895):268–82.

Schofield, Comdr. Frank H. "Military Character." *Journal of the United States Artillery* 46 (1916):297–318.

Schofield, Maj. Gen. John M. "Inaugural Address." *JMSIUS* 1 (1879):1–19.

Steele, Lt. Matthew Forney. "Military Reading: Its Use and Abuse." *Cavalry Journal* 8 (1895):93–104.

"The Study of Military History," *Nation* 93 (December 1912):556–57.

Swift, Eben. "An American Pioneer in the Cause of Military Education." *JMSIUS* 44 (1909):67–72.

———. "The Military Education of Robert E. Lee." *Virginia Historical Magazine* 30 (1927):99–166.

"Too Much Book Learning for Soldiers." *Army and Navy Journal* 49 (October 1911):212.

Totten, Lt. C. A. L. "Strategos: An American Game of War." *JMSIUS* 2 (1880): 186–202.

Wagner, 1st Lt. Arthur L. "An American War College." *JMSIUS* 10 (1889):287–304.

———. "The Military and Naval Policy of the United States." *JMSIUS* 7 (1886):371–403.

———. (Capt.). "Proper Military Instruction." *JMSIUS* 21 (1899):421–29.

"Who Shall Write Our Military History?" *Infantry Journal* 9 (1913):545–78.

Wisser, Lt. John P. "Practical Instruction of Officers at Posts." *JMSIUS* 9 (1888):198–221.

"Withholding Public Records." *Nation* 94 (January 1912):78–79.

Wood, A. E. "The Proper Employment of Cavalry in War." *Cavalry Journal* 4 (1891):114–36.

Government Documents

Annual Report of the American Historical Association. Washington, D.C.: Government Printing Office, 1899, 1900, 1908, 1912, 1919, 1920, 1924.

Annual Report of the Commandant of the U.S. Army School of the Line and Staff School (also appearing under other titles that reflect the frequent name changes of the Leavenworth schools between the Spanish-American War and World War I). Washington, D.C.: Government Printing Office, 1904, 1905, 1906, 1908, 1909, 1910, 1913, 1921.

Annual Report of the Secretary of War, 1878, 1879, 1881, 1898, 1902, 1913. Washington, D.C.: Government Printing Office, various years.

United States Army. *Cavalry Service Regulations.* Washington, D.C.: Government Printing Office, 1914.

———. Army. *Department of the Army Ad Hoc Committee Report on the Army Need for the Study of Military History.* 4 vols. West Point, N.Y.: N.p., 1971.

———. Army. Surgeon General's Office. *Medical and Surgical History of the War of the Rebellion.* 3 vols. in 6 parts. Washington, D.C.: Government Printing Office, 1877–1888.

———. Army. Surgeon General's Office. *The Medical Department of the United States Army in the World War.* 15 vols. in 17 parts. Washington, D.C.: Government Printing Office, 1921–1929.

———. Congress. House of Representatives. Reports. Washington, D.C.: Government Printing Office, 54th, 60th, 62d Congress.

———. Congress. Senate. Reports. Washington, D.C.: Government Printing Office, 62d Congress.

Unpublished Student Essays at USAMHI

Abernethy, Maj. Robert S. "The Advance of Grant's Army towards Spotsylvania, May 7, and the Recontre Battle of May 8, 1864." AWC 1911–12.

Anderson, Maj. Edward D. "The Second Battle of Bull Run." AWC 1913–14.

Atkinson, Lt. Col. B. W. "The Battle of Antietam." AWC 1912–13.

Buffington, Lt. Col. A. P. "The First Battle of Bull Run." AWC 1913–14.

Cabell, Maj. DeRussy. "The Operations about Spotsylvania, May 10–18, 1864." AWC 1912–13.

Dugan, Lt. Col. Thomas B. "Battle of Chancellorsville." AWC 1912–13.

Ely, Maj. Hanson. "The Antietam Campaign." AWC 1915–16.

Fergusson, Maj. F. K. "The Operations of May 10, 1864, at Spotsylvania." AWC 1911–12.

Gaston, Lt. Col. Joseph A. "The Gettysburg Campaign, to Include the Fighting of the First Day, July 1, 1863." AWC 1911–12.

Gerhardt, Maj. Charles R. "The Battle of Groveton and Second Bull Run." AWC 1912–13.

Harts, Maj. W. W. "Second Day of the Battle of Gettysburg." AWC 1911–12.

Hasbrouck, Lt. Col. Alfred. "The First Battle of Bull Run." AWC 1912–13.

Hickok, Capt. Howard R. "The Battle of Spotsylvania Court House, 9–12 May 1864." AWC 1909–10.

Howell, Maj. G. P. "Campaign and Battle of Gettysburg." AWC 1914–15.

Lincoln, Capt. Charles S. "The Chancellorsville Campaign." AWC 1911–12.

McDonald, Lt. Col. J. B. "Operations of the Federal and Confederate Cavalry in the Chancellorsville Campaign." AWC 1911–12.

Major, Capt. Duncan. "Battle of Chancellorsville, May 3, 1863, the Retreat of the Federal Army, May 5, 1863, the Federal Left in the Campaign of Chancellorsville, including the Second Battle of Fredericksburg, May 3, the Action at Salem Church, May 3 and 4." AWC 1911–12.

Naylor, Capt. W. K. "Second Battle of Bull Run." AWC 1909–10.

Noyes, Col. Charles R. "The Gettysburg Campaign, exclusive of the Battle." AWC 1913–14.

O'Ryan, Brig. Gen. John F. "The Battle of Gettysburg, July 1–2–3, 1863." AWC 1913–14.

Sigerfoos, Maj. Edward. "Campaign and Battle of Second Manassas." AWC 1914–15.

SECONDARY SOURCES

Books

Abel, Annie H. *The American Indian as Participant in the Civil War.* Cleveland: Arthur L. Clark Company, 1919.

Abrahamson, James L. *America Arms for a New Century: The Making of a Giant Military Power.* New York: Free Press, 1981.

Alexander, E. Porter. *Military Memoirs of a Confederate.* New York: C. Scribner's, 1907; reprint ed., Dayton, Ohio: Morningside Press, 1977.

Alger, John I. *The Quest for Victory: The History of the Principles of War.* Westport, Conn.: Greenwood Press, 1982.

Ambrose, Stephen E. *Upton and the Army.* Baton Rouge: Louisiana State University Press, 1964.

Anders, Leslie. *Gentle Knight: The Life and Times of Major General Edwin Forrest Harding.* Kent, Ohio: Kent State University Press, 1985.

Ashburn, Percy M. *A History of the Medical Department of the United States Army.* Boston: Houghton Mifflin and Company, 1929.

Ball, Harry P. *Of Responsible Command: A History of the U.S. Army War College.* Carlisle Barracks, Pa.: Alumni Association of the U.S. Army War College, 1983.

Bidwell, Bruce W. *History of the Military Intelligence Division, Department of the Army General Staff, 1775–1941.* Frederick, Md.: University Publications of America, 1986.

Bigelow, Donald N. *William Conant Church and the Army and Navy Journal.* New York: Columbia University Press, 1952.

Blakely, George T. *Historians on the Homefront: American Propagandists for the Great War.* Lexington: University Press of Kentucky, 1970.

Bledstein, Burton J. *The Culture of Professionalism: The Middle Class and the Development of Higher Education in America.* New York: W. W. Norton, 1976.

Bond, Brian. *The Victorian Army and the Staff College, 1854–1914*. London: Eyre Methuen, 1972.

Bradley, Omar N., with Clay Blair. *A General's Life: An Autobiography by General of the Army Omar N. Bradley*. New York: Simon and Schuster, 1983.

Bucholz, Arden. *Hans Delbrück and the German Military Establishment: War Images in Conflict*. Iowa City: University of Iowa Press, 1985.

Callwell, Maj. Gen. Sir C. E. *Field Marshal Sir Henry Wilson*. 2 vols. New York: C. Scribner's Sons, 1927.

Cincinnatus. *Self-Destruction: The Disintegration and Decay of the United States Army during the Vietnam Era*. New York: W. W. Norton, 1981.

Clapp, Margaret Antoinette. *Forgotten First Citizen: John Bigelow*. Boston: Little, Brown, 1947.

Coffman, Edward M. *The Old Army: A Portrait of the American Army in Peacetime, 1784–1898*. New York: Oxford University Press, 1986.

Connelly, Thomas L. *The Marble Man: Robert E. Lee and His Image in American Society*. New York: Alfred A. Knopf, 1977.

Dastrup, Boyd L. *The U.S. Army Command and General Staff College: A Centennial History*. Manhattan, Kans.: Sunflower Press, 1982.

Deutrich, Mabel E. *The Struggle for Supremacy: The Career of General Fred C. Ainsworth*. Washington, D.C.: Public Affairs Press, 1962.

Early, Jubal A. *Lieutenant General Jubal Anderson Early, C.S.A.: Autobiographical Sketch and Narrative of the War between the States*. Philadelphia: J. B. Lippincott, 1912.

Fisher, Sydney George. *The Struggle for American Independence*. 2 vols. Philadelphia: J. B. Lippincott, 1908.

———. *True History of the American Revolution*. Philadelphia: J. B. Lippincott, 1902.

Freeman, Douglas Southall. *Lee's Dispatches: Unpublished Letters of General Robert E. Lee, C.S.A., to Jefferson Davis and the War Department of the Confederate States of America, 1862–1865*. New York: G. P. Putnam's, 1915.

Gabriel, Richard A. *Military Incompetence: Why the American Military Doesn't Win*. New York: Hill and Wang, 1985.

Goerlitz, Walter. *History of the German General Staff, 1657–1945*. Translated by Brian Battershaw. New York: Praeger, 1959.

Greenfield, Kent Roberts. *The Historian and the Army*. New Brunswick, N.J.: Rutgers University Press, 1954.

Haskell, Thomas L. *The Emergence of Professional Social Science: The American Social Science Association and the Nineteenth-Century Crisis of Authority*. Urbana: University of Illinois Press, 1977.

Hattaway, Herman, and Archer Jones. *How the North Won: A Military History of the Civil War*. Urbana: University of Illinois Press, 1983.

Hattendorf, John B., B. Mitchell Shipton III, and John R. Wadleigh. *Sailors and Scholars: The Centennial History of the Naval War College*. Newport, R.I.: Naval War College Press, 1985.

Herbst, Jurgen. *The German Historical School in American Scholarship*. Ithaca, N.Y.: Cornell University Press, 1965.

Hewes, James E., Jr. *From Root to McNamara: Army Organization and Administration, 1900–1963*. Washington, D.C.: Center of Military History, 1975.

Higham, John. *History*. Englewood Cliffs, N.J.: Prentice-Hall, 1965.

Hofstadter, Richard. *Anti-Intellectualism in American Life*. New York: Alfred A. Knopf, 1963.

Holley, I. B., Jr. *General John M. Palmer, Citizen Soldiers, and the Army of a Democracy*. Westport, Conn.: Greenwood Press, 1982.

Hunt, Elvid, and Walter E. Lorence. *History of Fort Leavenworth, 1827–1937*. 2d ed. Fort Leavenworth, Kans.: Command and General Staff College Press, 1937.

Huntington, Samuel P. *The Soldier and the State*. Cambridge, Mass.: Harvard University Press, 1957.

Janowitz, Morris. *The Professional Soldier: A Social and Political Portrait*. 2d ed. New York: Free Press, 1971.

Johnston, Joseph E. *Narrative of Military Operations*. New York: D. Appleton, 1874.

Lupfer, Capt. Timothy T. *The Dynamics of Doctrine: The Changes in German Tactical Doctrine during the First World War*. Leavenworth Paper 4. Fort Leavenworth, Kans.: Combat Studies Institute, 1981.

Luvaas, Jay. *The Education of an Army: British Military Thought, 1815–1940*. Chicago: University of Chicago Press, 1964.

——. *The Military Legacy of the Civil War: The European Inheritance*. Chicago: University of Chicago Press, 1959.

Millett, Allan R. *Military Professionalism and Officership in America*. Mershon Center Briefing Paper 2. Columbus, Ohio: Mershon Press, 1977.

Millis, Walter. *Military History*. American Historical Association Pamphlet 39. Washington, D.C.: American Historical Association, 1961.

Nenninger, Timothy K. *The Leavenworth Schools and the Old Army: Education, Professionalism, and the Officer Corps of the United States Army, 1881–1918*. Westport, Conn.: Greenwood Press, 1978.

Pappas, George S. *Prudens Futuri: The U.S. Army War College, 1901–1967*. Carlisle Barracks, Pa.: Alumni Association of the U.S. Army War College, 1967.

Perkins, Dexter. *Yield of the Years*. Boston: Little, Brown, 1969.

Pogue, Forrest C. *George C. Marshall: The Education of a General, 1880–1939*. New York: Viking Press, 1963.

Posen, Barry R. *The Sources of Doctrine: France, Britain, and Germany between the World Wars*. Ithaca, N.Y.: Cornell University Press, 1984.

Roman, Alfred. *The Military Operations of General Beauregard*. 2 vols. New York: Harper & Brothers, 1884.

Schindler, Henry, and E. E. Booth. *History of the Army Service Schools*. Fort Leavenworth, Kans.: Staff College Press, 1908.

Sears, Stephen W. *Landscape Turned Red*. New Haven, Conn.: Ticknor and Fields, 1983.

Shafer, Boyd C. *Faces of Nationalism: New Realities and Old Myths*. New York: Harcourt Brace Jovanovich, 1972.

Snyder, Jack. *The Ideology of the Offensive: Military Decision Making and the Disasters of 1914*. Ithaca, N.Y.: Cornell University Press, 1984.

Stackpole, Edward J. *Chancellorsville: Lee's Greatest Battle*. Harrisburg, Pa.: Stackpole Company, 1958.

Tucker, Glenn. *Lee and Longstreet at Gettysburg*. Indianapolis: Bobbs-Merrill, 1968.

Weigley, Russell F. *A History of the United States Army*. New York: Macmillan, 1967.

——. *Towards an American Army: Military Thought from Washington to Marshall*. New York: Columbia University Press, 1962.

Wiebe, Robert H. *The Search for Order, 1877–1920*. New York: Hill and Wang, 1967.

Wish, Harvey. *The American Historian: A Social-Intellectual History of the Writing of the American Past*. New York: Oxford University Press, 1960.

Wrezin, Michael. *Oswald Garrison Villard: Pacifist at War*. Bloomington, Ind.: Indiana University Press, 1965.

ARTICLES

Alexander, E. Porter. "The Great Charge and Artillery Fighting at Gettysburg." In *Battles and Leaders of the Civil War*, 4 vols., edited by Robert Underwood Johnson and Clarence Clough Buel, 3:357–68. New York: Century Press, 1888.

"Arthur Latham Conger." In *Harvard Class of 1894, Fiftieth Anniversary Report*. Cambridge, Mass.: Harvard University Press, 1944.

Bacevich, Andrew J. "Emory Upton: A Centennial Assessment." *Military Review* 61 (1981): 21–28.

———. "Family Matters: American Civilian and Military Elites in the Progressive Era." *Armed Forces and Society* 8 (1982):418–25.

———(Capt.). "Progressivism, Professionalism, and Reform." *Parameters* 9 (1979):66–71.

Baltzly, Alexander. "Robert Matteson Johnston and the Study of Military History." *Military Affairs* 21 (1957):26–30.

Carlson, Robert E. "Professor Fred Fling: His Career and Conflicts at Nebraska University." *Nebraska History* 62 (1981):481–96.

Carter, Clarence E. "The United States and Documentary Historical Publications." *Mississippi Valley Historical Review* 25 (1938):3–24.

Coddington, Edwin B. "The Strange Reputation of General George G. Meade: A Lesson in Historiography." *The Historian* 23 (1962):145–66.

Coffman, Edward M. "American Command and Commanders in World War I." In *New Dimensions in Military History*, edited by Russell F. Weigley, pp. 177–95. San Rafael, Calif.: Presidio Press, 1972.

———. "The American Military Generation Gap in World War I: The Leavenworth Clique in the AEF." In *Command and Commanders in Modern Warfare: Proceedings of the Second Military History Symposium, U.S. Air Force Academy*, edited by William Geffen, pp. 35–43. Washington, D.C.: Government Printing Office, 1969.

Conger, Arthur L. "Robert Matteson Johnston, 1867–1920," *Journal of the American Military History Foundation* 1 (Summer 1937):45–46.

Craig, Gordon A. "Delbrück: The Military Historian." In *Makers of Modern Strategy: Military Thought from Machiavelli to Hitler*, edited by Edward Mead Earle, pp. 260–83. Princeton, N.J.: Princeton University Press, 1943.

de Czege, Col. Huba Wass. "How to Change an Army." *Military Review* 64 (November 1984):32–49.

Gates, John M. "The Alleged Isolation of U.S. Army Officers in the Late Nineteenth Century." *Parameters* 10 (1980):32–45.

Geffen, Lt. Col. William. "The Leavenworth Clique in World War I: A Military View." In *Command and Commanders in Modern Warfare: Proceedings of the Second Military History Symposium, U.S. Air Force Academy*, edited by William Geffen, pp. 48–61. Washington, D.C.: Government Printing Office, 1969.

Grattan, C. Hartley. "The Historians Cut Loose." *American Mercury* 11 (August 1927): 414–30.

Howard, Michael. "Men against Fire: Expectations of War in 1914." In *Military Strategy and the Origins of the First World War*, edited by Steven Miller, pp. 41–57. Princeton, N.J.: Princeton University Press, 1985.

Imboden, John. "Incidents of the First Bull Run." In *Battles and Leaders of the Civil War*, 4 vols., edited by Robert Underwood Johnson and Clarence Clough Buel, 1:229–39. New York: Century Press, 1888.

Irvine, Dallas D. "The Genesis of the *Official Records*." *Mississippi Valley Historical Review* 24 (1937–38):221–29.

Karsten, Peter. "Armed Progressives: The Military Reorganizes for the American Century."

In *Building an Organizational Society*, edited by Jerry Israel, pp. 196–232. New York: Free Press, 1972.

Klegon, Douglas. "The Sociology of Professions: An Emerging Perspective." *Sociology of Work and Occupations* 5 (1978):259–82.

Krause, Maj. Michael D. "Arthur L. Wagner: Doctrine and Lessons from the Past." *Military Review* 58 (1978):53–59.

Lane, Jack C. "American Military Past: The Need for New Approaches." *Military Affairs* 41 (1977):109–14.

Longstreet, James. "The Invasion of Maryland." In *Battles and Leaders of the Civil War*, 4 vols., edited by Robert Underwood Johnson and Clarence Clough Buel, 2:663–74. New York: Century Press, 1888.

Luvaas, Jay. "Military History: An Academic Historian's Point of View." In *New Dimensions in Military History*, edited by Russell F. Weigley, pp. 19–36. San Rafael, Calif.: Presidio Press, 1972.

Mencken, H. L. "Star Spangled Men." *New Republic* 24 (September 1927):119.

Millett, Allan R. "American Military History: Over the Top." In *The State of American History*, edited by Herbert J. Bass, pp. 157–82. Chicago: Quadrangle Books, 1970.

Morton, Louis. "The Historian and the Study of War." *Mississippi Valley Historical Review* 48 (1962):599–613.

"Our Military Propagandists." *Nation* 99 (July 1914):63–64.

Rainey, James W. "Ambivalent Warfare: The Tactical Doctrine of the AEF in World War I." *Parameters* 8 (Fall 1983):34–46.

Riepma, Siert F. "Portrait of an Adjutant General." *Journal of the American Military History Foundation* 2 (1937):26–35.

Ryan, Garry D. "Disposition of AEF Records of World War I." *Military Affairs* 30 (1966): 212–19.

Spiller, Roger J. "The Beginnings of the Kindergarten." *Military Review* 61 (1981):2–12.

Talcott, T. M. R. "General Lee's Strategy at the Battle of Chancellorsville." *Southern Historical Society Papers* 34 (1906):1–27.

VanTassel, David D. "From Learned Society to Professional Organization: The American Historical Association, 1884–1900." *American Historical Review* 89 (1984):929–56.

Weigley, Russell F. "The Elihu Root Reforms and the Progressive Era." In *Command and Commanders in Modern Warfare: Proceedings of the Second Military History Symposium, U.S. Air Force Academy*, edited by William Geffen, pp. 11–27. Washington, D.C.: Government Printing Office, 1969.

Wilensky, Harold L. "The Professionalization of Everyone?" *American Journal of Sociology* 70 (1964):137–58.

DISSERTATIONS AND UNPUBLISHED WORKS

Ahern, Lt. Col. George P. "A Chronicle of the Army War College, 1899–1919." Undated typescript, USAMHI.

Griess, Thomas E. "Dennis Hart Mahan: West Point Professor and Advocate of Professionalism, 1830–1871." Ph.D. diss., Duke University, 1969.

Skirbunt, Peter D. "Prologue to Reform: The 'Germanization' of the United States Army, 1865–1890." Ph.D. diss., Ohio State University, 1983.

Stansfield, George James. "A History of the Army War College at Washington, D.C., 1899–1940." Typescript, 1964, USAMHI.

INDEX

Abel, Annie H., 163
Adams, Byron S., 116, 119, 121–22
Adjutant General's Office, 7, 29; book endorsement policy of, 100–12; document access policy of, 145, 148–52; and purchases of military books, 99; Revolutionary War documents in, 153; as site of early army historical efforts, 184
Ainsworth, Gen. Frederick C., 148–53, 162
Airplane, as a military innovation, 143
Alexander, Gen. E. Porter, 80, 104, 117, 132, 133, 160
American Campaigns (Steele), 88, 109–24, 129, 199, 208
American Historical Association (AHA): advice of for Historical Branch after World War I, 196–97; advisory committee on Revolutionary War documents of, 157–59; and *American Historical Review*, 177; Boston convention of 1912, 75, 77, 164, 166–70, 185–86; Charleston convention of 1913, 155, 157–58, 164, 170–74, 186; Chicago convention of 1914, 174; and document access question, 145, 148–52, 162–63; Military and Naval History Committee of, 67, 163, 166–77, 180, 182; Military History Writing Prize Committee of, 75, 163, 170, 172–73, 177–80; praise for Staff College source method course of, 171; professionalization of, 5, 6–7, 29–30, 147; relations of with army after World War I, 199–200; and Revolutionary War documents issue, 148, 153–59; and Staff College graduates as faculty at civilian universities, 175–76; and supervision of government documentary editing projects, 159–62, 163; survey of historical work of government agencies after World War I, 197
American Kriegsspiel, The (Livermore), 43
American Military Institute, 181
American Statistical Association, 151
Anderson, Prof. F. M., 179
Anderson, Col. George S., 23
Andrews, Gen. George, 155, 156
Antietam: as model for map exercises and map maneuvers, 42, 44; staff rides to, 47–48, 58, 59, 65; student evaluations of

generalship at, 62, 131, 133, 134, 140, 142
Anti-intellectualism, 23–26, 45, 90–91, 110–11
Applicatory method: limitations of, 67–69; resurgence of, after World War I, 204; use of in army schools
Armies of Asia and Europe (Upton), 36
Army and Navy Gazette (London), 38, 107
Army and Navy Journal, 92, 120, 167, 185
Army War College: Class of 1907, 40, 47–48; Class of 1908, 41, 46; Class of 1909, 41–42, 44–45, 64; Class of 1910, 57–58, 119, 128; Class of 1911, 47, 62, 128; Class of 1912, 22, 128; Class of 1913, 62, 65–66, 76, 77; Class of 1914, 76, 78, 129; Class of 1915, 76, 122, 129, 130; Class of 1916, 76, 79; Class of 1917, 76, 78–79, 83, 84; Class of 1921, 204; curricular reform of after World War I, 204; founding of, 15–16, 35, 38; graduates of, in World War I, 201–2; historical rides at, 55, 57–58, 60–66, 204, 212; *kriegsspiel* at, 43–45; map exercises at, 40–42; official history of Civil War of, 75, 77–78, 128–44, 204; and Revolutionary War documentary editing project, 154; source-method research at, 75–84, 204; tactical rides at, 46–48
Artillery School, U.S. Army, 13–14, 35, 37
Atkinson, Lt. Col. B. W., 131
Atlanta campaign (1864), 55, 96, 112
Austro-Prussian War, 35, 51, 53, 95, 138
Azan, Col. Paul, 190

Baker, Newton D., 189, 192, 194, 198–99
Balloons, military, 104
Bancroft, Frederick, 151, 158, 162
Battles and Leaders of the Civil War (Century), 110
Beauregard, Gen. P. G. T., 132
Bell, Harry, 74
Bell, Gen. J. Franklin, 111–12
Biddle, Col. John, 187
Bigelow, Maj. John, Jr., 13, 211; on AHA Revolutionary War documents committee, 158; as military author, 95–101, 108, 112, 120; in World War I, 192, 193
Bigelow, John, Sr., 99
Bigelow, Poultney, 99

35.00